Judgment and Decision Making at Work

Employees are constantly making decisions and judgments that have the potential to affect themselves, their families, their work organizations, and on some occasions even the broader societies in which they live. A few examples include: deciding which job applicant to hire, setting a production goal, judging one's level of job satisfaction, deciding to steal from the cash register, agreeing to help organize the company's holiday party, forecasting corporate tax rates two years later, deciding to report a coworker for sexual harassment, and predicting the level of risk inherent in a new business venture. In other words, a great many topics of interest to organizational researchers ultimately reduce to decisions made by employees.

Yet, numerous entreaties notwithstanding, industrial and organizational psychologists typically have not incorporated a judgment and decision-making perspective into their research. The current book begins to remedy the situation by facilitating cross-pollination between the disciplines of organizational psychology and decision making. The book describes both laboratory and more "naturalistic" field research on judgment and decision making, and applies it to core topics of interest to industrial and organizational psychologists: performance appraisal, employee selection, individual differences, goals, leadership, teams, and stress, among others. The book also suggests ways in which industrial and organizational psychology research can benefit the discipline of judgment and decision making. The authors of the chapters in this book conduct research at the intersection of organizational psychology and decision making, and consequently are uniquely positioned to bridge the divide between the two disciplines.

Scott Highhouse is a Professor and Ohio Eminent Scholar in the Department of Psychology, Bowling Green State University. He received his PhD in 1992 from the University of Missouri at St. Louis. Scott served as Associate Editor of *Organizational Behavior and Human Decision Processes* (*OBHDP*) from 2001–2007, and as Associate Editor of the *Journal of Occupational and Organizational Psychology* from 2007–2009. He is currently co-editor, with Neal Schmitt, of the *Industrial-Organizational Psychology* volume of Wiley's *Handbook of Psychology*.

Reeshad S. Dalal received his PhD from the University of Illinois at Urbana-Champaign in 2003. He is now an associate professor of Industrial/Organizational Psychology and Chair-Elect of the psychology department at George Mason University in Fairfax, Virginia.

Eduardo Salas is Trustee Chair and Pegasus Professor of Psychology at the University of Central Florida (UCF). He also holds an appointment as Program Director for the Human Systems Integration Research Department at UCF's Institute for Simulation & Training. Previously, he was a Senior Research Psychologist and Head of the Training Technology Development Branch of NAVAIR-Orlando for fifteen years. During this period, Dr. Salas served as a principal investigator for numerous R&D programs focusing on teamwork, team training, simulation-based training, decision making under stress, learning methodologies, and performance assessment.

The Organizational Frontiers Series

SIOP Organizational Frontiers Series

Series Editor

Eduardo Salas
University of Central Florida

Coovert/Thompson: (2013) *The Psychology of Workplace Technology*
Highhouse/Dalal/Salas: (2013) *Judgment and Decision Making at Work*
Cortina/Landis: (2013) *Modern Research Methods for the Study of Behavior in Organizations*
Olson-Buchanan/Koppes Bryan/Foster Thompson: (2013) *Using Industrial-Organizational Psychology for the Greater Good: Helping Those Who Help Others*
Eby/Allen: (2012) *Personal Relationships: The Effect on Employee Attitudes, Behavior, and Well-being*
Goldman/Shapiro: (2012) *The Psychology of Negotiations in the 21st Century Workplace: New Challenges and New Solutions*
Ferris/Treadway: (2012) *Politics in Organizations: Theory and Research Considerations*
Jones: (2011) *Nepotism in Organizations*
Hofmann/Frese: (2011) *Error in Organizations*
Outtz: (2009) *Adverse Impact: Implications for Organizational Staffing and High Stakes Selection*
Kozlowski/Salas: (2009) *Learning, Training, and Development in Organizations*
Klein/Becker/Meyer: (2009) *Commitment in Organizations: Accumulated Wisdom and New Directions*
Salas/Goodwin/Burke: (2009) *Team Effectiveness in Complex Organizations*
Kanfer/Chen/Pritchard: (2008) *Work Motivation: Past, Present, and Future*
De Dreu/Gelfand: (2008) *The Psychology of Conflict and Conflict Management in Organizations*
Ostroff/Judge: (2007) *Perspectives on Organizational Fit*
Baum/Frese/Baron: (2007) *The Psychology of Entrepreneurship*

Weekley/Ployhart: (2006) *Situational Judgment Tests: Theory, Measurement, and Application*

Dipboye/Colella: (2005) *Discrimination at Work: The Psychological and Organizational Bases*

Griffin/O'Leary-Kelly: (2004) *The Dark Side of Organizational Behavior*

Hofmann/Tetrick: (2003) *Health and Safety in Organizations*

Jackson/Hitt/DeNisi: (2003) *Managing Knowledge for Sustained Competitive Knowledge*

Barrick/Ryan: (2003) *Personality and Work*

Lord/Klimoski/Kanfer: (2002) *Emotions in the Workplace*

Drasgow/Schmitt: (2002) *Measuring and Analyzing Behavior in Organizations*

Feldman: (2002) *Work Careers*

Zaccaro/Klimoski: (2001) *The Nature of Organizational Leadership*

Rynes/Gerhart: (2000) *Compensation in Organizations*

Klein/Kozlowski: (2000) *Multilevel Theory, Research and Methods in Organizations*

Ilgen/Pulakos: (1999) *The Changing Nature of Performance*

Earley/Erez: (1997) *New Perspectives on International I-O Psychology*

Murphy: (1996) *Individual Differences and Behavior in Organizations*

Guzzo/Salas: (1995) *Team Effectiveness and Decision Making*

Howard: (1995) *The Changing Nature of Work*

Schmitt/Borman: (1993) *Personnel Selection in Organizations*

Zedeck: (1991) *Work, Families, and Organizations*

Schneider: (1990) *Organizational Culture and Climate*

Goldstein: (1989) *Training and Development in Organizations*

Campbell/Campbell: (1988) *Productivity in Organizations*

Hall: (1987) *Career Development in Organizations*

Judgment and Decision Making at Work

Edited by

Scott Highhouse
Bowling Green State University

Reeshad S. Dalal
George Mason University

Eduardo Salas
University of Central Florida

Routledge
Taylor & Francis Group

NEW YORK AND LONDON

First published 2014
by Routledge
605 Third Avenue, New York, NY 10017
4 Park Square, Milton Park, Abingdon, Oxon OX14 4RN

Routledge is an imprint of the Taylor & Francis Group, an informa business

© 2014 Taylor & Francis

Library of Congress Cataloging in Publication Data
Judgment and decision making at work/edited by Scott Highhouse, Reeshad S. Dalal & Eduardo Salas.
   pages cm
   Includes bibliographical references and index.
   1. Decision making. 2. Judgment. 3. Industrial psychology. 4. Work—
   Psychological aspects. 5. Employees—Psychology. I. Highhouse, Scott.
   II. Dalal, Reeshad S. III. Salas, Eduardo.
   HD30.23J83 2013
   153.8′3—dc23
   2013000566

ISBN: 978-1-138-80171-4 (pbk)
ISBN: 978-0-415-88686-4 (hbk)
ISBN: 978-0-203-76705-4 (ebk)

Typeset in Minion and Optima
by Florence Production Ltd, Stoodleigh, Devon, UK

To Bob Guion and Frank Landy

Scott Highhouse

To my wife, Carra (my best decision!).
And to my parents, Myrna & Sam

Reeshad S. Dalal

To Gary Klein, whose ideas and views brought new
thinking on decision-making theory and practice . . .

Eduardo Salas

Contents

Commentary

Series Foreword

From the moment we wake up, we make decisions. We make decisions about what to have for breakfast, what to wear, what route to use to get to work or school, how long to stay at work, and so on. These are just a few examples of everyday life. But, we also make decisions at work–on what, how, when, to execute a task or perform an activity or interact with someone. These decisions vary along many lines. Some decisions are easy, some are hard and complex. Some have severe consequences, some not necessarily. Some need to be made in seconds, others in months or longer. Some are individual, others with a team. Some with lots of information available, others with little information. Some with clear information, other with lots of ambiguity. This is, indeed, a complex phenomenon; one that needs a science. And that is the motivation of this book–to describe and push the science of judgment and decision making.

In this volume, Scott, Reeshad, and I have tried to illustrate some relevant topics that help us understand the complex, dynamic, and multi-level aspects of judgment and decision making. We hope we have represented topics, issues, theories, approaches, and trends that cover the state-of-the-science now and where we are headed. We hope these topics inform practice and generate everyday-based principles applicable to many situations and organizations. We hope there is more to come on this topic from our organizational science and practice.

We would like to thank the SIOP Organizational Frontier Series Editorial Board for their support and encouragement as well as all the authors of this volume. We can all be proud of this contribution to our science and SIOP.

Eduardo Salas
Series Editor
University of Central Florida

About the Editors

Scott Highhouse is a Professor and Ohio Eminent Scholar in the Department of Psychology, Bowling Green State University. He received his PhD in 1992 from the University of Missouri at St. Louis. Scott served as Associate Editor of Organizational Behavior and Human Decision Processes (OBHDP) from 2001–2007, and as Associate Editor of the *Journal of Occupational and Organizational Psychology* from 2007–2009. He is currently co-editor, with Neal Schmitt, of the *Industrial-Organizational Psychology* volume of Wiley's *Handbook of Psychology*.

Scott has been named a Fellow of the American Psychological Association (APA), the Association for Psychological Science (APS), and the Society for Industrial-Organizational Psychology (SIOP). And, he served on SIOP's Executive Board from 2009–2012.

Scott formerly worked in organizational development at Anheuser Busch Companies in St. Louis, Missouri. His primary areas of expertise are assessment/selection for employment, and human judgment/decision making. His work has been featured in the *Washington Post, Wall Street Journal, The Guardian, Christian Science Monitor*, and *Chronicle for Higher Education*.

Reeshad S. Dalal received his PhD from the University of Illinois at Urbana-Champaign in 2003. He is now an associate professor of Industrial-Organizational Psychology and Chair-Elect of the psychology department at George Mason University in Fairfax, Virginia, USA. His research interests are in the areas of employee performance (primarily deviant/counterproductive behavior, citizenship behavior, safety behavior, and within-person variability in performance), decision making (primarily decision making in the workplace, decision-making competence/skill, and the giving and taking of advice during decision making), personality and its interactions with the work situation (primarily situational "strength"), job attitudes (primarily job satisfaction, employee engagement, and employee moods/emotions), and research methods (primarily policy capturing designs and longitudinal designs such as ecological momentary assessment). He currently serves on the editorial board of the *Academy of Management Journal*, and he formerly served on the editorial boards of the *Journal of Applied Psychology* and the *Journal of Business and Psychology*. In addition to his academic work, he has been involved in applied projects related to job attitudes and work experiences, standard-setting, program evaluation, content validity, and forecasting.

Eduardo Salas is Trustee Chair and Pegasus Professor of Psychology at the University of Central Florida (UCF). He also holds an appointment as Program Director for the Human Systems Integration Research Department at UCF's Institute for Simulation & Training. Previously, he was a Senior Research Psychologist and Head of the Training Technology Development Branch of NAVAIR-Orlando for fifteen years. During this period, Eduardo served as a principal investigator for numerous R&D programs focusing on teamwork, team training, simulation-based training, decision making under stress, learning methodologies, and performance assessment.

About the Contributors

Silvia Bonaccio, University of Ottawa, Ottawa, Ontario, Canada

Margaret E. Brooks, Bowling Green State University, Bowling Green, Ohio, USA

Reeshad S. Dalal, George Mason University, Fairfax, Virginia, USA

Michael A. Daniels, Bowling Green State University, Bowling Green, Ohio, USA

Budd Darling, University of Central Florida, Orlando, Florida, USA

James E. Driskell, Florida Maxima, Winter Park, Florida, USA

Tripp Driskell, University of Central Florida, Orlando, Florida, USA

David Dunning, Cornell University, Ithaca, New York, USA

Gary J. Greguras, Singapore Management University, Singapore

Rebecca Grossman, University of Central Florida, Orlando, Florida, USA

Scott Highhouse, Bowling Green State University, Bowling Green, Ohio, USA

Edgar E. Kausel, Universidad de Chile, Santiago, Chile

Kristine M. Kuhn, Washington State University, Pullman, Washington, USA

Christopher J. Lake, Bowling Green State University, Bowling Green, Ohio, USA

Shenghua Luan, Singapore Management University, Singapore

Kevin R. Murphy, Lamorinda Consulting LLC and Colorado State University, Fort Collins, Colorado, USA

Lisa Ordóñez, University of Arizona, Tucson, Arizona, USA

Jochen Reb, Singapore Management University, Singapore

Ramón Rico, University of Central Florida, Orlando, Florida, USA

Eduardo Salas, University of Central Florida, Orlando, Florida, USA

Marissa L. Shuffler, University of Central Florida, Orlando, Florida, USA

Jerel E. Slaughter, University of Arizona, Tucson, Arizona, USA

Shirley Sonesh, University of Central Florida, Orlando, Florida, USA

Jacqueline M. Spencer, University of Central Florida, Orlando, Florida, USA

Cynthia Kay Stevens, University of Maryland, College Park, Maryland, USA

Daan van Knippenberg, Erasmus University, Rotterdam, The Netherlands

Lyn Van Swol, University of Wisconsin-Madison, Wisconsin, USA

George Wu, University of Chicago, Chicago, Illinois, USA

Stephanie Zajac, University of Central Florida, Orlando, Florida, USA

Abbreviations

ACDM	Assessment of Career Decision Making
CRM	crew resource management
DMIDI	Decision Making Individual Differences Inventory
ETS	Educational Testing Service
GDMS	General Decision-Making Style
I-O	industrial-organizational
ISC	illusory shared cognition
JDM	judgment and decision making
KSAs	knowledge, skills, and abilities
MS	Maximization Scale
MTS	Maximizing Tendency Scale/multiteam system
NDM	naturalistic decision making
OB	organizational behavior
OJT/L	on-the-job training/learning
OpSim	Operational Simulation
PA	performance appraisal
RPD	recognition-primed decision
SA	Selective Accessibility/situation assessment/situation awareness
SBT	simulation-based training
SDS	social decision scheme
SET	stress exposure training
SEU	subjective expected utility
SHRM	Society for Human Resource Management
SJT	situational judgment test
SME	subject matter expert
SMM	shared mental model
SP/A	security-potential/aspiration
STAT	swift starting action team
SWAT	special weapons and tactics
TMM	team mental model
TMS	transactive memory system
TSA	team situation awareness
TSM	team situation model

1

Introduction to Judgment and Decision Making

Scott Highhouse, Reeshad S. Dalal, and Eduardo Salas

Most introductory chapters begin with a definition of the research area they are summarizing and applying. It seems difficult, however, to come up with a definition of judgment and decision making (JDM) research that is not tautological. We chose, therefore, to borrow (i.e., steal) a definition from another book on the topic. In Goldstein and Hogarth's (1997) excellent book on the trends and controversies in JDM, the authors defined the psychology of judgment and decision making as *the field that investigates the processes by which people draw conclusions, reach evaluations, and make choices.* That seems as good as anything we might have come up with. But, there is something sterile and dissatisfying about this definition. It glosses over what Goldstein and Hogarth acknowledged is the broad and sometimes puzzling nature of a field that contains "a number of schools of thought that identify different issues as interesting and deem different methods as appropriate" (p. 3).

The three editors of this volume, if pressed, will confess to being influenced by different streams of research and different perspectives on how JDM should be studied. The first and second editors (Highhouse and Dalal, respectively) identify most with the bounded rationality (Simon, 1957) perspective that is best exemplified by the heuristics and biases program of Kahneman, Slovic, and Tversky (1982) and the "everyday irrationality" perspective of Dawes (1988, 2001). These approaches see considerable value in understanding and improving JDM by focusing on how it may go wrong. This is often done in a decontextualized environment where specific processes may be isolated.

Yet, the second editor is also somewhat sympathetic to approaches that focus on the adaptive nature of heuristics. These perspectives are similar in spirit to a long tradition of research on Brunswik's lens model (Hammond, 1955), and are often associated with Gigerenzer (1993) and his ABC group at the Max Planck Institute. This group is concerned with "fast and frugal" heuristics that make us smart. These traditions focus on judgment and decision performance in a contextualized environment, and have revealed that some of the biases identified by Kahneman, Tversky and colleagues (e.g., Kahneman et al., 1982) are attenuated, though not completely eliminated, when presented in contexts familiar to research participants.

The third editor (Salas) takes a radical departure from these perspectives. He focuses on real-world decision making, particularly in crisis situations. This perspective has its roots in dynamic decision making (Brehmer, 1990) and naturalistic decision making (Klein et al., 1993), and focuses on decisions involving extreme time pressure, complexity, expertise, and high stakes. Of the various approaches to studying judgment and decision making, this approach has arguably made the greatest inroads into industrial-organizational (I-O) psychology (Salas, Rosen, & DiazGranados, in press), perhaps because it emphasizes field research in occupational contexts—or perhaps because the third editor is so productive.

RECOGNITION IN PSYCHOLOGY

Whereas the field of industrial-organizational psychology has been around for over 100 years, the psychological study of judgment and decision making is considerably younger. Table 1.1 shows a timeline of important milestones in the JDM field. Although some might quibble with an inclusion here or an exclusion there, most scholars of JDM would agree that this table captures the important events that have shaped the field. As the timeline shows, early research in this area was stimulated by important contributions in the 1950s, especially the piece by Ward Edwards, who is widely recognized as the founder of behavioral decision theory. Edwards introduced psychologists to the expected utility model, and challenged them to consider whether decision makers actually behaved this way.

With the normative model as a standard against which decision making can be compared, the field of JDM has enjoyed an enormously fruitful youth. Studies over the 1960s, 1970s, and 1980s drew from economics, psychophysics, social psychology, and elsewhere to identify a profusion of

TABLE 1.1

Important Milestones in the History of Judgment and Decision Making (JDM)

1950s	• Ward Edwards (1954) defines the domain of JDM in a classic 1954 *Psychological Bulletin* article • Paul Meehl (1954) publishes the classic *Clinical Versus Statistical Prediction* • Kenneth Hammond (1955) applies Egon Brunswik's lens model to clinical prediction • Herbert Simon (1955) introduces the concept of "bounded rationality" • Luce and Raiffa (1957) publish *Games and Decisions* • Leon Festinger (1957) presents the theory of cognitive dissonance
1960s	• Ellsberg paradox (1961) stimulates interest in psychology of ambiguity • Allen Parducci (1966) introduces range-frequency theory • James Stoner (1968) introduces the risky shift phenomenon (the initial impetus for the broader group polarization phenomenon) in group decision making • Amos Tversky (1969) publishes "Intransitivity in preferences"
1970s	• Barry Staw (1976) introduces escalation of commitment • Janis and Mann (1977) publish *Decision Making* • Kahneman and Tversky (1979) introduce prospect theory • Robyn Dawes (1979) publishes the "The robust beauty of improper linear models"
1980s	• First JDM meeting is held in 1980 • Richard Thaler (1980) introduces mental accounting • Nisbett and Ross (1980) publish *Human Inference: Strategies & Shortcomings of Social Judgment* • Norman Anderson (1981) introduces information integration theory • Kahneman, Slovic, and Tversky (1982) publish the classic *Judgment Under Uncertainty: Heuristics and Biases* • Naylor (1985) changes the name of his journal to *Organizational Behavior and Human Decision Processes* • Society for Judgment and Decision Making (SJDM; www.sjdm.org) is established in 1986 • Calderwood, Crandall, and Klein (1987) define the field of naturalistic decision making • *Journal of Behavioral Decision Making* introduced in 1988 • Robyn Dawes (1988) publishes first edition of *Rational Choice in an Uncertain World*
1990s	• Gerd Gigerenzer (1991) challenges heuristics and biases paradigm • Max Bazerman (1991) publishes first edition of *Judgment in Managerial Decision Making* • Tetlock (1991) introduces "people as politicians" perspective on JDM • Shafir, Simonson, and Tversky (1993) introduce reason-based choice • Klein, Orasanu, Calderwood, and Zsambok (1993) publish *Decision Making in Action* • Scott and Bruce (1995) publish *Decision-Making Style: The Development and Assessment of a New Measure*
2000s	• Daniel Kahneman wins Nobel Prize in Economics in 2002 • SJDM open-access journal *Judgment and Decision Making* introduced in 2006 • Blackwell *Handbook of Judgment and Decision Making* published in 2007

shortcomings associated with everyday judgment and decision making. The list of cognitive biases includes ambiguity aversion, anchoring and adjustment, availability, base rate neglect, certainty effect, confirmation trap, conjunction fallacy, decoy effect, denominator neglect, dilution in prediction, duration neglect, endowment, evaluability weighting, focusing effect, framing effect, gambler's fallacy, hindsight, honoring sunk costs, illusion of validity, illusory correlation, loss aversion, omission, outcome prejudice, overconfidence, phantom effect, planning fallacy, probability neglect, pseudodiagnosticity, representativeness, small-sample error, status quo effect, subadditivity, temporal discounting, and probably more. Moreover, explaining these phenomena to the general public has resulted in best-selling books by prominent JDM scholars (see Table 1.2). The success of these endeavors shows that: (a) JDM has permeated popular culture and our everyday language, and (b) JDM topics have considerable relevance to everyday life, including life at work. The applied relevance of JDM research is one reason that authors have seen considerable potential for it to inform research and practice in I-O psychology and related fields (Dalal et al., 2010; Moore & Flynn, 2008; Rosen, Shuffler, & Salas, 2010).

TABLE 1.2

Judgment and Decision Making (JDM) Scholars with Popular Press Books

Title	Author(s)	Affiliation
Predictably Irrational	Dan Ariely	Duke
Switch	Chip Heath and Dan Heath	Stanford and Duke
Nudge	Richard Thaler and Cass Sunstein	University of Chicago
Thinking, Fast and Slow	Daniel Kahneman	Princeton
Expert Political Judgment	Philip Tetlock	University of Pennsylvania
The Power of Intuition	Gary Klein	Applied Research Associates
The Art of Choosing	Sheena Iyengar	Columbia
The Paradox of Choice	Barry Schwartz	Swarthmore College
Gut Feelings	Gerd Gigerenzer	Max Planck Institute
How We Know What Isn't So	Thomas Gilovich	Cornell
Everyday Irrationality	Robyn Dawes	Carnegie Mellon

RELEVANCE TO WORKPLACE JUDGMENTS AND DECISIONS

As Dalal and Brooks (this volume) note, much of what happens in the workplace can ultimately be reduced to judgments and decisions made by individuals acting alone or in collectives (such as teams). Indeed, the topics covered in this book (performance appraisal, employee selection, job choice, goal setting and striving, and leadership, to name just a few) are, at heart, specific kinds of judgments or decisions. Yet, organizational researchers have not really studied decisions *as* decisions. Nor have JDM researchers paid much attention to the workplace. Given the outsized importance of work, and working, to human existence and dignity (Hulin, 2002), these omissions seem inexplicable. In the remainder of this section, we introduce organizational researchers to aspects of the field of JDM that are likely to make cross-fertilization more challenging but also, ultimately, more fruitful.

Moore and Flynn (2008; see also Dalal et al., 2010) argued that the use of a normative benchmark, a defining feature of JDM research, has allowed the field to prosper. They suggest that researchers of organizational behavior would do well to adopt a similar approach. By recognizing things that *should* govern judgments and decisions in the workplace, organizational researchers could examine how actual judgments and decisions *systematically* deviate from these principles (rather than deviating based on random error; see Dawes, 1998). When choosing among finalists for a job, for example, the characteristics of a person you are no longer considering should not affect your preference between two remaining finalists. There is very strong evidence, however, that irrelevant candidates will systematically affect preference among relevant ones (Highhouse, 1996; Highhouse & Johnson, 1996). Understanding that this may occur allows us to debias the decision-making environment in hopes of preventing it from happening in high-stakes settings (Arkes, 1991).

Some have argued that traditional JDM has limited relevance to organizational research because it uses a paradigm that is incompatible with making applied inferences. Staw (2010, p. 411), for example, noted:

> In its search for parsimonious cause-effect relationships, JDM research often misses (or willfully avoids) many of the most crucial elements of work behavior, making judgment and decision research less interesting and relevant to organizational researchers.

The issue of whether the low-fidelity experimental approach can be reconciled with common field approaches such as passive observation is extremely complicated (see Borsboom et al., 2009), and we will not tackle it here. We do agree with Staw (2010) that realistic (yet relatively controlled) techniques such as the managerial "in-basket" could be profitably used to systematically study decision making in the workplace (see also Byham, 2010).

Another common criticism of traditional JDM research is that it creates a caricature of the decision maker, and has become preoccupied with identifying new kinds of errors and mistakes. Kahneman (1991, p. 144) defended the JDM focus on deviations from rationality by noting that:

> Memory is understood by investigating forgetting, and visual illusions contribute to the understanding of visual constancies. In the present context, the heuristics of judgment and choice are identified by the biases they tend to produce.

Kahneman noted that the advantage of using a normative standard is that it avoids the pitfalls of tearing down competing theoretical positions. The normative standard is immune to destruction because it is not based on behavioral observations. According to Moore and Flynn (2008) JDM research "thrives in the productive tension between what *is* and what *ought to be*" (p. 420, italics in original).

As we noted earlier, naturalistic decision making (NDM) has prospered within I-O psychology. This has especially occurred in the team literature, where concern is focused on sensemaking in coordinated environments. The NDM approach also emphasizes expertise, and the study of experts. According to Rosen, Shuffler, and Salas (2010) experts provide "naturally occurring models of how effective decisions can be made in complex and demanding situations" (p. 439). This perspective has not received adequate attention in I-O psychology or in traditional JDM (cf., Shanteau, 1992).

The NDM approach, however, is not immune to criticism. Connolly and Ordóñez (2003, p. 509) observed about research approaches used in this area:

> The tasks themselves are quite complex, even if they are greatly over-simplified versions of real-world analogs. Amateur subjects are thus easily overwhelmed, whereas expert subjects object to the unreality of the tasks. Findings thus tend to be task specific and difficult to aggregate over different studies.

Also, whereas intuition is celebrated within the NDM perspective (Salas, Rosen, & DiazGranados, 2010), it is treated with considerable trepidation within behavioral decision research (Camerer & Johnson, 1991) and within I-O (Highhouse, 2008). Clearly, collaboration among these different perspectives could help us understand the boundary conditions on expertise and intuition.

OVERVIEW

The purpose of this edited volume is to provide research-based perspectives from JDM on traditional areas of interest to I-O psychologists. Our goal was to bring together excellent scholars who have one foot planted in JDM and another in I-O psychology (or a related discipline) and have them imagine how specific areas within I-O psychology could benefit from the application of ideas from JDM. The first section of the book is on personnel decision making, and examines the application of traditional JDM research to topics including performance evaluation, management development, employee selection, individual differences, and job choice. The second section of the book applies traditional JDM research and theory to topics typically associated with organizational psychology, including goal setting, leadership, compensation, and integrated judgments. This section also includes an NDM approach to studying team decision making. Finally, the third section focuses on decision making in action, and examines NDM approaches to decision under stress, expertise, and training. It also includes a chapter on how I-O psychologists have typically gone about assessing decision-making competence in managers. Overall, this book provides a timely application of JDM to I-O topics by scholars doing cutting-edge work in the field. We believe this volume will contribute meaningfully to the literature by articulating new and valuable perspectives on important I-O topics.

REFERENCES

Arkes, H.R. (1991). Costs and benefits of judgment errors: Implications for debiasing. *Psychological Bulletin*, *110*, 486–498.

Borsboom, D., Kievit, R.T., Cervone, D., and Hood, B. (2009). The two disciplines of scientific psychology, or: The disunity of psychology as a working hypothesis. In

J. Valsiner, P. Molenaar, M. Lyra, and N. Chaudhary (Eds.) *Dynamic Process Methodology in the Social and Developmental Sciences* (Chapter 4). New York: Springer Science and Business Media.

Brehmer, B. (1990). Strategies in real-time, dynamic decision making. In R.M. Hogarth (Ed.) *Insights in Decision Making: A Tribute to Hillel J. Einhorn*. Chicago, IL: University of Chicago Press.

Byham, W.C. (2010). Assessment centers are an excellent way of studying decision making. *Industrial and Organizational Psychology, 3*, 443–444.

Camerer, C.F. and Johnson, E.J. (1991). The process-performance paradox in expert judgment: How can experts know so much and predict so badly? In K.A. Ericsson and J. Smith (Eds.) *Toward a General Theory of Expertise: Prospects and Limits* (pp. 195–217). Cambridge: Cambridge University Press.

Connolly, T. and Ordóñez, L. (2003). Judgment and decision making. In W.C. Borman, D.R. Ilgen, and R.J. Klimoski (Eds.) *Handbook of Psychology* (vol. 12, pp. 493–518). Hoboken, NJ: John Wiley & Sons.

Dalal, R.S., Bonaccio, S., Highhouse, S., Ilgen, D.R., Mohammed, S., and Slaughter, J.E. (2010; focal article). What if industrial-organizational psychology decided to take workplace decisions seriously? *Industrial and Organizational Psychology, 3*, 386–405.

Dawes, R.M. (1988). *Rational Choice in an Uncertain World*. San Diego, CA: Harcourt Brace Jovanovich.

Dawes, R.M. (1998). Behavioral decision making and judgment. In D.T. Gilbert and S.T. Fiske (Eds.) *The Handbook of Social Psychology* (4th ed., vol. 2, pp. 497–548). Boston, MA: McGraw-Hill.

Dawes, R.M. (2001). *Everyday Irrationality*. Boulder, CO: Westview Press.

Gigerenzer, G. (1993). The bounded rationality of probabilistic mental models. In K.I. Manktelow and D.E. Over (Eds.) *Rationality: Psychological and Philosophical Perspectives*. London: Routledge.

Goldstein, W.M. and Hogarth, R.M. (1997). *Research on Judgment and Decision Making: Currents, Connections, and Controversies*. Cambridge: Cambridge University Press.

Hammond, K.R. (1955). Probabilistic functionalism and the clinical method. *Psychological Review, 62*, 255–262.

Highhouse, S. (1996). Context-dependent selection: The effects of decoy and phantom job candidates. *Organizational Behavior and Human Decision Processes, 65*, 68–76.

Highhouse, S. (2008). Stubborn reliance on intuition and subjectivity in employee selection. *Industrial and Organizational Psychology, 1*, 333–342.

Highhouse, S. and Johnson, M. (1996). Gain/loss asymmetry and riskless choice: Loss aversion in choices among job finalists. *Organizational Behavior and Human Decision Processes, 68*, 225–233.

Hulin, C.L. (2002). Lessons from industrial and organizational psychology. In J.M. Brett and F. Drasgow (Eds.) *The Psychology of Work: Theoretically Based Empirical Research* (pp. 3–22). Mahwah, NJ: Lawrence Erlbaum Associates.

Kahneman, D. (1991). Judgment and decision making: A personal view. *Psychological Science, 2*, 142–145.

Kahneman, D., Slovic, P., and Tversky, A. (1982). *Judgment under Uncertainty: Heuristics and Biases*. Cambridge: Cambridge University Press.

Klein, G.A., Orasanu, J., Calderwood, R., and Zsambok, C.E. (Eds.). (1993). *Decision Making in Action: Models and Methods*. Norwood, NJ: Ablex Publishing Corporation.

Moore, D.A. and Flynn, F.J. (2008). The case for behavioral decision research in organizational behavior. *Academy of Management Annals, 2*, 399–431.

Rosen, M.A., Shuffler, M., and Salas, E. (2010). How experts make decisions: Beyond the JDM paradigm. *Industrial and Organizational Psychology, 3*, 438–442.

Salas, E., Rosen, M.A., and DiazGranados, D. (2010). Expertise-based intuition and decision making in organizations. *Journal of Management, 36*, 941–973.

Salas, E., Rosen, M.A., and DiazGranados, D. (in press). Naturalistic decision making in individuals and teams. In S.W.J. Kozlowski (Ed.) *Oxford Handbook of Industrial and Organizational Psychology*. New York: Oxford University Press.

Shanteau, J. (1992). Competence in experts: The role of task characteristics. *Organizational Behavior and Human Decision Processes, 53*, 252–266.

Simon, H. (1957). A behavioral model of rational choice. *The Quarterly Journal of Economics, 69*, 99–118.

Staw, B.M. (2010). The trouble with JDM: Some limitations to the influence of JDM on organizational research. *Industrial and Organizational Psychology, 3*, 411–416.

Part I

Personnel Decision Making

2

Performance Appraisals as Heuristic Judgments under Uncertainty

Jochen Reb, Gary J. Greguras, Shenghua Luan, and Michael A. Daniels

INTRODUCTION

JDM and the Performance Appraisal Process

Performance appraisals (PAs) are nearly universal in modern organizations and influence important decisions concerning compensation, promotion, termination and others. Typically, performance is appraised via subjective evaluations by supervisors, peers, or self in the form of performance ratings (Landy & Farr, 1980). We believe that this process can be fruitfully viewed from a judgment and decision making (JDM) perspective. This perspective highlights that raters need to search, integrate, and evaluate information to make judgments and decisions about employees' performance. A major concern for researchers and practitioners alike has been that performance ratings and actual performance are not perfectly correlated, suggesting that raters are less than perfect in their appraisals. Why this is so can easily be understood from a JDM perspective. This body of research suggests that performance appraisals are judgments made under uncertainty using heuristic processes rather than purely "cold," analytical, perfectly rational cognition.

Historically, judgment and decision research had a strong influence on PA research through the famous "heuristics and biases" program and related work in social psychology on biases in social judgment (Kahneman, Slovic, & Tversky, 1982; Nisbett & Ross, 1980). This has led to many contributions such as work on halo bias or leniency bias (for an excellent review of this work, see Landy & Farr, 1980). Over time, interest waned and other research questions became more central to performance appraisal research, partly inspired by the more social and motivational framework proposed in Murphy and Cleveland (1995). The waning interest was also justified by a narrow view on the part of PA researchers as well as many behavioral decision researchers of JDM as essentially the study of biases. However, we believe that now is a good time to reinvigorate JDM research on PA from a broader perspective of heuristic processing that goes beyond biases by including affect, attention, cognition, and contextual factors.

The purpose of this chapter is to present some JDM research and ideas relevant to PA in a selective rather than comprehensive manner focusing on areas we believe are promising for future research. We discuss these under the sections on perception and cognition, emotions, and context and environment. Our overarching framework is of PA as a heuristic process under uncertainty and in the next section we discuss this framework in more detail.

Performance Appraisal as a Heuristic Process under Uncertainty

Arguably, few concepts have had a stronger impact on the study of judgment and decision making than Herbert Simon's *bounded rationality*. The essence of bounded rationality is captured concisely by Simon's "scissors" metaphor: "Human rational behavior is shaped by a scissors whose two blades are the structure of task environments and the computational capabilities of the actor" (1990, p. 7). It is out of the necessity to cope with these two constraints that our mind has adopted various heuristics to solve most problems (e.g., Gigerenzer, 2008; Newell & Simon, 1972; Tversky & Kahneman, 1974). On one side, heuristic processing is faster and requires fewer attentional, cognitive, and computational capabilities than optimization algorithms. Due to its "shortcut" nature, such processing can lead to systematic deviations from normative standards, resulting in the so-called "biases." This aspect of bounded rationality has been studied extensively in JDM under the heuristics and biases paradigm (Gilovich, Griffin, & Kahneman, 2002).

On the other side, task environments may differ in many aspects, such as their levels of uncertainty and complexity and how information and goals are structured. These differences call for a repertoire of heuristics that can be selected flexibly for tasks with distinct features (e.g., Gigerenzer & Selten, 2002). Although this aspect of bounded rationality has received less attention, the study of it is essential to understand the nature and effects of heuristic processing and we shall return to it later.

From our perspective, PA is fundamentally similar to other JDM tasks: Based on some relevant information of the ratee, the rater needs to either derive a judgment on a criterion variable that can take multiple values (e.g., selecting one response option on a performance rating scale) or make a decision, that is, a choice among two or more options that has concrete consequences (e.g., promoting an employee or not). This task can be complicated due to its uncertain nature. Specifically, facing a myriad of information, raters may not know which pieces are relevant to the appraisal criterion and which are not (see, for example, our discussion on the dilution effects in performance judgment). Even if raters were able to focus on information that is useful, it is often not clear how important each piece of information is relative to others, and how one should utilize such information to come up with a sound judgment or decision.

These difficulties stem in part from an uncertain environment, in which cues (e.g., employee behaviors) are only probabilistically related to the criterion (e.g., performance; Brehmer & Joyce, 1988), and in part from raters who are usually limited in their skill and knowledge concerning the rating task. Various heuristics that direct raters' attention to some but not all information in the environment and utilize information with some simple but effective methods (e.g., Gigerenzer, Todd, & the ABC Research Group, 1999; Luan, Schooler, & Gigerenzer, 2011) are common tools employed by decision makers in dealing with uncertainties such as those encountered in the PA process.

In summary, PA can be viewed as a heuristic process under uncertainty. While raters typically use heuristic processing, they may not be aware of some of the limitations of such heuristics and the impossibility to always make accurate performance judgments given the uncertainty involved in this task. The next section describes some important work within a "traditional" heuristics frame that focuses on perception and cognition.

PERCEPTION AND COGNITION IN THE PERFORMANCE APPRAISAL PROCESS

Framing Effects on Performance Judgments

It has long been recognized that how a decision is framed can have a huge influence on which option is chosen. Even two logically equivalent statements (e.g., 80 percent fat-free vs. 20 percent fat) may lead to different decisions because of the difference in framing. An important finding in JDM has been the difference between gain and loss framing. According to prospect theory (Kahneman & Tversky, 1979), options are evaluated relative to the decision maker's reference point such that values above the reference point are perceived as gains whereas values below are perceived as losses. Generally, losses are weighed more heavily and are perceived relatively more unfavorably than gains are, a phenomenon called "loss aversion." Further, as objective gains or losses increase, the increase in subjective value (i.e., perceived gain or loss) decreases (i.e., S-shape function of the subjective value function).

Applying this idea to performance evaluations, Wong and Kwong (2005) investigated whether employee evaluations are influenced by the framing of the performance information. Using a scenario-based study, results indicated that the same objective performance information was evaluated more favorably when it was framed positively (e.g., presence rate of 97 percent) than when it was framed negatively (e.g., absence rate of 3 percent). Results further indicated that the performance differences between two individuals were perceived to be larger when the performance information was expressed with smaller compared to larger numbers, consistent with the S-shape function of the subjective value function. Similarly, Levin (1987) observed that basketball players' performances were evaluated more favorably when participants were presented with the percentage of shots made compared to participants who were presented with percentage of shots missed.

Future research on framing effects and performance evaluations could examine the boundary conditions of such effects. For example, some research suggests that framing effects are weakened for individuals who have strongly held beliefs or high personal involvement with respect to the evaluated attribute (Levin, Schneider, & Gaeth, 1998). Similarly, research indicates that framing effects may not be observed if one has to justify the decision to others (Miller & Fagley, 1991) or has a close relationship with the person that the decision will affect (Wang & Johnston, 1995). In applied settings where a manager may have high personal involvement in appraisals, may have to justify appraisal ratings to employees, and may have a close relationship with the employee, framing effects might be greatly reduced or eliminated.

Decoy Effects in Performance Judgments

A famous effect that is similar to framing effects is the decoy effect. Consider a choice between two non-dominated options (i.e., each option is better on at least one attribute). Huber, Payne, and Puto (1982) found that introducing a third, "decoy" option that is dominated by only one of the original options significantly increases the frequency with which the dominating option is chosen. This effect violates the normative principle of regularity. For example, let us say a supervisor evaluates the performance of three subordinates. Subordinate A produces high quantity and medium quality work. Subordinate B produces medium quantity and high quality work. Subordinate C (the decoy) produces high quantity and low quality work. Subordinate C is "asymmetrically dominated" by Subordinate A, which should increase the latter's evaluation relative to a situation in which only A and B are compared (e.g., Highhouse, 1996). If Subordinate C (the decoy) produced low quantity and high quality products, Subordinate C would now be asymmetrically dominated by Subordinate B, and B's performance evaluation would improve.

Numerous explanations have been offered to explain the decoy effect. For example, Wedell and Pettibone (1996) note that the presence of a decoy may influence the relative weighting of attributes or the subjective value attributed to an attribute, or may add value to an alternative choice. Other research has focused on moderating variables. For example, Slaughter, Bagger, and Li (2006) found that the effect is stronger under pressure to justify the decision to others (accountability). Connolly, Reb, and Kausel (2010), in contrast, found that a focus on self-justification (through increased regret salience) reduces the effect, apparently making decision makers rely less on the shallow justification provided by the irrelevant decoy option. Future research could examine whether and under which conditions decoy options influence performance ratings as well as decisions on whom to promote or to whom to give the largest raise.

Dilution Effects in Performance Judgments

Like decoy effects, dilution effects occur because additional information is presented to the decision maker, which in this case leads to less extreme judgments (Nisbett, Zukier, & Lemley, 1981). More specifically, dilution effects occur when purely non-diagnostic information tempers, or dilutes, the effect of diagnostic information when making judgments. For example, a supervisor might evaluate a service employee receiving high customer satisfaction ratings much more positively than an employee receiving poor customer ratings. However, when the supervisor is provided with other, non-diagnostic information (such as the type of car the employees drives), the dilution effect suggests that the difference between the two performance ratings is reduced as the supervisor's judgments become less extreme.

Tetlock and Boettger (1989) found that the dilution effect is exacerbated when people are held accountable for their judgments. This is interesting given that one might expect accountability to lead to less biased decisions (but consistent with the amplifying effect of accountability on the decoy effect discussed above) (for an excellent review of the accountability effect, see Lerner & Tetlock, 1999). Apparently, when accountability is high *and* non-diagnostic information is presented, people focus more heavily on the irrelevant information and try to make sense of it leading to diluted (regressive) judgments (Tetlock & Boettger, 1989). There is some evidence that this may, in part, be due to conversational norms. People naturally try to ascribe relevance to information that is presented during conversation and thus may be likely to construe non-diagnostic information as diagnostic (Grice, 1975). When participants were told that conversational norms were going to be broken during the study, the effect disappeared with the accountable subjects, though the effect persisted with the unaccountable subjects (Tetlock, Lerner, & Boettger, 1996). This indicates that both the conversational norm and judgmental bias explanations work to cause dilution in judgment.

Dilution effects are important to study in the PA setting because the rater often has a lot of non-diagnostic information concerning employees' personal life, hobbies, interests, and background. Arguably, most of that information will not be relevant when a manager needs to make judgments about job performance. According to the dilution effect, that irrelevant information would actually dilute the influence of diagnostic information, such as performance-relevant behaviors. As a result, strong performers are rated less positively and weak performers less negatively. This could also have implications when the assessor has more non-diagnostic information about some employees than others. In this case employees performing at the same level may receive different evaluations due to the differential influence of irrelevant information. More research is needed to understand the mechanisms by which this phenomenon occurs in a PA context as well as determine the utility of debiasing techniques.

Anchoring Effects in Performance Judgments

In the anchoring and adjustment heuristic, a final judgment is the result of an initial anchor from which the judgment is adjusted (Kahneman et al., 1982). Although the judgment and decision-making literature typically focuses on information that is clearly irrelevant, the PA literature typically has focused on how potentially relevant information influences evaluations (Thorsteinson et al., 2008). For example, this literature has investigated how information about an employee's previous performance, self-ratings or peer ratings, and other employees' performance levels influences evaluations of that employee's current performance (e.g., Foti & Hauenstein, 1993; Klimoski & Inks, 1990; Smither, Reilly, & Buda, 1988). More recently, consistent with the majority of research on anchoring effects, researchers have examined how clearly irrelevant information may influence performance ratings. For example, athletes with higher numbers printed on their jerseys were evaluated to be more likely to perform better in a future game than were athletes with lower numbers on their jerseys (Critcher & Gilovich, 2008).

In the most comprehensive study to date on irrelevant anchors' effects on performance evaluations, Thorsteinson et al. (2008) had participants view an example of a performance rating form that indicated either the highest or lowest possible rating. Results indicated that the low anchor decreased ratings and the high anchor increased ratings compared to a control group that did not receive any anchoring information. In a follow-up, participants viewed anchors that were more (sample evaluation of an employee) or less (sample evaluation of a product) applicable to the participants' task of evaluating an employee. Results revealed a main effect for anchoring such that high anchors produced higher ratings than the ratings of a control group that did not receive any anchoring information, whereas the low anchors did not differ from the control ratings. Whether or not the anchor was relevant (i.e., product or performance anchor) did not influence ratings. To assess the generalizability of their findings to a field context, they asked students to evaluate their class professor late in the semester for research purposes. Using high or low anchors on a sample performance rating form, results indicated that the high anchor produced higher ratings but that the low anchor did not affect ratings when compared to a control group.

Anchoring effects frequently occur even when the anchor is completely irrelevant, so extreme that it is implausible, or presented subliminally (Mussweiler & Englich, 2005). For example, Tversky and Kahneman (1974) generated an anchor by spinning a wheel of numbers and observed that the number that the wheel stopped on (i.e., the anchor) affected subsequent decisions in the direction of the anchor (i.e., either a high or low number). Interestingly, anchoring effects occur for domain experts and novices alike, regardless of whether or not the individual could recall the anchor value

(Critcher & Gilovich, 2008), despite warnings about the biasing effects of anchors (Tversky & Kahneman, 1974), and even when participants are offered incentives to provide accurate judgments (Kahneman et al., 1982). Further, research suggests that two anchors with the same semantics but different absolute values (e.g., 7300 m versus 7.3 km) produce different effects such that anchors with larger absolute values produced larger effects (Wong & Kwong, 2000).

According to the Selective Accessibility (SA) model of anchoring, anchors are believed to influence judgments because the anchor increases the accessibility of anchor-consistent knowledge about the object (Mussweiler & Strack, 2001). According to the SA model, for example, when a supervisor is exposed to an anchor and is then asked to evaluate an employee, the supervisor assesses whether the employee is equal to the anchor value. When making this comparison, the supervisor will access anchor-consistent knowledge from one's memory and rely on this inform-ation when evaluating the employee thereby producing an assimilation effect. It is worth noting that, although the performance appraisal literature discusses contrast, primacy, or recency effects, anchoring effects differ because they may result from completely irrelevant information and do not require a comparison to another ratee.

Evaluation of Dynamic Performance

Employee performance is dynamic and changes over time (Hofmann, Jacobs, & Gerras, 1992). Changes in employee performance occur for a variety of reasons and may be temporary or relatively permanent. For example, temporary performance changes may result from fluctuations in one's daily affective state, whereas relatively permanent changes may occur as a result of employees learning or developing skills that are required for effective performance. Considering both short-term and long-term changes in performance, employee performance profiles may differ on at least three primary characteristics: (a) performance mean, (b) performance variation, and (c) performance trend (i.e., the trajectory of performance such as an improving, deteriorating, or flat trend). When faced with the task of providing an overall performance rating for an appraisal period, raters must somehow integrate these dynamic features of performance into one summary evaluation.

Reb and Cropanzano (2007) argued that, in a heuristic process, raters draw on salient Gestalt characteristics of a dynamic performance profile to arrive at their summary performance ratings. In a laboratory experiment using hypothetical dynamic performance profiles, they manipulated performance mean, trend, and variability (within-subjects) as well as display format, that is, whether performance information was displayed in tables or as graphs (between-subjects). In addition to an effect of performance mean (i.e., higher ratings for higher mean performance), and consistent with predictions, results showed an effect for performance trend such that performance ratings were most favorable for an improving trend, followed by a flat trend, followed by a deteriorating trend (see also DeNisi & Stevens, 1981). Interestingly, they also found that display format moderated results consistent with the idea that ratings are influenced by salient Gestalt characteristics: performance trend had a stronger effect when performance information was displayed as a graph and the trend information was most salient; performance mean had a stronger effect when information was given in a table and average performance was more salient. (Similarly, Lee & Dalal (2011) found a stronger effect of negative performance extremities in the more salient graphic display condition.) The effect of trend on evaluations of performance has been established in both student and manager samples and in western (U.S.) and eastern (Singapore) samples (Reb & Cropanzano, 2007; Reb & Greguras, 2010).

Future research could examine moderating conditions for this effect. For example, Reb and Greguras (2010) found that the trend effect was stronger when performance ratings were made for developmental purposes as compared to administrative purposes and the reverse was true for the effect of performance mean. They argued that this makes sense given that trend is more relevant for developmental purposes. Future research should also move beyond laboratory scenario studies and examine the influence of performance dynamics on actual performance ratings over real time. A first step in this direction was taken by Barnes, Reb and Ang (2010), who showed that performance trend predicts compensation decision in NBA basketball players over and above performance mean.

Decision Makers' Hubris

As the above examples of cognitive heuristics and biases show, raters do not perfectly assess ratee performance. Indeed, it is typically impossible for the rater to know *for sure* how well an employee performed. Given the difficulty of the task as well as the limitations to human judgment (i.e., bounded rationality), this imperfection is not surprising. What is surprising is decision makers' hubris. Despite the inherent difficulty of making accurate judgments under uncertainty, people have been shown to exhibit a remarkable (over)confidence in their judgment (see Dunning, this volume, for a more comprehensive review).

A number of factors seem to be contributing to lacking appreciation of making judgments under uncertainty and the resulting decision-making hubris: judgmental miscalibration, or an inability to accurately estimate the precision of one's judgment (Alpert & Raiffa, 1982; Griffin & Brenner, 2004); a tendency to seek confirmatory evidence that supports one's hypotheses and to discount or filter out evidence that contradicts one's hypotheses (confirmation bias; Koriat, Lichtenstein, & Fischhoff, 1980); and decision makers' tendency to believe that they are capable (better-than-average effect; Taylor & Brown, 1988) and in control (illusion of control; Langer, 1975) and that the world is more certain than it actually is (illusion of certainty; Fischhoff, Slovic, & Lichtenstein, 1977). Such illusions can also lead to an inflated view of one's own judgment ability and can reduce raters' reliance on decision aids, which have been shown to allow for more accurate assessments than one's own intuition or holistic judgment (Highhouse, 2008; Sieck & Arkes, 2005).

A few remedies have been suggested to reduce decision makers' overconfidence: providing detailed calibration feedback and asking subjects to reflect on and process that feedback (Sieck & Arkes, 2005), making people aware of the pervasiveness of overconfidence (McGraw, Mellers, & Ritov, 2004), and asking participants to specifically generate reasons that support the alternative hypothesis (Hoch, 1985). However, there is some evidence that the latter tactic could actually entrench the participants' confidence if few alternative views are accessed (due to the availability heuristic; Fox, 2006). Research should examine in more detail how raters can avoid hubris and become more aware of the limitation of their performance ratings.

EMOTIONS IN THE PERFORMANCE APPRAISAL PROCESS

Analytical vs. Emotional Decision Making

Research on the role of emotion in judgment and decision-making processes is a relatively recent contribution to the literature. Historically, decision making was seen as a purely cognitive, analytical endeavor and JDM research focused on discovering and explaining cognitive heuristics and biases (Kahneman et al., 1982). Current theory and empirical work has shifted to include emotion as part of decision processes and out-comes. This shift seems particularly relevant for the PA context as evaluating performance is an inherently affective-laden process. For example, supervisors may experience emotions such as anxiety, regret, or guilt as part of the PA process, whereas employees may similarly experience emotions such as worry, anger, and frustration.

The role of emotions in the decision-making process is compellingly illustrated in the work of neurologist Antonio Damasio and colleagues. Damasio studied patients who had damaged the part of the brain that is responsible for the experience of emotions. Even though all other brain regions were intact and the people were otherwise fully functioning, they were unable to make intelligent decisions that served their own interests (Damasio, Tranel, & Damasio, 1990). Thus, while the decision-making process may appear to be fully cognitive in nature, it appears that emotions are crucial in moving us toward the best option or judgment.

Damasio (1994) argues that over time we learn to associate certain stimuli with affective states, called somatic markers. Sometimes, cognitively weighing the pros and cons of the individual attributes of stimuli becomes computationally cumbersome (e.g., when an assessor is too busy to process and evaluate an observed behavior of a subordinate). In this case, he/she may quickly call up a particular somatic marker from previous experience that will evoke a positive or negative emotion (e.g., frustration), which will then guide behavior (e.g., make a negative evaluation of that employee) and ease the cognitive load. This pool of somatic markers used to short-cut more algorithmic information processing is called the *affect heuristic* (Slovic et al., 2002).

A complementary account of affective processes in cognitive reasoning distinguishes System 1 from System 2 processing (Kahneman, 2003; Stanovich & West, 2000). The former is characterized by fast, heuristic-based, emotional processing and is generally social and personal in nature. The latter is characterized by slower, controlled, analytic processing and is less social and less contextualized. Because System 2 processing is much more effortful, people typically rely on System 1 processing despite its potentially biased processing. Thus, judgments and decisions tend to be the result of System 1 processing unless both motivation and available resources are present to allow System 2 processing to override System 1. It stands to reason that System 1 processes have significant influence on performance evaluations. Raters often are occupied by a variety of tasks, limiting the amount of attentional and cognitive resources available for making performance judgments. Also, the multiple complex stimuli common in organizational settings favor System 1 processing because it is quicker and less effortful.

Anticipated Emotions in the Appraisal Process

Baumeister and colleagues (2007) argued that decisions are guided by anticipated emotion and that without the anticipation of emotions, particularly regret, people are more likely to make poor decisions that they will later feel sorry about. Gilbert and Wilson (2007) have called the process of anticipating emotions "pre-feeling" and have argued that it is similar to (but less intensive than) the experience of actual emotion. One anticipated emotion that has received particular attention is anticipated regret (Zeelenberg & Pieters, 2007). Because regret is an aversive emotion evoked by a bad decision, people are motivated to avoid it. Regret avoidance has been found in practical domains such as negotiation (Larrick & Boles, 1995), consumer behavior (Simonson, 1992), and sexual behavior (Richard, de Vries, & van der Pligt, 1998), and in laboratory gambling tasks (Reb & Connolly, 2010).

Connolly and Zeelenberg (2002) have argued for two components of regret. A first component, *outcome regret*, is associated with the evaluation of the outcome resulting from one's choice as worse than some reference standard such as the actual or imagined outcome of a foregone option. A second component, *self-blame regret*, is associated with a judgment that one made an unjustified decision—for example, that one decided hastily or used poor information. Considerable evidence supports the idea of self-blame regret. For example, Pieters and Zeelenberg (2005) found in a series of studies that intention-behavior inconsistency can increase experienced regret over a bad outcome. They also found that self-reported amount of thinking about the decision, an indicator of decision process carefulness, was negatively related to experienced regret. Further, Reb and Connolly (2010) provided evidence for a mediating role of justifiability perceptions in the effect of self-blame regret.

Applying these ideas to the PA context, one can wonder whether raters will be influenced by any anticipated emotions they might experience during the PA process. For example, raters might anticipate regret or guilt for providing low ratings, thereby negatively affecting ratee outcomes (e.g., bonus, promotion). At the same time, raters might anticipate regret and self-blame for unduly favorable ratings that are unfair relative to the evaluations of other employees. The balance of these two anticipated regrets may determine the location of the final rating on a rating scale. Another interesting question is what will happen when emotions such as regret are particularly salient during the appraisal process. Research suggests that increasing the salience (explicitly or implicitly) of self-blame regret can lead to more careful, justifiable decision processes (Reb, 2008; Reb & Connolly, 2010). This suggests that prompting raters to anticipate the self-blame and regret they might experience as a result of giving a wrong rating might lead to more careful, accurate ratings.

Experienced Emotions in the Appraisal Process

Emotions are not only influential as anticipated consequences in the performance appraisal process, but also influence the process itself. The Affect Infusion Model is a promising theory of how affect influences our behaviors and judgments (Forgas, 1995; Forgas & George, 2001). This model proposes that affective states are more likely to influence judgment when the task is complex and requires substantial processing than when it is relatively straightforward. This is because when judgment is difficult to make, the assessor searches pre-existing knowledge and experiences, which are emotion-laden, to help make a decision. Also, when the judgment is not straightforward (e.g., the assessor has not had much experience with the employee), the assessor relies on more constructive and generative processes that are likely to utilize affective structures.

So, how do experienced emotions affect the performance judgment process? The affect-as-information hypothesis states that experienced affect assigns value to whatever is interpreted as the cause of that affect (e.g., Clore, 1992). This affect is then interpreted as useful information about how one feels about the object of judgment (e.g., the performance of an employee). As previously mentioned, this affect heuristic is fast and powerful in terms of its effect on judgment. One important aspect of this phenomenon is that when the person is aware of an emotion that was caused by something other than the judgment task, it is unlikely to affect the judgment much. However, if the cause of the emotion is ambiguous, it may erroneously be used as information in the judgment task (Kadous, 2001). Thus, a rater who is, for unknown reasons, in a bad mood may attribute this mood to information about the performance of the employee and as a result give a more negative performance rating.

Emotions and moods can also affect which memories are recalled while making performance judgments (see Rusting, 1998, for a review). This mood-congruency hypothesis states that the assessor is more likely to recall past events that are congruent with his/her current mood. Thus, a rater with a positively valenced mood is more likely to recall employee behavior that also elicited positive feelings at the time (Sinclair, 1988). Interestingly, interpersonal affect (a like–dislike relationship between rater and ratee) rather than mood has been found to influence the recall and weighting of congruent performance information (Robbins & DeNisi, 1998). This is because a long affective history that exists between two people is likely to be more salient than a transient mood state. Additionally, this effect has been shown to be stronger for upward and peer ratings rather than top-down assessments. The reason for this is because raters in these cases typically have less experience in making performance judgments of others and are also less accountable for those judgments (Antonioni & Park, 2001).

Felt emotions in the performance appraisal process can also affect the depth of information processing used by the rater (Schwarz, 1990). More specifically, negative emotions tend to lead to more in-depth processing of information compared to positive emotions. This is because negative emotions are a signal that something is wrong and requires more attention. Positive emotions indicate that all is well and are more likely to promote the use of heuristics so that attention can be allocated elsewhere.

Example: Escalation of Commitment

Escalation of commitment refers to the allocation of additional resources (e.g., time, money) to a failing project (Staw, 1976). Escalation of commitment can be considered irrational because these additional resources are unlikely to result in a successful project ("throwing good money after bad"). Several explanations have been proposed to explain decision makers' escalation of commitment, for example: (a) *self-justification*—individuals want to be viewed favorably and therefore these additional resources justify their prior decisions (Staw, 1976), (b) *closing costs*—individuals are willing to accept risks in an attempt to avoid the sure loss of resources by quitting the project (Arkes & Blumer, 1985), and (c) *norm for consistency*—individuals prefer to appear consistent in their support for a project or in their beliefs that the project will succeed (Staw & Ross, 1980).

Although most demonstrations of escalation of commitment involve allocating additional financial resources to a failing project, this phenomenon has also been observed in a PA context. For example, Slaughter and Greguras (2009) found a positive escalation effect, that is, more favorable performance evaluations from raters initially responsible for hiring the employee than from raters not involved in the hiring decision. However, they found no negative escalation effect, that is, no worse ratings for raters who had initially recommended *not* hiring the employee. Extending these studies, recent research has investigated the role that emotions might play in influencing one's escalation of commitment when evaluating employee performance.

Wong, Yik, and Kwong (2006) examined the role of negative affect in escalating decisions. Participants were informed that they were or were not responsible for the hiring of a certain employee who was now performing poorly. Trait negative affect and whether one was responsible for hiring the employee interacted to predict performance ratings such that the relationship between negative affect and performance ratings was strongly negative in the responsible condition but not significant in the not responsible condition. Wong et al. (2006) argued that individuals with high negative affect are more likely to withdraw from stressful situations (e.g., receiving negative feedback that the employee they chose is performing poorly) in order to reduce unpleasant feelings, and therefore they are less likely to escalate commitment to a failing and stressful project than individuals lower on negative affect.

Research also demonstrates that other emotions or anticipated emotions influence one's escalation of commitment. For example, Tsai and Young (2010) examined how fear and anger may influence escalation of commitment. Tsai and Young argued that anger is associated with a sense of control (optimism), whereas fear is associated with a sense of lack of control (pessimism). Consistent with their hypotheses, participants in the fear-induced condition perceived their hiring decision as being more risky (pessimism) than participants in the anger-induced condition (optimism). Further, risk perception mediated the relationships between emotion (fear or anger) and escalation such that risk perception negatively predicted escalation of commitment in the form of performance ratings. Other research on escalation of commitment and emotions (but not necessarily in a performance appraisal context) has observed, for example, that anticipating positive emotions if the project succeeds positively relates to escalation of commitment (Harvey & Victravich, 2009), that experiencing regret from escalating in one situation can decrease escalation in a different context (Ku, 2008), and that anticipating experiencing regret for quitting a project positively predicts the amount that one escalates (Wong & Kwong, 2007).

O'Neill (2009) extended the above studies by examining how the expressions of anger and guilt *by others* in one's workplace might influence escalation of commitment. O'Neill reasoned that employees learn appropriate emotional expressions from their coworkers. If one's coworkers frequently express anger, O'Neill hypothesized that individuals will be more likely to escalate commitment because they may wish to avoid the consequences of angry coworkers if one admits to making a bad initial decision. In contrast, individuals will be less likely to escalate commitment when coworkers frequently express guilt because guilt is an expression that something went wrong and that it is acceptable to admit mistakes to one's coworkers. Results from two of her three studies supported these hypotheses.

CONTEXTUAL AND ENVIRONMENTAL INFLUENCES

Culture as Moderator of Performance Judgments

The increasing diversity of the global workforce adds another layer of influence on interpersonal and group dynamics in the workplace (Triandis, Kurowski, & Gelfand, 1994). A particularly salient source of diversity in the modern workplace is national culture, yet there has been surprisingly little research on the effects of culture on performance appraisal processes (Fletcher & Perry, 2001). The scant literature that exists is primarily descriptive and fails to examine the underlying processes that cause differences in judgment and behavior. Because of this, the performance appraisal literature has been criticized for lacking generalizability to cultures outside the U.S. and Northwestern Europe (e.g., Triandis, 1999). Some work has looked at the effects of culture on general decision-making styles, which is a step in the right direction. Weber, Ames, and Blais (2004) developed a culturally differentiated taxonomy of decision-making "modes," or preferences in the ways people arrive at decisions. For example, they found that the Chinese are less inclined to use analytical/calculation-based reasoning at coming to decisions than Americans. More research is needed, however, to determine how these modes of decision making affect the performance appraisal process cross-culturally.

In the performance appraisal context, Li and Karakowsky (2001) found culture to affect PA accuracy in samples of Asian- and Caucasian-Americans. They found that when an observer views behavior as undesirable, based on cultural values, that behavior becomes more salient and is given more weight in overall performance judgments. For example, a rater from a culture that values high power distance would be more sensitive to undesirable behaviors such as insubordination or showing a lack of respect to superiors. This has important implications from a JDM perspective because multiple observers may rate the same behavior differently depending on their cultural lenses. Thus, the criteria used for assessing rater accuracy should be considered in the cultural context of both the rater and ratee.

Some work in social psychology has also looked at appraisal processes in general from a cross-cultural perspective. Morris and Peng (1994) found that the Americans and Chinese have different attribution styles, which is likely to differentially affect performance judgments. They found that the American sample was much more susceptible to the fundamental attribution error (the under-attribution of others' behavior to contextual or situational factors) than the Chinese sample. This is likely due to the American individualistic value that places less emphasis on the social-relational aspects of behavior than the Chinese collectivist values.

One cultural difference that may affect performance appraisals is that of lay theories of change. North Americans tend to hold the view that things remain stable over time and that rates of change are fairly con-tinuous, whereas Eastern cultures (particularly Chinese) expect trajectories to change or even reverse with time (Ji, 2008). This is likely the result of a difference in temporal focus, with westerners focusing more on the present and easterners focusing more on the future and past (Ji et al., 2009). Surprisingly, there has been very little research as to how these differences might affect performance appraisals. For example, it is possible that someone with a more cyclical or variable theory of change might be better able to perceive changes in performance over time. Someone with a more stable theory of change might be more susceptible to the confirmation bias as they are less likely to perceive disconfirming information as indicative of a change in employee performance. It could also be that those with a variable theory of change are more influenced by past behavior than current behavior, which could bias performance judgments. More work is needed in this area.

Finally, there has also been some research that has looked at the effects of culture on appraisal mechanisms from the ratee perspective. Brockner and Chen (1996) analyzed culture as a moderator of the relationship between self-esteem and self-protection after a threat to the self. In a U.S. sample (with more independent self-construal) this relationship held, but in a Chinese sample (with more interdependent self-construal), it did not. Thus, cultural values seem also to affect how people construe and respond to negative feedback. More research is needed in this area to better understand how culture also affects the ratee to maximize the benefits of feedback interventions.

Ecological Rationality of Performance Appraisal Heuristics

Recall that the structure of task environments and limitation of our cognitive capacities are the two "blades" in Simon's scissors metaphor. Whereas the latter has been studied extensively in JDM, especially by the heuristics and biases program (e.g., Gilovich et al., 2002; Tversky & Kahneman, 1974), the former did not receive much attention until Gigerenzer and colleagues started their ecological rationality program more recently (e.g., Gigerenzer et al., 1999). The core of the program, as its name suggests, is to understand the environment or ecology under which a cognitive task is undertaken and how different strategies—optimization models or heuristics—should be selected to maximize their fit to the task ecology.

The spirit of the program is exemplified by the "take-the-best" heuristic. Take-the-best is a heuristic designed for the paired-comparison tasks in which one needs to infer which option of a pair has a larger criterion value (e.g., which employee of two has better managerial potential). Its algorithm is simple: It searches cues related to the criterion (e.g., employees' personalities, education, past performance, etc.) in the order of their predictive validities and stops searching whenever there is a difference between the two options on a cue. A decision is then made in favor of the option that has a larger value on the stopping cue. This simple heuristic has been shown to perform remarkably well against other, more complex strategies (e.g., Czerlinski, Gigerenzer, & Goldstein, 1999). However, this is more so in environments where cues differ largely in their validities, but less in environments where cue validities are rather close (e.g., Martignon & Hoffrage, 2002). In addition, take-the-best is a heuristic designed specifically for one type of tasks: paired-comparison. For other tasks, such as judgment of a continuous variable's value or choice among multiple options with varied feature values, other heuristics or strategies must be applied in its place (e.g., Gigerenzer, 2008). The multiplicity of heuristics in the face of the complexity of task ecologies is summarized by the "toolbox" metaphor: The mind is like a handyman who likes to carry a toolbox at work; depending on the task at hand, either a hammer or a screwdriver is applied to maximize the job efficiency but seldom both (e.g., Gigerenzer & Selten, 2002).

What can we learn from the ideas of ecological rationality in the study of performance appraisal? First, it would be interesting to know what tools are placed in the appraisal toolbox. A rich set of heuristics, fast-and-frugal or quick-and-dirty, that have already been studied widely in the JDM community may serve as possible starters. Second, knowing the tools, the next step would be to study structures of different task ecologies. Besides the informational structure that is emphasized by the ecological rationality program (e.g., Gigerenzer et al., 1999), cultural, social, and organizational structures should be critical in the context of performance appraisal, as well. Third, a claim made frequently by the ecological rationality program is that simple heuristics can often achieve as high levels of performance as optimization models (e.g., multiple regression and Bayesian models). Some approaches not entirely familiar to the management community, such as computer simulations and model comparison techniques based on models' *predictive* but not fitting performance, have been used to support this claim (e.g., Luan et al., 2011). Adopted to study the workings of performance appraisal heuristics, these approaches could facilitate our understanding of the heuristics in both descriptive- and prescriptive-oriented research.

CONCLUSION AND OUTLOOK

Much too often, there has been an unfortunate equating of judgment and decision making with "cognitive heuristics and biases." This equating is unfortunate because it limits the contribution a JDM perspective can make to our understanding of the performance appraisal process. From our perspective, a decision can be thought of as a bottleneck into which a variety of factors, such as personality, values, beliefs, judgments, and preferences, are condensed through the decision process (see Reb, 2010). Thus, a JDM perspective can be useful in advancing theory-based, process-oriented research. Importantly, such a perspective is not limited to studying cognition but can integrate other factors, such as affect, culture, and context, as we have shown above. We hope that our chapter contributes to such a broader understanding of JDM and more research in this direction.

REFERENCES

Alpert, M. and Raiffa, H. (1982). A progress report on the training of probability assessors. In D. Kahneman, P. Slovic, & A. Tversky (Eds.) *Judgment Under Uncertainty: Heuristics and Biases* (pp. 294–305). New York: Cambridge University Press.

Antonioni, D. and Park, H. (2001). The relationship between rater affect and three sources of 360-degree feedback ratings. *Journal of Management, 27*(4), 479–495.

Arkes, H.R. and Blumer, C. (1985). The psychology of sunk cost. *Organizational Behavior and Human Decision Processes, 35,* 124–140.

Barnes, C.M., Reb, J., and Ang, D. (2010). More than just the mean: Moving to a dynamic view of performance-based compensation. Working paper, Virginia Tech.

Baumeister, R.F., Vohs, K.D., DeWall, C.N., and Zhang, L.Q. (2007). How emotion shapes behavior: Feedback, anticipation, and reflection, rather than direct causation. *Personality and Social Psychology Review, 11,* 167–203.

Brehmer, B. and Joyce, C.R.B. (1988). *Human Judgment: The SJT View.* North-Holland: Elsevier Science Publishers.

Brockner, J. and Chen, Y-R. (1996). The moderating roles of self-esteem and self-construal in reaction to a threat to the self: Evidence from the People's Republic of China and the United States. *Journal of Personality and Social Psychology, 71,* 603–615.

Clore, G.L. (1992). Cognitive phenomenology: Feelings and the construction of judgment. In L.L. Martin and A. Tesser (Eds.) *The Construction of Social Judgment* (pp. 133–164). Hillsdale, NJ: Lawrence Erlbaum Associates.

Connolly, T., Reb, J., and Kausel, E.E. (2010). Intuitive politicians or intuitive penitents? Regret aversion, accountability and justification in the decoy effect. Working paper, University of Arizona.

Connolly, T. and Zeelenberg, M. (2002). Regret in decision making. *Current Directions in Psychological Science, 11,* 212–216.

Critcher, C.R. and Gilovich, T. (2008). Incidental environmental anchors. *Journal of Behavioral Decision Making, 21,* 241–251.

Czerlinski, J., Gigerenzer, G., and Goldstein, D.G. (1999). How good are simple heuristics? In G. Gigerenzer, P.M. Todd, & the ABC Research Group (Eds.) *Simple Heuristics That Make Us Smart* (pp. 97–118). New York: Oxford University Press.

Damasio, A.R. (1994). *Descartes' Error: Emotion, Reason, and the Human Brain.* New York: Grosset/Putnam.

Damasio, A.R., Tranel, D., and Damasio, H. (1990). Individuals with sociopathic behavior caused by frontal damage fail to respond autonomically to social stimuli. *Behavioural Brain Research, 41*(2), 81–94.

DeNisi, A. and Stevens, G.E. (1981). Profiles of performance, performance evaluations, and personnel decisions. *Academy of Management Journal, 24,* 592–602.

Fischhoff, B., Slovic, P., and Lichtenstein, S. (1977). Knowing with certainty: The appropriateness of extreme confidence. *Journal of Experimental Psychology: Human Perception and Performance, 3,* 522–564.

Fletcher, C. and Perry, E. (2001). Performance appraisal and feedback: A consideration of national culture and a review of contemporary and future trends. In N. Anderson, D. Ones, H. Sinangil, and C. Viswesvaran (Eds.) *International Handbook of Industrial, Work, and Organizational Psychology.* Beverly Hills, CA: Sage.

Forgas, J.P. (1995). Mood and judgment: The affect infusion model (AIM). *Psychological Bulletin, 117*(1), 39–66.

Forgas, J.P. and George, J.M. (2001). Affective influences on judgments and behavior in organizations: An information processing perspective. *Organizational Behavior and Human Decision Processes*, 86(1), 3–34.

Foti, R.J. and Hauenstein, N.M.A. (1993). Processing demands and the effects of prior impressions on subsequent judgments: Clarifying the assimilation/contrast debate. *Organizational Behavior and Human Decision Processes*, 56, 167–189.

Fox, C.R. (2006). The availability heuristic in the classroom: How soliciting more criticism can boost your course ratings. *Judgment and Decision Making*, 1, 86–90.

Gigerenzer, G. (2008). Why heuristics work. *Perspectives on Psychological Science*, 3, 20–29.

Gigerenzer, G. and Selten, R. (Eds.) (2002). *Bounded Rationality: The Adaptive Toolbox*. Cambridge, MA: MIT Press.

Gigerenzer, G., Todd, P.M., and the ABC Research Group. (1999). *Simple Heuristics That Make Us Smart*. New York: Oxford University Press.

Gilbert D.T. and Wilson T.D. (2007). Prospection: Experiencing the future. *Science, 317*, 1351–1354.

Gilovich, T., Griffin, D., and Kahneman, D. (2002). *Heuristics and Biases: The Psychology of Intuitive Judgment*. New York: Cambridge University Press.

Grice, H.P. (1975). Logic and conversation. In P. Cole and J.L. Morgan (Eds.) *Syntax and Semantics* (vol. 3, pp. 41–58). New York: Academic Press.

Griffin, D. and Brenner, L. (2004). Perspectives on probability judgment calibration. In D.J. Koehler and N. Harvey (Eds.) *Blackwell Handbook of Judgment and Decision Making* (pp. 177–199). Malden, MA: Blackwell.

Harvey, P. and Victoravich, L.M. (2009). The influence of forward-looking antecedents, uncertainty, and anticipatory emotions on project escalation. *Decision Sciences, 40*, 759–782.

Highhouse, S. (1996). Context-dependent selection: The effects of decoy and phantom job candidates. *Organizational Behavior and Human Decision Processes*, 65, 68–76.

Highhouse, S. (2008). Stubborn reliance on intuition and subjectivity in employee selection. *Industrial and Organizational Psychology*, 1(3), 333–342.

Hoch, S.J. (1985). Counterfactual reasoning and accuracy in predicting personal events. *Journal of Experimental Psychology: Learning, Memory, and Cognition*, 11, 719–731.

Hofmann, D.A., Jacobs, R., and Gerras, S.J. (1992). Mapping individual performance over time. *Journal of Applied Psychology*, 77, 185–195.

Huber, J., Payne, J.W., and Puto, C. (1982). Adding asymmetrically dominated alternatives: Violations of regularity and the similarity hypothesis. *Journal of Consumer Research*, 9, 90–98.

Ji, L.J. (2008). The leopard cannot change his spots, or can he? Culture and the development of lay theories of change. *Personality and Social Psychology Bulletin*, 34, 613–622.

Ji, L.J., Guo, T., Zhang, Z., and Messervey, D. (2009). Looking into the past: Cultural differences in perception and representation of past information. *Journal of Personality and Social Psychology*, 96, 761–769.

Kadous, K. (2001). Improving jurors' evaluations of auditors in negligence cases. *Contemporary Accounting Research*, 18(3), 425–444.

Kahneman, D. (2003). A perspective on judgment and choice: Mapping bounded rationality. *American Psychologist*, 58, 697–720.

Kahneman, D., Slovic, P., and Tversky, A. (1982). *Judgment Under Uncertainty: Heuristics and Biases*. New York: Cambridge University Press.

Kahneman, D. and Tversky, A. (1979). Prospect theory: An analysis of decision under risk. *Econometrica: Journal of the Econometric Society*, 47(2), 263–291.

Klimoski, R. and Inks, L. (1990). Accountability forces in performance appraisal. *Organizational Behavior and Human Decision Processes, 45,* 194–208.

Koriat, A., Lichtenstein, S., and Fischhoff, B. (1980). Reasons for confidence. *Journal of Experimental Psychology: Human Learning and Memory, 6*(2), 107–118.

Ku, G. (2008). Before escalation: Behavioral and affective forecasting in escalation of commitment. *Personality and Social Psychology Bulletin, 34,* 1477–1491.

Landy, F.J. and Farr, J. (1980). Performance ratings. *Psychological Bulletin, 87,* 72–107.

Langer, E.J. (1975). The illusion of control. *Journal of Personality and Social Psychology, 32,* 311–328.

Larrick, R.P. and Boles, T.L. (1995). Avoiding regret in decisions with feedback: A negotiation example. *Organizational Behavior and Human Decision Processes, 63,* 87–97.

Lee, H. and Dalal, R.S. (2011). The effects of performance extremities on ratings of dynamic performance. *Human Performance, 24*(2), 99–118.

Lerner, J.S. and Tetlock, P.E. (1999). Accounting for the effects of accountability. *Psychological Bulletin, 125*(2), 255–275.

Levin, I.P. (1987). Associative effects of information framing on human judgments. Paper presented at the annual meeting of the Midwestern Psychological Association, Chicago, IL, May.

Levin, I.P., Schneider, S.L., and Gaeth, G.J. (1998). All frames are not created equal: A typology and critical analysis of framing effects. *Organizational Behavior and Human Decision Processes, 76,* 149–188.

Li, J. and Karakowsky, L. (2001). Do we see eye-to-eye? Implications of cultural differences for cross-cultural management research and practice. *Journal of Psychology, 135*(5), 501–517.

Luan, S., Schooler, L.J., and Gigerenzer, G. (2011). A signal detection analysis of fast-and-frugal trees. *Psychological Review, 118,* 316–338.

Martignon, L. and Hoffrage, U. (2002). Fast, frugal and fit: Lexicographic heuristics for paired comparison. *Theory and Decision, 52,* 29–71.

McGraw, A.P., Mellers, B.A., and Ritov, I. (2004). The affective costs of overconfidence. *Journal of Behavioral Decision Making, 17*(4), 281–295.

Miller, P.M. and Fagley, N.S. (1991). The effects of framing, problem variations, and providing rationale on choice. *Personality and Social Psychology Bulletin, 17,* 517–529.

Morris, M.W. and Peng, K. (1994). Culture and cause: American and Chinese attributions for social and physical events. *Journal of Personality and Social Psychology, 67,* 949–971.

Murphy, K.R. and Cleveland, J.N. (1995). *Understanding Performance Appraisal: Social, Organizational, and Goal-based Perspectives.* Thousand Oaks, CA: Sage.

Mussweiler, T. and Englich, B. (2005). Subliminal anchoring: Judgmental consequences and underlying mechanism. *Organizational Behavior and Human Decision Processes, 98,* 133–143.

Mussweiler, T. and Strack, F. (2001).The semantics of anchoring. *Organizational Behavior and Human Decision Processes, 86,* 234–255.

Newell, A. and Simon, H.A. (1972). *Human Problem Solving.* Englewood Cliffs, NJ: Prentice Hall.

Nisbett, R.E. and Ross, L.D. (1980). *Human Inference: Strategies and Shortcomings of Social Judgment.* Englewood Cliffs, NJ: Prentice-Hall.

Nisbett, R.E., Zukier, H., and Lemley, R.E. (1981). The dilution effect: Nondiagnostic information weakens the implications of diagnostic information. *Cognitive Psychology, 13*(2), 248–277.

O'Neill, O.A. (2009). Workplace expression of emotions and escalation of commitment. *Journal of Applied Social Psychology, 39*, 2396–2424.

Pieters, R. and Zeelenberg, M. (2005). On bad decisions and deciding badly: When intention-behavior inconsistency is regrettable. *Organizational Behavior and Human Decision Processes, 97*, 18–30.

Reb, J. (2008). Regret aversion and decision process quality: Effects of regret salience on decision process carefulness. *Organizational Behavior and Human Decision Processes, 105*, 169–182.

Reb, J. (2010). Integrating IOOB and JDM through process-oriented research. *Industrial and Organizational Psychology, 3*, 445–447.

Reb, J. and Connolly, T. (2010). The effects of action, normality, and decision carefulness on anticipated regret: Evidence for a broad mediating role of decision justifiability. *Cognition & Emotion, 24*, 1405–1420.

Reb, J. and Cropanzano, R. (2007). Evaluating dynamic performance: The influence of salient gestalt characteristics on performance ratings. *Journal of Applied Psychology, 92*, 490–499.

Reb, J. and Greguras, G.J. (2010). Understanding performance ratings: Dynamic performance, attributions, and rating purpose. *Journal of Applied Psychology, 95*, 213–220.

Richard, R., de Vries, N.K., and van der Pligt, J. (1998). Anticipated regret and precautionary sexual behavior. *Journal of Applied Psychology, 28*, 1411–1428.

Robbins, T.L. and DeNisi, A.S. (1998). Mood vs. interpersonal affect: Identifying process and rating distortions in performance appraisal. *Journal of Business & Psychology, 12*(3), 313.

Rusting, C.L. (1998). Personality, mood, and cognitive processing of emotional information: Three conceptual frameworks. *Psychological Bulletin, 124*(2), 165–196.

Schwarz, N. (1990). Feelings as information: Informational and motivational functions of affective states. In E.T. Higgins and R.M. Sorrentino (Eds.) *Handbook of Motivation and Cognition: Foundations of Social Behavior* (vol. 2, pp. 527–561). New York: Guilford Press.

Sieck, W.R. and Arkes, H.R. (2005). The recalcitrance of overconfidence and its contribution to decision aid neglect. *Journal of Behavioral Decision Making, 18*(1), 29–53.

Simon, H.A. (1990). Invariants of human behavior. *Annual Review of Psychology, 41*, 1–19.

Simonson, I. (1992). The influence of anticipating regret and responsibility on purchase decisions. *Journal of Consumer Research, 19*, 105–118.

Sinclair, R.C. (1988). Mood, categorization breadth, and performance appraisal: The effects of order of information acquisition and affective state on halo, accuracy, information retrieval, and evaluations. *Organizational Behavior and Human Decision Processes, 42*, 22–46.

Slaughter, J.E., Bagger, J., and Li, A. (2006). Context effects on group-based employee selection decisions. *Organizational Behavior and Human Decision Processes, 100*, 47–59.

Slaughter, J.E. and Greguras, G.J. (2009). Initial attraction to organizations: The influence of trait inferences. *International Journal of Selection and Assessment, 17*, 1–18.

Slovic, P., Finucane, M., Peters, E., and MacGregor, D.G. (2002). Rational actors or rational fools: Implications of the affect heuristic for behavioral economics. *Journal of Socio-Economics, 31*(4), 329–342.

Smither, J.W., Reilly, R.R., and Buda, R. (1988). Effect of prior performance information on ratings of present performance: Contrast versus assimilation revisited. *Journal of Applied Psychology, 73*, 487–496.

Stanovich, K.E. and West, R.F. (2000). Individual differences in reasoning: Implications for the rationality debate? *Behavioral and Brain Sciences*, 23(5), 645.

Staw, B.M. (1976). Knee deep in the big muddy: A study of escalating commitment to a chosen course of action. *Organizational Behavior and Human Performance, 16,* 27–44.

Staw, B.M. and Ross, J. (1980). Commitment in an experimenting society: A study of the attribution of leadership from administrative scenarios. *Journal of Applied Psychology,* 65, 249–260.

Taylor, S.E. and Brown, J.D. (1988). Illusion and well-being: A social psychological perspective on mental health. *Psychological Bulletin, 103*(2), 193–210.

Tetlock, P.E. and Boettger, R. (1989). Accountability: A social magnifier of the dilution effect. *Journal of Personality and Social Psychology, 57*(3), 388–398.

Tetlock, P.E., Lerner, J.S., and Boettger, R. (1996). The dilution effect: Judgmental bias, conversational convention, or a bit of both? *European Journal of Social Psychology, 26,* 915–934.

Thorsteinson, T.J., Breier, J., Atwell, A., Hamilton, C., and Privette, M. (2008). Anchoring effects on performance judgments. *Organizational Behavior and Human Decision Processes, 107,* 29–40.

Triandis, H.C. (1999). Cross-cultural psychology. *Asian Journal of Social Psychology, 2,* 127–143.

Triandis, H.C., Kurowski, L.L., and Gelfand, M.J. (1994). Workplace diversity. In H.C. Triandis, M.D. Dunnette, and L.M. Hough (Eds.) *Handbook of Industrial and Organizational Psychology* (pp. 769–827). Palo Alto, CA: Consulting Psychologists Press.

Tsai, M.H. and Young, M.J. (2010). Anger, fear, and escalation of commitment. *Cognition and Emotion, 24,* 962–973.

Tversky, A. and Kahneman, D. (1974). Judgment under uncertainty: Heuristics and biases. *Science, 185,* 1124–1131.

Wang, X.T. and Johnston, V.S. (1995). Perceived social context and risk preference: A re-examination of framing effects in a life–death decision problem. *Journal of Behavioral Decision Making, 8,* 279–293.

Weber, E.U., Ames, D., and Blais, A.R. (2005). How do I choose thee? Let me count the ways: A textual analysis of similarities and differences in modes of decision making in the USA and China. *Management and Organization Review, 1,* 87–118.

Wedell, D.H. and Pettibone, J.C. (1996). Using judgments to understand decoy effects in choice. *Organizational Behavior and Human Decision Processes, 67,* 326–344.

Wong, K.F.E. and Kwong, J.Y.Y. (2000). Is 7300 m equal to 7.3 km? Same semantics but different anchoring effects. *Organizational Behavior and Human Decision Processes, 82,* 314–333.

Wong, K.F.E. and Kwong, J.Y.Y. (2005). Between-individual comparisons in performance evaluation: A perspective from prospect theory. *Journal of Applied Psychology, 90,* 284–294.

Wong, K.F.E. and Kwong, J.Y.Y. (2007). The role of anticipatory regret in escalation of commitment. *Journal of Applied Psychology, 92,* 545–554.

Wong, K.F.E., Yik, M., and Kwong, J.Y.Y. (2006). Understanding the emotional aspects of escalation of commitment: The role of negative affect. *Journal of Applied Psychology, 91,* 282–297.

Zeelenberg, M. and Pieters, R. (2007). A theory of regret regulation 1.0. *Journal of Consumer Psychology, 17,* 3–18.

3

The Problem of Recognizing One's Own Incompetence: Implications for Self-assessment and Development in the Workplace

David Dunning

> *The greatest of faults, I should say, is to be conscious of none.*
> *(Thomas Carlyle, 1795–1881)*

In some firms, schools, and other organizations, managers ask their employees to complete a task that, at least at first blush, would seem to be straightforward. Employees, and often managers themselves, are requested to sit down and describe the personal strengths they bring to the job as well as any shortcomings that interfere with their performance. They may be asked to list their recent accomplishments and their disappointments. They may be prompted to discuss their positive contributions to a firm's livelihood, and to list missed opportunities that they will pay attention to in the future. They list core competencies they can rely on as well as areas they are prioritizing for improvement.

In this chapter, I describe how this task of self-assessment is anything but straightforward. Self-assessment is a little like wandering into a hall of funhouse mirrors. People look at their reflections and typically see an image staring back at them that nowhere near matches the reality of themselves. Decades of research in social, personality, education, health, and organizational psychology describes just how distorted the reflections are when people try to perceive who they are.

FLAWS IN SELF-ASSESSMENT

Evidence of self-assessment distortion comes in two flavors. First, the assessments people give themselves typically bear only a meager to moderate relationship, at best, to reality. In an omnibus review of self-assessment research, Mabe and West (1982) found that the typical correlation between self-rating and objective performance lay around .29—a result echoed by Harris and Schaubroeck (1988) in the realm of organizational behavior and Hansford and Hattie (1982) in educational settings. To be sure, when objective criteria of performance are visible and unambiguous, such as they are in sports, the correlation between self-perception and reality rises to an enviable level ($r = .47$; Mabe & West, 1982). But in other complex social domains in which objective criteria are more complex, obscured, and ambiguous, such as in managerial competence and social skills, the correlations are much lower to nonexistent ($rs = .04$ and .17, respectively; see Dunning, 2005; Dunning, Heath, & Suls, 2004, for reviews).

Further, people's ratings fail to correlate strongly with their objective achievement even though there appears to be some clear signal that they should recognize. In many areas, the ratings that peers and supervisors provide lay more in agreement with each other and with objective outcomes than self-ratings do (Harris & Schaubroeck, 1988). For example, the self-ratings of surgical residents fail to predict how well they will do on board exams, but the ratings of instructors and peers strongly predict such performance (Risucci, Torolani, & Ward, 1989). Self-ratings among naval officers fail to predict who will receive early promotion as much as ratings from their peers do (Bass & Yammarino, 1991).

But it is the second flavor of distortion in the funhouse mirror of self-assessment that is the most pervasive. When people look at their reflections during self-assessment, they tend to see a person who is more skilled, ethical, hardworking, capable, popular, and giving than is actually the case. For example, Barnsley et al. (2004) asked medical residents to perform various standard medical procedures while being observed and graded by their supervisors. Often, the residents felt these were so proficient that they could teach the procedure to others (e.g., 80 percent thought they could instruct others how to catheterize a male patient). Their instructors tended to disagree (e.g., none thought any student was ready to teach others; in fact, 50 percent of students were rated as still needing supervision given flaws in their performance). In the workplace, Zenger (1992) surveyed engineers in two different software development companies and asked them to rate their skill relative to those of their peers. In one company, a full 32 percent placed themselves in the top 5 percent of engineers at the company. At the second firm, the comparable figure was 42 percent.

THE INVISIBILITY OF ONE'S OWN INCOMPETENCE

In our lab, one primary task is to learn why people are so often wrong about themselves. Why do self-ratings wander so far away from objective performance? Why do people hold beliefs about their skill and expertise that defy objective evidence—even the constraints of mathematical possibility and logical coherence? One important, and central, finding from our studies has to do with people's deficits and shortcomings. Data from our lab suggest people frequently commit the "greatest fault," as defined by Thomas Carlyle in the quotation that opens the chapter. People appear largely unable to spot limitations in their expertise, flaws in their knowledge. When they act incompetently, they seem not to know it (Dunning, 2011; Dunning et al., 2003; Ehrlinger et al., 2008; Kruger & Dunning, 1999).

To be sure, there are arenas in life where people's flaws are painfully obvious to them. A golfing duffer with a yawning slice is an agonizing witness as his or her drive curls grandly away from the fairway and into the woods where the poison ivy grows. But in many arenas in life, mistakes and errors are not so obvious because of a vexing paradox: The skills necessary to recognize error in those arenas are the exact same ones needed to avoid error in the first place. To recognize a faulty logical argument, a person must draw on the same expertise and knowledge that they draw upon to craft a logically sound argument. To recognize a winning ad campaign, a person must draw on the same expertise and savvy needed to create such a campaign in the first place.

In sum, in many intellectual and social domains, the skills and expertise needed to recognize superior and inferior performance are exactly the same skills and expertise needed to produce a superior performance. This creates a problem when a person's expertise is incomplete or corrupt. A person, of course, will strive to create the best performance that he or she can recognize. However, flaws in expertise mean that the person will often produce an inferior response, product, or performance. But those same flaws mean that he or she will not be able to recognize just what makes his or her product or performance so substandard. Thus, people are left thinking their actions are quite reasonable when, in fact, they are riddled with flaws and mistaken choices that render their performances, for lack of a better term, incompetent. In essence, Carlyle's greatest of faults is not only common, it is intrinsically difficult to avoid.

In theory, this fact about incompetence is true of all people. People all have a level of competence within which they do quite well—in terms of both producing appropriate responses and judging how appropriate those responses are. But, at some level, people's competence begins to dissipate, leaving them unable to spot the further imperfections of their ways. However, this is not intuitive, nor should it be. What I am arguing is that our ignorance and incompetence are often invisible to us. The limits of our knowledge and expertise are hidden, and we do not know the exact boundary when we begin to act out of ignorance rather than appropriate knowledge. Our boundaries of knowledge remain invisible for two reasons.

Unknown Unknowns

By definition, deficits in knowledge fall into two categories, one of which is familiar to us and one of which—by definition—is not. First, when people lack knowledge, they can be aware of it. For example, if you ask me how to achieve better gas mileage in my car, there are certain principles I know I do not know. These are, in the parlance of engineering and design, *known unknowns*, which are questions I am aware I do not know the answers to (for a fuller discussion, see Dunning, 2011). I do not know, for example, whether I should turn off my car at stoplights to save gas, whether my gas mileage would be better if I bought premium grade, and what exact speed I should be driving to best conserve fuel. In theory, I can look up the answers to these questions that I have identified.

But beyond these known unknowns lies another class of knowledge deficits, *unknown unknowns*. These are questions I do not even know to ask. These are pieces of information of which I am completely unaware. Let us return to saving gas. I am unaware I should be asking questions about tire care (tires should be fully inflated in order to save gas) and about my trunk (I should clean out all the junk I have left in the trunk, since its weight reduces gas mileage efficiency every time I drive). By definition, people are unaware of their unknown unknowns. And to the extent that they ignore even the possibility of unknown unknowns in their self-evaluations, they will make evaluations that are infused with too much confidence.

We have shown in our lab that people do not possess magical access to the number of unknown unknowns they are missing. In one study, we asked participants to complete a word puzzle known as Boggle, in which people look through a 4 × 4 array of letters to find words they can construct from adjacent letters. Participants' guesses of how many words in the puzzle they missed bore no relation to the reality. Once more, on average, participants thought they had missed eighteen words when in fact they had missed more than 150. Shown the list of unknown unknowns they had missed, participants became less favorable in their self-evaluations of performance, bet less money on their performances, and became more accurate (given criteria they endorsed as the best measures of accuracy) in their self-assessments (Caputo & Dunning, 2005). In another study, graduate students in psychology programs across the United States were asked to find flaws in several research studies that we described to them. Once again, participants were unable to anticipate how many methodological flaws they had missed. Once those flaws were pointed out to them, they provided more humble, and accurate, self-evaluations of methodological expertise (with one exception; participants continued to believe in their expertise when it came to their own research) (Caputo & Dunning, 2005, Study 4).

Reach-around Knowledge

But there is another reason why people fail to recognize when they have crossed from knowledge to ignorance. Often, people can call upon knowledge that looks like it is relevant to a problem they face, but that knowledge is either irrelevant or misleading. For example, suppose I asked you your opinion of Barjolet cheeses, or of Yamajitsu stereo systems. Most readers will not know about these brands, but some will offer an opinion.

Which is a curious fact. Barjolet cheeses and Yamajitsu stereos do not exist, and so any opinion is one that grows out of ignorance. But, in one study, depending on condition, between 25 and 87 percent of respondents expressed an opinion about nonexistent products such as these, even though a "don't know the product" option was available to them (Graeff, 2003). Presumably, respondents reached back to background knowledge they had to *construct* what they thought would be an appropriate response—information I have termed *reach-around knowledge* elsewhere (Dunning, 2011). "Barjolet," for example, sounds French, and respondents could reach back to their knowledge about French cheeses to form a response. Similarly, "Yamajitsu" sounds Japanese, and so respondents could refer back to any knowledge about Japanese electronics to reach a response.

This state of affairs can lead to a paradox. Often, people have rationales for their decisions, and use those rationales as sources of confidence. The problem is that those rationales might be accurate ones, but they also might be ones fraught with "bugs" and mistakes. Thus, those mistaken rationales lead to confidence while they also lead individuals to systematic error.

For example, in a reanalysis of data from Study 4 of Kruger and Dunning (1999), we looked at the confidence with which participants endorsed their solutions to a type of logical problem known as a Wason selection task. Quite naturally, participants who always followed the right algorithm and solved all the problems correctly were quite confident in their solutions. Not so participants who were more haphazard in their application of any algorithm and who achieved lower scores. But, the paradox in the pattern of data lay with participants who got virtually every problem wrong. Often, those individuals followed a systematic algorithm to find a solution—it just happened to be incorrect—and those individuals tended to be rather confident in their performance. In fact, those who consistently applied an incorrect algorithm, and thus got every single problem wrong, were indistinguishable in terms of confidence and performance evaluation from those who got every single item right (Williams & Dunning, 2011).

The issue is that it is often possible to find some sort of reach-around or "fig leaf" knowledge to apply to a problem and to formulate a response. The issue is that the value of such fig leaf knowledge is often dubious, and so using it can lead people to make errors that they do not anticipate. This is why, for example, people make such worrying claims such as stating they can sense when their blood pressure is high when in fact there are no known observable symptoms (other than strapping on the cuff) that can be used to assess hypertension (Baumann & Leventhal, 1985). This is why people looking for a date in the bar can claim they can spot people who are HIV positive, when in fact there are many HIV-positive individuals who display no visible symptoms (Williams et al., 1992).

THE DUNNING-KRUGER EFFECT

The argument here is that people's ignorance is often and typically invisible to them—and that holds true for everyone as they cross the border from knowledge to its absence. The acid test of this assertion, however, centers on those who have the least knowledge and thus the most ignorance. Are those, relative to their peers, who are, for lack of a better term, incompetent unaware of just how incompetent they are?

Data from our lab suggest that the incompetent are, indeed, largely unaware. In a phenomenon that has come to be known as the Dunning-Kruger effect, we have shown that people who display the lowest levels of expertise tend to remain confident—and inappropriately so—in the responses they make. In a typical study, we might ask college students as they leave the classroom after an exam how well they have done. Figure 3.1 shows the data from a typical experiment, in which we split students into quartiles based on their objective performance. As can be seen in the figure, students on average overestimate how well they have performed on the exam. Participants on average think they have performed in the 68th percentile among their peers when in fact their average performance, by definition, lay in the 50th percentile. They also significantly overestimated their raw test score. In addition, if one takes a close look at Figure 3.1, one sees that there is a rather shallow relationship between perceptions of performance and actual performance.

But key to the Dunning-Kruger effect are the perceptions provided by those in the bottom 25 percent of performance. Their exam scores put them in the 12th percentile among their peers, but they rate themselves as in the 60th percentile in terms of performance on the specific exam. To be sure, their self-perceptions were not as favorable as those of top performers, but relative to the reality they were overestimating quite a bit.

We, and others, have replicated this lack of awareness among the incompetent in a variety of settings, and placed the idea under a wide array of tests. Bottom performers fail to recognize the deficiencies in their answers even if paid up to $100 for accurate assessment or even if they have to justify their answers to another person. Bottom performers in real-life settings also show the same pattern. Hunters at a trap-skeet competition fail to understand when they are performing poorly on a quiz of firearm usage and safety. Debate teams in a regional college tournament fail to identify when their performances are putting them toward the bottom of the competition (Ehrlinger et al., 2008). Medical lab techs taking a quiz on material related to their jobs fail to recognize when they are making mistakes (Haun et al., 2000). Poorly performing medical students in clinical internships involving obstetrics and gynecology overestimate their grades by two full marks, thinking they will receive a B+ when their actual grade, on average, is a D+ (Edwards et al., 2003).

Such mistakes in self-perception cause misguided choices in behavior. Ferraro (2010) offered students taking his course two types of "insurance"

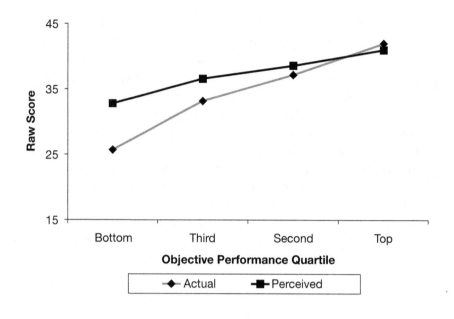

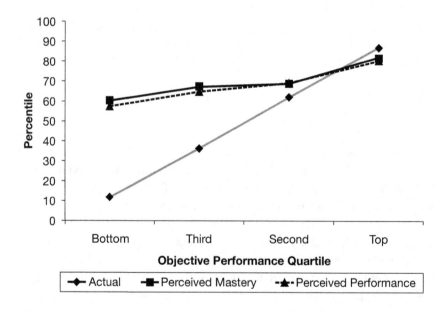

FIGURE 3.1
Perceived performance as a function of objective performance on a class exam.
Top panel presents percentile ratings for perceived mastery of course material and
performance on the exam. The bottom panel presents perceived raw score on the exam
(out of 45 points). From Dunning, D. et al. (2003). Why people fail to recognize their
own incompetence. *Current Directions in Psychological Science, 12,* 83–86, by SAGE
Publications. Adapted with permission.

against their final exam grade. For 10 points on the exam, participants could purchase an insurance policy that would add 20 points to their exam if they fell within the bottom 50 percent of students. For only 4 points, participants could buy a policy that would bump up their grade by 8 points if their score fell within the 50th and 75th percentile. Logic would dictate that the first policy would be more popular—if people had accurate self-views of competence. The first policy would profit twice as many people and offer twice the benefit, relative to the second policy. However, twice as many students bought the second policy as the first. And of those buying the second policy, 80 percent would have profited if they had bought the first policy instead. That is, they fell within the bottom 50 percent of performers when they projected they would fall within the 50th to 75th percentile.

Two notes should be made about these misperceptions among the incompetent. As far as we can tell, they are honest misperceptions. People truthfully believe that they are proficient when they are not. These are not cases of self-deception or denial. To be sure, self-deception and denial exist, but those psychological dynamics are not a necessary condition for lack of recognition among the incompetent. In fact, in one study on logical reasoning, when we trained participants to become proficient in their reasoning skills, they were quite willing to look back at their past performances and provide scathing evaluations of them (Kruger & Dunning, 1999, Study 4). The key was not that they were denying their incompetence in the first place; the trick was that they did not have the knowledge or skill needed to recognize that incompetence.

Second, a careful reader will notice that top performers often make errors in self-evaluation as well, often underestimating their performance relative to their peers. This error seems to spring from a different source than self-perception errors among the incompetent. The incompetent, because they cannot recognize flaws in their reasoning, are largely mistaken about their own skill and expertise. Top performers are more accurate about the self. Who they are wrong about are other people. Because they find the right solutions so straightforward, they assume everyone else does, too. As a consequence, they overestimate the competence of their peers. One can disabuse them of this error, however, by showing them how their peers handle the same problems. This intervention typically leads top performers to better recognize just how special their competencies are. This intervention, however, does nothing to rid the incompetent of their overly inflated self-assessments. Being incompetent, they largely fail to recognize how other people respond to situations in a superior way, and so cannot take advantage of this opportunity to correct their self-evaluations (Kruger & Dunning, 1999, Study 3).

CONSEQUENCES FOR ORGANIZATIONS

What does the inability of the incompetent to recognize their deficits mean for organizational life? If one translates the issues described above into the challenges and tasks that face organizational members on a day-to-day basis in any firm, what settings and activities are the most implicated? Herein, let me discuss three workplace challenges for which this work potentially bears direct implications.

Recognizing Expertise in Groups

Much work in organizations gets done not by individuals but by teams of individuals working together. It is almost a truism in the organizational literature that groups must be able to assess accurately the knowledge and skill that each member possesses. Only then will the group harness all the intellectual resources at its disposal to place it on the most efficient path to an optimal solution (Yetton & Bottger, 1982).

With that as background, the organizational literature presents a cautionary tale. People in groups show either only a modest (Henry et al., 1996; Libby, Trotman, & Zimmer, 1987) to virtually no skill (Littlepage et al., 1995; Miner, 1984) at recognizing who among them is an expert. To be sure, people do give much weight to the opinions of knowledgeable members if those members are explicitly identified for them, but left to their own devices they seem largely incapable of making the same identification (Bonner, Baumann, & Dalal, 2002). Complicating the picture, people lean on status cues, such as gender (Thomas-Hunt & Phillips, 2004) and manner of speech (Ng & Bradac, 1993), to assess who is an expert. Such indicators, however, can be misleading rather than diagnostic.

Our work on the Dunning-Kruger effect suggests one fundamental barrier that prevents people from recognizing experts: their own competence. People who suffer the double-burden of incompetence are largely unable to recognize competence and incompetence within others. When asked to judge who is performing well versus poorly, they do a significantly worse job than their more competent peers (Kruger & Dunning, 1999, Study 3). Thus, it is not a surprise that significant numbers of group members fail to recognize expertise and skill when it is evident. They fail to possess the intellectual tools and resources necessary to make the identification.

There is, however, a more general problem that arises when groups try to discern the experts in their midst. It is not only poor performers who have problems recognizing top performers. In a sense, all group members share the problem, in that their competence reaches only a certain level, beyond which their judgments become unreliable and more inaccurate. People suffer a social cognitive Peter Principle, to invoke that old phrase from the 1970s, in that their ability to judge the competence of others remains trustworthy up to some level associated with their own level of competence, but after that point their judgments of others become more and more untrustworthy. Ultimately, this means that performers at the very top—the experts—are most likely to be misjudged by their less competent peers. Their "genius," for lack of a better term, will go unrecognized.

In recent data, we have demonstrated that the skill of "geniuses" is often misjudged and underestimated. In one study, we asked participants to complete a quiz on logical reasoning (Cone & Dunning, 2011). We then gave them quizzes filled out by six other participants and asked them to judge how many items each peer had gotten right. One of the tests represented a perfect score, but participants on average thought this person had achieved only a 65 percent score. If one thought of this test in terms of "IQ," and converted scores on the quizzes to LQ (logical reasoning) scores the way the WAIS IQ test is calculated, this perfect score represented an LQ of roughly 145, but was judged to be an LQ of roughly 106. Participants judged the LQ of this perfect score to be even lower to the extent they themselves performed badly. Top-performing participants still underestimated the performance of this individual, but did so to a significantly reduced degree. Both groups, top and bottom performers alike, did a much better job judging the tests of individuals who had posted weak scores. An individual with a 20 percent score, for example, was perceived to have scored 30 percent (in LQ terms, a score of 55 was seen as a 66).

The consequences of a group's inability to recognize expertise have yet to be fully mapped, but one implication is rather easy to conclude: Often, groups will fail to recognize the most expert person, instead identifying some other individual as the one to take the lead. Nagel (2010) ran a simulation of elections in which the individuals could identify leadership skill only up to the level of their own skill, after which their choices were more random. He found, under these conditions, that people would typically elect as a leader a person who was above average in leadership skill, but not at the genius level of leadership skill.

Advice Seeking

Our work on the Dunning-Kruger effect also carries implications for the seeking and giving of advice in organizational levels. Often, it is customary for leaders and managers to seek out information, analysis, and suggestions about important decisions (Bonaccio & Dalal, 2006). Advice-seeking behavior, however, must largely be influenced by a manager's beliefs about his or her knowledge or belief. To the extent that managers believe themselves to be fully informed, with no questions to ask or uncertainties to settle, they will not bother to seek out advice—even if they are, in fact, incompetent, and facing any number of invisible unknown circumstances.

Self-beliefs about competence could also determine how much weight participants give to advice from other individuals. It is interesting to note that one central finding in the advice-seeking literature is that individuals tend to give too little weight to the opinions of others. Often, decision makers would have made more accurate decisions had they shifted their opinions more in the direction of their advice givers (Bonaccio & Dalal, 2006; Yaniv & Kleinberger, 2000). One can imagine that self-perceptions of competence can influence the degree to which people pay heed to or discount the suggestions of others, and may lead to unfortunate mistakes when people have too much confidence in their decision-making acumen.

In addition, as the Dunning-Kruger effect suggests, competent performers might be better judges of the worth of advice than are poor performers (Kruger & Dunning, 1999). To the extent that top performers can better separate inferior suggestions from superior ones, top performers might be in a better position to take advantage of the advice of others than are poor performers. Their advantage in accuracy is advantaged even further. In contrast, incompetent individuals may place their confidence in misguided advice, leading to errors in judgment or even worse.

Finally, the Dunning-Kruger effect suggests implications for the person giving advice rather than receiving it. According to the central analysis describing the effect, top performers tend to think that their expertise is nothing special. They underestimate how much they know relative to their peers, thinking that everyone else must know what they themselves know. That inadvertent humility can inhibit top performers from giving crucial advice to other people. Assuming that other people already know what they know, they may assume that any advice they might give would be superfluous, or might think that they need not completely explain the rationale or nuances contained in their advice. Thus, their peers may suffer by not receiving all the wise counsel that those with expert knowledge have available.

Feedback and Self-improvement

One might think that the issue of incompetence and the Dunning-Kruger effect would be self-correcting. After all, if one is making mistakes, one must be receiving feedback from the world that one has to work on improving skills and know-how. There is growing evidence, however, that incompetence has a way of entrenching itself, that people show a facility at failing to recognize their deficiencies. Students, for example, receive clear and compelling feedback every time they receive an exam score, but data suggest that poor performers tend not to correct their inappropriately optimistic forecasts of performance over multiple exams (Ferraro, 2010; Hacker et al., 2000). In fact, classic research in medical education shows that the self-assessments of medical students ending their medical school careers do not correlate with their board scores. Instead, those self-assessments largely echo the opinions medical students held of their skills *during the middle of their first year in school* (Arnold, Willoughby, & Calkins, 1985).

The psychological mechanisms underlying the intransigence of incompetence come as no surprise. Sometimes, feedback from the world is not clear or compelling, but is ambiguous, absent, invisible, or bathed in the warm glow of social politeness. Furthermore, any poker player will tell you that feedback does not necessarily follow the worth of one's decisions: good moves are sometimes severely punished, and naive moves are richly rewarded (see Carter & Dunning, 2008, for a discussion of the problems associated with feedback).

The lessons that people draw from feedback also tend to be imperfect. First, relative to a Bayesian analysis, people are too conservative in their reactions to feedback, clinging to preconceived notions of ability and not shifting their impressions as much as the feedback suggests they should. People also give much more weight to positive feedback than they do to its negative counterpart. If, for example, people initially believe their IQ lies among the bottom 10 percent of their peers, but then hear they have scored in the top half on a short IQ quiz, they raise their self-estimate of IQ almost 15 percentile points. However, if they instead think they are in the top 10 percent among their peers, they shift their impression down only 8 percentile points if they hear they have scored in the bottom half of the quiz (Mobius et al., 2011).

People also avoid situations that involve their deficits. In one recent study on emotional intelligence, we told participants about how well they had scored relative to a national sample. We also offered them a book about "the emotionally intelligent manager" to purchase at half-price. Of those performing in the top quartile, 64 percent bought the book. Of those in the bottom quartile, only 19 percent did so (Sheldon, Ames, & Dunning, 2011). This finding echoes other research showing that people will pay less for information about their IQ scores if they suspect those scores will be low, irrespective of the reality of their performance (Mobius et al., 2011).

DESIGNING FEEDBACK FOR THE UNAWARE

Accurate self-impressions prove essential for thriving in an organizational environment. Middle managers who mistakenly overestimate their job skills often prove at risk to derailment from a once-promising career. Those who, as a consequence, fail to improve upon those skills are often more likely to be fired or demoted, or to plateau into a position below expectations. In contrast, those who examine themselves, seeking out feedback to look at their skills more objectively, are provided more opportunity to recover (Shipper & Dillard, 2000). Further, successful managers who are held in esteem by superiors, subordinates, and peers tend to be those who seek feedback—especially corrective feedback—and, thus, tend to hold relatively accurate opinions of their exact strengths and shortcomings (Ashford & Tsui, 1991).

These findings suggest that successful self-reflection and assessments, which at first may seem to be a most personal and private task, may actually be more of a collective enterprise than an individual one. One must seek out outside sources of feedback and observation if one is to arrive at an accurate view of self. This outside feedback can come in many forms. It can come in the form of multisource feedback, in which managers and employees receive input from supervisors, subordinates, and peers (Rothstein, 1990). It can come as executive coaching (Feldman & Lankau, 2005), or in the guise of informal mentorship (Halai, 1998; Murray, 1991).

Feedback programs, however, are not simple panaceas when it comes to providing employees with self-insight and making their work more effective. To be sure, the presence of the Dunning-Kruger effect suggests that feedback can be essential. If people are simply not aware of areas in which they are deficient, a word or two from a colleague or consultant might hold immeasurable value. Yet, in a comprehensive review of over 100 years of research on providing feedback, Kluger and DeNisi (1996) found that nearly 40 percent of feedback interventions not only failed to achieve their goals but were, instead, demotivating—that is, they prompted employees to perform worse after the program than they did before. In a separate review focused on multisource feedback regimens, researchers found that such programs tend to produce only small improvements in performance (Smither, London, & Reilly, 2005). Thus, if feedback is theoretically so valuable, why does it so frequently fail to produce marked enhancements in performance?

To be effective, any feedback program must not only provide information to employees but must do so with three goals in mind, lest its value be called into question. First, any feedback given an employee should be accurate, which is not necessarily a given. Individuals charged with providing performance evaluations often succumb to leniency biases, in which they rate employees too highly, halo effects, in which they allow the favorability of core evaluations to contaminate their other performance ratings, and unreliability, in which they fail to give the same employee behavior consistently the same rating (Woehr & Huffcutt, 1994). In multisource feedback, the agreement among people giving feedback can be at times quite low, making one wonder if feedback givers are talking about the same individual. This is particularly true when feedback giver and employee have not been acquainted for long (Rothstein, 1990). Raters have much less insight about traits or behaviors that are internal to the individual (e.g., shyness) or happen privately (e.g., counterproductive work behavior) (Dalal, 2005; Vazire, 2010). Thus, it is not a surprise that careful training for performance raters is a necessary condition for feedback to achieve some better degree of accuracy (Woehr & Huffcutt, 1994).

Second, any feedback program must be designed to avoid a defensive reaction on the part of the person receiving the feedback (Audia & Locke, 2003). Feedback serves the goal of self-improvement, but feedback also arouses goals of protecting one's ego and reputation (Ashford, Blatt, & VandeWalle, 2003). There are many ways to lessen the potential threat posed by feedback. First, the giving of feedback can be a more frequent event, thus making it a smaller and more ordinary occasion (Ashford, 1989). Second, feedback can be decoupled from other decisions that carry consequences, such as a person's salary or bonus. Third, feedback can concentrate on behaviors of the individual rather than on their overall competence and character (DeNisi & Kluger, 2000). Fourth, feedback can be timely. Often, managers will put off giving feedback about an employee's errors until the error finally makes the manager angry. This is not the best time or manner for a manager to discuss an employee's shortcomings in an effective manner that circumvents defensive blowback (Larson, 1989). Finally, researchers could explore whether self-affirmation exercises dispel the threat of negative feedback (Steele, 1988). In health, for example, self-affirmation interventions prompt people to accept that their health may be more at risk and that they need to do something about it (Sherman, Nelson, & Steele, 2000).

Finally, feedback requires follow-up. Just simply receiving feedback will not spontaneously cause employees to improve. They further need to know that change is necessary. They need specific goals of improvement to shoot for. There need to be incentives for them to change. Finally, a roadmap needs to be given of how to improve. Often, people will perceive a need to change, but not know how to effect it. Without knowledge of the "how," people often fail to succeed in changes they are quite motivated to pursue (Locke & Latham, 1990). Thus, it is a classic message from social psychology that explicit and specific instructions about how to institute a personal change may be the crucial information that leads people to improve (Leventhal, Singer, & Jones, 1965).

CONCLUDING REMARKS

It may be the case, as Thomas Carlyle suggests, that the worst fault among humans is admitting to none, but I hope the material herein convinces the reader that this fault is not one that people pursue knowingly. Often, people's ignorance and incompetence are invisible to them. They think they are doing just fine when, in fact, they are doing anything but.

This innocence of ignorance presents challenges for any organization, and I have outlined just a few. But, as well, if there are challenges for organizations, there are also challenges to be met by researchers who study organizations. How best can organizations help employees and managers to discover shortcomings that are imperceptible to them? How do organizations best identify experts and the best advice? More to the point, how do organizations learn about their own ignorance at a collective level? There are many challenges of insight to surmount, but the first step of any challenge is gaining the insight that out there might be a host of knowledge one does simply yet not know, but that is out there to harvest.

ACKNOWLEDGMENT

The writing of this chapter was supported by National Science Foundation Grant 0745806. The views expressed in this review do not necessarily reflect those of the Foundation.

REFERENCES

Arnold, L., Willoughby, T.L., and Calkins, E.V. (1985). Self-evaluation in undergraduate medical education: A longitudinal perspective. *Journal of Medical Education, 60,* 21–28.

Ashford, S.J. (1989). Self-assessments in organizations: A literature review and integrative model. In B.M. Staw and L.L. Cummings (Eds.) *Research in Organizational Behavior* (vol. 11, pp. 133–174). Greenwich, CT: JAI Press.

Ashford, S.J., Blatt, R., and VandeWalle, D. (2003). Reflections on the looking glass: Review of research on feedback-seeking behavior in organizations. *Journal of Management, 29,* 733–799.

Ashford, S.J. and Tsui, A.S. (1991). Self-regulation for managerial effectiveness: The role of active feedback-seeking. *Academy of Management Journal, 34,* 251–280.

Audia, P.G. and Locke, E.A. (2003). Benefiting from negative feedback. *Human Resource Management Review, 13,* 631–646.

Barnsley, L., Lyon, P., Ralson, S., Hibbert, E., Cunningham, I., Gordon, F., and Field, M.J. (2004). Clinical skills in junior medical officers: A comparison of self-reported confidence and observed competence. *Medical Education, 38,* 358–367.

Bass, B.M. and Yammarino, F.J. (1991). Congruence of self and others' leadership ratings of Naval officers for understanding successful performance. *Applied Psychology, 40,* 437–454.

Baumann, L. and Leventhal, H. (1985). I can tell when my blood pressure is up, can't I. *Health Psychology, 4,* 203–218.

Bonaccio, S. and Dalal, R.S. (2006). Advice taking and decision-making: An integrative literature review, and implications for the organizational sciences. *Organizational Behavior and Human Decision Processes, 101,* 127–151.

Bonner, B.L., Baumann, M.R., and Dalal, R.S. (2002). The effects of member expertise on group decision-making and performance. *Organizational Behavior and Human Decision Processes, 88,* 719–736.

Caputo, D.D. and Dunning, D. (2005). What you don't know: The role played by errors of omission in imperfect self-assessments. *Journal of Experimental Social Psychology, 41,* 488–505.

Carter, T.J. and Dunning, D. (2008). Faulty self-assessment: Why evaluating one's own competence is an intrinsically difficult task. *Personality and Social Psychology Compass, 2,* 346–360.

Cone, J. and Dunning, D. (2011). Does genius go unrecognized? Unpublished manuscript, Cornell University.

Dalal, R.S. (2005). A meta-analysis of the relationship between organizational citizenship behavior and counterproductive work behavior. *Journal of Applied Psychology, 90,* 1241–1255.

DeNisi, A.S. and Kluger, A.N. (2000). Feedback effectiveness: Can 360-degree appraisals be improved? *Academy of Management Executive, 14,* 129–139.

Dunning, D. (2005). *Self-insight: Roadblocks and Detours on the Path to Knowing Thyself.* New York: Psychology Press.

Dunning, D. (2011). The Dunning-Kruger effect: On being ignorant of one's own ignorance. In J. Olson and M.P. Zanna (Eds.) *Advances in Experimental Social Psychology* (vol. 44, pp. 247–296). New York: Elsevier.

Dunning, D., Heath, C., and Suls, J. (2004). Flawed self-assessment: Implications for health, education, and the workplace. *Psychological Science in the Public Interest, 5,* 69–106.

Dunning, D., Johnson, K., Ehrlinger, J., and Kruger, J. (2003). Why people fail to recognize their own incompetence. *Current Directions in Psychological Science, 12,* 83–86.

Edwards, R.K., Kellner, K.R., Sistrom, C.L., and Magyari, E.J. (2003). Medical student self-assessment of performance on an obstetrics and gynecology clerkship. *American Journal of Obstetrics and Gynecology, 188,* 1078–1082.

Ehrlinger, J., Johnson, K., Banner, M., Dunning, D., and Kruger, J. (2008). Why the unskilled are unaware? Further explorations of (lack of) self-insight among the incompetent. *Organizational Behavior and Human Decision Processes, 105,* 98–121.

Feldman, D.C. and Lankau, M.J. (2005). Executive coaching: A review and agenda for future research. *Journal of Management, 31,* 829–848.

Ferraro, P.J. (2010). Know thyself: Competence and self-awareness. *Atlantic Economic Journal, 38,* 183–196.

Graeff, T.R. (2003). Exploring consumers' answers to survey questions: Are uninformed responses truly uninformed? *Psychology & Marketing, 20,* 643–667.

Hacker, D.J., Bol, L., Horgan, D.D., and Rakow, E.A. (2000). Test prediction and performance in a classroom context. *Journal of Educational Psychology, 92,* 160–170.

Halai, A. (1998). Mentor, mentee and mathematics: A story of professional development. *Journal of Mathematics Teacher Education, 1,* 295–315.

Hansford, B.C. and Hattie, J.A. (1982). The relationship between self and achievement/performance measures. *Review of Educational Research, 52,* 123–142.

Harris, M.M. and Schaubroeck, J. (1988). A meta-analysis of self-supervisor, self-peer, and peer-supervisor ratings. *Personnel Psychology, 41,* 43–62.

Haun, D.E., Zeringue, A., Leach, A., and Foley, A. (2000). Assessing the competence of specimen-processing personnel. *Laboratory Medicine, 31,* 633–637.

Henry, R.A., Strickland, O.J., Yorges, S.L., and Ladd, D. (1996). Helping groups determine their most accurate member: The role of outcome feedback. *Journal of Applied Social Psychology, 26,* 1153–1170.

Kluger, A.N. and DeNisi, A. (1996). The effects of feedback interventions on performance: A historical review, a meta-analysis, and a preliminary feedback intervention theory. *Psychological Bulletin, 119,* 254–284.

Kruger, J.M. and Dunning, D. (1999). Unskilled and unaware of it: How difficulties in recognizing one's own incompetence lead to inflated self-assessments. *Journal of Personality and Social Psychology, 77,* 1121–1134.

Larson, J.R. Jr. (1989). The dynamic interplay between employees' feedback-seeking strategies and supervisors' delivery of performance feedback. *Academy of Management Review, 14,* 408–422.

Leventhal, H.R., Singer, R., and Jones, S. (1965). Effects of fear and specificity of recommendations upon attitudes and behavior. *Journal of Personality and Social Psychology, 2,* 20–29.

Libby, R., Trotman, K.T., and Zimmer, I. (1987). Member variation, recognition of expertise, and group performance. *Journal of Applied Psychology, 72*, 81–87.

Littlepage, G.E., Schmidt, G.W., Whisler, E.W., and Frost, A.G. (1995). An input-process-output analysis of influence and performance in problem-solving groups. *Journal of Personality and Social Psychology, 69*, 877–889.

Locke, E.A. and Latham, G.P. (1990). Work motivation and satisfaction: Light at the end of the tunnel. *Psychological Science, 1*, 240–246.

Mabe, P.A. III and West, S.G. (1982). Validity of self-evaluation of ability: A review and meta-analysis. *Journal of Applied Psychology, 67*, 280–286.

Miner, F.C. (1984). Group versus individual decision making: An investigation of performance measures, decision strategies, and process losses/gains. *Organizational Behavior and Human Performance, 33*, 112–124.

Mobius, M.M., Niederle, M., Niehaus, P., and Rosenblat, T.S. (2011). *Managing Self-confidence: Theory and Experimental Evidence.* Working Paper No. 17014. Cambridge, MA: NBER.

Murray, M. (1991). *Beyond the Myths and Magic of Mentoring: How to Facilitate an Effective Mentoring Program.* San Francisco, CA: Jossey-Bass/Pfeiffer.

Nagel, M. (2010). A mathematical model of democratic elections. *Current Research Journal of Social Sciences, 2*, 255–261.

Ng, S.H. and Bradac, J.J. (1993). *Power in Language: Verbal Communication and Social Influence.* Newbury Park, CA: SAGE.

Risucci, D.A., Torolani, A.J., and Ward, R.J. (1989). Ratings of surgical residents by self, supervisors and peers. *Surgical Gynecology and Obstetrics, 169*, 519–526.

Rothstein, H.R. (1990). Interrater reliability of job performance ratings: Growth to asymptote level with increasing opportunity to observe. *Journal of Applied Psychology, 75*, 322–327.

Sheldon, O., Ames, D., and Dunning, D. (2011). Self-assessments of emotional intelligence. Unpublished manuscript, Rutgers University.

Sherman, D.A.K., Nelson, L.D., and Steele, C.M. (2000). Do messages about health risks threaten the self? Increasing the acceptance of threatening health messages via self-affirmation. *Personality and Social Psychology Bulletin, 26*, 1046–1058.

Shipper, F. and Dillard, J.E. Jr. (2000). A study of impending derailment and recovery of middle managers across career stages. *Human Resource Management, 39*, 331–345.

Smither, J.W., London, M., and Reilly, R.R. (2005). Does performance improve following multisource feedback? A theoretical model, meta-analysis, and review of empirical findings. *Personnel Psychology, 58*, 33–66.

Steele, C.M. (1988). The psychology of self-affirmation: Sustaining the integrity of the self. In L. Berkowitz (Ed.) *Advances in Experimental Social Psychology* (vol. 21, pp. 261–302). San Diego, CA: Academic Press.

Thomas-Hunt, M.C. and Phillips, K.W. (2004). When what you know is not enough: Expertise and gender dynamics in task groups. *Personality and Social Psychology Bulletin, 30*, 1585–1598.

Vazire, S. (2010). Who knows what about a person? The Self-Other Knowledge Asymmetry (SOKA) model. *Journal of Personality and Social Psychology, 98*, 281–300.

Williams, E. and Dunning, D. (2011). From formulae to faith: Rational errors underlying mistaken confidence among the incompetent. Unpublished manuscript, University of Florida.

Williams, S.S., Kimble, D.L., Covell, N.H., Weiss, L.H., Newton, K.J., Fisher, J.D., and Fisher, W.A. (1992). College students use implicit personality theory instead of safer sex. *Journal of Applied Social Psychology, 22,* 921–933.

Woehr, D.J. and Huffcutt, A.I. (1994). Rater training for performance appraisal: A quantitative review. *Journal of Occupational and Organizational Psychology, 67,* 189–205.

Yaniv, I. and Kleinberger, E. (2000). Advice taking in decision making: Egocentric discounting and reputation formation. *Organizational Behavior and Human Decision Processes, 83,* 260–281.

Yetton, P. and Bottger, P. (1982). Individual versus group problem solving: An empirical test of a best-member strategy. *Organizational and Human Performance, 29,* 307–321.

Zenger, T.R. (1992). Why do employers only reward extreme performance? Examining the relationships among performance, pay, and turnover. *Administrative Science Quarterly, 37,* 198–219.

4

Employee Selection Decisions

Jerel E. Slaughter and Edgar E. Kausel

The majority of employee selection research is focused on the development, assessment, and relative predictive efficacy of predictor constructs and methods (e.g., Schmidt & Hunter, 1998). Also receiving considerable research attention are validation support for selection strategies (Schmitt & Sinha, 2011) and applicant reactions to selection systems (Hauskenecht, Day, & Thomas, 2004). Comparatively less work, however, has focused on the *decisions* that employers make during the selection process. This is despite the fact that virtually all employee selection scenarios come down to decisions about applicants, such as the decision to invite an applicant for an on-site interview, to reject the candidate from further consideration, or to make an employment offer. Thus, the lack of attention to the specific decisions is somewhat unfortunate, from both a scientific perspective and a practical one.

Fortunately, there is an enormous amount of research within the area of judgment and decision making (JDM) that has already begun to provide much insight into employee selection. JDM is an exciting and inter-disciplinary field that is highly relevant to employee selection decisions (e.g., Dalal et al., 2010; Highhouse, 1997, 2001). The goal of this chapter is to summarize what we know about decision making that can help us to understand why selection decision makers behave the way they do, as well as the outcomes that result from such behavior. The chapter is divided into three sections. In the first section, we outline some strategies that selection decision makers use and why they use them. People tend to place substantial weight on intuitive judgment, despite a preponderance of evidence that shows that the performance of statistical formulas far exceeds the performance of intuition for predicting job performance (Kleinmuntz, 1990). We offer several reasons for why this occurs. In the second section, we discuss some negative consequences of relying on intuition. Finally, in the third section, we discuss some practical considerations: How can we improve employee selection decision making? We discuss how research findings might be communicated in a manner that is more persuasive to hiring managers, as well as our ideas about how to compensate for the fact that managers are unlikely to fully surrender their use of intuition when making selection decisions.

HOW SELECTION DECISIONS ARE MADE

Potential Methods of Making Selection Decisions

Before we discuss how people typically *do* make selection decisions, it is worth considering the possible ways that they *can* use to make decisions. Table 4.1 (adapted from Gatewood, Feild, & Barrick, 2008) presents these methods. The far left column of the table represents how information about applicants, or *predictor* information, is collected. The final two columns represent the possibilities that different pieces of predictor information can either be combined mechanically, with a predetermined formula, or judgmentally, where the decision maker decides how to integrate the information to make final decisions.

When predictor information is purely judgmental, it means that only the subjective judgment of the decision maker is used to form opinions of applicants' information. Examples of this include judgments made from standard employment applications, résumés, and unstructured interviews. When predictor information is purely mechanical, this means that

TABLE 4.1

Methods of Collecting and Combining Predictor Information for Making Selection Decisions

Method of Collecting Predictor Information	Method of Combining Predictor Information	
	Mechanical	**Judgmental**
Judgmental	Trait Ratings	Pure Judgment
Mechanical	Pure Statistical	Profile Interpretation
Both	Mechanical Composite	Judgmental Composite

Source: Adapted from Gatewood, Feild, and Barrick (2008). *Human Resource Selection* (6th ed., p. 227). Cincinnati, OH: Southwestern. Table is abridged version of the original.

subjective judgment plays no part in applicant scores on the predictors. Examples of mechanical predictor information collection include standardized tests of cognitive ability, personality, and situational judgment. Of course, there are many times when both types of information are collected, such as when both tests and interviews are used, and these possibilities are represented in the third row of the table. A mechanical composite takes both kinds of predictor information and combines formulaically. Finally, a judgmental composite is used when decision makers have both mechanical and judgmental predictor information available to them and choose to make decisions by combining information judgmentally.

Judgmental composites are likely the most common method of making selection decisions (Gatewood, Feild, & Barrick, 2008). Prevailing conventional wisdom goes something like this: It's a good idea to collect some standardized information about candidates with published tests. It's easy and relatively inexpensive. But in the end, if you're going to accept a person into your organization, and invest the time required to train and socialize that employee, you want to have a say in the matter, and not have the candidate selected by a formula. As stated by Debra Cohen, the chief knowledge officer of the Society for Human Resource Management (SHRM), on the hiring practices used at SHRM:

> At the end of the day, however, hiring managers have to use their judgment as to which candidates make the cut for further predictive testing and must ultimately select individuals who will fit the organization as well as have the technical capability to do the job. A person who is smart and who gets "results" may be a person who discriminates, bullies, or causes turnover in the organization. Practitioners are mindful of these issues because as HR professionals they see the fallout daily from poor fit or bad management practices and know that intelligence, personality, and goal setting are important but are not enough.
>
> (Cohen, 2007, p. 1014)

So often, hiring managers are given the final say in the decision, and use their own subjective judgment to combine the assessment information that has been collected. We want now to consider the question of why: Why do managers rely on their judgment to collect predictor information, and combine predictor information to make a final decision? Below, we suggest that this is a result of three processes that work together: lay theories about predicting job performance; decision-making biases that lead to persistence in the use of intuitive judgment; and practical considerations, such as organizational constraints and accountability systems.

Lay Theories about Predicting Job Performance

One reason why hiring managers rely on their subjective judgment for collecting predictor information is because of their beliefs about the ability to develop expertise in predicting job performance. Accounts suggest that experienced managers believe that the combination of years of interviewing experience and the richness of the information exchanged between interviewer and interviewee can lead to improved accuracy (Leonard & Swap, 2004). Anecdotal examples are also easy to find. For instance, we have heard managers in our executive MBA classes claim that (unstructured) interviews can help managers (a) tell if people were lying on their résumés or personality tests and (b) assess their personalities to see how well they will fit into the current organization or workgroup.

These assertions are probably best characterized as "half-truths." Research does suggest, in fact, that interview-based measures of personality predict performance. Huffcutt et al. (2001) observed meta-analytic, corrected correlations between job performance and interview-assessed conscientiousness ($\rho = .33$), extraversion ($\rho = .33$), emotional stability ($\rho = .47$), and agreeableness ($\rho = .51$). These are actually higher than meta-analytic validities for self-report personality measures (Barrick, Mount, & Judge, 2001). However, the more critical finding was that the validities for structured interview assessments of personality were much higher (around .44) than for unstructured interview assessments (around .25). Thus, in order to appropriately assess personality in an interview, one must develop questions that are specifically intended to measure these characteristics, develop rating scales with behavioral anchors, train interviewers, ask the same questions of all candidates, and so forth (Campion, Palmer, & Campion, 1997). Casual conversation that is not standardized across applicants is unlikely to give interviewers valuable information about applicant personality.

Managers also believe in their ability to predict future job performance based on interview performance because interviews contain rich and detailed information. Put simply, having access to more detailed information leads people to be more confident about their decisions (Heath & Gonzalez, 1995; Koriat, 2008; Oskamp, 1965). Unfortunately, this increased confidence is not associated with an increase in accuracy. Oskamp (1965) found that clinicians and graduate students increased their reported confidence in responses to multiple-choice questions about a patient's life history as they received successively more information (e.g., moving from just background information, to childhood information, to information about school years, to information about adult years), and yet the accuracy of their responses remained constant even as the amount of information increased. The same was true in more recent work by Hall, Ariss, and Todorov (2007) and Tsai, Klayman, and Hastie (2008) in predicting the outcome of basketball and football games. One reason posited for these effects is that people pay too much attention to irrelevant and nondiagnostic information, and this "crowds out" the more predictive, but mundane, statistical information. So, over the years, managers strengthen their belief that, once they have rich and detailed information, they can treat the prediction of job performance as a unique event and therefore not amenable to statistical prediction (Hall et al., 2007).

How do managers form these lay theories of influences on decision accuracy? Evidence suggests that two sources are responsible. One likely source is the training and guidance they receive from *other managers*. Rynes, Colbert, and Brown (2002) found that most high-ranking managers—those with the titles of manager, director, and vice president—answered incorrectly to true–false questions concerning the effectiveness of structured interviews, the validity of cognitive ability for low-skilled jobs, the superiority of intelligence over conscientiousness as a predictor of job performance, and the existence of the five-factor model of personality. Moreover, respondents reported that the most common source of assistance in solving HR problems was another HR professional in the same organization. This is sobering, given their average level of knowledge. This means that the untruths then get "passed down the line" to newer and less-experienced managers, along with increased confidence in their decision strategies (e.g., Heath & Gonzalez, 1995).

A second source of managers' lay theories is the information contained in the publications they read (Rynes, Giluk, & Brown, 2007). Rynes, Giluk, and Brown (2007) found that there was very little coverage of the efficacy of cognitive ability or personality in employee selection in *Harvard Business Review* and *HR Magazine*, two publications with large readerships that are meant to bridge science and practice. Even worse, they found that several of the articles that were published in these outlets presented information that was either inconsistent with published scientific HR findings or made claims that went beyond those findings (e.g., suggesting that personality can be assessed by evaluating interviewee behavior during a meal at a restaurant). Claims such as these may be particularly damaging, because they may be direct causes of managers' use of subjective judgment rather than validated selection tools.

Biases that Lead to the Persistence of Judgment Reliance

To this point, we have discussed several reasons why managers may initially choose to use judgment and intuition over more scientifically sound selection decision-making methods. However, it is also worth considering why managers *persist* in using such methods even when they might be presented with evidence that suggests that their strategies are not sound.

One potential reason for this persistence is that hiring managers are unlikely to engage in critical evaluations of their decisions. When people form an opinion or attitude, they favorably evaluate information that supports their initial opinion, while also disregarding or reacting negatively to unsupportive information (Hogan, 1987; Lord, Ross, & Lepper, 1979; Rothbart, Evans, & Fulero, 1979). For example, Lord, Ross, and Lepper (1979) found that college students who supported capital punishment evaluated experimenter-created synopses of research studies that suggested its deterrent effect as scientifically sound, while they easily found many problems with studies that suggested nondeterrence. The opposite was true for those who reported opposing capital punishment. Similarly, Hogan (1987) found that supervisors' initial expectations about how well subordinates would perform influenced their performance ratings. In a selection decision-making situation, what this means is that, when a manager decides to extend a job offer to an applicant, he or she becomes more likely to evaluate that person as a successful hire in the future. To justify the initial decision, managers may attend only to the employee's successful performance outcomes and overlook the unsuccessful ones. Moreover, because the manager expects the employee to perform well, the manager may also provide opportunities and assignments that actually encourage the employee to perform successfully (e.g., Eden, 1984; Rosenthal & Jacobson, 1968). Such behaviors would lend managers continued confidence in the efficacy of their current selection methods.

There are also some features of selection decisions that impose limits on hiring managers' ability and motivation to learn from their past decision-making experiences. In terms of selection decision making, we conceptualize *learning from experience* as being able to recognize the positive and negative aspects of one's previous actions, so that one can repeat what was done well and make improvements on what was not done well. Sometimes, by no fault of their own, managers are unable to learn from experience. Consider the case of when a manager rejects an applicant for a position because he didn't "click" with this applicant as well as he did with another, and therefore felt that the applicant wouldn't fit with him and other members of the team (even though the rejected applicant had relevant work experience and high scores on the organization's test battery). In this case, even if that applicant goes on to be successful at a similar job, and would have been successful had they been chosen, the manager likely cannot and will not be aware of this. The manager is likely to be unaware he has made a poor decision, and could not correct his error in the future— even if he wanted to do so.

There are also many things that limit managers' *motivation* to learn from situations in which the chosen employee turned out to be unsuccessful. One is that people fall prey to self-serving explanations and rationalizing, such as unrealistically blaming the failure on others, or on supposedly unforeseeable circumstances (Zuckerman, 1979; Russo & Schoemaker, 1989). For example, a manager might blame a weakening economy or lack of coworker support for the poor performance of a salesperson whom she had selected. Decision makers have also been found to fall prey to the hindsight bias, in which people have a hard time divorcing themselves from the knowledge they have after an event occurred (Fischhoff, 1975; Hawkins & Hastie, 1990). This leads decision makers to believe that they knew the outcome "all along." In such cases, managers may erroneously recall that they had a smaller role in the selection decision than was actually the case, or they might inappropriately remember having had information that would have led them to make a different selection decision. For example, they may discover that the employee had been let go from a previous sales job for poor performance, and then falsely remember perceiving that the person might not be very persuasive and would have a hard time closing deals. Alternatively, they may blame the unsuccessful hire on candidate misrepresentation of qualifications (Phillips & Gully, 2008). Finally, even if managers accept that they have made decision-making errors, they may be likely to forget them altogether. When managers reflect on their previous decisions, they are also likely to remember them in a more favorable light than is deserved, as people tend to remember their successes and forget their failures (Tversky & Kahneman, 1973).

Practical Considerations

Methods of selection decision making are also impacted by situational forces. The patterns we describe above result not only from individual tendencies.

The root cause is often more systemic, because circumstances are often not conducive to making optimal decisions. For example, selection decision makers may not have resources such as a large amount of uninterrupted time and knowledge of regression analysis when they make decisions. Instead, many have been thrust into supervisory roles with relatively little training on the human resource aspects of their jobs. Hiring managers also have to consider the views of higher-level managers to whom they might have to explain the decisions, and the preferences of subordinates with whom the new hire will be working closely (Gilliland & Cherry, 2000). Such accountability pressures (Frink & Klimoski, 1998) are likely to cause decision makers to rely on easily justifiable reasons for choosing candidates, perhaps to the neglect of more important factors (Shafir, Simonson, & Tversky, 1993). Finally, because selection decisions in organizations are often influenced by panels, committee, or groups (Sessa & Taylor, 2000), it is important to understand that group processes and preferences may influence individual managerial decision-making strategies.

Summary

In this section, we have discussed various ways that selection decisions might be made. These include combinations of (a) mechanical or judgment predictor information that is (b) combined either mechanically or judgmentally. Evidence suggests that those making selection decisions are likely to use a judgmental combination of mechanical and judgmental predictor information. We followed this with discussion of some potential reasons why this occurs, including managers' ideas about how information gathered during the selection process influences predictability. Finally, we also discussed some reasons why people might persist in their use of judgment, or why they continue to "stubbornly rely" on their intuition to the neglect of methods that are more scientifically sound (Highhouse, 2008). In the section that follows, we discuss some consequences of relying on intuitive judgment.

SOME NEGATIVE CONSEQUENCES OF RELIANCE ON JUDGMENT

One of the earliest questions studied in the field of JDM was whether experts' predictions were better than mechanical combinations of data

(Morera & Dawes, 2006). In an influential book, Paul Meehl (1954) reviewed twenty studies comparing intuitive (judgmental) predictions made by clinical psychologists with predictions based on statistical models. In all studies that Meehl reviewed, he found that the statistical method provided more accurate forecasts than judgments, or a combination of the two. More than five decades of research—and hundreds of studies—have consistently shown that in virtually every type of possible forecast (e.g., political and economic trends, criminal recidivism, marital satisfaction, job performance), judgmental predictions are inferior to statistical predictions (Grove et al., 2000; Tetlock, 2005). In the following paragraphs, we consider some of the negative consequences of intuitive judgment that explain this poor performance.

Neglecting Base Rates

Decision makers are rationally bounded (Simon, 1956) and are particularly poor at incorporating information such as base rates in their judgment (Kahneman & Tversky, 1973). Consider the following scenario. Job applicants in a retail company are required to take an integrity test to detect potentially dishonest individuals (i.e., individuals who have engaged in employee theft). Extensive research with the test suggests it correctly identifies dishonest individuals 80 percent of the time (i.e., 80 percent of employees who failed the test had engaged in employee theft). Twenty percent of the time the test incorrectly identifies a dishonest individual (i.e., 20 percent of individuals who failed the test had not engaged in employee theft). In addition, research shows that about 5 percent of applicants are dishonest (e.g, Ash, 1988).

Suppose a given candidate fails the integrity test. What is the probability that this candidate is in fact dishonest? Most people would answer that the probability is pretty high. In an undergraduate HR class we have taught, more than 90 percent of the students stated that the probability would be over 75 percent, and that given the risk it would be reasonable not to hire the applicant. Using Bayes' Theorem, however, the normative correct answer is only 17 percent. In other words, the odds are roughly 5:1 that the candidate is honest! This gap between human judgment and the Bayesian answer is not limited to business undergraduates. Eddy (1982) found that physicians made errors of similar magnitude when presented with a comparable problem involving cancer diagnosis.

Why is human judgment so far off? One critical issue is that people tend to ignore base rates. In the scenario above, they tend to disregard the fact that there are few dishonest individuals (5 percent) in the population of applicants. This is essential in Bayesian reasoning. If there are 1,000 applicants, we would expect that 50 individuals would be dishonest, and that 40 (80 percent) of them would fail the test. The problem is what occurs with the remaining 950 applicants, as 190 of these (950 × .20) would unfairly fail the test. Thus, a total of 230 (40 + 190) applicants would fail the test and, as noted, only 17 percent of these would be accurately identified as dishonest. We encourage the reader to perform these computations assuming that 50 percent of the applicants are dishonest. Under this assumption, things change dramatically: Eighty percent of individuals would be accurately identified as dishonest. In this case, most students in our class would have been right in their estimations.

Adjusting for Task Difficulty

Decision makers also have a hard time comparing "apples to oranges." Consider a situation in which a manager compares the past performance of two candidates. In previous jobs, the first candidate achieved impressive numbers selling a product from a reputable brand (i.e., high performance in an easy job); the second candidate achieved lower numbers by selling a product from an unknown brand (i.e., average performance in a difficult job). Can employers adjust their judgment for this differential difficulty?

Moore et al. (2010) examined this issue in the context of graduate admission decisions. Undergraduate institutions vary in their grading standards and this is known (Rojstaczer, 2010). High grades are easier to earn in some institutions and thus are less indicative of high performance than are the same grades earned from an institution with lower average grades. Moore et al. (2010) found that admissions committees failed to adjust their interpretation of grades based on the leniency of grading, even after controlling for a number of factors such as institutional quality. As a result, students from universities who provided higher grades were favored in selection. This finding is consistent with a broader phenomenon, the correspondence bias, which suggests that people are unable to sufficiently discount information about others' situations when assessing their outcomes (Gilbert & Malone, 1995).

Relations among Choice Options

People can also make inconsistent choices because of how judgments and decisions are elicited. Lichtenstein and Slovic (2006) argue that one of the most important findings in JDM over the last several decades is that people seldom "have" preferences; rather, preferences are constructed in the process of making a particular choice (Payne, Bettman, & Johnson, 1992). This construction of preference often leads to reversals in choice: Sometimes people prefer option A to option B; sometimes they prefer B to A.

There is a growing literature on choice-set effects in personnel decisions, which suggests that decisions in these contexts are highly sensitive to the way the choice is framed. For example, Highhouse and Gallo (1997) found that participants who observed a candidate performing poorly at the end of a work sample exercise rated the candidate's overall performance as worse than those who observed the candidate performing poorly at the beginning of the exercise. Schuh (1978) demonstrated contrast effects in employment interviews, in which a job candidate's rating depended on the previous candidate's performance.

Decisions about job candidates may also be influenced by decoys (Huber, Payne, & Puto, 1982). The decoy effect occurs when choices between two options that are similarly attractive change by introducing a third option (the decoy). For example, consider a case in which a general manager is deciding among three applicants for a plant manager in a manufacturing company. The three final candidates differ on only two assessments: a work sample assessment and a promotability assessment (see Table 4.2). A is clearly superior to C, and therefore choosing C doesn't make much sense. However, the choice between A and B is tough to make. Which candidate is the general manager more likely to choose? Highhouse (1996) presented these options to participants. As expected, nobody chose Candidate C; most people (68 percent) chose Candidate A. Now, imagine a second scenario in which Candidate A and B had received the same assessment as above, but Candidate C had scored low on the work sample test (4) and high on the promotability interview (80). Again, Candidate C is clearly inferior to

TABLE 4.2

Candidate Assessment

Candidate Name	Work Sample	Promotability
Candidate A	7	66
Candidate B	5	80
Candidate C	7	54

Source: Adapted from Highhouse (1996).

option B, and Highhouse (1996) found that no one chose this option. But here, most people (65 percent) chose participant B. Despite never being chosen, the decoy—Candidate C—induced a preference reversal of the other two options!

The decoy effect seems to be robust. Slaughter, Sinar, and Highhouse (1999) found the effect even when decision makers had to make inferences about each candidate's performance on each dimension (i.e., candidate performance was videotaped and had to be inferred). Slaughter, Bagger, and Li (2006) found the decoy effect to be stronger when selection decisions were made by groups. Interestingly, Bonaccio and Reeve (2006) found that, when asked about why they made their choice, decision makers seemed to be unaware of the decoy's influence.

Summary

There are several factors that make human judgment imperfect. Selection decision makers who base their judgment solely on intuition tend to neglect information, have difficulty in adjusting information, and fall prey to context effects that lead to preference reversals. The overall conclusion from this section is that, whenever possible, it is better to use mechanical combinations of data rather than intuitive judgment. This position is shared by many authors in the behavioral sciences. As Meehl (1986) stated, in reference to the clinical versus mechanical controversy, "there is no controversy in social science which shows such a large body of qualitatively diverse studies coming out so uniformly in the same direction as this one" (p. 373).

IMPROVING SELECTION DECISION MAKING

In this section, we provide some suggestions for improving selection decision making. Frankly, the causes of less-than-optimal decision making we have discussed—such as naiveté and misinformation, pervasive cognitive and motivational biases, and organizational accountability systems—are rather far reaching, and it is beyond the scope of this chapter to suggest ways of fixing all of these problems. Thus, in this section, we provide a relatively modest set of suggestions for improvement. Much as we hate to admit it, these are closer to conventional corrective medicine than they are to preventative lifestyle changes. The first set of suggestions deals with how we might convince practitioners of the value of selection research findings and mechanical combinations of data. The second set helps to account for situations where it may not be possible to rely on mechanical combinations of data. In presenting these, we recognize that managers will be reluctant to give up control over the selection process and to entirely ignore their intuitive judgment (e.g., Posthuma, Morgeson, & Campion, 2002).

Persuading Selection Decision Makers

Use simple statistics. Although selection researchers obviously have a strong grasp of the meaningfulness of r and r^2 values, we recommend avoiding their use for trying to convince managers of the usefulness of validated selection tools. In general, managers either do not understand these coefficients, or they use them to criticize selection decision aids (and thus rely exclusively on their intuition). As Kuncel (2008) states, "[t]he unfortunate reality is that 4 percent of the variance can save some organizations a fortune but will rarely get anyone excited" (p. 345).

A better strategy may be to present validity information in terms of expectancy charts and performance differences between low and high scorers (Bridgeman, Burton, & Cline, 2009). These authors offered a strategy of presenting validity information where scores on the predictor (GRE scores) were divided into three groups (top 25 percent, middle 50 percent, and bottom 25 percent), and scores on the criterion were divided into two groups (highly successful, 3.8 or higher GPA in the first year of graduate school; and not highly successful, or less than 3.8 GPA). Their analysis showed that, for doctoral students in biology, 39 percent of those in the highest-scoring group were highly successful. This compared favorably to 22 percent in the middle-GRE group, and 15 percent in the low-GRE group. This presentation is likely be much more convincing to decision makers than would an analysis showing an r^2 of .09.

Moreover, we recommend that, when communicating base rates to managers, a frequency format is preferred over a percentage format. People have an easier time dealing with frequencies than they do with percentages (Gigerenzer, Hell, & Blank, 1988), because the natural way that people tend to learn about contingencies is through the sequential coding and updating of frequencies (Cosmides & Tooby, 1996). Gigerenzer and Hoffrage (1995) found that Bayesian reasoning (necessary to solve the potentially dishonest applicant scenario described above) was much improved when using frequency formats (e.g., 5 of every 100 applicants are dishonest) as opposed to probability formats (0.05 probability of an applicant being dishonest) or even percentage formats (5 percent of the applicants are dishonest). Presenting base-rate information as frequencies may thus improve managers' accuracy when thinking about statistics.

Use easily-understood utility estimates and causal chain analysis. Most readers are likely to be at least somewhat familiar with utility analysis, which translates the impact of human resource procedures into dollar values (Boudreau & Ramstad, 2003). Utility formulas attempt to estimate the dollar value of the gain in employee performance that results from using selection procedures that correlate with performance, or HR interventions that improve performance, such as performance appraisal and training programs. Presumably, such information should be convincing to managers because they take into account the dollar cost and dollar benefit of the HR practice and allow them, with relatively easy manipulation, to determine how much money can be gained (or saved) by implementing certain procedures. However, research on managers' acceptance of utility estimates suggests that, unless utility formulas are significantly simplified, estimates derived from these formulas are unlikely to be convincing to managers (Hazer & Highhouse, 1997). Utility formulas include as their components selection ratios, the dollar estimate of a standard deviation difference in job performance, and the expected standardized difference in performance between a group subjected to the HR practices and a no-treatment control group. Not surprisingly, managerial reactions to these estimates have not been very favorable. In fact, Whyte and Latham (1997) found that adding utility analysis estimates using these types of formulas led to lower acceptance of the HR practice. It will be important for future researchers to continue to experiment with simpler forms of utility analysis and determine whether selection decision makers' reactions may be improved.[1]

Fortunately, conclusions from recent research using a more simplified version of utility analysis, termed *causal chain analysis,* have been more encouraging (Winkler, Köenig, & Kleinmann, 2010). Causal chain analysis demonstrates the linkage of the implementation of HR practices to increases in profits through mediating variables such as employee attitudes and customer satisfaction (of course, these paths to profit are also likely to be indirect, and mediated by variables such as effort and work withdrawal for attitudes, and repeat business and positive word-of-mouth advertising for customer satisfaction). The presentation to decision makers is similar to figures that researchers use to depict path models, except that the paths are depicted as percentages in the dependent variable that result from a set increase in the independent variable, as established by prior research.

For example, Figure 4.1 shows the expected increase in profits resulting from a 10 percent increase in training participation. All that needs to be added is an explanation of the cost of the program ($150,000) and the dollar value of an 8 percent increase in profits ($600,000) to calculate the expected return on investment (400 percent). In Figure 4.2, we have adapted the situation to a selection situation that involves using tests of extraversion to select customer service employees (e.g., Liao & Chuang, 2004). Winkler, Köenig, and Kleinmann (2010) found that, compared to utility analysis with the same training program and the same level of profit, managers perceived the causal chain analysis to be more understandable, felt that the information was of higher quality, were more satisfied with the information, and indicated stronger intention to use the program. Such results are promising for the future of convincing practitioners of the monetary value of scientific selection.

Present information to others in terms of narratives. As noted, managers are more likely to rely on personnel selection aids—and therefore make better decisions—if they can see the value of the method. One effective way in which a prediction method can gain acceptance is through the use of narratives (Kuncel, 2008). People seldom use raw evidence (e.g, numerical information) to make intuitive decisions; rather, they use narrative story structures to organize and interpret evidence (Pennington & Hastie, 1988). Narratives allow people to mentally simulate situations (Tversky & Kahneman, 1982). In employee selection, for example, narratives could allow individuals to imagine situations in which a candidate may behave in certain ways. Narratives also allow the presentation of information in

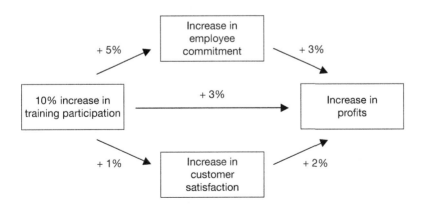

FIGURE 4.1
Causal chain analysis (adapted from Winkler, Köenig, & Kleinmann, 2010).

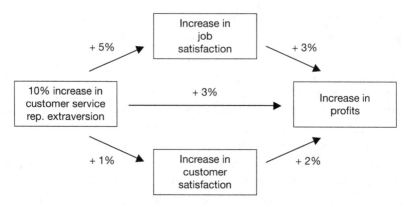

FIGURE 4.2
Causal chain analysis adapted to employee selection.

the form of causal arguments, which are more readily assimilated and more easily recalled than information presented in the form of statistical summaries (Slusher & Anderson, 1996). For example, one could present the information of Candidate A in a table, showing a score at the 90th percentile on a general mental ability test. Alternatively, this information could be presented in a narrative format: "C. Underwood has high general mental abilities, and thus she is likely to process information in an efficient way. This may help her prepare accurate financial reports." Presenting information about a candidate in terms of a narrative rather than with only numerical information could greatly increase the perceived importance of a particular assessment.

Accounting for the Use of Intuition

Offer decision support based on statistical predictions. Decisions and predictions are more likely to be accepted if there is input from human judgment. From this perspective, it is unrealistic to expect that organizational decision makers will accept taking human judgment "out of the loop" and leave selection forecasts (i.e., predictions of candidates' job performance) entirely to mechanical combinations of predictors. Furthermore, people are unwilling to use decision aids when they perceive their own autonomy to be violated (Goldsmith, 2000). This suggests that people may react unfavorably if told to pick the option that the statistical method recommends. A different strategy that is likely to create less reactance is to offer *decision support*, in which decision makers are not told *what* to choose, but *how* to choose (Dalal & Bonaccio, 2010) based on statistical methods. For example, decision makers may be advised on how to combine the information they face, as suggested by a weighed additive model. Dalal and Bonaccio (2010, Study 2) found that decision support was well perceived in terms of both accuracy and autonomy.

Use a limited number of important cues. There may be cases in which statistical methods such as regression analysis are so strongly opposed that they cannot be used at all. Even so, fortunately, there is substantial research on the best predictors of job performance (e.g., Schmidt & Hunter, 1998). We recommend using a small set of valid predictors (or cues) such as scores from general mental ability tests and assessment centers. Using too much information, especially when information is vivid and irrelevant (e.g., whether someone *looks* competent; Todorov et al., 2005), makes people lose their focus and rely less on the more valid predictors (Hall, Ariss, & Todorov, 2007).

Ask decision makers to make precise estimates, and provide unambiguous feedback. Together with the decision of hiring or rejecting a candidate, decision makers should make precise, numerical predictions. For example, a decision maker could predict that he or she is 50 percent confident that candidate A will be in the top decile of all employees' performance; or that he or she is 90 percent confident that candidate B will be in the top decile of all employees' performance. Note that there are two important issues that make these estimates precise: (a) They include a numerical confidence interval (e.g., 90 percent), and (b) they include a specific criterion (e.g., the top decile of all employees' performance).

Precise predictions such as these can be contrasted with actual performance, which allows computing calibration and overconfidence indices (Yates, 1990). Of course, this only applies to accepted candidates, as it is impossible to receive feedback from rejected candidates. Using precise estimates makes individuals less likely to be vulnerable to hindsight bias (Fischhoff, 2001). This allows decision makers to realize the limitations of their predictive skills, and to learn from feedback (Arkes, 2001). As a result, they may be more willing to rely on selection decision aids, which should improve their hiring decisions.

Promote thinking about reasons why the initial judgment may be wrong. In addition to precise estimates and feedback, a second way to reduce overconfidence is to think about (and write down) reasons why the initial judgment may be wrong (Arkes, 1991). This works as a debiasing strategy, because the individual focuses on contrary evidence that would not otherwise be considered (Larrick, 2004). Thinking and listing these reasons can help make more accurate judgments.

Summary

In this section, we have discussed a number of ways to try to convince managers of the value of evidence-based decision making for employee selection, including simplifying the presentation of validity and utility information. We have also discussed ways to improve decision making when managers are resistant to using mechanical predictor information and mechanical combination of predictors. We do need to sound a note of caution here. Many of the suggestions we have made are based on what is known from laboratory-based decision-making research. Thus, whether they will be effective in the field, in terms of improving decision making and improving user reactions, is an empirical question. We urge researchers to continue to experiment with different methods for improving the quality of selection decisions.

CONCLUDING COMMENTS

In this chapter, we have discussed selected research on judgment and decision making and its relation to employee selection. Given the close relationship between these two processes, we are hopeful that the information we have presented leads to more research at the intersection of these topics and creative ideas about how to improve selection decision making in organizations. As a result of the brevity of the chapter, we want to leave with the warning that there are many influences on decision making not discussed here. If the reader is so inclined, we encourage a closer look at other works in decision making that will provide more complete information (e.g., Loewenstein, 1996).

We want to leave the reader with two thoughts. One is directed toward practitioners and managers, and the other is directed toward researchers. In his most recent book, Ariely (2010) writes about testing one's intuition. Many practitioners believe in the power of their intuitive judgments because they do not dare to act *against* their intuition. As a result, they are never able to test the hypothesis that their intuitions might be wrong. Most managers seriously underestimate the value of experimentation, however (Staw & Ross, 1987). Managers should test their intuition every so often, by ignoring their gut feelings and choosing on the basis of objective information. For example, they might choose job candidates whose scores on objective assessments are highest but who do not rank first on their intuitive assessment of rapport and fit. They may well find that acting against intuition and relying on validated methods is a pretty good method after all.

Finally, missing from research on selection decision making is descriptive information on how such decisions are made. Many of the assumptions we have made here, in terms of how often intuition is used or our ideas about exactly why managers cling to intuition, have not been fully substantiated empirically. We encourage researchers to collect information from managers on how they make selection decisions, as well as the reasons for the methods they use. Qualitative research—paradoxically, in the form of interviews—can be especially helpful in this regard. Before we can be confident about providing solutions, we need to know more about the basic "problem."

NOTE

1. There are certainly other reasons beyond complexity that may be causing negative reactions to utility estimates. First, utility estimates might seem absurdly high in terms of raw dollars gained. Second, utility estimates are often computed without input from other organizational decision makers. In such cases, it is unlikely that this analysis will be convincing (Jayne & Rauschenberger, 2000). These issues are also important to consider when using causal chain analysis.

REFERENCES

Ariely, D. (2010). *The Upside of Irrationality: The Unexpected Benefits of Defying Logic at Work and at Home.* New York: HarperCollins.

Arkes, H.R. (1991). Costs and benefits of judgment errors: Implications for debiasing. *Psychological Bulletin, 110,* 486–498.

Arkes, H.R. (2001). Overconfidence in judgmental forecasting. In J.S. Armstrong (Ed.) *Principles of Forecasting: A Handbook for Researchers and Practitioners* (pp. 157–176). Boston, MA: Kluwer Academic.

Ash, P. (1988). *Honesty Test Scores, Biographical Data, and Delinquency Indicators.* Paper presented at the 96th Annual Convention of the American Psychological Association, Atlanta, GA, August.

Barrick, M.R., Mount, M.K., and Judge, T.A. (2001). Personality and performance at the beginning of the new millennium: What do we know and where do we go next? *International Journal of Selection and Assessment, 9,* 9–30.

Bonaccio, S. and Reeve, C.L. (2006). Consideration of preference shifts due to relative attribute variability. *Organizational Behavior and Human Decision Processes, 101,* 200–214.

Boudreau, J.W. and Ramstad, P.M. (2003). Strategic HRM measurement in the 21st century: From justifying HR to strategic talent leadership. In M. Goldsmith, R.P. Gandossy, and M.S. Efron (Eds.) *HRM in the 21st Century* (pp. 79–90). New York: John Wiley.

Bridgeman, B., Burton, N., and Cline, F. (2009). A note on presenting what predictive validity numbers mean. *Applied Measurement in Education, 22*, 109–119.

Campion, M.A., Palmer, D.K., and Campion, J.E. (1997). A review of structure in the selection interview. *Personnel Psychology, 50*, 655–702.

Cohen, D.J. (2007). The very separate worlds of academic and practitioner publications in human resource management: Reasons for the divide and concrete solutions for bridging the gap. *Academy of Management Journal, 50*, 1013–1019.

Cosmides, L. and Tooby, J. (1996). Are humans good intuitive statisticians after all? Rethinking some conclusions from the literature on judgment under uncertainty. *Cognition, 58*, 1–73.

Dalal, R.S. and Bonaccio, S. (2010). What types of advice do decision-makers prefer? *Organizational Behavior and Human Decision Processes, 112*, 11–23.

Dalal, R.S., Bonaccio, S., Ilgen, D.R., Highhouse, S., Mohammed, S., and Slaughter, J.E. (2010). What if industrial–organizational psychology decided to take workplace decisions seriously? *Industrial and Organizational Psychology: Perspectives on Science and Practice, 3*, 386–405.

Eddy, D.M. (1982). Probabilistic reasoning in clinical medicine: Problems and opportunities. In D. Kahneman, P. Slovic, and A. Tversky (Eds.) *Judgment under Uncertainty: Heuristics and Biases* (pp. 249–267). Cambridge: Cambridge University Press.

Eden, D. (1984). Self-fulfilling prophecy as a management tool: Harnessing Pygmalion. *Academy of Management Review, 9*, 64–73.

Fischhoff, B. (1975). Hindsight ≠ foresight: The effect of outcome knowledge on judgment under uncertainty. *Journal of Experimental Psychology: Human Perception and Performance, 104*, 288–299.

Fischhoff, B. (2001). Learning from experience: Coping with hindsight bias and ambiguity. In J.S. Armstrong (Ed.) *Principles of Forecasting: A Handbook for Researchers and Practitioners* (pp. 543–554). Boston, MA: Kluwer Academic.

Frink, D.D. and Klimoski, R.J. (1998). Toward a theory of accountability in organizational and human resources management. *Research in Personnel and Human Resources Management, 17*, 1–51.

Gatewood, R.D., Feild, H.S., and Barrick, M.R. (2008). *Human Resource Selection*. Cincinnati, OH: Southwestern.

Gigerenzer, G., Hell, W., and Blank, H. (1988). Presentation and content: The use of base rates as a continuous variable. *Journal of Experimental Psychology: Human Perception and Performance, 14*, 513–525.

Gigerenzer, G. and Hoffrage, U. (1995). How to improve Bayesian reasoning without instruction: Frequency formats. *Psychological Review, 102*, 684–704.

Gilbert, D.T. and Malone, P.S. (1995). The correspondence bias. *Psychological Bulletin, 117*, 21–38.

Gilliland, S.W. and Cherry, B. (2000). Managing "customers" of selection processes. In J. Kehoe (Ed.) *Managing Selection in Changing Organizations* (pp. 158–196). San Francisco, CA: Jossey-Bass.

Goldsmith, D.J. (2000). Soliciting advice. The role of sequential placement in mitigating face threat. *Communications Monographs, 67*, 1–19.

Grove, W.M., Zald, D.H., Lebow, B.S., Snitz, B.E., and Nelson, C. (2000). Clinical versus mechanical prediction: A meta-analysis. *Psychological Assessment, 12*, 19–30.

Hall, C.C., Ariss, L., and Todorov, A. (2007). The illusion of knowledge: When more information reduces accuracy and increases confidence. *Organizational Behavior and Human Decision Processes, 103,* 277–290.

Hauskenecht, J.P., Day, D.V., and Thomas, S.C. (2004). Applicant reactions to selection procedures: An updated model and meta-analysis. *Personnel Psychology, 57,* 639–683.

Hawkins, S.A. and Hastie, R. (1990). Hindsight: Biased judgments of past events when outcomes are known. *Psychological Bulletin, 107,* 311–327.

Hazer, J.T. and Highhouse, S. (1997). Factors influencing managers' reactions to utility analysis: Effects of SD_y method, information frame, and focal intervention. *Journal of Applied Psychology, 82,* 104–112.

Heath, C. and Gonzalez, R. (1995). Interaction with others increases decision confidence but not decision quality: Evidence against information collection views of interactive decision making. *Organizational Behavior and Human Decision Processes, 61,* 305–326.

Highhouse, S. (1996). Context-dependent selection: The effects of decoy and phantom job candidates. *Organizational Behavior and Human Decision Processes, 65,* 68–76.

Highhouse, S. (1997). Understanding and improving job-finalist choice: The relevance of behavioral decision research. *Human Resource Management Review, 7,* 449–470.

Highhouse, S. (2001). Judgment and decision making research: Relevance to industrial and organizational psychology. In N. Anderson, D.S. Ones, H.K. Sinangil, and C. Viswesvaran (Eds.) *Handbook of Industrial, Work and Organizational Psychology* (pp. 314–332). Thousand Oaks, CA: Sage.

Highhouse, S. (2008). Stubborn reliance on intuition and subjectivity in employee selection. *Industrial and Organizational Psychology: Perspectives on Science and Practice, 1,* 333–342.

Highhouse, S. and Gallo, A. (1997). Order effects in personnel decision making. *Human Performance, 10,* 31–46.

Hogan, E.A. (1987). Effects of prior expectations on performance ratings: A longitudinal study. *Academy of Management Journal, 30,* 354–368.

Huber, J., Payne, J.W., and Puto, C. (1982). Adding asymmetrically dominated alternatives: Violations of regularity and the similarity hypothesis. *Journal of Consumer Research, 9,* 90–98.

Huffcutt, A.I., Conway, J.M., Roth, P.L., and Stone, N.J. (2001). Identification and meta-analytic assessment of psychological constructs measured in employment interviews. *Journal of Applied Psychology, 86,* 897–913.

Jayne, M.E.A. and Rauschenberger, J.M. (2000). Demonstrating the value of selection in organizations. In J.F. Kehoe (Ed.) *Managing Selection in Changing Organizations* (pp. 123–157). San Francisco, CA: Jossey-Bass.

Kahneman, D. and Tversky, A. (1973). On the psychology of prediction. *Psychological Review, 80,* 237–251.

Kleinmuntz, B. (1990). Why we still use our heads instead of formulas: Toward an integrative approach. *Psychological Bulletin, 107,* 296–310.

Koriat, A. (2008). Subjective confidence in one's answers: The consensuality principle. *Journal of Experimental Psychology: Learning, Memory, and Cognition, 34,* 945–959.

Kuncel, N.R. (2008). Some new (and old) suggestions for improving personnel selection. *Industrial and Organizational Psychology, 1,* 343–346.

Larrick, R.P. (2004). Debiasing. In D. Koehler and N. Harvey (Eds.) *Blackwell Handbook of Judgment and Decision Making* (pp. 316–337). Oxford: Blackwell.

Leonard, D. and Swap, L. (2004). Deep smarts. *Harvard Business Review, 82,* 88–97.

Liao, H. and Chuang, A. (2004). A multilevel investigation of factors influencing employee service performance and customer outcomes. *Academy of Management Journal, 47*, 41–58.

Lichtenstein, S. and Slovic, P. (Eds.) (2006). *The Construction of Preference.* Cambridge, MA: Cambridge University Press.

Loewenstein, G. (1996). Out of control: Visceral influences on behavior. *Organizational Behavior and Human Decision Processes, 65*, 272–292.

Lord, C., Ross, L., and Lepper, M.R. (1979). Biased assimilation and attitude polarization: The effects of prior theories on subsequently considered evidence. *Journal of Personality and Social Psychology, 37*, 2098–2109.

Meehl, P.E. (1954). *Clinical Versus Statistical Prediction: A Theoretical Analysis and a Review of the Evidence.* Minneapolis, MN: University of Minnesota.

Meehl, P.E. (1986). Causes and effects of my disturbing little book. *Journal of Personality Assessment, 50*, 370–375.

Moore, D.A., Swift, S.A., Sharek, Z.S., and Gino, F. (2010). Correspondence bias in performance evaluation: Why grade inflation works. *Personality and Social Psychology Bulletin, 36*, 843–852.

Morera, O.F. and Dawes, R.M. (2006). Clinical and statistical prediction after 50 years: A dedication to Paul Meehl. *Journal of Behavioral Decision Making, 19*, 409–412.

Oskamp, S. (1965). Overconfidence in case-study judgments. *Journal of Consulting Psychology, 23*, 23–33.

Payne, J.W., Bettman, J.R., and Johnson, E.J. (1992). Behavioral decision research: A constructive processing perspective. *Annual Review of Psychology, 43*, 87–131.

Pennington, N. and Hastie, R. (1988). Explanation-based decision making: Effects of memory structure on judgment. *Journal of Experimental Psychology: Learning, Memory, and Cognition, 14*, 521–533.

Phillips, J.M. and Gully, S.M. (2008). The role of perceptions versus reality in managers' choice of selection decision aids. *Industrial and Organizational Psychology: Perspectives on Science and Practice, 1*, 361–363.

Posthuma, R.A., Morgeson, F.P., and Campion, M.A. (2002). Beyond employment interview validity: A narrative review of recent research and trends over time. *Personnel Psychology, 55*, 1–81.

Rojstaczer, S. (2010). Grade inflation at American colleges and universities. Retrieved December 21, 2010, from www.gradeinflation.com/.

Rosenthal, R. and Jacobson, L. (1968). *Pygmalion in the Classroom.* New York: Holt, Rhinehart & Winston.

Rothbart, M., Evans, M., and Fulero, S. (1979). Recall for confirming events: Memory processes and the maintenance of social stereotyping. *Journal of Experimental Social Psychology, 15*, 343–355.

Russo, J.E. and Schoemaker, P.J.H. (1989). *Decision Traps: The Ten Barriers to Brilliant Decision-making and How to Overcome Them.* New York: Doubleday.

Rynes, S.L., Colbert, A.E., and Brown, K.G. (2002). HR professionals' beliefs about effective human resources practices: Correspondence between research and practice. *Human Resource Management, 41*, 149–174.

Rynes, S.L., Giluk, T.L., and Brown, K.G. (2007). The very different worlds of academic and practitioner periodicals in human resource management: Implications for evidence-based management. *Academy of Management Journal, 50*, 987–1008.

Schmidt, F.L. and Hunter, J.E. (1998). The validity and utility of selection methods in personnel psychology: Practical and theoretical implications of 85 years of research findings. *Psychological Bulletin, 124*, 262–274.

Schmitt, N. and Sinha, R. (2011). Validation support for selection procedures. In S. Zedeck (Ed.) *APA Handbook of Industrial and Organizational Psychology* (vol. 2, pp. 421–444). Washington, DC: American Psychological Association.

Schuh, A. (1978). Contrast effects in the interview. *Bulletin of the Psychonomic Society, 11,* 195–196.

Sessa, V.I. and Taylor, J.J. (2000). Choosing leaders: More cooks make a better broth. *Consulting Psychology Journal: Research and Practice, 52,* 218–225.

Shafir, E., Simonson, I., and Tversky, A. (1993). Reason-based choice. *Cognition, 49,* 11–36.

Simon, H.A. (1956). Rational choice and the structure of the environment. *Psychological Review, 63,* 129–138.

Slaughter, J.E., Bagger, J., and Li, A. (2006). Context effects on group-based employee selection decisions. *Organizational Behavior and Human Decision Processes, 100,* 47–59.

Slaughter, J.E., Sinar, E.F., and Highhouse, S. (1999). Decoy effects and attribute-level inferences. *Journal of Applied Psychology, 84,* 823–828.

Slusher, M.P. and Anderson, C.A. (1996). Using causal persuasive arguments to change beliefs and teach new information: The mediating role of explanation availability and evaluation bias in the acceptance of knowledge. *Journal of Educational Psychology, 88,* 110–122.

Staw, B.M. and Ross, J. (1987). Behavior in escalation situations: Antecedents, prototypes, and solutions. In L.L. Cummings and B.M. Staw (Eds.) *Research in Organizational Behavior* (vol. 9, pp. 39–78). Greenwich, CT: JAI Press.

Tetlock, P.E. (2005). *Expert Political Judgment: How Good Is It? How Can We Know?* Princeton, NJ: Princeton University Press.

Todorov, A., Mandisodza, A.N., Goren, A., and Hall, C.C. (2005). Inferences of competence from faces predict election outcomes. *Science, 308,* 1623–1626.

Tsai, C.I., Klayman, J., and Hastie, R. (2008). Effects of amount of information on judgment accuracy and confidence. *Organizational Behavior and Human Decision Processes, 107,* 97–105.

Tversky, A. and Kahneman, D. (1973). Availability: A heuristic for judging frequency and probability. *Cognitive Psychology, 5,* 207–232.

Tversky, A. and Kahneman, D. (1982). Evidential impact of base rates. In D. Kahneman, P. Slovic, and A. Tversky (Eds.) *Judgment Under Uncertainty: Heuristics and Biases.* New York: Cambridge University Press.

Whyte, G. and Latham, G. (1997). The futility of utility analysis revisited: When even an expert fails. *Personnel Psychology, 50,* 601–610.

Winkler, S., Köenig, C.J., and Kleinmann, M. (2010). Single-attribute utility analysis may be futile, but this can't be the end of the story: Causal chain analysis as an alternative. *Personnel Psychology, 63,* 1041–1065.

Yates, J.F. (1990). *Judgment and Decision Making.* Englewood Cliffs, NJ: Prentice Hall.

Zuckerman, M. (1979) *Sensation Seeking: Beyond the Optimal Level of Arousal.* Hillsdale, NJ: Erlbaum.

5

Individual Differences in Decision-making Skill and Style

Reeshad S. Dalal and Margaret E. Brooks

> In a knowledge-based economy, we propose that a knowledge worker's
> primary deliverable is a good decision.
> (Milkman, Chugh, & Bazerman, 2009, p. 379)

As you read this sentence, employees are making decisions and judgments that have the potential to affect themselves, their families, their work organizations, and on some occasions even the broader societies in which they live. A few examples include deciding which job applicant to hire, rating the job performance of a subordinate, setting a production goal, deciding whether to speed up the assembly line, judging one's level of job satisfaction, deciding to steal from the cash register, agreeing to help organize the company's holiday party, forecasting corporate tax rates two years later, deciding to report a coworker for sexual harassment, predicting how long a project will take to complete, deciding whether it would be acceptable to leave work early in order to attend a daughter's soccer match, and predicting the level of risk inherent in a new business venture. In other words, a great many topics of interest to organizational researchers ultimately reduce to decisions made by employees (Dalal et al., 2010).

The importance of decision making can additionally be seen through job analysis. An O*NET skill search (see www.onetonline.org), conducted on November 12, 2011, revealed that the skill of "judgment and decision-making" is important for 644 occupations. Accompanying the usual suspects on this list (e.g., "chief executives," "umpires, referees, and other sports officials," "surgeons," and "loan officers") are numerous occupations whose inclusion may at first glance be surprising: for instance, "parking lot attendants," "upholsterers," "pest control workers," "poets, lyricists and creative writers," and "coroners." Several other skills listed on O*NET (e.g., "complex problem solving," "troubleshooting") are also closely related to decision making.

Within the broader field of judgment and decision making (Koehler & Harvey, 2004; Stevenson, Busemeyer, & Naylor, 1990), one specific area—namely, individual differences in decision-making—should be of particular interest to organizational researchers (Bonaccio et al., 2010; Dalal et al., 2010; Mohammed & Schwall, 2009). Decision-making style and skill may be useful in employee selection, particularly if researchers are able to demonstrate incremental validity beyond commonly used selection tools (intelligence tests, personality inventories, etc.). A focus on individual differences in decision making therefore has the potential to be very useful, particularly at the upper echelons of the organization where decisions are likely to have an organization-wide impact.

THE PRESENT CHAPTER

The study of individual differences in decision making has the potential to improve organizational decision making, particularly with regard to personnel functions. In order to realize this promise, though, we need more research dedicated to understanding the role of these individual differences at work. Our call is for an organized and theoretical approach to investigating how individual differences in decision making affect important work outcomes. Some researchers have begun laying the foundation for this endeavor.

Mohammed and Schwall (2009) wrote a comprehensive review of research on cognitive-, personality-, and motivation-based individual differences and decision making. Their review and guide to future research calls for more emphasis on the role of individual differences in judgment and decision making, and provides researchers some direction, including ideas about how we might better design our research to capture the impact of individual differences on decision making (Mohammed & Schwall, 2009).

In addition, the Decision Making Individual Differences Inventory (DMIDI), an extensive online database, gives researchers free access to many measures of individual differences in decision making. In their paper that introduces the DMIDI and presents "guidelines for the more productive pursuit of individual differences research within [the field of judgment and decision making]," Appelt and colleagues (2011) lament that, although research exists on numerous individual differences that may be important to decision making, researchers have not systematically examined the role these differences play in the decision-making process. They argue for a more systematic, theoretical, and nuanced approach to the study of individual differences in the area of decision making—one that targets theoretically important individual difference variables and considers interactions of these variables with situational and contextual factors.

The scope of the current chapter is narrower than that of Mohammed and Schwall (2009) and Appelt et al. (2011). We limit our review and commentary to individual differences *in* decision making; that is, to differences between people in how they make decisions. We address individual differences in decision-making style and skill, to the exclusion of other individual differences (e.g., personality, self-presentation motives, cognitive ability, risk taking) that might affect decision-making outcomes. In addition, though we readily acknowledge that individual differences in decision making have the potential to influence outcomes in a wide variety of domains (e.g., family, health), we restrict our purview to outcomes in the workplace.

In this chapter, we discuss, in turn, decision-making styles, decision-making skill, and the relationships between them. We subsequently discuss the relationship between decision-making styles and other non-cognitive traits, the relationship between decision-making skill and intelligence, the role of situations, and the criterion problem vis-à-vis decision-making style and skill.

DECISION-MAKING STYLES

Definition and Overview

The concept of decision-making style has some of its earliest roots in the cognitive style literature, as an application of the concept of style to the process of decision making (Kozhevnikov, 2007). The "style" idea was transported to research in managerial fields to try to categorize managerial decision makers in terms of their typical approach to decision making (e.g., Agor, 1984; Kirton, 1976; Rowe & Mason, 1987). Most of the more recent work on decision-making styles, however, emerged not from the managerial literature, but from the vocational decision-making area. The foundational decision-making styles work in vocational decision making was a series of attempts to develop a comprehensive set of decision-making styles (e.g., Arroba, 1977; Harren, 1979; Harren et al., 1978; Jepsen & Dilley, 1974; Johnson, 1990). In the late 1970s, Harren articulated a model of career decision making and developed a measure called the Assessment of Career Decision Making (ACDM; Harren, 1979; Harren et al., 1978). In this work, he defined decision-making style as "the individual's characteristic mode of perceiving and responding to decision-making tasks," or, more simply, "the manner in which the person goes about making decisions" (Harren, 1979, p. 125). Within the larger ACDM, Harren developed three decision-making style subscales—*rational, intuitive,* and *dependent*—that, according to Chartrand and Camp (1991), became the primary measures of decision-making styles in the career development and vocational decision-making areas. Two of these three—rational and intuitive—derived in part from literature in psychology on modes or systems of information processing (e.g., Chaiken, 1980; Tversky & Kahneman, 1983). All three styles, along with two others, would later emerge in Scott and Bruce's (1995) commonly used measure.

We now define several decision-making styles that have promise for contributing to our understanding of decision making at work. All are individual differences in the way people make decisions, and, despite their seeming relevance to the workplace, all have thus far received very limited attention in this context.

General Decision-making Styles

Scott and Bruce (1995) drew from the career development and vocational behavior literatures to develop a measure of decision-making styles. In their scale development paper, Scott and Bruce defined decision-making style as "the learned, habitual response pattern exhibited by an individual when confronted with a decision situation" (p. 820). They derived four decision-making styles from previous research and theorizing: *rational, intuitive, avoidant,* and *dependent.* A fifth style, *spontaneous* decision making, emerged from their factor analysis and was consequently added to their General Decision-Making Style (GDMS) instrument.

Rational decision making involves thorough evaluation, logic, and careful thought. Its cognitive roots are in the rational mode of information processing, which is characterized by conceptual, analytical, and systematic thinking (Epstein et al., 1996). Intuitive (experiential) decision making is a more instinctual, hunch-based approach. Like the rational decision-making style, the intuitive style is based in part on research that describes a mode of information processing—in this case, a heuristic, experiential, implicit mode (Epstein et al., 1996). Dependent decision making is a style that involves reliance on others for direction and decision support. Avoidant decision making involves postponing, procrastinating, or otherwise avoiding making a decision. Spontaneous decision making is characterized by impulsivity and spur-of-the-moment decision making.

Maximizing/Satisficing

More than fifty years ago, Simon (1955, 1956) wrote about the concept of maximizing in decision making. He argued that, given the complexity of decision making and the limitations of human cognition, maximizing (or optimizing) decisions may not be a realistic goal. Instead, seeking a good enough alternative (i.e., satisficing) might be a reasonable approach. Schwartz et al. (2002) took a trait approach to the idea of maximizing. They developed the Maximization Scale (MS) to measure differences in maximizing—that is, to differentiate people who would be likely to maximize from those who would take a satisficing approach to decision making.

Indecisiveness

Indecisiveness is dispositional avoidance of, and difficulty making, decisions across contexts (Germeijs & De Boeck, 2002). It has traditionally been of most interest in the clinical psychology domain because of its relationship to clinical diagnoses and diagnostic criteria (e.g., obsessive compulsive disorder, perfectionism and hoarding; Frost & Gross, 1993; Frost & Shows, 1993), as well as in the vocational counseling area because of its relationship to career indecision; yet, it can be measured as a tendency that pervades multiple domains (Germeijs & De Boeck, 2002).

Reliability and Validity

Decision-making styles have been described as an applied offshoot or subcategory of cognitive styles—differentiated from basic research on cognitive styles, which has been more theoretical and has more of a focus on individual differences in broader cognitive functioning (Kozhevnikov, 2007). Decision-making styles would best fit into the subcategory of cognitive styles that Sternberg and Grigorenko (1997) refer to as "the activity-centered approach" to cognitive styles. This category includes learning styles and teaching styles, and is characterized in part by its more applied bent and regrettable lack of theory and validation. The next sections review the reliability and limited criterion-related validity information available for a number of measures of decision-making styles.

General Decision-making Style (GDMS) Instrument

Scott and Bruce (1995) describe their five decision-making styles as independent, but not mutually exclusive. An initial factor analysis suggested a five-factor structure, and this structure was replicated with two independent samples. Loo (2000) did additional work to establish the psychometric properties of the measure, including a confirmatory factor analysis that supported the same five-factor structure. Several studies have found similar patterns of inter-correlations among the five styles. The rational style is negatively related to the intuitive, avoidant, and dependent styles; the dependent and avoidant styles are positively correlated, as are the spontaneous and intuitive styles (Loo, 2000; Scott & Bruce, 1995; Thunholm, 2004, 2009). Cronbach's alpha estimates of internal consistency ranged across studies and samples from .77 to .85 for rational decision style, .78 to .84 for the intuitive style, .62 to .86 for the dependent style, .84 to .94 for the avoidant style, and .83 to .87 for the spontaneous style.

Rational decision style. A rational decision style has been linked positively to outcomes including person–job fit (Singh & Greenhaus, 2004), job satisfaction and satisfaction with the job search process (Crossley & Highhouse, 2005), and high school GPA (Baiocco, Laghi, & D'Alessio, 2009). Galotti et al. (2006) examined the role of decision styles in undergraduates' choice of college major, and found that undergraduates high in rational decision style reported more planning behavior, more positive feelings about their decision process, and a final decision more congruent with their values than their low-rational-style counterparts.

Intuitive decision style. In a study of the cognitive styles of managers, managing directors' and owner-managers' intuitive decision-making style was positively related to firm performance (Sadler-Smith, 2004). Crossley and Highhouse (2005) found that an intuitive decision-making style was positively related to employees' satisfaction with their job and their job search process. Intuitive decision making was also related to positive feelings about the decision process and a final decision that was consistent with their values in undergraduates choosing a college major (Galotti et al., 2006). Lodato, Highhouse, and Brooks (2011) found that intuitive decision making was strongly related to a preference for intuition-based hiring (relying on instincts or feelings to make hiring decisions).

Dependent decision style. In their studies of "real-life choices," Galotti and colleagues (Galotti et al., 2006; Galotti & Tinkelenberg, 2009) found that dependent decision making was related to negative feelings about the decision process in undergraduate students choosing a major and in parents choosing their child's first grade placement.

Avoidant decision style. Avoidant decision making has also been associated with a number of outcomes, including numbers of school absences in adolescents (Baiocco, Laghi, & D'Alessio, 2009), less planning behavior and value-incongruent decision making and negative feelings about the decision process in undergraduates choosing a major (Galotti et al., 2006), and negative stress in military officers (Thunholm, 2008).

Spontaneous decision style. Outcomes related to a spontaneous decision style include a larger number of school absences in adolescents (Baiocco, Laghi, & D'Alessio, 2009), less negative stress in military officers (Thunholm, 2008), and less self-reported planning in undergraduates.

Maximization Scale (MS) and Maximizing Tendency Scale (MTS)

Maximizing and satisficing are treated as different ends of one maximizing continuum. A high scale score identifies one as a maximizer and a low score identifies one as a satisficer. The original Maximization Scale (MS; Schwarz et al., 2002) had some notable psychometric shortcomings, including Cronbach's alphas that ranged from .54 to .75 across different samples, items with very low factor loadings, and numerous items with very low item-total correlations (Diab, Gillespie, & Highhouse, 2008; Nenkov et al., 2008).

In response to psychometric shortcomings of the scale, two alternatives to the MS were introduced. Nenkov and colleagues reduced the MS to a six-item short form (2008). The authors recommended using the short version of the scale in future research because of superior psychometric properties, including better nomological validity and superior CFA goodness-of-fit indices. Reliabilities for the shortened scale ranged from .36 to .60 across samples. Authors of the MS consider it a multidimensional scale with three sub-dimensions (i.e., alternative search, decision difficulty, and high standards). Diab, Gillespie, and Highhouse (2008) developed a new instrument, a unidimensional measure of maximizing they termed the Maximizing Tendency Scale (MTS); they suggested that the MTS is both more psychometrically sound and "more faithful to the theory of the attribute" than the MS (p. 365). Diab, Gillespie, and Highhouse (2008) compared the original MS with the MTS and found the MTS to have superior psychometric characteristics, including higher Cronbach's alpha (.80 for the MTS and .68 for MS), higher item-total correlations, and both more and higher magnitude correlations with decision-making behaviors.[1]

The MTS and the original version of the MS also show different patterns of relationships with other variables. Most notably, the MS shows relationships with maladaptive personal characteristics, whereas the MTS does not. Diab, Gillespie, and Highhouse (2008) contend that the multidimensional MS includes items that measure closely related but distinct constructs such as indecisiveness, and that it is these items that are responsible for the positive relationship found between maladaptive personal characteristics and the MS.

Research has connected maximizing to several affective and behavioral outcomes. Chowdhury, Ratneshwar, and Mohanty (2009) studied maximizers in the context of consumer decision making. They asked people to shop online for a Christmas gift and gave them three minutes to make a choice from among an assortment of options. Maximizers perceived more time pressure and were more likely to change their decision when given the opportunity to reconsider after time had elapsed. Iyengar, Wells, and Schwartz (2006) examined the effect of maximizing on the job search process and found that maximizers were more fixated on options they had not pursued, relied more on external influences, experienced more negative feelings about the process, and were less satisfied with their job offers. Yet, maximizers received higher salary offers ($7,340 more on average) than did satisficers.

Indecisiveness Scales

The Frost and Shows (1993) Indecisiveness Scale is a 15-item measure that was developed in the clinical area and shows expected relationships with a number of maladaptive personality characteristics; the Cronbach's alphas range from .88 to .90 across several samples (Frost & Gross, 1993; Frost & Shows, 1993; Spunt, Rassin, & Epstein, 2009). Spunt, Rassin, and Epstein (2009) argued that two factors underlie indecisiveness—avoidant indecisiveness (difficulty with and general avoidance of decision making) and aversive indecisiveness (negative feelings associated with decision making). Their factor analysis supported this factor structure and both subscales had acceptable Cronbach's alphas (avoidant was .85 and aversive was .82). In 2002, Germeijs and De Boeck developed a new measure of indecisiveness because of concerns that available measures were confounded with other variables and included domain-specific items. Their 22-item scale of indecisiveness is intended to measure only indecisiveness (and not elements of other related variables), and is intended to be relevant to any decision-making context. Their research showed a test-retest reliability of .67 across four months and a Cronbach's alpha of .91.

In terms of validity, people who score high on indecisiveness have been shown to take longer to make decisions, experience more decision-making difficulty (Frost & Shows, 1993), are more likely to defer decisions (Rassin & Muris, 2005), and ignore the risk of lost opportunities (Patalano & Wengrovitz, 2007).

Relevance to the Workplace

The above discussion suggests that there is very little extant research on decision-making styles in workplace settings, even though these styles appear quite relevant to workplace settings (especially vis-à-vis jobs that require considerable decision making). Perhaps the most likely workplace application is in the area of employee selection. However, to our knowledge no studies have examined whether these decision-making styles provide incremental value beyond commonly used predictors (e.g., intelligence and personality) in the prediction of job performance. Therefore, this represents an important area of opportunity for future research.

Research in applied settings such as the workplace would also, paradoxically, be aided by basic research establishing a comprehensive taxonomy of decision-making styles. Clearly, there exist both conceptual connections (e.g., between avoidant indecisiveness and avoidant decision-making style) and empirical relationships (e.g., between intuitive and spontaneous decision-making styles) among the plethora of decision-making styles that have thus far been identified. A taxonomy would winnow down the decision-making styles to a manageable number, thus aiding I-O psychologists and other applied researchers.

DECISION-MAKING SKILL OR COMPETENCE

Definition and Overview

A small but growing body of research has been concerned with individual differences in decision-making skill or competence. Incompetent (or biased) decision making is usually defined in terms of consistent, systematic departures from normative models of decision making (e.g., violations of the rational choice axiom of transitivity; Bruine de Bruin, Parker, & Fischhoff, 2007; Stanovich, West, & Toplak, 2011). Stated differently, research on decision-making skill adopts the famous program of research on heuristics and biases articulated over several decades by numerous researchers (most notably Amos Tversky & Daniel Kahneman), but with the additional proviso that there exist individual differences in the extent to which people fall prey (or not) to these biases. Preliminary theoretical and empirical work suggests that between one and four underlying (i.e., latent) factors of decision-making skill may exist (e.g., Arkes, 1991; Bazerman & Moore, 2009; Bruine de Bruin, Parker, & Fischhoff, 2007; Finucane & Gullion, 2010; Parker & Fischhoff, 2005; Stanovich, Toplak, & West, 2008; Tversky & Kahneman, 1974).

In perhaps the best extant work in this area, Bruine de Bruin, Parker, and Fischhoff (2007) and Parker and Fischhoff (2005) concluded that a single underlying factor of overall decision-making skill was sufficient to represent performance in seven domains: Resistance to Framing (i.e., providing consistent responses despite logically irrelevant changes in the way problems are described), Recognizing Social Norms (i.e., accurately assessing social norms among peers), (the absence of) Under/ Overconfidence (i.e., being neither less nor more confident than is warranted on the basis of one's accuracy level), Applying Decision Rules (i.e., correctly applying various decision-making strategies when presented with a display of information), Consistency in Risk Perception (i.e., applying the laws of probability consistently), Resistance to Sunk Costs (i.e., considering only future consequences rather than unrecoverable past investments when making decisions), and Path Independence (i.e., providing consistent responses to normatively equivalent choices, regardless of whether the choices are made in one step or two). The complete list of items used by Bruine de Bruin, Parker, and Fischhoff (2007) is available at http://sds.hss.cmu.edu/risk/ADMC.htm. Examples of items reflecting several other domains of decision-making skill (e.g., Anchoring and Adjustment, Outcome Bias, Risk–Reward Relationships) are provided in Stanovich and West (2008).

Reliability and Validity

In the area of decision-making skill or competence, Parker and Fischhoff (2005) reported a Cronbach's alpha of .76 and Bruine de Bruin, Parker, and Fischhoff (2007) reported a Cronbach's alpha of .85 for overall decision-making skill. However, there is cause for concern regarding the reliabilities reported for some of the component measures of decision-making skill—in particular, Resistance to Sunk Costs and Resistance to Framing (Bruine de Bruin, Parker, & Fischhoff, 2007; Del Missier, Mäntylä, & Bruine de Bruin, 2011; Parker & Fischhoff, 2005).

Evidence of the validity of measures of decision-making skill is not yet widespread. Bruine de Bruin, Parker, and Fischhoff (2007) developed a self-report measure of decision-making success, which was once again defined in the negative—as the *avoidance* of suboptimal outcomes. Examples included missing a flight (for those respondents who had taken at least one airplane trip), getting divorced (for those respondents who had ever been married), consuming so much alcohol that the respondent vomited (for those respondents who had ever had an alcoholic drink), "[being] in a public fight or screaming argument," and "[breaking] a bone because [the respondent] fell, slipped, or misstepped." They found that overall decision-making skill and five of its seven components were significantly positively associated with avoiding suboptimal outcomes—and that these relationships were attenuated only slightly after controlling for intelligence.

Parker and Fischhoff (2005), who studied adolescents, assessed the following categories of risky behavior measured two to five years *before* the assessment of decision-making skill (i.e., a *post*dictive study): behavior consistent with antisocial disorder (using a clinical diagnostic instrument), externalizing behavior (reported by mothers), delinquency (reported by mothers), alcohol and marijuana consumption (self-reported), and amount of sex and number of sexual partners (self-reported). The authors noted that, although decisions by adolescents to engage in these behaviors "need not be irrational," these decisions "would be poor choices in a society that proscribes them and for individuals who fully understand their consequences" (p. 10). Overall decision-making skill and one of its seven components (Under/Overconfidence) were negatively related to almost all the forms of risky behavior—and these relationships were attenuated only slightly after controlling for intelligence.

A few studies have also used a "known groups" validation technique. Results indicate that: (1) economists reported engaging in less escalation of commitment to sunk costs than did biologists, presumably due to disciplinary training (Larrick, Morgan, & Nisbett, 1990; Larrick, Nisbett, & Morgan, 1993), (2) students with multiple school suspensions adhered less to cost-benefit rules than did their peers (Stanovich, Grunewald, &

West, 2003), and (3) high-level government and military leaders out-performed adult residents from the Pittsburgh area in three domains of decision-making skill studied (Resistance to Framing, Consistency in Risk Perception, and Resistance to Sunk Costs), though there were no differences in a fourth domain (Under/Overconfidence; Carnevale, Inbar, & Lerner, 2011).

Thus, the available validity evidence, though scant, is promising. Several directions for future research in organizational settings are readily apparent. In the current section, in the interest of space, we present only two. First, a domain of behavior *at work* that parallels some of the behavior studied by Parker and Fischhoff (2005) and Bruine de Bruin, Parker, and Fischhoff (2007) is counterproductive or deviant work behavior (Spector et al., 2006). Second, supervisor reports of employee task performance (behavior that is included in job descriptions and recognized by organizational reward systems; Williams & Anderson, 1991) should be associated with decision-making skill—and this should especially be true for jobs that require considerable decision making (as identified, say, by O*NET).

RELATIONSHIP BETWEEN DECISION-MAKING SKILL AND DECISION-MAKING STYLES

How is decision-making skill or competence related to decision-making style? Stanovich (e.g., Stanovich, West, & Toplak, 2011) has argued that decision-making skill is likely to be related to dispositional thinking styles, such as the need for cognition (the extent to which people engage in and enjoy thinking; Cacioppo & Petty, 1982), that are associated with heuristical thinking being overridden by analytical thinking. Empirical results are generally supportive of the idea that some aspects of decision-making skill—Resistance to Framing and Resistance to Sunk Costs—are related positively to the need for cognition (Carnevale, Inbar, & Lerner, 2011; see also Mohammed & Schwall, 2009). Other results (Bruine de Bruin, Parker, & Fischhoff, 2007; Parker & Fischhoff, 2005; see also Mohammed & Schwall, 2009) suggest that overall decision-making skill and some of its components are related positively to the rational decision-making style and are related negatively to the spontaneous and avoidant decision-making styles.

OTHER ISSUES

Relationship Between Decision-making Styles and Other Non-cognitive Traits

The decision-making styles reviewed here have relationships with numerous non-cognitive traits. Most of the literature in this area has not systematically and theoretically examined these relationships; rather, most findings are reports of simple correlations. Future research should more closely examine whether these decision styles exhibit incremental value beyond other non-cognitive traits in the prediction of important outcomes. Here, we note some of the relationships that may be most promising for further development.

Several researchers have looked at the relationship between the Big 5 personality traits and decision-making or cognitive styles (e.g., Bacanli, 2006; Diab, Gillespie, & Highhouse, 2008; Pacini & Epstein, 1999). Extraversion, openness to experience and conscientiousness are all positively related to both rational and intuitive decision-making styles. Agreeableness is positively related to intuitive decision-making style. Neuroticism is positively related to avoidant decision-making style, maximizing and indecisiveness, and is negatively related to rational decision-making style.

Other variables of potential interest that are related to decision-making styles include social desirability, control orientation, optimism, and regret. Social desirability is positively related to the rational decision-making style and negatively related to the intuitive, avoidant, and spontaneous styles (Thunholm, 2004). Internal control orientation is positively related to rational decision-making style; external control orientation is positively related to dependent and spontaneous styles (Scott & Bruce, 1995) and indecisiveness (Bacanli, 2006). Optimism is positively related to intuitive decision-making style and negatively related to rational decision-making style (Epstein et al., 1996) and maximizing (Nenkov et al., 2008). Finally, regret is positively related to maximizing and indecisiveness (Diab, Gillespie, & Highhouse, 2008; Spunt, Rassin, & Epstein, 2009).

Relationship Between Decision-making Skill and Intelligence

A growing consensus in various areas of psychology asserts that there exist two broad cognitive processes or systems: a heuristical system (fast, low in computational power, requiring little concentration, and not interfering with other ongoing cognition) and an analytical system (slow, high in computational power, requiring much concentration, and interfering with other ongoing cognition; Chaiken & Trope, 1999; Kahneman, 2011; Stanovich, West, & Toplak, 2011).[2] Reliance on the heuristical system is the default, and can frequently lead to good decisions. The problem is that people often tend to rely on the heuristical system even in cases where an analytical response is called for.

In such cases, to make a good decision, a person must: (1) be capable of overriding the heuristical system with the analytical system, (2) detect the need for such an override, and (3) possess the cognitive capacity to accomplish the override. Stanovich, West, and Toplak (2011) maintain that the first and third of these steps are related to conventionally assessed intelligence, but that the second step is not (rather, it is related to dispositional thinking styles such as the need for cognition). In other words, intelligence appears to be necessary but not sufficient for decision-making skill.

Empirically, Stanovich, West, and Toplak (2011) note that decision biases are at most moderately but frequently only trivially associated with intelligence (a few examples from the latter category are the anchoring effect, the sunk cost effect, and risk/benefit confounding), and that the magnitude of empirical relationship between each bias and intelligence is a function of the specific combinations of the three steps required for the avoidance of that bias. As I-O psychologists, we speculate that the empirical relationships obtained in the studies reviewed by Stanovich, West, and Toplak (2011) may be somewhat understated due to measurement artifacts such as range restriction and unreliability. Yet, it seems doubtful that decision-making skill is redundant with intelligence. For example, intelligent people outperform less intelligent people on a rational thinking task only when told what the bias is and what they can do to avoid it (Stanovich, West, & Toplak, 2011). Moreover, decision-making skill appears to predict decision outcomes even after controlling for intelligence (e.g., Bruine de Bruin, Parker, & Fischhoff, 2007; Parker & Fischhoff, 2005). In fact, Stanovich (2009, p. 35) has gone so far as to coin the term "dysrationalia" to indicate "the inability to think and behave rationally despite having adequate intelligence." Nonetheless, future research on decision-making skill should continue to examine the relationship of this construct with intelligence and the incremental validity, vis-à-vis workplace outcomes, of this construct beyond intelligence.

The Role of Situations

In decision making, as in psychology as a whole, the effects of individual differences are believed to be contextual—that is, conditional on the situation (Appelt et al., 2011; Mohammed & Schwall, 2009). Although a comprehensive and universally acknowledged taxonomy of situations does not yet exist, among the candidates for the most important psychological dimension underlying situations is "situational strength" (Snyder & Ickes, 1985). Situational strength is defined as the set of "implicit or explicit cues provided by external entities regarding the desirability of potential behaviors" (Meyer, Dalal, & Hermida, 2010, p. 122). Strong situations have the effect of reducing variance in criteria and consequently constraining relationships between individual differences and criteria (Meyer, Dalal, & Hermida, 2010; Meyer et al., in press; Mischel, 1977). In other words, individual differences in decision-making style and skill are likely to exert stronger influences on decision outcomes in weak than in strong situations.

From a conceptual standpoint, two facets of situational strength described by Meyer, Dalal, and Hermida (2010) appear especially relevant to individual differences in decision-making style and skill: constraints ("the extent to which an individual's freedom of decision and action is limited by forces outside his or her control"; p. 126) and consequences ("the extent to which [an individual's] decisions or actions have important positive or negative implications for any relevant person or entity"; p. 127). It therefore seems reasonable to expect that individual differences in decision-making style and skill will have a greater impact on decision-making outcomes in situations involving weak rather than strong constraints (i.e., high rather than low decision latitude) and weak rather than strong consequences (i.e., low rather than high decision importance).

Interestingly, it has been posited that the laboratory, where most judgment and decision-making research (including much research on individual differences in decision making) has been conducted, is itself a strong situation (Weiss & Adler, 1984). Consequently, it may be that individual differences in decision making exert less impact in traditional laboratory studies than in laboratory studies that are specifically designed as weak situations or in field studies that happen to involve weak situations (Weiss & Adler, 1984).

Yet, regardless of whether research on situational moderators is carried out in the laboratory or the field, it is wise to recall methodological factors that have bedeviled previous research on person–situation interactions (Chaplin, 1997). To maximize their chances of detecting interactions, researchers should use large samples, reliable measures, research designs that minimize range restriction, and so forth. Like Appelt et al. (2011), we suggest the use of multilevel studies, in which situations and decision outcomes are assessed at the within-person level and individual differences are, by definition, assessed at the between-person level. In such designs, statistical power can be enhanced by increasing either the number of people studied or the number of measurements per person. Such studies can be conducted either in the field (as experience sampling studies; see Bolger, Davis, & Rafaeli, 2003) or in the laboratory (as multi-trial studies; see, e.g., Schreiber & Kahneman, 2000).

It is worth noting, however, that the so-called "competitive" interaction discussed in the above paragraphs—a type of interaction in which individual difference variables and situation variables compete to explain variance in outcomes—is not the only way of conceiving an interaction (Buss, 1977; Funder, 2008). Much less studied but equally meaningful from a psychological perspective is the "cooperative" interaction, which involves the reciprocal impact of individual differences and situations on each other (Buss, 1977; Funder, 2008). Thus, for example, a chronically indecisive person may actively seek out work situations where he or she is not required to make many decisions (i.e., impact of individual differences on situations); conversely, long-term exposure to work situations that do not require much decision making may increase a person's indecisiveness (i.e., impact of situations on individual differences). Studying such interactions, however, requires a different mindset on the part of researchers (i.e., a systems approach; Buss, 1977; Funder, 2008) as well as different research designs (at the very least, cross-lagged designs in which the lags are determined by theory regarding the amount of time required for individual differences to start and stop influencing situations, and vice versa).

We close this section by noting that, although the study of situational factors associated with decision making is of great importance theoretically (e.g., in helping to explain when individual differences in decision making are likely to exert more versus less impact), an understanding of relevant situational factors also lends itself to *interventions* of considerable practical (i.e., applied) importance. For instance, situational interventions can attenuate the impact of undesirable scores on individual differences in decision making (e.g., low scores on measures of decision-making skill). Specifically, organizations can strategically introduce constraints by requiring decision makers to follow strategies designed to overcome low skill in decision making. Simple constraints such as requiring decision makers to "consider the opposite" (Lord, Lepper, & Preston, 1984) and compare the current project to a "reference class" consisting of relevant previous projects (Lovallo & Kahneman, 2003) have proven quite effective in reducing chronically biased decision making (for reviews, see Bazerman & Moore, 2009; Larrick, 2004). Heath, Larrick, and Klayman (1998) provide numerous examples of how these and other strategies can be implemented effectively in organizational settings.

The Criterion Problem

> The criterion, if properly understood, could give us further insights into the effect of the independent variable, and perhaps even help identify some of the intervening variables.
>
> (Weitz, 1961, p. 231)

Although most researchers acknowledge that performance is multi-dimensional, a major problem is that performance criteria and their inter-relationships are not well understood (Austin & Villanova, 1992; Dalal & Hulin, 2008). Previously, we suggested counterproductive work behavior and task performance as potential performance criteria associated with individual differences in decision making (to this list, one might add organizational citizenship behavior; Dalal, 2005). However, the true value of individual differences in decision making is likely to be found at a more molecular level—that is, in criteria that reflect decision-making performance rather than broader job performance.

Decisions can be evaluated in terms of criteria such as accuracy, consistency, ethicality, and conformity with the predictions from a normative model. However, even these criteria are overly restrictive (Dalal et al., 2010; Mohammed & Schwall, 2009). Pre- and post-decision criteria are also important. Examples of pre-decision criteria are the level of situation awareness, the manner in which the decision problem is formulated, the quantity of alternatives (options) generated, the quality of alternatives generated, and the creativity of alternatives generated. Examples of post-decision criteria are satisfaction with the chosen alternative, post-decision regret, and implementation intentions.

Future research should therefore attempt to generate theory to map specific decision-making criteria on to specific individual differences in decision-making style and skill. Regardless of the specific criterion under consideration, however, it should be noted that the impact of individual differences in decision making is most likely to be observed vis-à-vis *habitual* decision-making performance on the job rather than performance on a single job-related decision (e.g., Epstein, 1980).

CONCLUSION

We have argued that individual differences in decision-making style and skill are a ripe area for research exploration in the intersection between decision making and the workplace. Although there has historically been some attention to decision-making styles, the research is largely atheoretical and has not been systematically applied to potentially fruitful areas such as personnel selection. Decision-making skill has received some recent attention in the judgment and decision-making literature, and initial research suggests that it has potential to add insight to the area of workplace psychology. JDM researchers and workplace psychology researchers alike have much to contribute to these promising areas of exploration.

NOTES

1. The short version of the MTS has not yet been compared to the MS.
2. To be clear, these "systems" should be interpreted not as explanatory but rather as merely descriptive. Stated differently, it would be incorrect to identify the systems either as being associated with distinct parts of the brain or as agents that cause behavior. Instead, the systems are "useful fictions"—terminological shorthand adopted for ease of understanding (Kahneman, 2011, p. 28).

REFERENCES

Agor, W.H. (1984). *Intuitive Management.* Englewood Cliffs, NJ: Prentice Hall.

Appelt, K.C., Milch, K.F., Handgraaf, M.J.J., and Weber, E.U. (2011). The Decision Making Individual Differences Inventory and guidelines for the study of individual differences in judgment and decision-making research. *Judgment and Decision Making, 6,* 252–262.

Arkes, H.R. (1991). Costs and benefits of judgment errors: Implications for debiasing. *Psychological Bulletin, 110,* 486–498.

Arroba, T.Y. (1977). Decision-making style as a function of occupational group, decision content and perceived importance. *Journal of Occupational Psychology, 51,* 219–226.

Austin, J.T. and Villanova, P. (1992). The criterion problem: 1917–1992. *Journal of Applied Psychology, 77,* 836–874.

Bacanli, F. (2006). Personality characteristics as predictors of personal indecisiveness. *Journal of Career Development, 32,* 320–332.

Baiocco, R., Laghi, F., and D'Alessio, M. (2009). Decision-making style among adolescents: Relationship with sensation seeking and locus of control. *Journal of Adolescence, 32,* 963–976.

Bazerman, M.H. and Moore, D. (2009). *Judgment in Managerial Decision Making* (7th ed.). Hoboken, NJ: Wiley.

Bolger, N., Davis, A., and Rafaeli, E. (2003). Diary methods: Capturing life as it is lived. *Annual Review of Psychology*, 54, 579–616.

Bonaccio, S., Dalal, R.S., Highhouse, S., Ilgen, D.R., Mohammed, S., and Slaughter, J.E. (2010). Taking workplace decisions seriously: This conversation has been fruitful! *Industrial and Organizational Psychology*, 3, 455–464.

Bruine de Bruin, W., Parker, A.M., and Fischhoff, B. (2007). Individual differences in adult decision-making competence. *Journal of Personality and Social Psychology*, 92, 938–956.

Buss, A.R. (1977). The trait-situation controversy and the concept of interaction. *Personality and Social Psychology Bulletin*, 3, 196–201.

Cacioppo, J.T. and Petty, R.E. (1982). The need for cognition. *Journal of Personality and Social Psychology*, 42, 116–131.

Carnevale, J.J., Inbar, Y., and Lerner, J.S. (2011). Individual differences in need for cognition and decision-making competence among leaders. *Personality and Individual Differences*, 51, 274–278.

Chaiken, S. (1980). Heuristic versus systematic information processing and the use of source versus message cues in persuasion. *Journal of Personality and Social Psychology*, 39, 752–766.

Chaiken, S. and Trope, Y. (Eds.) (1999). *Dual-process Theories in Social Psychology*. New York: Guilford.

Chaplin, W.F. (1997). Personality, interactive relations, and applied psychology. In R. Hogan, J. Johnson, and S. Briggs (Eds.) *Handbook of Personality Psychology* (pp. 873–890). San Diego, CA: Academic Press.

Chartrand, J.M. and Camp, C.C. (1991). Advances in the measurement of career development constructs: A 20-year review. *Journal of Vocational Behavior*, 39, 1–39.

Chowdhury, T., Ratneshwar, S., and Mohanty, P. (2009). The time-harried shopper: Exploring the differences between maximizers and satisficers. *Marketing Letters*, 20, 155–167.

Crossley, C.D. and Highhouse, S. (2005). Relation of job search and choice process with subsequent satisfaction. *Journal of Economic Psychology*, 26, 255–268.

Dalal, R.S. (2005). A meta-analysis of the relationship between organizational citizenship behavior and counterproductive work behavior. *Journal of Applied Psychology*, 90, 1241–1255.

Dalal, R.S., Bonaccio, S., Highhouse, S., Ilgen, D.R., Mohammed, S., and Slaughter, J.E. (2010). What if industrial-organizational psychology decided to take workplace decisions seriously? *Industrial and Organizational Psychology*, 3, 386–405.

Dalal, R.S. and Hulin, C.L. (2008). Motivation for what? The criterion question. In R. Kanfer, G. Chen, and R. Pritchard (Eds.) *Work Motivation: Past, Present and Future* (pp. 63–100). New York: Routledge.

Del Missier, F., Mäntylä, T., and Bruine de Bruin, W. (2011). Decision-making competence, executive functioning, and general cognitive abilities. *Journal of Behavioral Decision Making*, in press.

Diab, D.L., Gillespie, M.A., and Highhouse, S. (2008). Are maximizers really unhappy? The measurement of maximizing tendency. *Judgment and Decision Making*, 3, 364–370.

Epstein, S. (1980). The stability of behavior: II. Implications for psychological research. *American Psychologist*, 35, 790–806.

Epstein, S., Pacini, R., Denes-Raj, V., and Heier, H. (1996). Individual differences in intuitive–experiential and analytical–rational thinking styles. *Journal of Personality and Social Psychology, 71*, 390–405.

Finucane, M.L. and Gullion, C.M. (2010). Developing a tool for measuring the decision-making competence of older adults. *Psychology and Aging, 25*, 271–288.

Frost, R.O. and Gross, R.C. (1993). The hoarding of possessions. *Behaviour Research and Therapy, 31*, 367–381.

Frost, R.O. and Shows, D.L. (1993). The nature and measurement of compulsive indecisiveness. *Behaviour Research and Therapy, 31*, 683–692.

Funder, D.C. (2008). Persons, situations, and person-situation interactions. In O.P. John, R.W. Robins, and L.A. Pervin (Eds.) *Handbook of Personality: Theory and Research* (3rd ed., pp. 568–580). New York: Guilford.

Galotti, K.M., Ciner, E., Altenbaumer, H.E., Geerts, H.J., Rupp, A., and Woulfe, J. (2006). Decision structuring in important real-life choices. *Psychological Science, 18*, 320–325.

Galotti, K.M. and Tinkelenberg, C.E. (2009). Real-life decision making: Parents choosing a first-grade placement. *The American Journal of Psychology, 122*, 455–468.

Germeijs, V. and De Boeck, P. (2002). A measurement scale for indecisiveness and its relationship to career indecision and other types of indecision. *European Journal of Psychological Assessment, 18*, 113–122.

Harren, V.A. (1979). A model of career decision making for college students. *Journal of Vocational Behavior, 14*, 119–133.

Harren, V.A., Kass, R.A., Tinsley, H.E., and Moreland, J.R. (1978). Influence of sex role attitudes and cognitive styles on career decision making. *Journal of Counseling Psychology, 25*, 390–398.

Heath, C., Larrick, R.P., and Klayman, J. (1998). Cognitive repairs: How organizational practices can compensate for individual shortcomings. *Research in Organizational Behavior, 20*, 1–37.

Iyengar, S.S., Wells, R.E., and Schwartz, B. (2006). Doing better but feeling worse. *Psychological Science, 17*, 143–150.

Jepsen, D.A. and Dilley, J.S. (1974). Vocational decision-making models: A review and comparative analysis. *Review of Educational Research, 44*, 331–349.

Johnson, D.P. (1990). Indecisiveness: A dynamic, integrative approach. *The Career Development Quarterly, 39*, 34–39.

Kahneman, D. (2011). *Thinking, Fast and Slow.* New York: Farrar, Straus, and Giroux.

Kirton, M. (1976). Adaptors and innovators: A description and measure. *Journal of Applied Psychology, 61*, 622–629.

Koehler, D.J. and Harvey, N. (Eds.) (2004). *Blackwell Handbook of Judgment and Decision Making.* Malden, MA: Blackwell.

Kozhevnikov, M. (2007). Cognitive styles in the context of modern psychology: Toward an integrated framework of cognitive style. *Psychological Bulletin, 133*, 464–481.

Larrick, R.P. (2004). Debiasing. In D.J. Koehler and N. Harvey (Eds.) *Blackwell Handbook of Judgment and Decision Making* (pp. 316–337). Malden, MA: Blackwell.

Larrick, R.P., Morgan, J.N., and Nisbett, R.E. (1990). Teaching the use of cost-benefit reasoning in everyday life. *Psychological Science, 1*, 362–370.

Larrick, R.P., Nisbett, R.E., and Morgan, J.N. (1993). Who uses the cost-benefit rules of choice? Implications for the normative status of microeconomic theory. *Organizational Behavior and Human Decision Processes, 56*, 331–347.

Lodato, M.A., Highhouse, S., and Brooks, M.E. (2011). Predicting professional preferences for intuition-based hiring. *Journal of Managerial Psychology, 26*, 352–365.

Loo, R. (2000). A psychometric evaluation of the general decision-making style inventory. *Personality and Individual Differences, 29,* 895–905.

Lord, C.G., Lepper, M.R., and Preston, E. (1984). Considering the opposite: A corrective strategy for social judgment. *Journal of Personality and Social Psychology, 47,* 1231–1243.

Lovallo, D. and Kahneman, D. (2003). Delusions of success: How optimism undermines executives' decisions. *Harvard Business Review, 81,* 56–63.

Meyer, R.D., Dalal, R.S., and Hermida, R. (2010). A review and synthesis of situational strength in the organizational sciences. *Journal of Management, 36,* 121–140.

Meyer, R.D., Dalal, R.S., José, I., Hermida, R., Chen, T.R., Vega, R.P., Brooks, C.K., and Khare, V. (in press). Measuring job-related situational strength and assessing its interactive effects with personality on voluntary work behavior. *Journal of Management.*

Milkman, K.L., Chugh, D., and Bazerman, M.H. (2009). How can decision making be improved? *Perspectives on Psychological Science, 4,* 379–383.

Mischel, W. (1977). The interaction of person and situation. In D. Magnusson and N.S. Endler (Eds.) *Personality at the Crossroads: Current Issues in Interactional Psychology* (pp. 333–352). Hillsdale, NJ: Lawrence Erlbaum.

Mohammed, S. and Schwall, A. (2009). Individual differences and decision making: What we know and where we go from here. *International Review of Industrial and Organizational Psychology, 24,* 249–312.

Nenkov, G.Y., Morrin, M., Ward, A., Schwarz, B., and Hulland, J. (2008). A short form of the Maximization Scale: Factor structure, reliability and validity studies. *Judgment and Decision Making, 3,* 371–388.

Pacini, R. and Epstein, S. (1999). The relation of rational and experiential information processing styles to personality, basic beliefs, and the ratio-bias phenomenon. *Journal of Personality and Social Psychology, 76,* 972–987.

Parker, A.M. and Fischhoff, B. (2005). Decision-making competence: External validation through an individual-differences approach. *Journal of Behavioral Decision Making, 18,* 1–27.

Patalano, A.L. and Wengrovitz, S.M. (2007). Indecisiveness and response to risk in deciding when to decide. *Journal of Behavioral Decision Making, 20,* 405–424.

Rassin, E. and Muris, P. (2005). To be or not to be . . . indecisive: Gender differences, correlations with obsessive-compulsive complaints, and behavioural manifestation. *Personality and Individual Differences, 38,* 1175–1181.

Rowe, A.J. and Mason, R.O. (1987). *Managing with Style: A Guide to Understanding, Assessing, and Improving Decision Making.* San Francisco, CA: Jossey-Bass.

Sadler-Smith, E. (2004). Cognitive style and the management of small and medium-sized enterprises. *Organization Studies, 25,* 155–181.

Schreiber, C.A. and Kahneman, D. (2000). Determinants of the remembered utility of aversive sounds. *Journal of Experimental Psychology: General, 129,* 27–42.

Schwartz, B., Ward, A., Monterosso, J., Lyubomirsky, S., White, K., and Lehman, D.R. (2002). Maximizing versus satisficing. *Journal of Personality and Social Psychology, 83,* 1178–1197.

Scott, S.G. and Bruce, R.A. (1995). Decision-making style: The development and assessment of a new measure. *Educational and Psychological Measurement, 55,* 818–831.

Simon, H.A. (1955). A behavioral model of rational choice. *Quarterly Journal of Economics, 69,* 99–118.

Simon, H.A. (1956). Rational choice and the structure of the environment. *Psychological Review, 63,* 129–138.

Singh, R. and Greenhaus, J.H. (2004). The relation between career decision-making strategies and person–job fit: A study of job changers. *Journal of Vocational Behavior, 64,* 198–221.

Snyder, M. and Ickes, W. (1985). Personality and social behavior. In G. Lindzey and E. Aronson (Eds.) *Handbook of Social Psychology* (3rd ed., pp. 883–948). New York: Random House.

Spector, P.E., Fox, S., Penney, L.M., Bruursema, K., Goh, A., and Kessler, S. (2006). The dimensionality of counterproductivity: Are all counterproductive behaviors created equal? *Journal of Vocational Behavior, 68,* 446–460.

Spunt, R.P., Rassin, E., and Epstein, L.M. (2009). Aversive and avoidant indecisiveness: Roles for regret proneness, maximization, and BIS/BAS sensitivities. *Personality and Individual Differences, 47,* 256–261.

Stanovich, K.E. (2009). The thinking that IQ tests miss. *Scientific American Mind, 20,* 34–39.

Stanovich, K.E., Grunewald, M., and West, R.F. (2003). Cost-benefit reasoning in students with multiple secondary school suspensions. *Personality and Individual Differences, 35,* 1061–1072.

Stanovich, K.E., Toplak, M.E., and West, R.F. (2008). The development of rational thought: A taxonomy of heuristics and biases. *Advances in Child Development and Behaviour, 36,* 251–285.

Stanovich, K.E. and West, R.F. (2008). On the relative independence of thinking biases and cognitive ability. *Journal of Personality and Social Psychology, 94,* 672–695.

Stanovich, K.E., West, R.F., and Toplak, M.E. (2011). Individual differences as essential components of heuristics and biases research. In K. Manktelow, D. Over, and S. Elqayam (Eds.) *The Science of Reason: A Festschrift for Jonathan St.B.T. Evans* (pp. 355–396). Hove, UK: Psychology Press.

Sternberg, R.J. and Grigorenko, E.L. (1997). Are cognitive styles still in style? *American Psychologist, 52,* 700–712.

Stevenson, M.K., Busemeyer, J.R., and Naylor, J.C. (1990). Judgment and decision-making theory. In M.D. Dunnette and L.M. Hough (Eds.) *Handbook of Industrial and Organizational Psychology* (pp. 283–374). Palo Alto, CA: Consulting Psychologists Press.

Thunholm, P. (2004). Decision-making style: Habit, style or both? *Personality and Individual Differences, 36,* 931–944.

Thunholm, P. (2008). Decision-making styles and physiological correlates of negative stress: Is there a relation? *Scandinavian Journal of Psychology, 49,* 213–219.

Thunholm, P. (2009). Military leaders and followers—Do they have different decision styles? *Scandinavian Journal of Psychology, 50,* 317–324.

Tversky, A. and Kahneman, D. (1974). Judgment under uncertainty: Heuristics and biases. *Science, 185,* 1124–1131.

Tversky, A. and Kahneman, D. (1983). Extensional versus intuitive reasoning: The conjunction fallacy in probability judgment. *Psychological Review, 90,* 293–315.

Weiss, H.M. and Adler, S. (1984). Personality and organizational behavior. *Research in Organizational Behavior, 6,* 1–50.

Weitz, J. (1961). Criteria for criteria. *American Psychologist, 16,* 228–231.

Williams, L.J. and Anderson, S.E. (1991). Job satisfaction and organizational commitment as predictors of organizational citizenship and in-role behaviors. *Journal of Management, 17,* 601–617.

6

A Decade of Job Choice Research

Cynthia Kay Stevens

A recent chapter reviewing empirical job choice research (Highhouse & Hoffman, 2001) emphasized the need to integrate insights from the judgment and decision making (JDM) literature and to explore more fully job seekers' perspectives, rather than focusing so heavily on employers' concerns. In the decade since, these recommendations have proven prescient. The developed nations have weathered a series of financial bubbles (e.g., mortgage and housing meltdown, sovereign and municipal debt crises) that first shrank unemployment rates to unimaginably low levels and then threw millions of employees out of work while making jobs scarce for millions more new labor market entrants and job changers. This global phenomenon highlights a pressing need to understand job seekers' and decision makers' perspectives and choices not just when alternatives are plentiful and attractive, but also when they are distasteful or not easily comparable (e.g., take a position below one's capabilities, continue to search, retire early, get more education, start a business).

Job choice research during the past decade has offered many new insights into how job seekers make decisions, such as the central role of job seekers' pre-existing knowledge about employers' brands and reputations (e.g., Cable & Turban, 2001) and the impact of various recruitment practices that precede formal interviews on job seekers' attraction (e.g., Collins, 2007). Moreover, several cross-over studies that combine theories from JDM and applied problems in job choice have emerged (e.g., Tenbrunsel & Diekmann, 2002; Wells & Iyengar, 2005). Yet in many respects, the potential benefits of fuller integration of the JDM–job choice research literatures remain unrealized. JDM research has typically been conducted in laboratory settings with college students who are given information about a few attributes for multiple alternatives and who then evaluate these simultaneously. In contrast, recruitment and job choice studies usually involve surveys of graduating college students or unemployed job seekers in which they recall attribute or search activity information from memory and reconstruct what were often sequential decision processes. Designing empirical work that synthesizes both disciplines holds promise for the development of sharper, more dynamic theories that can inform consequential public policy debates.

Toward that end, this chapter offers a summary of the past decade of job choice research along with a critique of it using the lens of JDM theories and findings. I begin with a definition of job choice and an overview of research trends in past reviews. I then summarize recent studies of the factors that affect job seekers' knowledge of and attraction to job opportunities and how they process such information when making decisions. Finally, I consider how relevant JDM theories, methods, and key constructs might inform the next decade of job choice research.

PAST RESEARCH TRENDS IN JOB CHOICE RESEARCH

Barber (1998) defined *job choice* as the final decision job seekers make to accept or reject job offers, and differentiated it from similar screening decisions that occur earlier in the search process (e.g., whether or not to pursue additional information about job opportunities). Although her reasoning is valid (i.e., early screening decisions do not require job seekers to forego all other job alternatives), the past decade of recruitment and job choice research has begun to focus on these earlier decisions. Moreover, alternatives that survive earlier screening decisions comprise job seekers' consideration sets when they make final acceptance/rejection decisions, so these earlier decisions can have a profound impact by setting the context for final choices. For these reasons, I follow Highhouse and Hoffman (2001) in considering *job choice* as the cognitions that job seekers generate both to screen potential job opportunities and to accept or reject job offers.

Both Rynes (1991) and Highhouse and Hoffman (2001) organized their reviews around *content* (what attributes affect job seekers' attraction?) and *process* issues (how do job seekers weight and combine information into decisions?). Both reviews noted that cues and signals provided by prospective employers provide input into job seekers' perceptions of job attributes, which researchers had loosely categorized into objective (e.g., pay, type of work, coworkers, training) and subjective factors (e.g., whether recruiters or recruitment activities have much impact on job seekers' preferences). Note that job seekers' assessments of "objective" attributes included some subjectivity in evaluating their own chances for promotion and whether coworkers or the work environment would be pleasant. In general, job seekers' evaluations of these objective attributes were seen as the key driver of their attraction and choices, although subjective factors pertaining to recruiter and organizational treatment showed relationships with actual decisions.

With regard to job seekers' decision processes, both prior reviews noted the general acceptance of expected value models (such as expectancy theory and subjective expected utility (SEU) theory) as a basis for predicting job seekers' choices. These models propose that job seekers undergo a methodical evaluation process in which they first form judgments about the attractiveness of each alternative. Such judgments are assumed to be *compensatory* in that several desirable attributes (e.g., short commute, pleasant work environment, interesting work) may offset an undesirable attribute (e.g., low pay) in forming this overall judgment. Job seekers are predicted to choose the alternative that *maximizes* their chances of obtaining the most desirable mix of attributes. While these process models are predicated on the assumption that decision makers have multiple simultaneous job alternatives from which to choose, economists have developed a variation, optimal-stopping models, to handle situations in which job seekers must choose between a single job offer or continuing to search (e.g., Devine & Kiefer, 1991). Optimal-stopping models are also based on the assumption that job seekers desire to maximize outcomes, and propose that they set a reservation wage to benchmark job offers (i.e., reject those with salaries below the reservation wage and accept the first offer at or above it).

The early methodologies used to explore job choices largely followed the guidelines implicit in expected value models. Aside from a few studies that obtained rankings of job attribute importance (e.g., Jurgensen, 1978), most early research adopted one of three basic approaches: policy capturing, surveys of job seekers mid-way or near the end of their searches, or archival analyses of unemployment data. Policy capturing studies provided the best test of expectancy/SEU theory predictions because respondents rated the attractiveness of multiple hypothetical alternatives that varied attribute values systematically; they permitted within-subject analyses that captured individual differences in preferences and policies. In contrast, survey studies correlated job seekers' perceptions of job attributes with their attraction levels, usually for a single organization, and often obtained both pre- and post-interview measures to assess changes in attraction attributable to recruiters' influence. Finally, archival data enabled economists to evaluate the impact of various model parameters (e.g., availability of unemployment compensation) on search duration.

Although the available data indicate that expected-value models correctly predict job seekers' decisions at greater than chance rates (see Devine & Kiefer, 1991; Wanous, Keon, & Latack, 1983), Barber (1998) criticized the validity of their underlying assumptions, particularly those pertaining to compensatory tradeoffs leading to maximization as key elements in job choices. More recent studies (e.g., Osborn, 1990) found evidence that some attributes are decidedly non-compensatory, in that alternatives that fail to meet some minimum values (e.g., minimal salary levels, preferred geographic areas) are discarded regardless of their attractiveness on all other attributes. Likewise, Highhouse and Hoffman (2001) noted that expected-value models are of limited value in explaining both how job seekers prescreen alternatives (either during search or at the end, if there are many job offers) and how they make "tough choices" in situations where the set of available job alternatives does not contain one that clearly dominates the others in terms of providing preferred attributes. These critiques have been useful in stimulating a broader range of theories and methodologies within recent studies.

RECENT TRENDS IN JOB CHOICE RESEARCH

During the past decade, empirical research on the factors affecting job seekers' attraction to organizations has focused less on parsing the relative importance of objective versus subjective attributes and more on the role of pre-existing knowledge about employers and factors that affect job seekers' chances of securing employment. Empirical studies of their decision processes have begun to explore both how job seekers resolve "tough choices" and how the longitudinal context inherent in job search affects decision making. I summarize the findings pertaining to each of these trends below.

Determinants of Job Seekers' Attraction to Organizations

Researchers examining the factors that attract job seekers to organizations have pursued three distinct but overlapping paths: (a) how job seekers acquire information about job opportunities, (b) the factors that affect their perceptions of job and organizational attributes, and (c) personality and motivational factors that lead to employment.

How do job seekers gain information about job attributes? Job choice researchers have long borrowed from economic theories on market signals (Spence, 1973) as a basis for understanding where job seekers learn about the job attributes that form the basis for their choices. Although the early work on recruitment implicitly or explicitly assumed that recruiters conveyed the relevant information about job attributes during interviews and site visits, later research has recognized that job seekers actually begin search with pre-existing beliefs about employers that derive from their own and others' prior exposure to organizational marketing efforts (Cable & Turban, 2003a). Such exposure may occur in the form of product or service advertising (Collins, 2007; Turban, 2001), corporate sponsorships of campus events (Collins & Han, 2004), news stories and other exposure in the media (e.g., Slaughter et al., 2004), word-of-mouth discussions with friends or those who work for the organization (e.g., Turban, 2001), prior personal experience working for the organization (Cable et al., 2000), and studying the organization in school (Turban, 2001).

Exposure to such information increases job seekers' familiarity with prospective employers, which in turn affects accurate recall of firm information (Cable & Turban, 2003b) and attraction to the firm (Lemmink, Schuijf, & Streukens, 2003). Interestingly, however, Cable et al. (2000) found that applicants who relied on word-of-mouth information or prior work experience in the organization were no more accurate in their perceptions of company culture (as measured by congruence with executives' perceptions of company culture) than were those who relied on the unrealistically positive information conveyed in company brochures. It may be that perceptions of company culture are variable across stakeholder groups and thus unable to be conveyed in a unitary way to prospective employees. More generally, few studies have considered the extent to which job seekers' knowledge of organizational attributes corresponds with their actual attributes. This is a curious oversight, given (a) prior extensive work on realistic job previews as a way to correct misinformation, and (b) the notion that job search intensity and information sources might affect job seekers' knowledge accuracy, which in turn may have a significant impact on later person–organization fit, performance, job satisfaction, adjustment, and turnover.

What factors affect perceived job and organizational attributes? In recent years, researchers have abandoned the practice of eliciting detailed applicant ratings on lists of various job attributes (e.g., salary, benefits, work environment, coworkers, promotion opportunities) and have begun focusing instead on tapping three more global perceptions that comprise their knowledge about employers: familiarity, organizational images, and perceived organizational reputation (Cable & Turban, 2001). *Familiarity* refers to the level of awareness that job seekers have of organizations, and can range from a complete lack of awareness to recognition (i.e., prompted recall) to unaided recall and to top-of-mind awareness (Cable & Turban, 2001). As such, familiarity reflects how accessible employer information is in memory (Turban, 2001), which in turn is linked with greater attraction (Chapman et al., 2005; Turban, 2001). Cable and Turban (2001) proposed that familiarity serves as a signal of employer legitimacy, leading to inferences about organizational stability and desirability. Yet, Brooks et al. (2003) found that familiarity enables job seekers to recall both more positive and more negative information, depending on what type of memory they are prompted to retrieve. For example, respondents are more likely to cite highly (versus less) familiar firms as both most admirable and most contemptible, and they provide more reasons for and against working for highly (versus less) familiar firms. That said, virtually all studies of organizational familiarity effects on job seekers' attraction have considered only recognizable, easily recalled, and top-of-mind organizations; as a result, little is known about how job seekers perceive or evaluate unfamiliar organizations as prospective employers. This represents a substantial oversight given statistics indicating that half of all American workers are employed by six million small (i.e., fewer than 500 employees) businesses,[1] in comparison with 18,311 large firms (U.S. Small Business Administration FAQ).

Organizational images refer to the contents of job seekers' beliefs about an organization's attributes as an employer, the jobs it offers, and the people who work there (Cable & Turban, 2001). Cable and Yu (2006) found that job seekers begin their searches with preformed organizational images that are linked to the images they hold following exposure to media presentations about those organizations. Similarly, job seekers' more general images about a given corporation are related to their images of that corporation as a potential employer, which in turn are positively related to their intentions to apply for jobs (Lemmink, Schuijf, & Streukens, 2003).

Based on theory and findings in cognitive psychology and marketing, job choice researchers have proposed that the beliefs comprising organizational images may be based both on job seekers' own inferences and on their knowledge of verifiable information. Both elements factor into attraction. For example, Lievens and Highhouse (2003) predicted and found that job seekers' organizational images comprised both instrumental (i.e., attributes pertaining to functional needs such as pay or work hours) and symbolic content (i.e., attributes related to intangible assessments, such as organizational traits). Moreover, job seekers used symbolic inferences as a basis for differentiating prospective employers from each other. In a study that more directly investigated job seekers' trait ascriptions to organizations, Slaughter et al. (2004) found five organizational personality dimensions: boyscout (i.e., solid, reliable, well-intentioned), dominant, innovative, style, and thrift. The first four organizational personality types tend to be linked with positive evaluations, whereas the fifth is associated with negative evaluations (Slaughter et al., 2004), although subsequent work found that perceptions of these organizational personalities interact with job seekers' own personalities in affecting attraction (Slaughter & Greguras, 2009).

A final component of job seekers' employer knowledge, *reputation*, refers to global or general temporally stable evaluative judgments about organizations that are believed to be shared by multiple constituencies (Highhouse, Brooks, & Greguras, 2009). Note that job seekers' individual perceptions of organizational reputations are distinct from but related to corporate reputations, which reflect aggregated perceptions within or across constituency groups (Highhouse, Brooks, & Greguras, 2009; Rindova et al., 2005). As such, the perceived reputation construct captures job seekers' impressions of how *other people* regard the organization and thus how others might perceive them as individuals if they were to join the organization. Given the social-identity implications of organizations' reputations, Highhouse, Thornbury, and Little (2007) proposed that job seekers use market cues to draw two types of symbolic inferences about organizations that affect their attraction: the extent to which a given organization is impressive to others, and the extent to which it is seen as respectable by others.

Empirical studies have linked job seekers' perceptions of reputation to organizations' media exposure as well as to attributes such as its industry and profitability (Cable & Graham, 2000). In addition, perceived organizational familiarity is related to pride in becoming an employee of the firm (Turban et al., 2001), although as noted earlier, Brooks et al. (2003) reported that more familiar firms can be seen as both more *and* less reputable, depending on whether positive or negative memory content is accessed. Cable and Turban (2003b) found in a policy capturing study that job seekers were willing to accept identical jobs with 7 percent lower salaries at a firm with a positive (versus a negative) reputation based on *Fortune* magazine ratings. Similarly, Cable and Turban (2003a) reported that firms that had been included on *Fortune, Business Week, 100 Best Companies,* and *Working Mother* lists of top firms had higher numbers of attendees at information sessions, applicants and interview bids as well as applicants with higher GPAs, more foreign language skills, and stronger interviewer ratings of quality.

How do individual differences affect the process of securing employment? Finally, researchers have considered the role of both personality and motivational factors in the extent to which job seekers obtain and accept job offers. These studies provide indirect evidence of the impact of individual differences on job choice, in the sense that observed relationships between these factors and individuals' employment status (i.e., employed versus not employed) comprise both the effort associated with search and generating job offers as well as the willingness or desire to accept one of the offers extended. The mechanisms underlying the relationship between personality and motivational variables, on one hand, and job choice, on the other hand, have not been explored. It appears that many personality and motivational variables do increase job seekers' attractiveness to employers and elicit job offers, but it is also possible that some variables might also predispose them to accept offers more readily rather than continue to search via other cognitive mechanisms.

Available data indicate that personality factors such as extraversion, conscientiousness (Kanfer, Wanberg, & Kantrowitz, 2001), positive affectivity (Côté, Saks, & Zikic, 2006), and proactive personality (Brown et al., 2006) are positively related to job seekers' employment status (i.e., having accepted a job offer). In addition, motivational factors, which include situational needs and more enduring self-motivation characteristics, are also predictive of employment status. Specifically, employment commitment (i.e., the extent to which one perceives paid employment as important for reasons beyond simply the pay), financial hardship, job search self-efficacy (Kanfer, Wanberg, & Kantrowitz, 2001; Saks, 2006; Wanberg, Kanfer, & Rotundo, 1999), core self-evaluations (Wanberg et al., 2005), goal orientation (Van Hooft & Noordzij, 2009), search strategy (e.g., focused versus exploratory approach to finding employment), and job seekers' objectives in searching (e.g., finding a new job versus objectives such as gaining bargaining leverage with one's employer, professional networking, or increasing awareness of potential opportunities; Van Hoye & Saks, 2008) have all been linked to employment status. It would be helpful for researchers to decompose the employment status criterion further into decision components such as attraction and risk preferences as a way to understand how personality and motivation influence job choices.

Factors Affecting How Job Seekers Process Information

Whereas studies in the preceding section focused on individual, information-source, and perceptual factors that influence job seekers' attraction to job alternatives, the research in this section considers how job seekers weigh and evaluate information when choosing how to respond (i.e., whether or not to pursue job alternatives; whether to accept or reject job offers). For example, Tenbrunsel and Diekmann (2002) explored how decision makers resolved "tough choices" in which all alternatives possessed different combinations of attractive and unattractive attributes. They found that participants preferred whichever job alternative was clearly superior to a decoy (i.e., a less attractive alternative in the consideration set that was unlikely to be chosen), despite the fact that the remaining feasible alternative had some superior attributes. They also found evidence to support the interpretation that the presence of an inferior alternative changes how people view the attractiveness of attribute values, possibly by giving rise to additional reasons that enable decision makers to justify their choices to others or by triggering loss aversion for attributes that would need to be sacrificed in making the choice.

Slaughter and Highhouse (2003) also explored whether "tough choices" are affected by the actual contingencies that operate on job seekers. Specifically, they examined attribute-salience effects, which occur when the attributes shared by fewer alternatives in the consideration set exert greater weight on choices, in comparison with attributes shared by greater numbers of alternatives. For example, if only one job alternative provides a short commute whereas several alternatives offer pleasant work environments, the short commute may come to outweigh pleasant work environment as a factor in choice. Slaughter and Highhouse (2003) found that the attribute-salience effect occurred most often in conditions where it was easy to compare the attributes across alternatives (e.g., all attribute information was presented in a matrix, versus scattered across several pages of information) and when job seekers had *not* first rated how important each attribute was to them (which could trigger a consistency bias).

Consistent with this pattern, several studies have demonstrated that job seekers' preferences are *not* stable throughout the job search process. For example, Boswell et al. (2003) found that the factors that job seekers rated as important in their choices shifted over time and also as a function of whether they were accepting/pursuing versus rejecting/not pursuing a job alternative. Likewise, Wells and Iyengar (2005) reported that job seekers perceived their preferences to be more stable than they actually were; moreover, those who believed erroneously that their preferences had not changed during search experienced more positive affect and greater success in finding and accepting job offers. The significance of changes in affective reactions was also noted by Wanberg, Zhu, and Van Hooft (2010), who found that job seekers who perceived lower search progress on a given day experienced negative affect but engaged greater search effort on the next day. It would be interesting to examine how such cycles of affect and effort influence how job seekers perceive and evaluate their preferences and job alternatives.

Finally, with regard to how individual differences affect job choices, little work has considered this question. Drawing from the theory of reasoned action as a basis for predicting job seekers' attraction to and choice of jobs, Van Hooft et al. (2006) did find that women and minorities were more influenced in their decisions by subjective norms (i.e., what others close to them thought about pursuing the job alternative) than were men or majority members, who were more influenced by their own personal attitudes about prospective employers.

FUTURE DIRECTIONS AND SYNTHESIS WITH JDM RESEARCH

As this summary suggests, job choice researchers have recognized that job seekers' pre-existing employer knowledge includes many inferences and that it plays a critical role in their evaluations. Another important insight from the past decade is that both preferences and evaluations are sensitive to context in that these may be swayed by the presence and range of attribute values of other alternatives under consideration. Yet, these advances could be dramatically enhanced through fuller integration of JDM research in the conceptualization and design of job choice studies. Toward this end, I summarize specific theoretical and methodological advancements that might be extended to the job choice domain, as well as findings pertaining to several key psychological processes (e.g., attention, memory).

JDM Theories and Methodologies

Prospect theory (Kahneman & Tversky, 1984) represents an enormously influential conceptualization that is curiously absent from the job choice literature. Similar to expectancy/SEU theory in predicting a compensatory-maximizing approach to evaluating attributes, prospect theory also explicitly considers decision makers' reference points (i.e., their starting points for evaluating alternatives, which often represent their status quo values), goals, and risk aversion in explaining choices. Prospect theory thus may help unify the fragmented literatures that have evolved for disparate job-seeking populations such that new labor market entrants, employed job seekers, and job losers could be expected to start search using dramatically different reference points and to exhibit quite different risk sensitivities. For example, new labor market entrants may frame alternatives as potential gains and take a conservative approach when considering job opportunities, whereas employed job seekers might view them as potential losses and become risk-seeking. Mapping group-level differences in reference points, aspirations, and loss aversion across these groups might thus fully or partially explain how and when employment status influences job choices.

A second conceptual advancement pertains to dual-process models to explain variations in decision makers' evaluations (Evans, 2008). Such models suggest that alternatives may be evaluated by either rapid, automatic, heuristic processes (often termed System 1) or slower, deliberative, effortful processes (System 2) as a function of the decision maker's goals and context. Despite well-documented problems linked to use of decision heuristics (Nisbett & Ross, 1980), however, research also suggests that heuristics are often reasonably accurate guides (Goldstein & Gigerenzer, 2002) and that, under some circumstances, deliberative decisions can even result in worse outcomes than reliance on heuristics (Dijkstra et al., 2012). Given that job choices unfold over time in a sequential series of smaller decisions (e.g., to pursue or discard a given opening) that cumulate to potentially life-changing outcomes, researchers would benefit from fuller consideration of the factors that trigger each type of processing as well as their consequences. For example, Goldstein and Gigerenzer (2002) have argued that reliance on the recognition heuristic produces reasonably accurate predictions in many contexts, yet its use and effectiveness in job choices (where organizational familiarity seems to influence decisions) is not well understood. Likewise, findings by Wells and Iyengar (2005) imply that job seekers who track shifts in their search criteria over time fare worse in emotional responses and outcomes than do those who remain unaware; the extent to which such outcomes result from differential reliance on System 1 versus System 2 processing should be investigated.

With regard to key JDM methodological innovations, Hastie and Dawes (2010) highlighted the development of the Iowa gambling task[2] and similar approaches as helping to clarify how decision makers learn from experience with positive and negative outcomes over series of related decisions. Given the longitudinal nature of job choices, this approach (in which decision makers must detect likely outcomes associated with each choice and change their behavior to obtain desired outcomes) seems especially well suited for identifying job seekers' strategies and adaptability. Likewise, experience-sampling methodologies, in which decision makers provide daily reports on their moods and decisions (see Seo & Barrett, 2007) represent a promising approach for understanding how job choices respond to incidental events and emotions. Several studies (e.g., Wanberg, Zhu, & Van Hooft, 2010) have adopted this method to study unemployed job seekers, and its use should be expanded both to a wider range of theoretically relevant variables and to other job-seeking populations.

Attentional Resources

With regard to important psychological processes, Weber and Johnson (2009) argued that decision makers' selective attention plays a central role in guiding the encoding, evaluation, and retrieval processes necessary in making judgments and choices. As a result, factors such as the task requirements (i.e., forming judgments versus making choices), environmental distractions, and personal goals and affect may all influence how job seekers attend to, recall, and assess available job alternatives. As one example, job seekers may construe their decision tasks differently in early versus later stages of search. Thus, screening alternatives in (or out) may trigger framing biases that direct attention differentially to positive (negative) attributes and elicit non-compensatory evaluations, whereas forming judgments about prospective employers may prompt controlled processing and compensatory weighting of attributes. Thus, changing the task early in search (e.g., asking job seekers to form judgments about early prospects) could shift their attention in ways that affect the size and composition of the consideration set available for later choices.

Similarly, job seekers' goals clearly influence their search intensity and outcomes (Van Hoye & Saks, 2008), but little is known about how such goals direct attention and choices. Given findings in the study of both motivated reasoning (Kunda, 1990) and goal orientations (Payne, Youngcourt, & Beaubien, 2007), it seems possible that differences in search goals (e.g., obtain a job with a prestigious employer, find a job that helps to manage dual career dynamics) would have profound effects on the employer information sought and retained in memory as well as how job alternatives are evaluated (e.g., focus on maximizing potential gains or minimizing potential losses, use of heuristic reasoning). Likewise, job seekers' affective reactions to their search progress influence their subsequent effort (Wanberg, Zhu, & Van Hooft, 2010), but findings in the JDM literature (Au et al., 2003; Seo & Barrett, 2007) demonstrate that affect and affect regulation may also have substantial effects on how job seekers evaluate their alternatives (e.g., accuracy in interpretation of information, use of heuristic shortcuts, confidence in judgments, time taken to process information). Thus, fuller consideration of how affect influences job seekers' attentional resources seems a promising direction for research.

Evaluation Context

One issue frequently sidestepped in recruitment and job choice research is that decision makers' evaluations are *relative*—that is, people have tremendous difficulty making absolute (i.e., solo) judgments, they are prone to reversing those judgments when reference points become available, and they use the attributes of available alternatives as references to differentiate them when making decisions (Hsee et al., 1999; Weber & Johnson, 2009). What this means in practice is that the *context* in which job seekers gather and evaluate information will always qualify interpretation of empirical findings and, as such, the context needs to be chosen deliberately and specified in advance to clarify interpretation.

Recent studies rarely ask job seekers to evaluate their attraction to a single organization, and it would be wise either to discontinue this practice or, if it is used, to elicit information about job seekers' idiosyncratic reference points (e.g., their ideal employer, an employer with whom they recently had contact). Given that job seekers rarely consider job opportunities in isolation, it would be preferable to ask for ratings of two or more job alternatives and to identify their attribute ranges. When multiple job alternatives are used, researchers should consider the effects of changes in attribute distributions on job seekers' preferences, evaluations, and choices. In this way, job choice researchers would be able to generate more accurate models of what attributes job seekers concentrate on and how these are likely to be evaluated in context.

Memory Processes

Some of the most important JDM concepts to integrate with job choice research concern the role of *memory processes* in guiding evaluations and decisions. Research has repeatedly shown, for example, that priming increases the accessibility of primed information in memory and thus influences later evaluations. Likewise, retrieval prompts such as implied default values (e.g., how does Employer X compare to Employer Y?) and implicit ordering of decision or evaluative tasks (e.g., what do you think of Employer 1? Employer 2? Employer 3?) can increase accessibility of some memory content at the expense of other competing memory content; as a result, both preference- and inference-construction processes are path-dependent (Weber & Johnson, 2009). Additionally, studies have found that decision makers have difficulty recalling important criteria for their decisions even when the decision domains (e.g., choosing MBA programs) are significant (Bond, Carlson, & Keeney, 2008), which suggests that memory processes play a vital part in understanding how and why job seeker preferences shift over time (Wells & Iyengar, 2005).

Because job search is nearly always a longitudinal process of investigating and pursuing job alternatives, most of the information used to choose jobs must be retrieved from memory. Thus, it would be helpful to explore job seekers' memories more closely by considering how information sources (e.g., product/service advertisements, job fairs, word-of-mouth discussions) affect the accuracy, encoding, salience, and retrieval of information as well as that information's later accessibility and malleability in memory. For example, do some sources lead to more accurate or accessible images than others and, if so, what are these sources? How do interventions that prime recollections of particular organizations affect job seekers' preferences? How do job seekers' inferences about organizations affect their evaluations—to what extent do they recognize or discount inferential content? And, importantly, under what conditions do job seekers reassess their positive or negative organizational images?

A related issue concerns the relationship between job seekers' familiarity with and knowledge of prospective employers. Familiarity reflects the accessibility of employer information in memory, and as such is correlated with employer knowledge. Yet, the concept of knowledge captures an additional feature, veracity, which is missing from existing studies of familiarity. As such, job seekers could perceive themselves as familiar with a given employer and use this perception heuristically to conclude that they possess more accurate employer knowledge than they actually do. In this way, familiarity may actually reduce job seekers' forecasting accuracy even as it increases their confidence (see Hall, Ariss & Todorov, 2007).

Individual Differences

Meta-analyses in job search and choice (e.g., Chapman et al., 2005; Kanfer, Wanberg, & Kantrowitz, 2001) have reported direct or moderated relationships between individual difference variables, such as demographic background and personality, with search behavior and outcomes. JDM researchers have also explored the relationship between many of these individual differences and decision making, particularly with regard to risk assessments. For example, women, older people, and individuals higher in introversion, conscientiousness, and neuroticism show tendencies toward greater risk aversion, which could explain some of the observed relationships between personality and demographics with employment status. Researchers might also increase understanding of job choice dynamics by including measures of cognitive style, such as propensity toward regret and promotion versus prevention regulatory focus.

Decision Avoidance

A final avenue for future research concerns *decision avoidance*, which Anderson (2003) described as the tendency to avoid making a decision either by postponing it or seeking an easy way out that involves no change or action. As such, this concept may provide helpful insights into why some job seekers reject job offers despite circumstances (e.g., unemployment) that might otherwise predict acceptance, as well as dysfunctional decision strategies to help resolve "tough choices." Anderson (2003) outlined several mechanisms underlying decision avoidance, including reliance on the status quo (i.e., desire for one's situation to remain the same), omission bias (preference for options that do not require action to be taken), inaction inertia (tendency to reject later alternatives after previously foregoing a similar alternative), and decision deferral (tendency to postpone making decisions). He proposed that preference stability and anticipated regret may both lead to decision avoidance, and that the consequences may include experienced regret and fear regulation. Incorporation of these variables into studies of tough choices and prolonged search may elucidate whether such processes are found in job choice settings.

CONCLUSION

In reviewing the past several decades of job choice research, it is clear that both our conceptual models and study designs have evolved considerably. Researchers are far more sophisticated in recognizing that organizational attraction both has roots that predate the onset of job search and is influenced by factors that extend beyond recruitment practices alone. Moreover, researchers have begun to appreciate the substantial role that context plays in affecting preferences and choices. By more fully integrating existing knowledge and concepts in the JDM literature, we are poised to capitalize on these insights in ways that dramatically increase the predictive and explanatory utility of our theories and models. Given the profound impact of fluctuations in our increasingly global economy on employment patterns, such work is sorely needed.

NOTES

1. Turban and Greening (1997) found that smaller firms are significantly less likely to be familiar to job seekers than are larger firms.
2. In the Iowa gambling task, respondents choose successive cards from one of four decks where each deck has different levels and distributions of rewards and penalties (e.g., high payoffs coupled with high and frequent penalties versus lower payoffs paired with infrequent and lower penalties). In this way, the expected value associated with each deck is not specified and must be learned over time.

REFERENCES

Anderson, C.J. (2003). The psychology of doing nothing: Forms of decision avoidance result from reason and emotion. *Psychological Bulletin, 129*(1), 139–167.

Au, K., Chan, F., Wang, D., and Vertinsky, I. (2003). Mood in foreign exchange trading: Cognitive processes and performance. *Organizational Behavior and Human Decision Processes, 91*, 322–338.

Barber, A.E. (1998). *Recruiting Employees: Individual and Organizational Perspectives.* Thousand Oaks, CA: Sage.

Bond, S.D., Carlson, K.A., and Keeney, R.L. (2008). Generating objectives: Can decision makers articulate what they want? *Management Science, 54*(1), 56–70.

Boswell, W.R., Roehling, M.V., LePine, M.A., and Moynihan, L.M. (2003). Individual job-choice decisions and the impact of job attributes and recruitment practices: A longitudinal study. *Human Resource Management, 42*(1), 23–37.

118 • *Cynthia Kay Stevens*

Brooks, M.E., Highhouse, S., Russell, S.S., and Mohr, D.C. (2003). Familiarity, ambivalence, and firm reputation: Is corporate fame a double-edged sword? *Journal of Applied Psychology*, *88*(5), 904–914.

Brown, D.J., Cober, R.T., Kane, K., Levy, P.E., and Shalhoop, J. (2006). Proactive personality and the successful job search: A field investigation with college graduates. *Journal of Applied Psychology*, *91*(3), 717–726.

Cable, D.M., Aiman-Smith, L., Mulvey, P.W., and Edwards, J.R. (2000). The sources and accuracy of job applicants' beliefs about organizational culture. *Academy of Management Journal*, *43*(6), 1076–1085.

Cable, D.M. and Graham, M.E. (2000). The determinants of job seekers' reputation perceptions. *Journal of Organizational Behavior*, *21*, 929–947.

Cable, D.M. and Turban, D.B. (2001). Establishing the dimensions, sources and value of job seekers' employer knowledge during recruitment. *Research in Personnel and Human Resources Management*, *20*, 115–163.

Cable, D.M. and Turban, D.B. (2003a). Firm reputation and applicant pool characteristics. *Journal of Organizational Behavior*, *24*, 733–751.

Cable, D.M. and Turban, D.B. (2003b). The value of organizational reputation in the recruitment context: A brand equity perspective. *Journal of Applied Social Psychology*, *33*(11), 2244–2266.

Cable, D.M. and Yu, K.Y.T. (2006). Managing job seekers' organizational image beliefs: The role of media richness and media credibility. *Journal of Applied Psychology*, *91*(4), 828–840.

Chapman, D.S., Uggerslev, K.L., Carroll, S.A., Piasentin, K.A., and Jones, D.A. (2005). Applicant attraction to organizations and job choice: A meta-analytic review of the correlates of recruiting outcomes. *Journal of Applied Psychology*, *90*(5), 928–944.

Collins, C.J. (2007). The interactive effects of recruitment practices and product awareness on job seekers' employer knowledge and application behaviors. *Journal of Applied Psychology*, *92*(1), 180–190.

Collins, C.J. and Han, J. (2004). Exploring applicant pool quantity and quality: The effects of early recruitment practice strategies, corporate advertising, and firm reputation. *Personnel Psychology*, *57*, 685–717.

Côté, S., Saks, A.M., and Zikic, J. (2006). Trait affect and job search outcomes. *Journal of Vocational Behavior*, *68*, 233–252.

Devine, T.J. and Kiefer, N.M. (1991). *Empirical Labor Economics: The Search Approach*. New York: Oxford University Press.

Dijkstra, K.A., van der Pligt, J., van Kleef, G.A., and Kerstholt, J.H. (2012). Deliberation versus intuition: Global versus local processing in judgment and choice. *Journal of Experimental Social Psychology*, *48*, 1156–1161.

Evans, J.St.B.T. (2008). Dual-processing accounts of reasoning, judgment, and social cognition. *Annual Review of Psychology*, *59*, 255–278.

Goldstein, D.G. and Gigerenzer, G. (2002). Models of ecological rationality: The recognition heuristic. *Psychological Review*, *109*(1), 75–90.

Hall, C.C., Ariss, L., and Todorov, A. (2007). The illusion of knowledge: When more information reduces accuracy and increases confidence. *Organizational Behavior and Human Decision Processes*, *103*, 277–290.

Hastie, R. and Dawes, R.M. (2010). *Rational Choice in an Uncertain World: The Psychology of Judgment and Decision Making*. Los Angeles, CA: Sage.

Highhouse, S., Brooks, M.E., and Greguras, G. (2009). An organization impression management perspective on the formation of corporate reputations. *Journal of Management*, *35*(6), 1481–1493.

Highhouse, S. and Hoffman, J.R. (2001). Organizational attraction and job choice. *International Review of Industrial and Organizational Psychology*, 16, 37–64.

Highhouse, S., Thornbury, E.E., and Little, I.S. (2007). Social-identity functions of attraction to organizations. *Organizational Behavior and Human Decision Processes*, 103, 134–146.

Hsee, C.K., Loewenstein, G.F., Blount, S., and Bazerman, M.H. (1999). Preference reversals between joint and separate evaluations of options: A review and theoretical analysis. *Psychological Bulletin*, 125(5), 576–590.

Jurgensen, C.E. (1978). Job preferences (What makes a job good or bad?). *Journal of Applied Psychology*, 63, 267–276.

Kahneman, D. and Tversky, A. (1984). Choices, values and frames. *American Psychologist*, 39, 341–350.

Kanfer, R., Wanberg, C.R., and Kantrowitz, T.M. (2001). Job search and employment: A personality-motivational analysis and meta-analytic review. *Journal of Applied Psychology*, 86(5), 837–875.

Kunda, Z. (1990). The case for motivated reasoning. *Psychological Bulletin*, 108(3), 480–498.

Lemmink, J., Schuijf, A., and Streukens, S. (2003). The role of corporate image and company employment image in explaining application intentions. *Journal of Economic Psychology*, 24, 1–15.

Lievens, F. and Highhouse, S. (2003). The relation of instrumental and symbolic attributes to a company's attractiveness as an employer. *Personnel Psychology*, 56, 75–102.

Nisbett, R.E. and Ross, L. (1980). *Human Inference: Strategies and Shortcomings of Social Judgment*. Englewood Cliffs, NJ: Prentice-Hall.

Osborn, D.P. (1990). A reexamination of the organizational choice process. *Journal of Vocational Behavior*, 36, 45–60.

Payne, S., Youngcourt, S.S., and Beaubien, J.M. (2007). A meta-analytic examination of the goal orientation nomological net. *Journal of Applied Psychology*, 92(1), 128–150.

Rindova, V.P., Williamson, I.O., Petkova, A.P., and Sever, J.M. (2005). Being good or being known: An empirical examination of the dimensions, antecedents and consequences of organizational reputation. *Academy of Management Journal*, 48(6), 1033–1049.

Rynes, S.L. (1991). Recruitment, job choice, and post-hire consequences: A call for new research directions. In M.D. Dunnette (Ed.) *Handbook of Industrial and Organizational Psychology* (2nd ed.). Palo Alto, CA: Consulting Psychologists.

Saks, A.M. (2006). Multiple predictors and criteria of job search success. *Journal of Vocational Behavior*, 68, 400–415.

Seo, M.G. and Barrett, L.F. (2007). Being emotional during decision making—good or bad? An empirical investigation. *Academy of Management Journal*, 50(4), 923–940.

Slaughter, J.E. and Greguras, G.J. (2009). Initial attraction to organizations: The influence of trait inferences. *International Journal of Selection and Assessment*, 17(1), 1–18.

Slaughter, J.E. and Highhouse, S. (2003). Does matching up features mess up job choice? Boundary conditions on attribute-salience effects. *Journal of Behavioral Decision Making*, 16, 1–15.

Slaughter, J.E., Zickar, M.J., Highhouse, S., and Mohr, D.C. (2004). Personality trait inferences about organizations: Development of a measure and assessment of construct validity. *Journal of Applied Psychology*, 89(1), 85–103.

Spence, M. (1973). Job market signaling. *Quarterly Journal of Economics*, 87, 355–374.

Tenbrunsel, A.E. and Diekmann, K.A. (2002). Job-decision inconsistencies involving social comparison information: The role of dominating alternatives. *Journal of Applied Psychology*, 87(6), 1149–1158.

120 • *Cynthia Kay Stevens*

Turban, D.B. (2001). Organizational attractiveness as an employer on college campuses: An examination of the applicant population. *Journal of Vocational Behavior, 58,* 293–312.

Turban, D.B. and Greening, D.W. (1997). Corporate social performance and organizational attractiveness to prospective employees. *Academy of Management Journal, 40,* 658–672.

Turban, D.B., Lau, C.-M., Ngo, H.-Y., Chow, I.H.S., and Si, S.X. (2001). Organizational attractiveness of firms in the People's Republic of China: A person–organization fit perspective. *Journal of Applied Psychology, 86*(2), 194–206.

U.S. Small Business Administration FAQ, retrieved September 22, 2011 from http://web.sba.gov/faqs/faqindex.cfm?areaID=24.

Van Hooft, E.A.J., Born, M.P., Taris, T.W., and Van der Flier, H. (2006). Ethnic and gender differences in applicants' decision-making processes: An application of the theory of reasoned action. *International Journal of Selection and Assessment, 14*(2), 156–166.

Van Hooft, E.A.J. and Noordzij, G. (2009). The effects of goal orientation on job search and reemployment: A field experiment among unemployed job seekers. *Journal of Applied Psychology, 94*(6), 1581–1590.

Van Hoye, G. and Saks, A.M. (2008). Job search as goal-directed behavior: Objectives and methods. *Journal of Vocational Behavior, 73,* 358–367.

Wanberg, C.R., Glomb, T.M., Song, Z., and Sorenson, S. (2005). Job-search persistence during unemployment: A 10-wave longitudinal study. *Journal of Applied Psychology, 90*(3), 411–430.

Wanberg, C.R., Kanfer, R., and Rotundo, M. (1999). Unemployed individuals: Motives, job-search competencies and job-search constraints as predictors of job seeking and reemployment. *Journal of Applied Psychology, 84*(6), 897–910.

Wanberg, C.R., Zhu, J., and Van Hooft, E.A.J. (2010). The job search grind: Perceived progress, self-reactions, and self-regulation of search effort. *Academy of Management Journal, 53*(4), 788–807.

Wanous, J.P., Keon, T.L., and Latack, J.C. (1983). Expectancy theory and occupational/organizational choices: A review and test. *Organizational Behavior and Human Performance, 32,* 66–86.

Weber, E.U. and Johnson, E.J. (2009). Mindful judgment and decision making. *Annual Review of Psychology, 60,* 53–85.

Wells, R.E. and Iyengar, S.S. (2005). Positive illusions of preference consistency: When remaining eluded by one's preferences yields greater subjective well-being and decision outcomes. *Organizational Behavior and Human Decision Processes, 98,* 66–87.

Part II

Organizational Decision Making

7

Goals and Decision Making

Lisa Ordóñez and George Wu

One of the most influential research areas in organizational behavior during the past forty years has been the investigation of goal setting theory (Locke & Latham, 1990, 2002). This research has shown, in both field and laboratory settings, across multiple tasks and contexts, that people work harder and persist longer to achieve a specific difficult goal relative to a vague or easy goal, such as "do your best." Locke and Latham (2006) conclude: "So long as a person is committed to the goal, has the requisite ability to attain it, and does not have conflicting goals, there is a positive, linear relationship between goal difficulty and task performance." Moreover, goal setting has become a frequently used motivational tool for professional managers who have access to a variety of websites, consultants, and computer programs. However, goal setting is not a magic motivational bullet and this extensive organizational use of goal setting has led to calls for restraint due to evidence of negative outcomes (Ordóñez et al., 2009a, 2009b; Schweitzer, Ordóñez, & Douma, 2004).

We use the term "goal" to refer specifically to a performance goal in which individuals strive to meet a specific, challenging goal based on outcomes of their performance. Thus, we do not consider goals that lack a clear end-state, such as "being healthy" or "being a good partner." Notions of this sort have been called "personal strivings" by Emmons (1986) and "life tasks" by Cantor et al. (1987). We also restrict ourselves to "all-or-nothing" goals. Thus, we do not discuss the interesting research on graded-goals (e.g., Soman & Cheema, 2004) in which value is attributed to progress towards a goal. Our definition naturally limits the scope of our discussion about goals. We do not include mastery or learning goals (Dweck 1986, 1992) in which individuals strive to master a set of skills. Research has indicated that mastery goals are more conducive to deeper processing of information (Nolen, 1988) and also lead to higher internal motivation (Elliot & Harackiewicz, 1996) compared to performance goals. Different theories have looked at various pieces of goals, including the dynamics of self-regulation (e.g., Carver & Scheier, 1998), the role of automatic control processes on goal pursuit (e.g., Trope & Fishbach, 2000), the effect of implementation intentions on goal achievement (e.g., Gollwitzer, 1999; Gollwitzer & Sheeran, 2006), or how motivation is influenced by whether behavior is self-determined or controlled (e.g., Deci, 1992; Deci & Ryan, 1985). These interesting ideas are beyond the scope of this chapter (for reviews of different goal concepts in cognitive, personality, and social psychology, see Austin & Vancouver, 1996; Fishbach & Ferguson, 2007; Pervin, 1989).

LINKING GOALS TO JDM RESEARCH

Our chapter focuses primarily on the intersection between specific, challenging performance goals and psychological models of decision making. The fertile field of judgment and decision making (JDM) has documented the processes people use in making judgments (e.g., Gilovich, Griffin, & Kahneman, 2002; Kahneman, Slovic, & Tversky, 1982), as well as how individuals evaluate options and make choices (e.g., Kahneman & Tversky, 2000; Shafir & LeBoeuf, 2004; Wu, Zhang, & Gonzalez, 2004). We argue that this vast literature provides insights into goal setting, as this research has for fields as varied as business and economics, law, and medicine (e.g., Camerer, 2000; Dowie & Elstein, 1988; Jolls, Sunstein, & Thaler, 1998).

It is clear that goals work (positively and negatively at times)—but precisely how do goals impact motivation? Heath, Larrick, and Wu (1999) directly connect goal setting theory to JDM by proposing that goals serve as reference points and thus inherit the properties of prospect theory's value function (Kahneman & Tversky, 1979; Tversky & Kahneman, 1992). Thus, the properties of the value function can help explain classic goal-setting results, as well as provide new behavioral predictions. By connecting goal setting to prospect theory, Heath, Larrick, and Wu (1999) provide a bridge between motivation (goals) and cognition (decision making) that will form the foundation for this chapter.

Although prospect theory was originally proposed as a model of risky decision making, researchers have used pieces of prospect theory to explain other aspects of decision making, such as mental accounting (Thaler,

1985). In a similar spirit, Heath, Larrick, and Wu (1999) propose that goals inherit three properties of the prospect theory value function:

1. *Reference dependence*: Reference points divide the set of outcomes into gains and losses (or successes and failures). Although the early empirical evidence looked primarily at status quo reference points, a number of recent papers have examined non-status quo reference points (e.g., Camerer et al., 1997; Genesove and Mayer, 2001; Heath, Huddart, & Lang, 1999; Pope & Schweitzer, 2011; Post et al., 2008). See also Koszegi and Rabin (2006).
2. *Loss aversion*: Losses are typically twice as painful as gains are pleasant. In the vernacular of prospect theory, "losses loom larger than gains." Loss aversion has been documented in risky choice settings (Abdellaoui, Bleichrodt, & Paraschiv, 2007; Tversky & Kahneman, 1992), as well as in riskless situations (Kahneman, Knetsch, & Thaler, 1990; Tversky & Kahneman, 1991).
3. *Diminishing sensitivity*: For both gains and losses, the value function is steeper close to the reference point, and shallower further from the reference point (for larger gains or larger losses).

The value function depicted in Figure 7.1 exhibits the three properties discussed above, and is concave for gains, convex for losses, and steeper for losses than gains. Note that the prospect theory value function differs from the classical expected utility models that evaluate utility of outcomes with respect to overall wealth and are typically concave everywhere (e.g., Pratt, 1964).

We illustrate the implications of this framework for motivation with a simple example. Suppose you establish a goal to read 100 pages this evening. Reference dependence suggests that any pages completed short of 100 pages will be seen as loss, while anything in excess of that goal will be coded as a gain. Loss aversion indicates that a reader will be more motivated when reading pages 95 to 100 than when reading pages 100 to 105. Finally, diminishing sensitivity suggests that motivation is higher when reading pages 95 to 100 than when reading pages 30 to 35. Similarly, a reader will work harder to finish pages 100 to 105 than to finish pages 160 to 165. Motivation can thus be seen as being proportional to the first derivative of the value function.

Heath, Larrick, and Wu (1999) show how the prospect theory value function explains the stylized findings in the goal-setting literature. This framework can accommodate the goal difficulty effect—performance

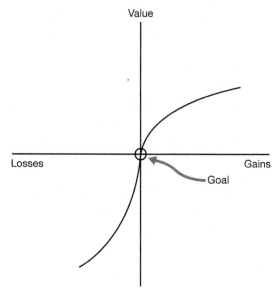

FIGURE 7.1
A typical prospect theory value function adapted to the "goals as reference points" framework. The function exhibits reference dependence, loss aversion, and diminishing sensitivity.

increases with goal difficulty and specific challenging goals lead to better performance than "do your best" goals. In addition, their setup accommodates Locke and Latham's (1990) proposed mechanisms for this effect: more difficult goals lead people to expend more effort, persist longer, and direct attention to the target goal relative to other objectives. Wu, Heath, and Larrick (2008) provide a formal framework to explain these as well as other results.[1]

IMPLICATIONS OF GOALS AS REFERENCE POINTS APPROACH

In this section, we discuss some implications of prospect theory for goal setting. The first set of implications follows directly from the shape of the value function shown in Figure 7.1. The "goals as reference points" approach explains how motivation shifts over the course of goal pursuit. Those who have not yet met a specific and challenging goal are in the loss domain and will be motivated to work harder and persist longer to meet the goal. Moreover, diminishing sensitivity indicates that the slope of the value function increases sharply the closer an individual is to a goal. This predicts the goal gradient effect (Hull, 1932; Kivetz, Urminsky, & Zheng, 2006) in which individuals increase effort the closer they are to the goal (or the mouse to the cheese in Hull's studies). Kivetz, Urminsky, and Zheng (2006) examine the goal gradient effect in the context of consumer loyalty programs. Cafés and car washes employ goals to encourage increased patronage through frequent buyer stamp cards (e.g., buy ten cups of coffee and the eleventh is free). In a field study at a local café, Kivetz, Urminsky, and Zheng (2006) demonstrate that consumers purchase coffee more frequently the closer they are to the goal of earning a free coffee. Purchasing behavior also slows down immediately after a card has been completed, consistent with the notion that consumers are now on a new goal and on the shallow part of the value function. Kivetz, Urminsky, and Zheng (2006) also show that relative progress contributes to the effect. Customers purchase coffee more when they are given two initial stamps on a "buy twelve/get one free" card than when they are given no bonus stamps on a standard "buy ten/get one free" card. Note that, in both cases, the customers are the same distance from the goal. Nevertheless, the former customers felt more progress to the goal and accelerated purchases relative to the latter customers.

The flip side of the goal gradient effect is a lack of motivation when individuals are far from a goal. Diminishing sensitivity implies that the value function is relatively flat far from the reference point. This means that stretch goals that are extremely challenging may lead to what Heath, Larrick, and Wu (1999) term the starting problem. An example from Cochran and Tesser (1996) is known as the "what the hell" effect: many dieters have had the experience of exceeding the daily calorie goal with a donut and then eating a couple more since the goal cannot be made on that day. Sales people may have a hard time getting started on the quarterly sales goal that seems almost impossible to achieve. Sitkin et al. (2011) summarize these and other disruptive effects of stretch goals in organizations. While previous researchers have observed a similar phenomenon, they have explained this starting problem as a lack of goal commitment (Erez & Zidon, 1984).

The shape of the value function also leads to predictions about risk taking. Kahneman and Tversky (1979) showed that the standard result of risk aversion for gains reverses for losses. The finding of risk seeking for losses led Kahneman and Tversky to posit a value function that was convex for losses. This aspect of the value function explains several empirical goal-setting results. Negotiators focusing on target price (a high goal) earned higher outcomes than those focusing on reservation price (a lower goal) (Galinsky, Mussweiler, & Medvec, 2002). Negotiators attained the better outcomes by making more aggressive first offers, which can be thought of as being more risky since they increase the possibility of an impasse. Higher goals also increased the demands individuals made in both one round (ultimatum) and multiple round (shrinking pie) bargaining games (Larrick, Heath, & Wu, 2009). In a computer simulation, tougher goals increased the strategic risk taken by participants (Knight, Durham, & Locke, 2001). However, Jeffrey, Onay, and Larrick (2010) demonstrate the "cushion effect" in which decision makers become *more* risk seeking when all options' outcomes exceed the stated goal (in direct contrast to the prediction of the goals as reference points approach).

If lying and cheating are seen as risky behaviors, then challenging goals may also lead to unethical behavior (Schweitzer, Ordóñez, & Douma, 2004). Indeed, a growing list of laboratory studies shows that adhering to specific, difficult goals can lead to lying and misrepresentation of performance. Scenario results suggest that people expect those who have not met a goal to cheat more than those who have met their goal (Schweitzer, Ordóñez, & Douma, 2002): respondents believe that consultants will over-represent hours worked, students will cheat on exams, salespeople will lie to customers to make sales, and joggers will lie even to themselves by logging more miles run when these individuals have not met goals as compared to those who have met their goals. These scenario results add even more credence to the "goals as reference points" perspective since they are consistent with prospect theory predictions. For example, respondents predicted that those individuals who were closer to meeting their goal were more likely to cheat than those who were farther from meeting the goal. In a lab study, participants were more likely to lie about their performance on an anagram task to meet a goal, even if doing so did not increase their experimental payment (Schweitzer, Ordóñez, & Douma, 2004; see also Cadsby, Song, & Tapon, 2010). Cameron and Miller (2009) further showed that individuals were more likely to cheat in the lab when put in a loss situation rather than a gain (note that the former group is in the prospect theory loss quadrant while the latter group is in the gain domain quadrant). Ordóñez et al. (2009a) present high profile business anecdotes that further support the case that goals can lead to unethical behavior. In fact, Barsky (2008) developed a theoretical model that predicts that not only can goals increase the chance of making unethical decisions to meet a goal, but these goals can also influence the evaluation of behavior leading those striving for the goal to view unethical behavior as appropriate.

The goals as reference points framework also makes some novel empirical predictions. Heath, Larrick, and Wu (1999) suggest that difficult but attainable goals might lead performance to "pile up" around the goal. Wu, Heath, and Larrick (2008) show that piling up follows directly from loss aversion: loss aversion implies that an individual is substantially more motivated when just short of a goal than farther away from meeting the goal. Thus, an individual may be motivated enough to reach a goal but not motivated enough to push on once that goal is reached. For example, sales people may meet their quarterly sales goals and then go golfing and take time off before the next quarter begins. In addition, due to the mere fact that goals are intended to focus attention on particular behaviors, effort may be allocated away from other important behaviors; thus, a focus on meeting quantitative sales goals may detract from customer service (Gilliland & Landis, 1992).

Finally, although most research in goal setting has looked at the effects of different assigned goal levels on performance, some research has investigated self-set goals (e.g., Locke et al., 1984; Williams, Donovan, & Dodge, 2000). Because more difficult goals lead to better performance on average, this raises the obvious question: What leads people to embrace more ambitious goals? Social psychology provides one simple answer: unrealistic optimism (e.g., Armor & Taylor, 2002). However, recent research has shown that optimism has a time course, with optimism reduced as the focal task approaches (Gilovich, Kerr, & Medvec, 1993). This reduction in optimism occurs in part because individuals are "bracing" for the possibility that performance may be disappointing relative to their expectations (Carroll, Sweeny, & Shepperd, 2006). In Sackett et al.'s (2013) recent study of marathon runners, some marathoners (the "goal group") were asked to indicate their finishing time goal approximately two weeks prior to the start of the marathon. In contrast, a control group was merely asked to report on their goal after completing the marathon. Even though almost 90 percent of marathoners in both conditions indicated that they had time goals, those in the goal group ran significantly faster than those in the control group. As predicted by the research on temporal attenuation of optimism, goals for the goal group were significantly more aggressive than goals for the control group, and goal level fully mediated the effect of asking for goals on finishing time.

SATISFACTION AND PERFORMANCE

The goals as reference points approach has implications for both goal pursuit and satisfaction. Garland (1984) suggested a satisfaction paradox in goal setting: Although higher goals lead to better performance, they also lead to lower satisfaction. Heath, Larrick, and Wu (1999) provide a straightforward explanation for this paradox—because goals act as reference points, performance is interpreted in relative terms. Although a more difficult goal may lead to better performance on average, it also increases the chance that an individual may fall short of the goal.

Research in judgment and decision making has put forth reasons why the value function that drives effort *could* differ from the value function that measures satisfaction. For example, research on affective forecasting and immune neglect has demonstrated that individuals make systematic mistakes in predicting their actual affective reactions to future events. Gilbert et al. (1998) showed that professors who were denied tenure were not nearly as unhappy as they anticipated being. Other work has suggested that, whereas aversion to losses clearly influences the decisions individuals make, losses do not actually loom larger than gains (Kermer et al., 2006).

Contrary to this research, it does appear that the properties of the prospect theory value function that drive motivation also govern satisfaction. Markle et al. (2013) provided one attempt to measure aggregate satisfaction as a function of goal performance. In this study, they asked marathoners to provide their time goals. They then looked at satisfaction as a function of relative performance, i.e., the number of minutes a runner exceeded or fell short of their time goal. The estimated satisfaction function resembled the value function in Figure 7.1. In particular, it exhibited both diminishing sensitivity as well as loss aversion, with a loss aversion coefficient of 2-to-1.

Goals are motivating since they increase satisfaction, self-efficacy, and competence after meeting them. Thus, people strive harder because they find pleasure in meeting their goals. Several studies have shown increased job satisfaction through meeting goals (Elliot & Harackiewicz, 1996), and satisfaction in classroom performance due to increased feeling of competence (Elliot & Sheldon, 1997). Consumers also have increased motivation and performance as they make progress toward their goals (Soman & Shi, 2003). In addition, goals are fulfilling and motivating if they are concordant with our self-concept (Judge et al., 2005). However, not meeting goals can lead to negative effects such as stress, lowered self-esteem, and demotivation (Cochran & Tesser, 1996; King & Burton, 2003; Soman & Cheema, 2004). Soman and Cheema (2004) showed that having missed a goal leads to further poor performance in a personal savings task and meeting deadlines for a proofreading task; for many participants, missing a goal led to worse behavior than having no goal at all.

MODERATING THE VALUE FUNCTION

We suggested that the value function has three properties: reference dependence, loss aversion, and diminishing sensitivity. Recent research has demonstrated that the shape of the value function varies across contexts as well as across people (e.g., Abdellaoui, Bleichrodt, & Paraschiv, 2007; Gächter, Johnson, & Hermann, 2007). For example, Dhar and Wertenbroch (2000) have shown that loss aversion is higher for affective than for utilitarian goods. (See Ariely, Huber, & Wertenbroch, 2005, for a discussion of other moderators of loss aversion.) More generally, we review some factors that might moderate the shape of the value function and hence the impact of goals on effort, persistence, and performance.

Markle et al. (2013) demonstrated that goal importance moderates loss aversion. They asked their marathoners to rate the importance of a time goal on a 1 to 7 scale. Though the loss aversion coefficient was approximately 2 for all marathoners, it differed substantially depending on how important marathoners regarded the time goal. Those who rated the goal as 5 or below showed no loss aversion (i.e., a loss aversion coefficient that was statistically indistinguishable from 1). The loss aversion coefficient was approximately 2-to-1 for those who rated the goal as 6 out of 7 in importance and approximately 6-to-1 for those who rated the goal as 7 out of 7 in importance.

Regulatory focus theory (Higgins, 1997) is a goal pursuit theory that has been used as a framework to explain, among other phenomena, the consumer decision-making process. The theory proposes two different foci or goals: promotion or prevention. Those with a promotion-focus orientation are more concerned with achieving their ideal desired end state; for example, some consumers may be motivated to achieve good health by buying products that promote wellness. However, those with a prevention-focus orientation may be attracted more to products that prevent illness, which would detract from safety and security. Regulatory focus theory can be combined with prospect theory to produce some interesting predictions on the impact of goals on performance and satisfaction. The prevention focus is a minimal goal that leads to more risk aversion and focus on avoiding losses (Idson, Liberman, & Higgins, 2000). Chernev (2004) modifies the prospect theory value function by proposing a steeper utility function in the domain of losses for individuals with a prevention focus compared to a promotion focus. However, Chernev (2004) further suggests that the promotion-focus curve is shallower in the domain of losses and much steeper in the domain of gains, which suggests a focus on achieving gains vis-à-vis the goal-defined reference point. Although Idson, Liberman, and Higgins (2000) note that there is not a direct correspondence between a promotion focus and risk seeking and between a prevention focus and risk avoidance, these differences in the steepness of the loss domain curves suggest that the starting problem and piling up would be much more severe with prevention vs. promotion individuals; this is a new behavioral prediction that is yet to be tested empirically.

Several studies suggest modifications of the basic goal as reference points approach. First, recall the Kivetz, Urminsky, and Zheng (2006) investigations on goal gradient. They proposed that, while a goal might act as a reference point, progress toward the goal is measured in relative rather than absolute terms. Second, Bonezzi, Brendl, and De Angelis (2011) propose a dual reference point model in which the evaluation of progress is governed by two frames, a "to-date" frame and a "to-go" frame. Thus, a reader with a goal of completing 100 pages would evaluate 70 pages read as both 70 pages completed (a "to-date" framing) and 30 pages remaining (a "to-go" framing). Since both reference points should exhibit the properties of the prospect theory value function, Bonezzi, Brendl, and De Angelis (2011) predict and find a U-shaped pattern of motivation, with motivation highest at the start as well as toward completion, but lowest in the middle (see also Koo & Fishbach, 2008). Note that a person who utilizes both "to-date" and "to-go" frames would not suffer from the starting problem discussed earlier.

Several other decision-making models include multiple reference points that could be thought of in terms of goals. March and Shapira (1992) developed a choice model that included reference points for survival and aspiration. Thus, individuals can think both about avoiding severe risk that might lead to death (survival reference point) and about the positive outcomes of pursuing even better outcomes (aspiration) in the decisions they make. In a similar manner, SP/A (security-potential/aspiration) theory (Lopes, 1987; Lopes & Oden, 1999) proposes a utility model with minimum (security-potential) and maximum (aspiration) reference points. Much more recently, the tri-reference point theory of risky choice (Koop & Johnson, 2012) incorporates minimum requirement, status quo, and goal reference points. In all three models, the goal reference point (aspiration or goal) is a desired value that is not necessarily a value that the decision maker expects to achieve.

More generally, goals might work alongside different reference points. For example, when goals differ from other natural performance standards (such as past performance, or a competitor's or colleague's performance), the goal, as well as the performance standards, might each act as a reference point. The result might be a temporal pattern of effort in which effort increases as an individual approaches a goal or another performance standard, but drops precipitously once that reference point is reached. More research is needed to understand how goals differ from these other standards in their implications for both motivation and satisfaction.

ORGANIZATIONAL IMPLICATIONS

There are many studies showing both the short-term and long-term value of goal-setting systems in organizations (Arvey, Dewhirst, & Brown, 1978; Latham & Yukl, 1975; Rodgers & Hunter, 1991; Wiese & Freund, 2005). Pritchard et al. (1988) showed that goal setting was effective in increasing performance in operation-type tasks, as were group-level feedback and incentives. There is evidence that goals help sales performance up to a point and then performance decreases when the goal is too extreme (Fu, Richards, & Jones, 2009). There is some debate whether or not self-set (personal) goals are better than goals set by superiors in an organization (Karakowsky & Mann, 2007), but little debate as to the positive impact of goals in organizational performance. One organizational field study (Mann, Samson, & Dow, 1998) showed that, while goal setting is valuable, bench marking (comparing performance to that of other organizations) led to superior performance.

However, goals do not work if improperly implemented. Organizations must play a balancing act between constantly pushing employees to perform at higher levels while, at the same time, not pushing too far. As indicated previously, employees who fall short of their goals have lower self-efficacy and increased stress, and can become demotivated (Cochran & Tesser, 1996; King & Burton, 2003; Soman & Cheema, 2004). If employees exceed goals, they (and presumably their managers) feel satisfaction. However, managers attempt to avoid the piling-up problem by constantly increasing the goals. This leads to a hedonic treadmill where employees and managers are not satisfied with performance for long and risk possible goal burnout. In addition, if organizations continue to increase the targets once they are met by employees, a ratchet effect can occur in which the employees decrease their performance to avoid the ever increasing goals (Frexias, Guesnerie, & Tirole, 1985). One possible solution lies in selecting multiple reference points to keep motivating effort (by selecting challenging goals not yet met) and satisfaction levels high (by selecting reference points succeeded). However, see Fishbach and Dhar (2005) for the potential negative impact of evaluating goal progress on multiple goals.

CONCLUSION

In this chapter, we have used the "goals as reference points" perspective to connect decision-making (cognition) and goal-setting (motivation) research. Thus, any decision-making model that proposes a utility function with respect to a reference point may provide new predictions for goal-setting research. For example, Heath, Larrick, and Wu (1999) found evidence for their new piling-up prediction based on the intersection between prospect theory and goal setting. We have reviewed some new findings that highlight the power of this framework for understanding the motivational power of goals. In addition, we have discussed findings that suggest some directions for extending and modifying this basic framework. The field of negotiation borrowed heavily from decision research to form new heuristic and biases predictions. For example, negotiators sometimes believe in the fixed-pie bias (Bazerman, 1983) and assume that there are no solutions in which both parties can be better off. In a similar vein, there may be new predictions in goal research in which particular goal levels are selected or performance relative to goals lead to systematic biases. Future research should continue to develop new predictions based on the intersection between the fields of motivation and decision research.

NOTE

1. Rablen (2010) builds on this framework and models intrinsic motivation within a principal–agent setup.

REFERENCES

Abdellaoui, M., Bleichrodt, H., and Paraschiv, C. (2007). Loss aversion under prospect theory: A parameter-free measurement. *Management Science, 53,* 1659–1674.

Ariely, D., Huber, J., and Wertenbroch, K. (2005). When do losses loom larger than gains? *Journal of Marketing Research, 42,* 134–138.

Armor, D.A. and Taylor, S.E. (2002). When predictions fail: The dilemma of unrealistic optimism. In T. Gilovich, D. Griffin, and D. Kahneman (Eds.) *Heuristics and Biases: The Psychology of Human Judgment* (pp. 334–347). Cambridge: Cambridge University Press.

Arvey, R.D., Dewhirst, H.D., and Brown, E.M. (1978). A longitudinal study of the impact of changes in goal setting on employee satisfaction. *Personnel Psychology, 31,* 595–608.

Austin, J.T. and Vancouver, J.B. (1996). Goal constructs in psychology: Structure, process, and content. *Psychological Bulletin, 120,* 338–375.

Barsky, A. (2008). Understanding the ethical cost of organizational goal-setting: A review and theory development. *Journal of Business Ethics, 81,* 63–81.

Bazerman, M.H. (1983). Negotiator judgment: A critical look at the rationality assumption. *The American Behavioral Scientist, 27,* 211–228.

Bonezzi, A., Brendl, C.M., and De Angelis, M. (2011). Stuck in the middle. *Psychological Science, 22,* 607–612.

Cadsby, C.B., Song, F., and Tapon, F. (2010). Are you paying your employees to cheat? *The BE Journal of Economic Analysis & Policy, 10,* 35.

Camerer, C. (2000). Prospect theory in the wild: Evidence from the field. In D. Kahneman and A. Tversky (Eds.) *Choices, Values and Frames* (pp. 288–300). New York: Cambridge University Press.

Camerer, C., Babcock, L., Loewenstein, G., and Thaler, R. (1997). Labor supply of New York City cabdrivers: One day at a time. *Quarterly Journal of Economics, 112,* 407–441.

Cameron, J.S. and Miller, D.T. (2009). Ethical standards in gain versus loss frames. In D. De Cremer (Ed.) *Psychological Perspectives on Ethical Behavior* (pp. 91–106). Charlotte, NC: Information Age Publishing.

Cantor, N., Norem, J.K., Niedenthal, P.M., Langston, C.A., and Brower, A.M. (1987). Life tasks, self-concept ideals, and cognitive strategies in a life transition. *Journal of Personality and Social Psychology, 53,* 1178–1191.

Carroll, P., Sweeny, K., and Shepperd, J.A. (2006). Forsaking optimism. *Review of General Psychology, 10,* 56–73.

Carver, C.S. and Scheier, M.F. (1998). *On the Self-Regulation of Behavior.* Cambridge: Cambridge University Press.

Chernev, A. (2004). Goal orientation and consumer preference for the status quo. *Journal of Consumer Research, 31,* 557–565.

Cochran, W. and Tesser, A. (1996). The "what the hell" effect: Some effects of goal proximity and goal framing on performance. In L.L. Martin (Ed.) *Striving and Feeling: Interactions Among Goals, Affect, and Self-regulation* (pp. 99–120). Hillsdale, NJ: Lawrence Erlbaum Associates.

Deci, E.L. (1992). Commentary: On the nature and functions of motivation theories. *Psychological Science, 3,* 167–171.

Deci, E.L. and Ryan, R.M. (1985). *Intrinsic Motivation and Self-determination in Human Behavior.* New York: Plenum.

Dhar, R. and Wertenbroch, K. (2000). Consumer choice between hedonic and utilitarian goods. *Journal of Marketing Research, 37,* 60–71.

Dowie, J. and Elstein, A. (1988). *Professional Judgment: A Reader in Clinical Decision Making.* Cambridge: Cambridge University Press.

Dweck, C. (1986). Motivational processes affecting learning. *American Psychologist, 41,* 1040–1048.

Dweck, C. (1992). The study of goals in psychology. *Psychological Science, 3,* 165–167.

Elliot, A.J. and Harackiewicz, J.M. (1996). Approach and avoidance achievement goals and intrinsic motivation: A mediational analysis. *Journal of Personality and Social Psychology, 70,* 461–475.

Elliot, A.J. and Sheldon, K.M. (1997). Avoidance achievement motivation: A personal goals analysis. *Journal of Personality and Social Psychology, 73,* 171.

Emmons, R.A. (1986). Personal strivings: An approach to personality and subjective well-being. *Journal of Personality and Social Psychology, 51,* 1058–1068.

Erez, M. and Zidon, I. (1984). Effect of goal acceptance on the relationship of goal difficulty to performance. *Journal of Applied Psychology, 69,* 69–78.

Fishbach, A. and Dhar, R. (2005). Goals as excuses or guides: The liberating effect of perceived goal progress on choice. *Journal of Consumer Research, 32,* 370–377.

Fishbach, A. and Ferguson, M.J. (2007). The goal construct in social psychology. In A.W. Kruglanski and E. Tory Higgins (Eds.). *Social Psychology: Handbook of Basic Principles* (2nd ed., pp. 490–515). New York: Guilford Press.

Frexias, X., Guesnerie, R., and Tirole, J. (1985). Planning under incomplete information and the ratchet effect. *Review of Economic Studies, 52,* 173–191.

Fu, F.Q., Richards, K.A., and Jones, E. (2009). The motivation hub: Effects of goal setting and self-efficacy on effort and new product sales. *Journal of Personal Selling and Sales Management, 29,* 277–292.

Gächter, S., Johnson, E.J., and Hermann, A. (2007). *Individual-level Loss Aversion in Riskless and Risky Choices.* IZA Discussion Paper No. 2961.

Galinsky, A.D., Mussweiler, T., and Medvec, V.H. (2002). Disconnecting outcomes and evaluations: The role of negotiator focus. *Journal of Personality and Social Psychology, 83,* 1131–1140.

Garland, H. (1984). Relation of effort-performance expectancy to performance in goal-setting experiments. *Journal of Applied Psychology, 69,* 79–84.

Genesove, D. and Mayer, C. (2001). Loss aversion and seller behavior: Evidence from the housing market. *Quarterly Journal of Economics, 116,* 1233–1260.

Gilbert, D.T., Pinel, E.C., Wilson, T.D., Blumberg, S.J., and Wheatley, T.P. (1998). Immune neglect: A source of durability bias in affective forecasting. *Journal of Personality & Social Psychology, 75,* 617–638.

Gilliland, S.W. and Landis, R.S. (1992). Quality and quantity goals in a complex decision task: Strategies and outcomes. *Journal of Applied Psychology, 77,* 672–681.

Gilovich, T., Griffin, D., and Kahneman, D. (2002). *Heuristics and Biases: The Psychology of Human Judgment.* Cambridge: Cambridge University Press.

Gilovich, T., Kerr, M., and Medvec, V.H. (1993). Effect of temporal perspective on subjective confidence. *Journal of Personality & Social Psychology, 64,* 552–560.

Gollwitzer, P.M. (1999). Implementation intentions: Strong effects of simple plans. *American Psychologist, 54,* 493–503.

Gollwitzer, P.M. and Sheeran, P. (2006). Implementation intentions and goal achievement: A meta-analysis of effects and processes. *Advances in Experimental Social Psychology, 38,* 69–119.

Heath, C., Huddart, S., and Lang, M. (1999). Psychological factors and stock option exercise. *Quarterly Journal of Economics, 114,* 601–627.

Heath, C., Larrick, R.P., and Wu, G. (1999). Goals as reference points. *Cognitive Psychology, 38,* 79–109.

Higgins, E.T. (1997). Beyond pleasure and pain. *The American Psychologist, 52,* 1280–1300.

Hull, C. (1932). The goal-gradient hypothesis and maze learning. *Psychological Review, 39,* 25–43.

Idson, L.C., Liberman, N., and Higgins, E.T. (2000). Distinguishing gains from nonlosses and losses from nongains: A regulatory focus perspective on hedonic intensity. *Journal of Experimental Social Psychology, 36,* 252–274.

Jeffrey, S.A., Onay, S., and Larrick, R.P. (2010). Goal attainment as a resource: The cushion effect in risky choice above a goal. *Journal of Behavioral Decision Making, 23,* 191–202.

Jolls, C., Sunstein, C., and Thaler, R. (1998). A behavioral approach to law and economics. *Stanford Law Review, 50,* 1471–1550.

Judge, T.A., Bono, J.E., Erez, A., and Locke, E.A. (2005). Core self-evaluations and job and life satisfaction: The role of self-concordance and goal attainment. *The Journal of Applied Psychology, 90,* 257–268.

Kahneman, D., Knetsch, J.L., and Thaler, R. (1990). Experimental tests of the endowment effect and the Coase theorem. *Journal of Political Economy, 98,* 1325–1348.

Kahneman, D., Slovic, P., and Tversky, A. (1982). *Judgment under Uncertainty: Heuristics and Biases.* Cambridge: Cambridge University Press.

Kahneman, D. and Tversky, A. (1979). Prospect theory: An analysis of decision under risk. *Econometrica, 47,* 263–291.

Kahneman, D. and Tversky, A. (2000). *Choices, Values, and Frames.* Cambridge: Cambridge University Press.

Karakowsky, L. and Mann, S.L. (2007). Setting goals and taking ownership: Understanding the implications of participatively set goals from a causal attribution perspective. *Journal of Leadership & Organizational Studies, 14,* 260–270.

Kermer, D.A., Driver-Linn, E., Wilson, T.D., and Gilbert, D.T. (2006). Loss aversion is an affective forecasting error. *Psychological Science, 17,* 649–653.

King, L.A. and Burton, C.M. (2003). The hazards of goal pursuit. In E.C. Chang and L.J. Sanna (Eds.) *Virtue, Vice, and Personality: The Complexity of Behavior* (pp. 53–69). Washington, DC: American Psychological Association.

Kivetz, R., Urminsky, O., and Zheng, Y. (2006). The goal-gradient hypothesis resurrected: Purchase acceleration, illusionary goal progress, and customer retention. *Journal of Marketing Research, 43,* 39–58.

Knight, D., Durham, C.C., and Locke, E.A. (2001). The relationship of team goals, incentives, and efficacy to strategic risk, tactical implementation, and performance. *The Academy of Management Journal, 44,* 326–338.

Koo, M. and Fishbach, A. (2008). Dynamics of self-regulation: How (un)accomplished goal actions affect motivation. *Journal of Personality and Social Psychology, 94,* 183–195.

Koop, G.J. and Johnson, J.G. (2012). The use of multiple reference points in risky decision making. *Journal of Behavioral Decision Making, 25,* 49–62.

Koszegi, B. and Rabin, M. (2006). A model of reference-dependent preferences. *Quarterly Journal of Economics, 121,* 1133–1165.

Larrick, R.P., Heath, C., and Wu, G. (2009). Goal-induced risk taking in negotiation and decision making. *Social Cognition, 27,* 342–364.

Latham, G.P. and Yukl, G.A. (1975). A review of research on the application of goal setting in organizations. *The Academy of Management Journal, 18,* 824–845.

138 • *Lisa Ordóñez and George Wu*

Locke, E.A., Frederick, E., Buckner, E., and Bobko, P. (1984). Effect of previously assigned goals on self-set goals and performance. *Journal of Applied Psychology, 69,* 694–699.
Locke, E.A. and Latham, G.P. (1990). *A Theory of Goal Setting & Task Performance.* Englewood Cliffs, NJ: Prentice Hall.
Locke, E.A. and Latham, G.P. (2002). Building a practically useful theory of goal setting and task motivation: A 35-year odyssey. *American Psychologist, 57,* 705–717.
Locke, E.A. and Latham, G.P. (2006). New directions in goal-setting theory. *Current Directions in Psychological Science, 15,* 265–268.
Lopes, L. (1987). Between hope and fear: The psychology of risk. *Advances in Experimental Social Psychology, 20,* 255–295.
Lopes, L. and Oden, G. (1999). The role of aspiration level in risky choice: A comparison of cumulative prospect theory and SP/A theory. *Journal of Mathematical Psychology, 43,* 286–313.
Mann, L., Samson, D., and Dow, D. (1998). A field experiment on the effects of benchmarking and goal setting on company sales performance. *Journal of Management, 24,* 73–96.
March, J.G. and Shapira, Z. (1992). Variable risk preferences and the focus of attention. *Psychological Review, 99,* 172–183.
Markle, A., Wu, G., White, R., and Sackett, A. (2013). Goals as reference points in marathon running: A novel test of reference dependence. Unpublished paper.
Nolen, S.B. (1988). Reasons for studying: Motivational orientations and study strategies. *Cognition and Instruction, 5,* 269–287.
Ordóñez, L.D., Schweitzer, M.E., Galinsky, A.D., and Bazerman, M.H. (2009a). Goals gone wild: The systematic side effects of overprescribing goal setting. *The Academy of Management Perspectives, 23,* 6–16.
Ordóñez, L.D., Schweitzer, M.E., Galinsky, A.D., and Bazerman, M.H. (2009b). On good scholarship, goal setting, and scholars gone wild. *The Academy of Management Perspectives, 23,* 82–87.
Pervin, L.A. (1989). Goal concepts: Themes, issues, and questions. In L.A. Pervin (Ed.) *Goal Concepts in Personality and Social Psychology* (pp. 473–479). Hillsdale, NJ: Lawrence Erlbaum Associates.
Pope, D.G. and Schweitzer, M.E. (2011). Is Tiger Woods loss averse? Persistent bias in the face of experience, competition, and high stakes. *American Economic Review, 101,* 129–157.
Post, T., van den Assem, M.J., Baltussen, G., and Thaler, R.H. (2008). Deal or no deal? Decision making under risk in a large-payoff game show. *American Economic Review, 98,* 38–71.
Pratt, J.W. (1964). Risk aversion in the small and in the large. *Econometrica, 32,* 122–136.
Pritchard, R.D., Jones, S.D., Roth, P.L., Stuebing, K.K., and Ekeberg, S.E. (1988). Effects of group feedback, goal setting, and incentives on organizational productivity. *Journal of Applied Psychology, 73,* 337–358.
Rablen, M.D. (2010). Performance targets, effort and risk-taking. *Journal of Economic Psychology, 31,* 687–697.
Rodgers, R. and Hunter, J.E. (1991). Impact of management by objectives on organizational productivity. *Journal of Applied Psychology, 76,* 322–336.
Sackett, A., Wu, G., Markle, A., and White, R. (2013). Harnessing optimism: How eliciting goals improve performance. Unpublished paper.
Schweitzer, M., Ordóñez, L., and Douma, B. (2002). The dark side of goal setting: The role of goals in motivating unethical decision making. *Best Paper Proceedings of the Academy of Management Conference,* 1–6.

Schweitzer, M., Ordóñez, L., and Douma, B. (2004). Goal setting as a motivator of unethical behavior. *Academy of Management Journal, 47*, 422–432.

Shafir, E. and LeBoeuf, R.A. (2004). Context and conflict in multiattribute choice. In D.J. Koehler and N. Harvey (Eds.) *Blackwell Handbook of Judgment and Decision Making* (pp. 341–359). Oxford: Blackwell.

Sitkin, S.B., See, K.E., Miller, C.C., Lawless, M.W., and Carton, A.M. (2011). The paradox of stretch goals: Organizations in pursuit of the seemingly impossible. *Academy of Management Review, 36*, 544–566.

Soman, D. and Cheema, A. (2004). When goals are counterproductive: The effects of violation of a behavioral goal on subsequent performance. *Journal of Consumer Research, 31*, 52–62.

Soman, D. and Shi, M. (2003). Virtual progress: The effect of path characteristics on perceptions of progress and choice. *Management Science, 49*, 1229–1250.

Thaler, R. (1985). Mental accounting and consumer choice. *Marketing Science, 4*, 199–214.

Trope, Y. and Fishbach, A. (2000). Counteractive self-control in overcoming temptation. *Journal of Personality and Social Psychology, 79*, 493–506.

Tversky, A. and Kahneman, D. (1991). Loss aversion in riskless choice: A reference dependent model. *Quarterly Journal of Economics, 106*, 1039–1061.

Tversky, A. and Kahneman, D. (1992). Advances in prospect theory: Cumulative representation of uncertainty. *Journal of Risk and Uncertainty, 5*, 297–323.

Wiese, B.S. and Freund, A.M. (2005). Goal progress makes one happy, or does it? Longitudinal findings from the work domain. *Journal of Occupational and Organizational Psychology, 78*, 287–304.

Williams, K.J., Donovan, J.J., and Dodge, T.L. (2000). Self-regulation of performance: Goal establishment and goal revision processes in athletes. *Human Performance, 13*, 159–180.

Wu, G., Heath, C., and Larrick, R. (2008). A prospect theory model of goal behavior. Unpublished paper.

Wu, G., Zhang, J., and Gonzalez, R. (2004). Decision under risk. In D.J. Koehler and N. Harvey (Eds.) *Blackwell Handbook of Judgment and Decision Making* (pp. 399–423). Oxford: Blackwell.

8

Leadership and Decision Making: Defining a Field

Daan van Knippenberg

By virtue of their position in the organizational hierarchy, leaders make decisions with considerable reach, affecting not only themselves but also others in the organization, and sometimes even the entire organization (Finkelstein, Hambrick, & Cannella, 2009; Useem, 2010). By the same token, leaders' position should allow leaders more than nonleaders to influence the decisions of others within the organization. Leadership and decision making thus would seem to be an important area of study in building our understanding of leadership's role in the functioning and performance of individuals, groups, and organizations. Somewhat suprisingly, however, leadership and decision making is a theme that is underrepresented in leadership research, even to the extent that it is debatable whether the study of leadership and decision making is commonly understood as an area of leadership research.

The purpose of this chapter therefore is twofold. First, it aims to take stock of the state of the science in leadership and decision making. Second, to the extent that any single individual can do such a thing for a scientific field of inquiry, it aims to define the field—to determine what the study of leadership and decision making could be, and perhaps should be, about: leader decision making, the role of leadership in shared decision making, and leadership's influence on followers' decisions. In a sense, this chapter thus is intended as much as a call to arms for research in leadership as to be a review of the state of the science in leadership and decision making.

LEADERSHIP AND DECISION MAKING?

The Psychological Study of Leadership

For behavioral research in leadership, the key question has always been what makes people in leadership positions effective in mobilizing and motivating subordinates ("followers") in pursuit of the objectives, mission, or vision the leader advocates for the collective (i.e., group, team, organization; van Knippenberg, 2012; Yukl, 2005). Influence on others thus is seen as the core of leadership, and effective influence is typically understood to be reflected first and foremost in follower performance outcomes such as task performance, citizenship behavior, and creativity and innovation, but also in perceptions of leadership (i.e., perceived leadership effectiveness, leadership satisfaction), and in work-related attitudes such as job satisfaction and organizational commitment (Kaiser, Hogan, & Craig, 2008). Leadership research has for instance abundantly studied the effectiveness of such aspects of leadership as charismatic and transformational leadership (e.g., Bass & Riggio, 2006), the quality of the social exchange relationship of leaders and followers (e.g., Martin et al., 2010), and task-oriented and relations-oriented leadership (e.g., Judge, Piccolo, & Ilies, 2004). In the wake of this research, there also is a burgeoning interest in the determinants of those leadership styles and behaviors that are identified as effective, even when the study of these determinants tends to be largely limited to personality and individual differences (e.g., Judge & Bono, 2000).

Perhaps because leadership is first and foremost understood in terms of a process of social influence and behavioral decision making research has a strong focus on the individual decision maker, leadership research has typically not asked questions regarding the role of leadership in decision making. Leader decision making typically is not understood as an influence on followers that would reflect or impact leadership effectiveness, and follower decision making is usually not considered as an outcome indicative of leadership influences. The limited research in participative leadership that is explicitly framed around the Vroom and Yetton (1973) and Vroom and Jago (1988) models is the exception here, but as outlined in the following most of participative leadership research is only tangentially related to behavioral decision making in that it concerns motivating influences of leadership more than decision quality or preferences.

As decision making in terms of actual decision outcomes hardly features as a 'topic' in leadership research, it would seem worthwhile to first establish what the study of leadership and decision making would be about, to set the stage for an assessment of the empirical evidence for the role of leadership in decision making in organizations.

Leadership Perspectives on Decision Making

From the perspective of the dominant focus on the individual decision maker in research in judgment and decision making (JDM) (e.g., Bazerman & Moore, 2009; Kahneman, Slovic, & Tversky, 1982), the obvious focus in research in leadership and decision making would be on the leader as decision maker. Indeed, even if leadership research has underplayed the importance of decision making, the issue is *not* that we know little about how leaders make decisions. There is a good case to be made that much research in JDM concerns such fundamental psychological processes that it applies to leaders and nonleaders alike, and leaders too should be subject to the heuristics and biases extensively documented in the JDM literature (e.g., Busenitz & Barney, 1997) and follow decision making strategies that have been documented for nonleaders (e.g., Hitt & Tyler, 1991).

For leader decision making to be a field of inquiry that is meaningfully different from the study of individual judgment and decision making per se, a unique leadership angle would be introduced in two ways. First, we may study if and how the leadership role affects individuals' decision making. At its most basic, the question would be: if faced with the same decision problem do leaders make different decisions (e.g., take more risk) or make decisions differently (e.g., more carefully and fully consider decision alternatives) than nonleaders? Related to this would be the question of how certain variables uniquely tied to leadership positions, such as span of control, level in the organizational hierarchy, or leadership experience, affect leader decision making. Second, this perspective on leadership and decision making would include the study of decision making for decisions uniquely tied to leadership, or at least strongly associated with leadership—decisions that would not be studied, or are unlikely to be studied for nonleaders. This would for instance include decisions concerning organizational strategy. We might call this first perspective on leadership and decision making the *leader decision making perspective*.

Decisions are not exclusively made by individuals, however. Decision making often is a collective activity—group decision making—because collective decision making in comparison to individual decision making may increase the pool of decision-relevant information, expertise, and perspectives available to the decision maker, because participation in decision making is expected to increase commitment to the decision that would benefit follow-up action, or because different individuals represent different interests that may be affected by the decision (e.g., De Dreu, Nijstad, & van Knippenberg, 2008; Kerr & Tindale, 2004). This too raises two issues in which leadership may play a role. First, leadership of decision making bodies may influence decision making process and outcomes—leadership can be studied as an influence in group decision making (e.g., how can leadership stimulate more careful consideration of decision-relevant information?). Second, the extent to which followers are involved in the decision making may be up to the leader's discretion, and the extent to which the leader invites participative decision making (i.e., participative leadership; Vroom & Yetton, 1973) may influence decisions. The extent to which a decision is made collectively (i.e., rather than by the leader) can thus also be studied as an influence on decision making (e.g., when is participative decision making positively related to decision quality?). This perspective on leadership and decision making we might call the *shared decision making perspective.*

Even though decision authority may be a hallmark of leadership, leaders are not the only ones making decisions in organizations—employees in nonleadership positions do too. From the perspective of leadership as social influence, the most obvious question then would be how leadership affects follower (employee) decision making. The study of this issue would include questions such as how leadership can stimulate better quality (e.g., more carefully considered) follower decisions or how leadership may influence decision outcomes to serve group or organizational ends (e.g., stimulate decisions that serve the collective interest more). We might call this the *follower decision making perspective.*

In the following I review the state of the science in these three perspectives on leadership and decision making. Given the somewhat uncertain status of leadership and decision making, the aim of this review is not just to assess what may be concluded on the basis of the empirical evidence available. The review aims as much to determine what we might want to pursue in future research to develop our understanding of the role of leadership in decision making in organizations.

THE EVIDENCE, AND WHERE TO GO FROM THERE

Leader Decision Making

How the leadership role affects leader decision making has been studied for decisions regarding the allocation of resources in terms of the extent to which leaders focus on the collective (i.e., team, group) or follower interest or, rather, make more self-serving decisions. This is an issue of no minor importance given the growing concern with instances in which individuals in leadership positions use their decision latitude to selfish ends, sometimes at great costs to the organization or society. A line of experimental research by De Cremer and van Dijk (De Cremer, 2003; De Cremer & van Dijk, 2005; van Dijk & De Cremer, 2006) addressed the basic question of how being a leader versus a group member affects such resource allocation decisions (i.e., even if in practice such decisions may be more likely to be made by leaders than by followers, the comparison is instructive in building our understanding of the psychology of leadership). De Cremer (2003) showed that leaders allocated more resources to self than to followers, especially when accountability was low. Delving deeper in the psychological mechanisms underlying this behavior, De Cremer and van Dijk (2005) showed that, as a result of feelings of greater entitlement, leaders took more from a common resource than nonleaders, and more than an equal share (i.e., individual resource decisions affected the resource from which others could draw). Van Dijk and De Cremer (2006) classified individuals as having self-interested or cooperative social values, and again showed that a greater sense of entitlement led leaders to make more self-serving resource decisions than nonleaders, but now mainly so when leaders held self-interested social values that would subjectively legitimize such behavior. De Cremer and van Dijk (2008) subsequently showed that the tendency of leaders to allocate resources to self at the expense of the availability of resources to others in the group is attenuated if feelings of social responsibility are induced (cf., cooperative, prosocial values).

The conclusion that emerges from the De Cremer and van Dijk studies is that the leadership role in and of itself may invite the perception that it is legitimate for a leader to benefit more from collective resources than nonleaders. While this is something that society seems happy to subscribe to up to a point (e.g., higher salaries or greater fringe benefits for leaders than for nonleaders are typically not seen as in principle problematic), there is a clear concern with how much more from collective resources leaders can appropriate for themselves, and an important question remains as to what leads people in leadership positions to show restraint in catering to their self-interest in resource allocation decisions. Prosocial values and a sense of social responsibility is one answer to this question emerging from the De Cremer and van Dijk studies. Rus, van Knippenberg, and Wisse (2010a) further addressed this question, focusing on self-definition as a leader—the extent to which the leadership role is part of an individual's identity—as an influence on the self-servingness of leader allocation decisions. Their research showed that stronger self-definition as a leader invites leaders to make their allocation decisions more contingent on their beliefs about good leadership and the decisions of other leaders as comparison standard (cf., injunctive and descriptive behavioral norms). The net result is that individuals who have a strong leader identity are more or less self-serving in their allocation decisions than leaders with weaker leader identities depending on whether their beliefs about effective leadership and the decisions of other leaders suggest restraint or entitlement. Complementing the focus on self-definition as a leader with a focus on self-definition as a member of the group, Giessner and van Knippenberg (2007) showed that leaders' allocation decisions are more group-serving when they see themselves more as group prototypical (i.e., representative of group identity). Leaders with fewer group prototypical self-perceptions were only relatively group-serving in their decisions when they were accountable to the group for their decisions, presumably because group prototypicality results in an internalization of group interests in the absence of which external motivators (i.e., accountability) would be necessary to invite group-oriented decisions.

As the power associated with leadership positions is often assumed to underlie leaders' derailing, Rus, van Knippenberg, and Wisse (2010b) also investigated how leader power impacts leader allocation decisions. Based on power approach theory, which states that power reduces individuals' sensitivity to external, social demands and increases their reliance on internal cues (Keltner, Gruenfeld, & Anderson, 2003), Rus, van Knippenberg, and Wisse (2010b) proposed and found that more powerful as compared with less powerful leaders' allocation decisions are more contingent on internal cues (i.e., effective leadership beliefs) and less contingent on external, social information (i.e., equity considerations suggested by the performance of subordinates). Further extending this rationale, Rus, van Knippenberg, and Wisse (in press) showed that accountability is more important in curbing leader self-serving decision tendencies the more powerful they are (i.e., and the less they are restrained by more social concerns).

Studies like these by De Cremer and van Dijk, Rus and colleagues, and Giessner and van Knippenberg suggest that there are leadership-specific influences on decision making both in terms of the information used as input in decision making and in terms of decision outcomes. Even so, in a sense they only scratch the surface of the issue as these studies all concern one particular type of decision—allocation decisions that can be understood to vary on a self-serving–group-serving continuum—and are limited to only a subset of influences associated with the leader role. One conclusion could thus be that these studies speak to the promise of a social psychological analysis of leader decision making, and invite systematic research that more fully develops the analysis of leadership-specific influences on leader decision making also in relationship to the type of decision under investigation. The latter can be understood to refer not only to other decisions strongly associated with leadership besides resource allocations (e.g., promotion decisions), but also to a comparison between decisions that are typically the domain of leadership and decisions that just happen to be made by a leader (i.e., does the leadership role affect decision making more generally, or only to the extent that decisions are associated with leadership?; the latter seems a reasonable hypothesis, but the proof of the pudding is in the eating).

While resource allocation decisions may be strongly associated with leadership, they are less unique to leadership than some other decisions may be, and decisions concerning organizational strategy probably stand out here as the kind of decisions that imply a leadership position. From the perspective of the study of leadership and decision making, strategic decisions thus constitute a prime example of the kind of decisions we may want to study within the leader decision making perspective. Organizational strategy has long enjoyed the interest of research in strategic management, and the role of leadership here has been acknowledged in the study of strategic leadership or strategic decision making, which focuses on the prediction of organizational strategy and performance on the basis of characteristics of the CEOs and top management teams of organizations (Finkelstein, Hambrick, & Cannella, 2009). From the perspective of behavioral decision making research, the problem faced by research in strategic leadership is that it hardly ever captures decision making itself. Indeed, by the very nature of the population studied, it may be very hard to assess the actual decisions made by CEOs or top management (Useem, 2010). This is no trivial point. While it does not seem unreasonable, for instance, to assume that differences in the extent to which organizations are focused on innovation reflect conscious decisions of the CEOs or top managements, it seems no less reasonable to assume that organizational innovation reflects the ability to innovate rather than (only) the decision to innovate (cf., West & Anderson, 1996). This is an important point for the study of behavioral decision making to remain meaningful and not be reduced to the claim that any behavior that is not completely automatic or habitual reflects behavioral decision making: in the absence of empirical evidence that directly speaks to decision making and to leadership's relationship with decision making, it is hard to reach conclusions regarding leadership and decision making on the basis of such studies even when decision making may be a plausible mediating process in the relationships observed.

Research in the area that does speak more directly to decision making, such as Busenitz and Barney's (1997) work suggesting that start-up entrepreneurs rely more on heuristics and biases than senior managers in large firms and Hitt and Tyler's (1991) demonstration that CEO characteristics such as work experience, age, and educational background affect the extent to which managers rely on more rational or more intuitive decision making, is very scarce. So scarce in fact, that it would seem to make little sense to try to draw integrative conclusions from these findings. Rather, I would propose that these studies point to some of the possibilities and obstacles in assessing top management decision making. Hitt and Tyler (1991), for instance, relied on a decision scenario approach to assess decision making styles, side-stepping the problem of capturing naturally occurring decisions. While this makes perfect sense, the downside is that such an approach does not allow for the assessment of the relationship between CEO or top management decision making and organizational performance—the ultimate interest in research in strategic leadership. As West and Anderson (1996) illustrate with their painstaking assessment of the innovativeness of top management teams by recording top management team decisions for several months, capturing such decisions in action is not impossible—but even then researchers face the hard task of distinguishing, for instance, innovation as a decision outcome from innovation as the outcome of creative capabilities (i.e., which is then subsequently rubber-stamped in a formal decision). The key challenge to develop the behavioral decision making aspect of this research area would thus seem to be to adequately capture and isolate the decision making component from its potential precursors and consequences (cf., Useem, 2010).

Where to go from here in the leader decision making perspective? Clearly, a case can be made for leadership-specific influences on leader decision making and for leadership-specific decision problems, and there is theory and evidence that directly or indirectly speaks to leader decision making. What is currently missing, however, is more integrative theory on leader decision making (i.e., as opposed to specific hypothesis development in individual studies) and a strong paradigm for the study of leader decision making in the field (as well as experimental paradigms to study other leader decisions than resource allocations in the lab). Developing these would seem key to further development of the leader decision making perspective.

Shared Decision Making

The role of team-based work in organizations has grown over the years and this development also assumes an active role of team members in decision making (Ilgen et al., 2005). Given the importance of teams and the long research tradition in group decision making (Kerr & Tindale, 2004), there actually is surprisingly little research on the role of leadership in shared decision making.

A study by Son Hing et al. (2007) takes the concern with the ethicality and self-servingness of leader decisions to the level of dyadic decision making. They showed that dyads with leaders high (rather than low) in social dominance orientation—a personality trait reflecting a belief in the value of hierarchy and a desire for power (Pratto et al., 1994)—made more unethical decisions, especially when follower personality was more conducive to acceptance of leadership. This study thus provides some cross-linkages with the work on social values, leadership beliefs, and power discussed previously, and suggests that such insights may extend to the domain of shared decision making.

There is also research on leadership and the quality of group decision making in terms of groups' ability to benefit from their distributed informational resources. As noted previously, an important reason to assign decision making to groups rather than individuals is the diversity of decision-relevant information, expertise, and perspectives groups can mobilize. Research in decision making with distributed information shows, however, that groups often fail to use their distributed informational resources adequately (Stasser, 1999). From this perspective then, an obvious question is how leadership may engender better use of distributed information. In answer to this question, van Ginkel and van Knippenberg (2012) proposed that one root cause for the suboptimal use of distributed information is that groups often have an understanding of their decision making task that puts too much emphasis on reaching an agreement and underplays the important role of information exchange and integration. Accordingly, group leaders advocating and role-modeling the importance of information exchange and integration should stimulate better use of distributed information and thus higher-quality decisions than groups would reach without a leader or with a leader espousing the importance of reaching agreement. This is exactly what their experimental study showed. Also addressing the use of distributed information in group decision making, Larson, Foster-Fishman, and Franz (1998; see also Larson et al., 1996) showed that participative leadership as compared with directive leadership resulted in more exchange of distributed information, as would be expected on the basis of the notion that participative leadership helps mobilize follower knowledge (Vroom & Yetton, 1973). Also consistent with Vroom and Yetton's analysis, participative leadership had no advantage over directive leadership when all decision-relevant information is already available to the leader.

Participative leadership as the sharing of decision authority is somewhat of a special case in this discussion. On the one hand, participative leadership has strong linkages to the leadership and decision making model proposed by Vroom and Yetton (1973) and extended by Vroom and Jago (1988). On the other hand, participative leadership has largely been studied in a way that only indirectly speaks to decision making at best, but is probably better understood through the lens of the motivating potential of follower empowerment. The Vroom and Yetton and Vroom and Jago models concern the impact on decision effectiveness of the extent to which leaders share their decision authority with their subordinates. They aim to capture the determinants of the optimal level of follower involvement in decision making—ranging from no involvement (autocratic leader decision making), via degrees of consultation to solicit followers' input without giving them equal decision authority, to fully shared decision making responsibility. The models would, for instance, advise sharing decision authority to the extent that followers have important information the leader lacks, follower commitment to the decision is important, and followers can be expected to pursue the same goals as the leader. Research has yielded some support for these models, suggesting that decisions made with a level of participation consistent with model prescriptions tend to be somewhat more effective than decisions made with levels of participation that deviate from model prescriptions, but the stronger tests that do not rely on managers' self-reports tend to yield weaker evidence (e.g., Field, 1982; Field & Andrews, 1998; Field & House, 1990).

Most studies of participative leadership have, however, focused on outcomes that are (much) more loosely connected to decision making, such as satisfaction with the decision and the leader, or follower performance. Korsgaard, Schweiger, and Sapienza (1995) and Peterson (1999), for instance, showed that leaders may increase satisfaction with and commitment to a decision when giving group members voice in the decision making process—a finding consistent with the more general notion from social justice research that voice (i.e., being heard or consulted) in decisions is associated with greater acceptance of and satisfaction with the decision and the decision making authority (Lind & Tyler, 1988). Other findings such as those of relationships of participative leadership and follower job performance (Leana, 1986) or creativity (Hirst et al., 2011) move further away from the discrete acts of decision making that are core to the study of behavioral decision making and toward the motivating effects of empowering leadership of which the sharing of decision authority can be considered an element (Kirkman & Rosen, 1999).

Aside from the fact that research in participative decision making has mostly revolved around the motivational-attitudinal and performance outcomes of participative leadership and not around its relationship with decision preferences or quality, participative leadership research is largely mute regarding the content of the decisions made. Viewed through the lens of the shared decision making perspective, it can therefore only be seen as indirectly speaking to leadership and decision making. The conclusion here thus is somewhat equivocal. On the one hand, there is a basis for the conclusion that participative leadership, understood as including shared decision making and consultation/voice, may contribute to leadership effectiveness as evidenced in attitudinal and behavioral outcomes, albeit probably only quite modestly so (Wagner, 1994). On the other hand, most of this evidence is unsatisfying from the shared decision making perspective as understood here, in that with few exceptions participative leadership studies do not speak to the decision(s) for which decision authority is shared nor to the outcome of these decisions. Moreover, to the extent that they do, they mostly concern evidence that only modestly supports the decision models advanced by Vroom and colleagues.

Where to go from here then in the shared decision making perspective? For leadership and group decision making the use of distributed information is important, but not all that is on the agenda. Distributed information often is linked to characteristics that differentiate group members from each other—group diversity. While studies of group diversity corroborate the notion that utilizing distributed informational resources is a core challenge in group decision making, they also point to the fact that greater informational diversity often goes hand in hand with differences that may inspire interpersonal tensions and reduce coordination and cooperation within the group (van Knippenberg, De Dreu, & Homan, 2004). An important challenge for leadership of group decision making may thus be to address interpersonal tension to prevent these from disrupting the effective use of the group's informational resources (cf., Kearney & Gebert, 2009), and the leadership that is effective in stimulating the exchange and integration of information in the absence of such tensions (Larson, Foster-Fishman, & Franz, 1998; van Ginkel & van Knippenberg, 2012) is not necessarily also effective in addressing such tensions (cf., van Knippenberg, De Dreu, & Homan, 2004). Moving from the study of distributed information in group decision making to the role of diversity more generally thus likely requires further development of leadership and decision making theory. Moreover, the challenges in group decision making also include dealing with differences in interests between group members, and effective group decision making may thus also include negotiation (De Dreu, Nijstad, & van Knippenberg, 2008). Here too may lie a unique leadership challenge in reaching integrative decisions.

For the study of participative leadership as the extent to which followers are involved in the decision making process it might be good to refocus on the key question the Vroom and Yetton (1973) and Vroom and Jago (1988) models aimed to address without necessarily feeling bound by these models or the research designs in which these were tested, and to study the quality of decision making in organizational units as a function of the extent to which decision making is shared in combination with characteristics of the decision problem, leader, and followers. Such research is not to deny the value of studying participative leadership, or the broader concept of empowering leadership, as a motivating and facilitating influence on follower functioning and performance, but rather to complement such more 'traditional' leadership research with a clearer focus on decision making as arguably one of the more important activities in organizations.

Follower Decision Making

Leadership research would typically not see follower decision making as an outcome of interest, and decision making research would typically not extend its scope to include influence on others' decisions. Probably as a consequence, follower decision making seems to be the least explored perspective in leadership and decision making, at least in the sense that research in this area is not explicitly framed in terms of follower decision making. Those studies that can be classified as concerning follower decision making concern leaders' influence on followers' decisions in social dilemmas.

Social dilemmas are situations in which self-interest and collective interest are partly at odds and partly converge, such as in the use of a scarce resource that can only be replenished at a certain rate or in the establishment of a collective good from which an entire group can benefit once group members have contributed enough to establish it. For collectives of people, this introduces a problem that can be understood from individuals' behavioral decisions to (what extent to) cooperate: individual payoff is maximized if the individual behaves selfishly (e.g., draws without restraint from the resource or does not contribute to the establishment of the collective good) while others in the group cooperate (show restraint in drawing from the resource or contribute to establish the collective good). However, if too many people follow this selfish route, all are worse off than when all had behaved more cooperatively: the resource will be exhausted or the collective good not established. As many resource decisions in organizations arguably have a social dilemma character (Kramer, 1991), a question for leadership is how it may stimulate follower cooperative choices in social dilemmas.

De Cremer and van Knippenberg (2002, 2005) addressed this question, focusing on leader self-sacrificing versus self-benefiting behavior—the extent to which the leader incurred personal costs for the collective good or pursued personal benefits at the expensive of the collective. They argued that leader self-sacrifice would build follower identification with the group by conveying the value of the group and its interests to followers, as well as build trust in the leader, and would thus motivate followers to make cooperative choices (De Cremer & van Knippenberg, 2005). Moreover, they proposed and found that this effect on follower cooperative decisions obtained primarily when follower identification with the collective was not built through other leadership actions (i.e., procedurally fair behavior; De Cremer & van Knippenberg, 2002), and when followers held self-interested rather than cooperative social values (i.e., when their social values would not motivate cooperation in and of themselves; De Cremer, 2002).

Developing the leader fairness aspect of this analysis further, De Cremer and van Knippenberg (2003) showed that leader procedural fairness was more important in motivating cooperative choices when outcomes received from the leaders where less favorable—a circumstance that can be expected to inspire closer attention to how one is treated (Brockner & Wiesenfeld, 1996). Shifting the emphasis to the moderating effect of group identification in the effects of leadership on cooperative decisions, De Cremer and van Vugt (2002) showed that leader commitment to the group and leader fairness were more strongly associated with follower cooperative choices when follower identification was high, whereas the perception that the leader possessed important leadership skills was more effective in engendering cooperative choice when identification was low. Van Vugt and De Cremer (1999) likewise showed that relational leadership was more predictive of cooperation when follower identification was high, whereas instrumental leadership (focused on punishing noncooperation) was more effective when identification was low.

In combination, these findings are consistent with an integrated social identity/fairness understanding of followers' motivation to cooperate, and leaders' role in building this motivation (cf., van Knippenberg & Hogg, 2003). In their focus on leader self-sacrificing behavior and leader fairness, they also provide a strong linkage with the research in leader decision making focused on the self-servingness and fairness of leader decisions. One straightforward conclusion here is that the combined conclusion of this research is that factors that motivate fairer, more group-serving leader decisions should result in more cooperative follower decisions—leader decision making affects follower decision making. Even so, we should be wary of the conclusion that, because A leads to B, and B leads to C, A leads to C—not all factors that inspire fair, ethical, and group-serving leader decisions may equally feed into desirable follower decisions. It is, for instance, not unreasonable to consider the possibility that fair decisions that are perceived to be externally enforced (e.g., because the leader is held accountable for the decisions) are less effective in motivating desirable follower decisions than fair decisions that are perceived to be intrinsically motivated (e.g., through a genuine sense of social responsibility as a leader). Such integrations of leader decision making and follower decision making perspectives thus warrant empirical tests—not just reviews of the literature.

Where to go from here in the follower decision making perspective? The previous paragraph already points to an obvious direction for further development of this research area: integrating leader decision making and follower decision making perspectives. While a reasonable 'base rate' proposition here may be that follower decisions are likely to reflect leader decisions, it would seem important to determine the contingencies of this relationship. Moreover, we may note that research in the follower decision making perspective is limited to one type of decision—cooperation in social dilemmas—and it would seem in order to cast a wider net in studying leadership influences on follower decisions.

IN CONCLUSION

The development of more integrative theory in an area of research seems often to require that the issue under consideration is recognized as an area of research to begin with. One simple aim this chapter hopes to achieve is to (more firmly) establish leadership and decision making as an area of research, in the hope to thus inspire theory development that is more broad-ranging and more integrative than the conceptual analysis found for any given empirical study. This is not to say, however, that all research in leadership and decision making needs is more integrative theory. Theory can only be as good as the empirical evidence supporting it (Ferris, Hochwarter, & Buckley, 2012), and research in leadership in decision making is scarce and slanted toward a limited number of perspectives. We need more empirical research not only to test more integrative theory but also to yield more material for integration.

In this respect, it is noteworthy that research in leadership and decision making predominantly concerns social decision making in the study of the fairness, group-servingness, or cooperativeness of leader and follower decisions. Given that leadership is a social and mostly group-based process, this is not necessarily surprising, but it does provide somewhat of a contrast with the long tradition in research in JDM focusing on heuristics, biases, and decision uncertainty. A fuller consideration of leadership and decision making should be able to position both these perspectives within a larger leadership and decision making nomological net.

Another issue that is potentially relevant here is the consideration of levels of analysis. As the Son Hing et al. (2007) study illustrates, the fairness/ethicality of leader decisions may not only be studied at the level of the individual leader as decision maker, but also at the level of shared decision making. The study of participative leadership likewise hints at issues of individual-collective comparisons, and research in strategic management seems to meander back and forth between a focus on the CEO as (potential) decision maker and the top management as a whole. While sometimes individual level processes may neatly extrapolate to dyadic or group decision making, comparisons of individual and group decision making suggest they often do not (e.g., Kerr & Tindale, 2004). Consideration of the same decisions across levels of analysis would thus also seem important in further developing leadership and decision making theory and research.

The challenges in developing these lines of research are clear—especially where it comes to gaining high-quality information about leadership in the field to complement experimental and scenario investigations. The argument for the important role that leadership and decision making should have in the functioning of individuals, groups, and organizations (e.g., Useem, 2010) stands as strong as before, however. The scientific payoff in meeting these challenges is clearly there.

REFERENCES

Bass, B.M. and Riggio, R.E. (2006). *Transformational Leadership*. Mahwah, NJ: Erlbaum.

Bazerman, M.H. and Moore, D. (2009). *Judgment in Managerial Decision Making*. Hoboken, NJ: Wiley.

Brockner, J. and Wiesenfeld, B.M. (1996). An integrative framework for explaining reactions to decisions: Interactive effects of outcomes and procedures. *Psychological Bulletin*, *120*, 189–208.

Busenitz, L.W. and Barney, J.B. (1997). Differences between entrepreneurs and managers in large organizations: Biases and heuristics in strategic decision making. *Journal of Business Venturing*, *12*, 9–30.

De Cremer, D. (2002). Charismatic leadership and cooperation in social dilemmas: A matter of transforming motives? *Journal of Applied Social Psychology*, *32*, 997–1016.

De Cremer, D. (2003). How self-conception may lead to inequality: An experimental investigation of the impact of hierarchical roles on the equality-rule when allocating organizational resources. *Group and Organization Management*, *28*, 282–302.

De Cremer, D. and van Dijk, E. (2005). When and why leaders put themselves first: Leader behaviour in resource allocations as function of feeling entitled. *European Journal of Social Psychology*, *35*, 553–563.

De Cremer, D. and van Dijk, E. (2008). Leader–follower effects in resource dilemmas: The roles of leadership selection and social responsibility. *Group Processes & Intergroup Relations*, *11*, 355–369.

De Cremer, D. and van Knippenberg, D. (2002). How do leaders promote cooperation: The effects of charisma and procedural fairness. *Journal of Applied Psychology*, *87*, 858–866.

De Cremer, D. and van Knippenberg, D. (2003). Cooperation with leaders in social dilemmas: On the effects of procedural fairness and outcome favorability in structural cooperation. *Organizational Behavior and Human Decision Processes*, *91*, 1–11.

De Cremer, D. and van Knippenberg, D. (2005). Cooperation as a function of leader self-sacrifice, trust, and identification. *Leadership and Organization Development Journal*, *26*, 355–369.

De Cremer, D. and van Vugt, M. (2002). Intergroup and intragroup aspects of leadership in social dilemmas: A relational model of cooperation. *Journal of Experimental Social Psychology, 38,* 126–136.

De Dreu, C.K.W., Nijstad, B.A., and van Knippenberg, D. (2008). Motivated information processing in group judgment and decision making. *Personality and Social Psychology Review, 12,* 22–49.

Ferris, G.R., Hochwarter, W.A., and Buckley, M.R. (2012). Theory in the organizational sciences: How will we know it when we see it? *Organizational Psychology Review, 2,* 94–106.

Field, R.H.G. (1982). A test of the Vroom-Yetton normative model of leadership. *Journal of Applied Psychology, 67,* 523–532.

Field, R.H.G. and Andrews, J.P. (1998). Testing the incremental validity of the Vroom-Jago versus Vroom-Yetton models of participation in decision making. *Journal of Behavioral Decision Making, 11,* 251–261.

Field, R.H.G. and House, R.J. (1990). A test of the Vroom-Yetton model using manager and subordinate reports. *Journal of Applied Psychology, 75,* 362–366.

Finkelstein, S., Hambrick, D.C., and Cannella, A.A. Jr. (2009). *Strategic Leadership.* New York: Oxford University Press.

Giessner, S.R. and van Knippenberg, D. (2007). *Leading FOR the Team: Situational Determinants of Team-oriented Leader Behavior.* Paper presented at the 2007 Annual Meeting of the Society of Industrial and Organizational Psychology, New York, April.

Hirst, G., van Knippenberg, D., Chen, C.-H., and Sacramento, C.A. (2011). How does bureaucracy impact on individual creativity? A cross-level investigation of team contextual influences on goal orientation–creativity relationships. *Academy of Management Journal, 54,* 624–641.

Hitt, M.A. and Tyler, B.B. (1991). Strategic decision models: Integrating different perspectives. *Strategic Management Journal, 12,* 327–351.

Ilgen, D.R., Hollenbeck, J.R., Johnson, M., and Jundt, D. (2005). Teams in organizations: From input-process-output models to IMOI models. *Annual Review of Psychology, 56,* 517–543.

Judge, T.A. and Bono, J.E. (2000). Five-factor model of personality and transformational leadership. *Journal of Applied Psychology, 85,* 751–765.

Judge, T.A., Piccolo, R.F., and Ilies, R. (2004). The forgotten ones?: A re-examination of consideration, initiating structure, and leadership effectiveness. *Journal of Applied Psychology, 89,* 36–51.

Kahneman, D., Slovic, P., and Tversky, A. (1982). *Judgment under Uncertainty: Heuristics and Biases.* New York: Cambridge University Press.

Kaiser, R.B., Hogan, R., and Craig, S.B. (2008). Leadership and the fate of organizations. *American Psychologist, 63,* 96–110.

Kearney, E. and Gebert, D. (2009). Managing diversity and enhancing team outcomes: The promise of transformational leadership. *Journal of Applied Psychology, 94,* 77–89.

Keltner, D., Gruenfeld, D.H., and Anderson, C. (2003). Power, approach, and inhibition. *Psychological Review, 110,* 265–284.

Kerr, N.L. and Tindale, R.S. (2004). Group performance and decision making. *Annual Review of Psychology, 55,* 623–655.

Kirkman, B.L. and Rosen, B. (1999). Beyond self-management: Antecedents and consequences of team empowerment. *Academy of Management Journal, 42,* 58–74.

Korsgaard, M.A., Schweiger, D.M., and Sapienza, H.J. (1995). Building commitment, attachment, and trust in strategic decision-making teams: The role of procedural justice. *Academy of Management Journal, 38,* 60–84.

Kramer, R. (1991). Intergroup relations and organizational dilemmas. *Research in Organizational Behavior, 13*, 191–228.

Larson, J.R. Jr., Christensen, C., Abbott, A.S., and Franz, T.M. (1996). Diagnosing groups: Charting the flow of information in medical decision-making teams. *Journal of Personality and Social Psychology, 71*, 315–330.

Larson, J.R., Foster-Fishman, P.G., and Franz, T.M. (1998). Leadership style and the discussion of shared and unshared information in decision-making groups. *Personality and Social Psychology Bulletin, 24*, 482–495.

Leana, C.R. (1986). Predictors and consequences of delegation. *Academy of Management Journal, 29*, 754–774.

Lind, E.A. and Tyler, T.R. (1988). *The Social Psychology of Procedural Justice.* New York: Plenum.

Martin, R., Thomas, G., Topakas, A., and Epitropaki, O. (2010). A review of leader–member exchange research: Future prospects and directions. *International Review of Industrial and Organizational Psychology, 25*.

Peterson, R.S. (1999). Can you have too much of a good thing? The limits of voice for improving satisfaction with leaders. *Personality and Social Psychology Bulletin, 25*, 313–324.

Pratto, F., Sidanius, J., Stallworth, L.M., and Malle, B.F. (1994). Social dominance orientation: A personality variable predicting social and political attitudes. *Journal of Personality and Social Psychology, 67*, 741–763.

Rus, D., van Knippenberg, D., and Wisse, B. (2010a). Leader self-definition and leader self-serving behavior. *Leadership Quarterly, 21*, 509–529.

Rus, D., van Knippenberg, D., and Wisse, B. (2010b). Leader power and leader self-serving behavior: The role of effective leadership beliefs and performance information. *Journal of Experimental Social Psychology, 46*, 922–933.

Rus, D., van Knippenberg, D., and Wisse, B. (in press). Leader power and self-serving behavior: The moderating role of accountability. *Leadership Quarterly.*

Son Hing, L.S., Bobocel, D.R., Zanna, M.P., and McBride, M.V. (2007). Authoritarian dynamics and unethical decision making: High social dominance orientation leaders and high right-wing authoritarianism followers. *Journal of Personality and Social Psychology, 92*, 67–81.

Stasser, G. (1999). The uncertain role of unshared information in collective choice. In L.L. Thompson, J.M. Levine, and D.M. Messick (Eds.) *Shared Cognition in Organizations: The Management of Knowledge* (pp. 49–69). Mahwah, NJ: Erlbaum.

Useem, M. (2010). Decision making as leadership foundation. In N. Nohria and R. Khurana (Eds.) *Handbook of Leadership Theory and Practice* (pp. 507–525). Boston, MA: Harvard University Press.

van Dijk, E. and De Cremer, D. (2006). Self-benefiting in the allocation of scarce resources: Leader–follower effects and the moderating role of social value orientation. *Personality and Social Psychology Bulletin, 32*, 1352–1361.

van Ginkel, W.P. and van Knippenberg, D. (2012). Group leadership and shared task representations in decision-making groups. *Leadership Quarterly, 23*, 94–106..

van Knippenberg, D. (2012). Leadership: A person-in-situation perspective. In K. Deaux and M. Snyder (Eds.) *Oxford Handbook of Personality and Social Psychology* (pp. 673–700). New York: Oxford University Press.

van Knippenberg, D., De Dreu, C.K.W., and Homan, A.C. (2004). Work group diversity and group performance: An integrative model and research agenda. *Journal of Applied Psychology, 89*, 1008–1022.

van Knippenberg, D. and Hogg, M.A. (2003). A social identity model of leadership effectiveness in organizations. *Research in Organizational Behavior, 25,* 243–295.

van Vugt, M. and De Cremer, D. (1999). Leadership in social dilemmas: Social identification effects on collective actions in public goods. *Journal of Personality and Social Psychology, 76,* 587–599.

Vroom, V.H. and Jago, A.G. (1988). *The New Leadership: Managing Participation in Organizations.* Englewood Cliffs, NJ: Prentice Hall.

Vroom, V.H. and Yetton, P.W. (1973). *Leadership and Decision-making.* Pittsburgh, PA: University of Pittsburgh Press.

Wagner, J.A. (1994). Participation's effects on performance and satisfaction: A reconsideration of research evidence. *Academy of Management Review, 19,* 312–330.

West, M.A. and Anderson, N.R. (1996). Innovation in top management teams. *Journal of Applied Psychology, 81,* 680–693.

Yukl, G. (2005). *Leadership in Organizations* (6th ed.). Englewood Cliffs, NJ: Prentice Hall.

9

Judgments about Pay

Kristine M. Kuhn

Although employment can provide people with many valuable outcomes, compensation is perhaps the most obvious and important. The decisions employers make about pay are crucial determinants of their ability to attract, motivate, and retain employees. Although motivational theories are the most common lenses applied to compensation, judgment and decision making research affords substantial opportunities to inform our understanding of how people evaluate their pay, and to offer practical insights to organizations on how best to compensate employees.

Two decades ago Kahneman and Thaler (1991) argued that an appreciation of the psychological principles of adaptation, loss aversion, contrast, and social comparison, as well as the underlying determinants of perceived fairness, could help employers design compensation packages that increased worker satisfaction without raising their dollar cost—the proverbial free lunch. Since then results from a number of laboratory and field studies have lent support to this proposition, yet they also suggest challenges to implementing successful plans, including possible unintended consequences. This chapter presents a broad but selective review of compensation research from the perspective of judgment and decision making (JDM) theory, drawn from a variety of methodologies and academic disciplines. Unfortunately, much human resource management research in compensation lacks awareness of related work in other areas. Researchers interested in applications of JDM to compensation would benefit from greater cross-fertilization across disciplinary boundaries, and attention to the multiple outcomes of interest to organizations and possible tradeoffs among them.

THE UTILITY FUNCTION OF INCOME

At the most basic level, the more money an employee receives, the greater the number of choices she can make to maximize her utility. In economics, income is therefore taken as essentially equivalent to well-being. When asked directly people rate pay as only moderately important in motivating their own work behavior (Heath, 1999), but policy-capturing and other indirect methods generally find compensation to be one of the most important factors driving judgments, particularly attraction to a job offer (Rynes, Gerhart, & Minette, 2004).

Yet there is little evidence that increasing income beyond basic subsistence levels increases reported happiness and life satisfaction. A focusing illusion leads people to exaggerate the impact of income on happiness (Kahneman et al., 2006). Substantial real income growth in Western countries over the past several decades has not been accompanied by any increase in happiness levels, and richer countries are generally no happier than poorer ones—the famous Easterlin paradox (Easterlin, 1973). Within a relatively well-off country, the correlation between income and well-being is positive but small (see Diener & Seligman, 2004). Although debate over the Easterlin paradox continues (Easterlin et al., 2010), both affect- and judgment-based measures of well-being show similar patterns of declining marginal utility with increasing income (Diener et al., 2009). Of more direct interest to organizational researchers and employers is any association between pay and job satisfaction. In a recent meta-analysis, Judge and his colleagues (2010) concluded that pay level is only marginally related to both job satisfaction and even to satisfaction with pay itself; on average, relatively well-paid individuals are only "trivially more satisfied" than poorly paid workers.

People's strong tendency to adapt can explain this finding. Whatever is viewed as normal is neutral, causing neither satisfaction nor pain (see Frederick & Loewenstein, 1999). Since people will very quickly adapt to a given pay level, no matter how high, it will not make them happy for long. For people able to afford basic needs, what matters is not their absolute level of income but their *relative* income, where value is defined as a gain or loss relative to a reference point. Income may be evaluated relative to oneself in the past (habituation) or relative to salient others (social comparison).

Changes in Pay

In a large-scale study of British employees who remained with the same organization in the same position, overall job satisfaction was positively correlated with their change in pay over the past year, particularly for younger and lower paid employees, but not with current level of pay (Clark, 1999). This provides evidence for habituation and a reference-dependent utility function, although the effect of any change in income may wear off quickly (Di Tella, Haisken-De New, & MacCulloch, 2010). In an experiment where students were hired to perform data entry, Gneezy and List (2006) found that paying a "gift" wage of almost twice as much per hour than advertised led to increased performance, but the beneficial impact on effort lasted only a couple of hours. It should be noted, however, that subjects in this study knew it was a one-time job of short duration and therefore had no motivation to secure its continuation, and their subjective attitudes were not assessed.

Mitra, Gupta, and Jenkins (1997) used a psychophysical approach to examine merit-based pay raises, and found that those below 7 percent evoked no noticeable cognitive or behavioral reactions. This finding should give employers pause, given that merit raises continue to be the most popular form of pay-for-performance and the 7 percent threshold is larger than what would typically be observed in practice. Surveys of U.S. employers before the recent recession found average merit-based pay raises for the *highest* performers to be less than 6 percent (Hansen, 2006, 2008), and only 4 percent in 2010 (Miller, 2011). Some studies, however, have found positive correlations between the size of a merit raise and attitudes for some types of employees under certain circumstances, i.e. if various individual differences and pay-for-performance perceptions are included in the analysis (Schaubroeck et al., 2008; Scott, Shaw, & Duffy, 2008; Shaw et al., 2003).

Even if small pay rises are unlikely to have much psychological impact, it matters that pay increase over time. People stubbornly prefer a wage profile that rises over those that are constant or declining, even if they are aware the rising profile has a lower economic value (Loewenstein & Sicherman, 1991). Such a pattern makes sense if utility is reference-dependent. It also helps to explain the robust economic finding that real wages climb more steeply than productivity. Notably, people evaluate pay changes in nominal rather than real terms, the well-known "money illusion" (Fisher, 1928). Thus a 5 percent raise in a time of 4 percent inflation is viewed as preferable to a 2 percent raise in a time of no inflation (Shafir,

Diamond, & Tversky, 1997). Even though people can evaluate this comparison in economic terms, the majority are strongly convinced that employees who receive the higher nominal raise will be both happier and likelier to stay with their employer (Shafir, Diamond, & Tversky, 1997). Workers experiencing stagnant wages may experience significant frustration. Reference-dependent utility and the money illusion suggest that most people would derive more utility from receiving a 3 percent raise in a time of 3 percent inflation (or possibly even 4 percent inflation) than from receiving no raise in a time of zero inflation.

But pay freezes will not be nearly as aversive as actual pay cuts. Loss aversion is one of the best established and most widely applied principles in the JDM literature. Prospect theory holds that losses loom larger than gains; at the margin, individuals are about twice as sensitive to losses as they are to gains of equivalent magnitude (Kahneman & Tversky, 1979; Tversky & Kahneman, 1991). While small raises may have little impact, small pay cuts will be quite distressing. Loss aversion helps explain the economically irrational phenomenon of "wage stickiness," wherein employers are reluctant to cut wages during times of high unemployment, believing that any savings would be offset by damage to morale and productivity (Bewley, 1999). Surveys of the general population find the vast majority of people perceive wage cuts to be unfair, although some factors (such as the money illusion) mitigate these perceptions (Charness & Levine, 2002; Kahneman, Knetsch, & Thaler, 1986).

Although many firms did cut wages and salaries along with hours and benefits during the recent recession (Dade & Tuna, 2008; Greenhouse, 2010a), actual reductions of nominal fixed pay have been historically rare and there are few data on their consequences. Greenberg (1990) observed increases in employee theft contemporaneous with a temporary pay cut, even when substantial effort was made to follow procedural justice precepts. In a recent field experiment, student workers who received a lower hourly wage than had been advertised (as a "projected" rate) were much less productive than those who received the expected rate, while workers who received a higher wage showed no improvement (Kube, Maréchal, & Puppe, 2010). In the Kahneman, Knetsch, and Thaler (1986) study, negative reactions to hypothetical pay cuts were lessened when the business was described as losing money, although high unemployment in and of itself did not mitigate perceptions of unfairness. The executives interviewed by Bewley (1999) in the early 1990s did not typically believe wage cuts would generate any net benefit to a firm, and only imposed pay cuts if they would actually save jobs, thereby rendering them more acceptable to employees.

Recently, however, at least some quite profitable firms have sought to justify proposed pay cuts with the presence of high unemployment and lower local wage rates, sparking considerable resentment (see Greenhouse, 2010b).

Mental accounting, the process by which people categorize and evaluate economic outcomes, offers a possible solution to the observed asymmetry in reactions to pay changes (see Kahneman & Thaler, 1991). Rather than change base pay, firms can award or not award bonuses (or adopt variable plans where compensation fluctuates with the ability of the firm to pay; see Klaas, 1999). If bonuses are not incorporated into the expected status quo, then their receipt should be rewarding as a distinct change from adaptation, whereas not receiving a bonus will be less aversive than overt wage cuts. There is substantial evidence that lump-sum bonuses are treated differently than regular income (Thaler, 1990), and some reason to believe that, for example, a \$40,000 salary with a \$2,000 bonus will be more satisfying than a \$42,000 salary.

In Kahneman, Knetsch, and Thaler (1986), 60 percent of respondents felt a 10 percent pay cut would be unfair if the business had not increased as before, whereas only 20 percent felt an equivalent pay reduction would be unfair if instead it was described as eliminating a usual bonus. In Charness and Levine's (2002) replication, however, over 40 percent of respondents still felt eliminating the bonus would be unfair. In practice, the extent to which a bonus is "usual" or expected, i.e. an entitlement, will matter a great deal. Heath, Knez, and Camerer (1993) present a model showing how both psychological limitations in judgment and strategic distortions in information exchanged lead employees to perceive their rewards as richer and more systematic than intended by their employer. Accordingly, in practice employees may quickly adapt to bonuses and treat non-receipt as a loss rather than a foregone gain. One way to lessen this tendency would be to segregate profit-sharing or other bonuses from regular paychecks. If happiness is determined by the frequency rather than the intensity of positive versus negative experiences (Diener, Sandvik, & Pavot, 2009), it would be better to award more frequent small bonuses rather than rare large ones. An unexpected bonus could also provide more utility than an expected one, although I am not aware of any field tests of this proposition. Of course, surprise bonuses would contravene the motivational logic of pay-for-performance, in which employees work hard because they are confident of receiving a known reward if a goal is achieved.

But if a firm wishes to begin awarding bonuses without increasing total compensation costs, base pay will have to be reduced. Whatever the firm's intentions, employees will experience this as a loss. Brown and Huber

(1992) studied the introduction of a pay-at-risk system where employees would be guaranteed to receive only 93 percent of their former salary. Not surprisingly, they reacted quite negatively, even though they could potentially receive a year-end performance bonus greater than 7 percent. Lee, Law, and Bobko (1999) also found that the introduction of a pay-at-risk plan generated widespread resentment; the plan was subsequently changed to ensure the majority of employees would earn a bonus such that total pay would be at least equal to previous salary.

Social Comparison

In addition to using their own previous pay as a reference point, employees also judge their compensation in relation to that of their peers. Job satisfaction is more strongly related to relative rather than absolute income (Clark & Oswald, 1996). If employees' co-workers are more salient reference points than the broader occupational labor market, a firm that chooses to be a pay leader will not see any improvement in employee attitudes or satisfaction (although recruitment may benefit). Rather, a policy of high internal pay dispersion will be more advantageous, as long as high performers, whom the organization most wishes to retain, are paid substantially more than their co-workers (as suggested by Judge et al., 2010, and others).

Yet such a recommendation ignores the likelihood that social comparison effects are, as with habituation, strongly asymmetric. Ordóñez, Connolly, and Coughlan (2000) asked subjects to evaluate a hypothetical MBA graduate's salary offer in light of those received by similar graduates; the pain associated with receiving a lower salary was much greater than the pleasure of receiving a higher offer. In a recent noteworthy field study, Card et al. (2010) randomly selected a subset of University of California employees to receive an email informing them of a new website that listed the pay of all University employees. All employees were subsequently surveyed about their job-related attitudes. Card et al. (2010) reported an asymmetric response to the information manipulation; employees who discovered their pay was below the median for their unit and job type were much less satisfied with their pay and job and more interested in leaving, while above-median earners were unaffected.

Asymmetry in social comparison implies possible benefits of greater wage compression. Pay dispersion has been linked to higher managerial turnover (Bloom & Michel, 2002) and to lower satisfaction and individual productivity (Pfeffer & Langton, 1993). But pay dispersion will influence attitudes and performance via pathways other than social comparison, and its effects will depend on whether spread is based on performance or seniority, the communication of pay policies, and the quality of the individual worker (Kepes, Delery, & Gupta, 2009; Shaw & Gupta, 2007). Based on their results, Card et al. (2010) suggest pay secrecy policies might be beneficial, despite their questionable legality, as pay openness can only decrease satisfaction. Pay secrecy is an understudied phenomenon (Colella et al., 2007), but a recent experiment that manipulated pay openness found its effects on an individual's performance to be contingent on her tolerance for inequity (Bamberger & Belogolovsky, 2010). In real-world organizations where the links between pay and performance are not completely objective or clear-cut, pay secrecy's effects on individual, unit-level, and organizational performance are likely to be even more contingent and complex. The extent to which the widespread availability of internet sites such as Glassdoor.com, which allow employees to see the purported compensation of peers at their own and competing firms, may have altered social comparison effects is an important topic for future research.

Assuming employees are aware of their co-workers' wages, the choices employers make about skew, as well as variance, may be key. Range frequency theory (Parducci, 1965, 1995) holds that negatively skewed event distributions are most conducive to happiness, and predicts that responses to a wage will be determined by its ordinal rank within a comparison set. If so, then variance-based measures of pay dispersion are not necessarily ideal for examining social comparison effects. Smith, Diener, and Wedell (1989) argued that happiness, both of each individual worker and the group average, would be greater if salaries are negatively rather than positively skewed. Brown et al. (2008) found that employee satisfaction depends more on ordinal rank rather than cardinal values (see also Clark, Masclet, & Villeval, 2010). Further support for range frequency theory is provided by the finding that turnover was lower in workplaces with more negatively skewed pay distributions (Brown et al., 2008).

Although the tension caused by incentivizing individual performance while also fostering employee cooperation and high morale may seem intractable, innovative approaches to compensation policies could help to minimize negative effects of social comparisons. For example, each year Fog Creek Software employees are assigned a level based on their experience, scope, and responsibility, and all employees at that level receive the same pay—no individual negotiating for raises is allowed (Spolsky, 2009). If employees feel their level assignment is fair, negative social comparison effects should be minimal. Such a policy would also prevent salary inversion, where new hires are paid more than existing employees of equal or higher rank, a problem of particular and perennial interest to academic faculty (e.g., *Chronicle of Higher Education*, 1990; Glassman & McAfee, 2005; June, 2011). Fog Creek also offers a profit-sharing plan. As discussed next, JDM research, so much of which concerns choices under uncertainty, has significant potential to inform our understanding of the likely effects of variable pay.

VARIABLE PAY AND RISK

Over the past few decades, increasing numbers of workers have begun to face some uncertainty about their expected pay. They may receive commissions, company equity, or bonuses based on various performance measures. In 2009 variable pay as a percentage of U.S. payroll for salaried employees was 12 percent, an all-time high since tracking began (Hewitt Associates, 2010). Wiseman, Gomez-Mejia, and Fugate (2000) observed that the vast literature on risk had been "virtually ignored" in the compensation literature, but their analysis, and subsequent work on compensation risk (see Gomez-Mejia, Berrone, & Franco-Santos, 2010), focused on executive pay. Organizations should be concerned with the reactions of non-executives to pay risk as well.

In a policy-capturing study of job attraction, Cable and Judge (1994) reported evidence for modal risk aversion, in that most student subjects preferred a fixed salary over one said to vary from 15 percent below to 25 percent above that amount contingent on organizational success. Expressed preferences for compensation risk, however, are likely to vary a great deal depending on context, methodology, and incentive basis. Kuhn and Yockey (2003) asked undergraduates in a series of experiments to choose between a job offer with a fixed salary and one with a lower certain component but some probability of earning a contingent-performance bonus that would provide higher total pay. In this study, most participants preferred the riskier option when the bonus would be based on individual performance, especially if they were high in self-efficacy; participants were more likely to choose the fixed salary option when the risky incentive would be based on team or organizational performance. Conceptualized as a risky choice, people were more willing to "bet" on their own performance than on collective performance because they were more confident of earning the bonus. The size and probability of the bonus also influenced preferences.

Kuhn and Yockey (2003) suggest, based on their findings, that organizations who offer lower fixed salaries but promise bonuses to top performers could attract self-confident new hires while lowering overall compensation costs, but they also speculate that disappointment and frustration from failure to earn expected rewards could lead to negative outcomes in the long term. In one experimental economics simulation, however, overconfident subjects were more likely to self-select into a convex incentive pay scheme (analogous to plans commonly used in sales in which a salesperson's commission percentage varies depending on her total sales) rather than a piece rate plan, and persisted in their economically irrational choice despite feedback (Larkin & Leider, 2011); these authors argue that firms could both attract and retain overconfident workers by the use of such non-linear incentives, lowering their overall wage bill.

Cadsby, Song, and Tapon (2007) found that risk-averse experimental participants, as measured by gamble choices, were more likely to choose a fixed wage over an individual piece rate, whereas more productive workers preferred the latter plan. Regardless of which compensation scheme they preferred, all subjects tended to be more productive under the pay-for-performance plan, although the risk-averse subjects were less responsive to this form of incentive. Pay-for-performance thereby lowered the unit costs of production via both sorting and incentive effects. In this laboratory experiment (Cadsby, Song, & Tapon, 2007), pay uncertainty derived from an individual not knowing exactly how many anagram problems she would be able to solve; in most organizational incentive schemes, uncertainty would also derive from many factors outside the employee's control (co-workers' relative performance, economic conditions, etc.). In general, the effect of financial incentives on performance has been studied using tasks where performance can be objectively measured (Camerer & Hogarth, 1999; Jenkins et al., 1998; Prendergast, 1999), whereas most employees are evaluated on subjective criteria.

There is little field research on the role pay risk plays in the attitudes and behaviors of actual employees. In one survey study of employed business students, risk aversion (measured by subjective ratings of work-related risk preferences) moderated the effects of a "control-by-pay" measure (Deckop, Merriman, & Blau, 2004). Risk-averse respondents reported lower satisfaction, fewer organizational citizenship behaviors, and more withdrawal cognitions if they felt their organization's pay system motivated them to work hard. There is no information provided, however, about the actual pay schemes under which respondents worked (Deckop, Merriman, & Blau, 2004).

Although research to date indicates substantial individual differences in how employees respond to the uncertainty associated with variable pay, the managerial implications are not necessarily clear. Recently the Google corporation announced that, in response to employee preferences, their compensation policy would be changed to reduce uncertainty:

> We've heard from your feedback on Googlegeist and other surveys that salary is more important to you than any other component of pay (i.e., bonus and equity). To address that, we're moving a portion of your bonus into your base salary, so now it's income you can count on, every time you get your paycheck.
>
> (CEO Eric Schmidt, quoted in Blodget, 2011)

This raises the interesting question of how much insight people have into the drivers of their own satisfaction, as well as what the ideal proportions of fixed and contingent pay might be. If individual employees vary in their preferences for pay risk, why not allow them to choose a personal risk level? Netflix is one of the rare companies that offers some such flexibility; employees can tailor the mix of salary and stock equity in their compensation package (Goldfarb & Holding, 2011).

Framing of Incentives

Incentive plans can be framed in either gain or loss terms, for example earn $10 with a $10 bonus for reaching a goal versus earn $20 with a $10 penalty if the goal is not reached. There is a substantial experimental literature in accounting that examines this kind of framing in contracts. Luft (1994) found that people are more likely to accept contracts described in bonus terms than functionally identical ones described in terms of penalties. But loss aversion also spurs people to work harder to avoid paying a penalty than they will to receive a bonus, and accordingly incentive contracts framed as losses actually increase task effort (Church, Libby, & Zhang, 2008; Hannan, Hoffman, & Moser, 2005), a result that seems contrary to conventional wisdom. Frederickson and Waller (2005) find that bonus framing may increase social learning in some situations, indicating possible advantages of offering carrots rather than sticks.

Outside of executive contracts, where clawback and other penalty provisions are becoming more common, loss-framed performance-contingent pay is relatively rare. But some workers may be penalized for defects, some commission-based salespeople have to pay the firm back from draws if they fail to meet a sales quota, and some law firms recruit new hires with a promised bonus that is not paid if they fall short of a billable hours target. Such penalties will be psychologically distinct from more conventional bonus plans, but research to date is too limited to offer much practical advice to employers. One study conducted at a Chinese electronics factory found an incentive plan framed as a bonus did not increase productivity as much as an isomorphic plan framed as a penalty did (Hossain & List, 2009). But while loss aversion may motivate employees to work especially hard to avoid penalties, they may also interpret them as signals of mistrust and experience lower satisfaction. Future research should examine the extent to which the acceptability of loss-framed pay varies due to culture, perceived controllability, and other factors.

Regardless of the overt framing of a compensation scheme, what matters most may be how employees perceive their variable pay. Do they view bonuses or other rewards as gains, or do they experience not receiving them as losses? Merriman and Deckop (2007) asked employees from a range of occupations and organizations to rate the extent to which they personally framed (non-receipt) of their future variable pay as a loss, with items such as "I have not achieved my annual income goal unless I earn some variable pay in addition to my base pay this year." Agreement with this measure correlated positively with self-rated effort and supervisor-rated performance, effects explainable by the motivating aspects of loss aversion (Merriman & Deckop, 2007). What remains to be examined more fully are the possible tradeoffs between performance gains due to loss aversion and lowered satisfaction and retention.

CONTEXT-DEPENDENT PREFERENCES

Even relatively basic questions about compensation, such as the impact of pay on an applicant's attraction to a job offer, have complicated answers. Salary expectations, at least for relatively inexperienced job seekers, can be strongly influenced by very simple changes in the contextual environment (Highhouse et al., 2003). Decision research also suggests that pay will have more of an impact on job choice decisions in labor markets where the pay range of available options is narrow than in those with wider ranges (Highhouse, Luong, & Sarkar-Barney, 1999). Even if most applicants are more attracted to a job offer with a specified variable pay component based on individual performance than to an equivalent one based on collective performance (as in Kuhn & Yockey, 2003), it does not necessarily follow that they will be more attracted to *firms* that emphasize individual incentives. Experimentally manipulating whether a company's recruitment advertisement mentions either a profit-sharing plan or an individual incentive plan leads readers to make different inferences about the organization's culture, and in this richer decision context no modal preference (as expressed by organizational attraction) for one type of incentive plan over the other is observed (Kuhn, 2009). Whether absolute pay level is more or less important than social comparison information about salaries depends on whether the job offer is evaluated separately or jointly with respect to other offers (Bazerman et al., 1994; Tenbrunsel & Diekmann, 2002).

Shaffer and Arkes (2009) present a series of experiments demonstrating another type of preference reversal in compensation, that between cash and non-cash incentives. Cash is, of course, fungible and rationally more desirable, and participants did in fact prefer cash in joint evaluation mode. Yet they gave higher ratings to non-cash incentives such as televisions when evaluated separately. Moreover, employees who received rewards from an incentive program felt that non-cash incentive recipients would enjoy their reward more and be more likely to tell friends (Shaffer & Arkes, 2009).

Heyman and Ariely (2004) compared the effects of non-monetary payments (candy) and cash in laboratory experiments, and found task effort to be sensitive to the amount of money but not to the magnitude of the non-cash gift. In this study, where pay was not contingent on performance, effort was actually higher when no payment was provided than when a low monetary payment was offered. These results are explained by differences in motivation between monetary and social markets (Heyman & Ariely, 2004). In an economic exchange framework performance is a specified return for money, whereas in a social exchange framework performance can be a tacit return for support and concern. Gneezy and Rustichini (2000) also found that low monetary incentives, which in this study were linked to performance, led to worse performance than did no incentives, leading them to conclude that pay should be "enough" or nothing. Given that very large contingent bonuses can have negative effects on performance (Ariely et al., 2009), it falls to employers to determine incentive bonus amounts that are not so low as to be insulting, and not so high as to generate undue pressure.

Heyman and Ariely (2004) suggest that in mixed monetary and social markets the monetary framing will dominate. But in one field experiment an unexpected wage increase of 20 percent failed to increase student workers' productivity, whereas an unexpected gift of a thermos bottle of equivalent monetary value did (Kube, Maréchal, & Puppe, 2008). This suggests that non-cash employee rewards may signal kindness or invoke social reciprocity. Conversely, making employees' pay highly contingent on their performance signals an economic exchange, highlighting the quid pro quo nature of the transaction. Pazy and Ganzach (2009) found that perceived organizational support, a measure that reflects social exchange in employment relationships, predicted performance under low, but not high, pay contingency.

Benefits constitute around 30 percent of U.S. payrolls, and represent another clear example of context dependency. Compensation in the form of health care or retirement contributions will not be viewed the same way as regular income. One early study that applied JDM theory to benefits found that employees' valuation of benefits anchored on their own contributions and were insufficiently adjusted for employer costs (Wilson, Northcraft, & Neale, 1985), but most subsequent research on benefits and employee attitudes has been based on organizational justice theory (see Williams, Malos, & Palmer, 2002). JDM research has been applied very productively to understanding and improving individual retirement savings behavior (see Benartzi & Thaler, 2007), and could also be applied to understanding the effects specific types of benefit plans have on employee attraction and retention. For example, consider a college senior choosing between two job offers. One offers $48,000 and a 401(k) plan that matches employee contributions up to 6 percent, whereas the other will pay $50,000 and offers a 401(k) plan with no match. Although the former is a better offer for a prudent saver, the larger salary of the latter may be more salient, and "presence of retirement plan" may just be evaluated categorically. Given that salaries are easy to compare, and benefits frequently are not, firms that offer generous benefits may not see any recruiting advantage. On the other hand, one field study found that leading the market in terms of overall percentage of payroll devoted to benefits was associated with a greater number of applicants, whereas leading the market in pay was not (Williams & Dreher, 1992).

RESEARCH NEEDS AND CONCLUSION

Risk and uncertainty are becoming more and more relevant to compensation, and so JDM-oriented research in this area has significant opportunity to make important contributions, both to theory and to practice. As noted earlier, explicit variable pay schemes are now common for many types of jobs at all organizational levels. Moreover, employee benefits increasingly have associated uncertainty as well. For example, many firms suspended matching contributions to 401(k) plans during the recent recession, and employees may make decisions about health care plans partly on the basis of subjective forecasts of health outcomes and costs. Perhaps most critically, a rapidly growing proportion of the labor force is contingent, as more people work as freelancers, independent contractors, or in other sorts of temporary arrangements. While there is substantial research on the attitudes and performance of contingent workers (Connelly & Gallagher, 2004), there is relatively little on their compensation, which can entail unique sources of uncertainty. Contractors paid for their time may have to make judgments about the likely duration of a project as well as pay rates; if they rationally seek other work as a project nears completion, their employers sometimes have to pay unplanned retention bonuses. Many freelancers who charge a flat fee complain about the difficulty of collecting promised compensation for their work.

Such issues are not typically addressed in compensation research, which generally studies college students or regular staff employees in one or two organizations. This limits both generalizability and the types of issues studied. One way to obtain data from more demographically diverse samples, and from people who work under a variety of compensation schemes, is via Amazon's Mechanical Turk. MTurk is an online marketplace for paying people around the world to perform computer-based tasks, including surveys and experiments, and has great potential as a social science research tool (Buhrmester, Kwang, & Gosling, 2011). These "workers" are primarily motivated by enjoyment rather than money (Paolacci, Chandler, & Ipeirotis, 2010), but their willingness to participate for small fees (e.g., 50 cents for a short survey) makes large sample sizes feasible. MTurk thus affords opportunities for both experiments and broad-based surveys (as respondents could also be asked about their regular employment, if any, and its compensation), as well as the potential for cross-cultural comparisons.

Getting compensation right, in terms of both how much to pay employees and how to determine their pay, is crucial to organizational success. But compensation plans that applicants and employees rate as desirable may not necessarily be those that would most increase effort, which in turn may not necessarily be those that maximize satisfaction, teamwork, or retention. While there may not be any truly free lunches in compensation, some types of plans are likely to provide better value. In particular, employers and compensation specialists could benefit from a greater appreciation of loss aversion and the asymmetric nature of responses to social comparison information.

REFERENCES

Ariely, D., Gneezy, U., Loewenstein, G., and Mazar, N. (2009). Large stakes and big mistakes. *Review of Economic Studies*, 76, 451–469.

Bamberger, P. and Belogolovsky, E. (2010). The impact of pay secrecy on individual task performance. *Personnel Psychology*, 63, 965–996.

Bazerman, M.H., Schroth, H.A., Shah, P.P., Diekmann, K.A., and Tenbrunsel, A.E. (1994). The inconsistent role of comparison others and procedural justice in reactions to hypothetical job descriptions: Implications for job acceptance decisions. *Organizational Behavior and Human Decision Processes*, 60, 326–352.

Benartzi, S. and Thaler, R.H. (2007). Heuristics and biases in retirement savings behavior. *The Journal of Economic Perspectives*, 21, 81–104.

Bewley, T.F. (1999). *Why Wages Don't Fall During a Recession*. Cambridge, MA: Harvard University Press.

Blodget, H. (2011). Google gives all employees surprise $1000 cash bonus plus 10% raise. *Business Insider*. Retrieved June 4, 2012 from www.businessinsider.com/google-bonus-and-raise-2010-11.

Bloom, M. and Michel, J.G. (2002). The relationships among organizational context, pay dispersion, and managerial turnover. *Academy of Management Journal*, 45, 33–42.

Brown, G.D., Gardner, J., Oswald, A.J., and Qian, J. (2008). Does wage rank affect employees' well-being? *Industrial Relations*, 47, 355–389.

Brown, K.A. and Huber, V.L. (1992). Lowering floors and raising ceilings: A longitudinal assessment of the effects of an earnings-at-risk plan on pay satisfaction. *Personnel Psychology*, 45, 279–311.

Buhrmester, M.D., Kwang, T., and Gosling, S.D. (2011). Amazon's Mechanical Turk: A new source of inexpensive, yet high-quality, data? *Perspectives on Psychological Science*, 6, 3–5.

Cable, D.M. and Judge, T.A. (1994). Pay preferences and job search decisions: A person–organization fit perspective. *Personnel Psychology*, 47, 317–348.

Cadsby, C.B., Song, F., and Tapon, F. (2007). Sorting and incentive effects of pay-for-performance: An experimental investigation. *Academy of Management Journal*, 50, 387–405.

Camerer, C.F. and Hogarth, R.M. (1999). The effects of financial incentives in experiments: A review and capital-labor-production framework. *Journal of Risk and Uncertainty*, 19, 7–42.

Card, D., Mas, A., Moretti, E., and Saez, E. (2010). Inequality at work: The effect of peer salaries on job satisfaction. Working Paper 16396. Cambridge, MA: National Bureau of Economic Research.

Charness, G. and Levine, D.I. (2002). Changes in the employment contract? Evidence from a quasi-experiment. *Journal of Economic Behavior & Organization*, 47, 391–405.

Chronicle of Higher Education (1990). New professors get more than old at business schools. *Chronicle of Higher Education*, April 4.

Church, B., Libby, T., and Zhang, P. (2008). Contracting frame and individual behavior: Experimental evidence. *Journal of Management Accounting Research, 20*, 153–160.

Clark, A.E. (1999). Are wages habit forming? Evidence from micro data. *Journal of Economic Behavior & Organization, 39*, 179–200.

Clark, A.E., Masclet, D., and Villeval, M.C. (2010). Effort and comparison income: Experimental and survey evidence. *Industrial and Labor Relations Review, 63*, 407–426.

Clark, A.E. and Oswald, A.J. (1996). Satisfaction and comparison income. *Journal of Public Economics, 61*, 359–381.

Colella, A., Paetzold, R., Zardkoohi, A., and Wesson, M. (2007). Exposing pay secrecy. *Academy of Management Review, 32*, 55–71.

Connelly, C.E., and Gallagher, D.G. (2004). Emerging trends in contingent work research. *Journal of Management, 30*, 959–983.

Dade, C. and Tuna, C. (2008). FedEx joins other firms cutting pay, retirement. *Wall Street Journal*, December 19, B1.

Deckop, J.R., Merriman, K.K., and Blau, G. (2004). Impact of variable risk preferences on the effectiveness of control by pay. *Journal of Occupational and Organizational Psychology, 77*, 63–80.

Diener, E., Kahneman, D., Arora, R., Harter, J., and Tov, W. (2009). Income's differential influence on judgments of life versus affective well-being. In E. Diener (Ed.) *Assessing Well-being: The Collected Works of Ed Diener* (pp. 233–246). New York: Springer Verlag.

Diener, E., Sandvik, E., and Pavot, W. (2009) Happiness is the frequency, not the intensity, of positive versus negative affect. In E. Diener (Ed.) *Assessing Well-being: The Collected Works of Ed Diener* (pp. 213–232). New York: Springer Verlag.

Diener, E. and Seligman, M.E.P. (2004). Beyond money: Toward an economy of well-being. *Psychological Science in the Public Interest, 5*, 1–31.

Di Tella, R., Haisken-De New, J., and MacCulloch, R. (2010). Happiness adaptation to income and to status in an individual panel. *Journal of Economic Behavior & Organization, 76*, 834–852.

Easterlin, R.A. (1973). Does money buy happiness? *The Public Interest, 30*, 3–10.

Easterlin, R.A., McVey, L.A., Switek, M., Sawangfa, O., and Zweig, J.S. (2010). The happiness–income paradox revisited. *Proceedings of the National Academy of Sciences of the USA, 107*, 22463–22468.

Fisher, I. (1928). *The Money Illusion*. New York: Adelphi.

Frederick, S. and Loewenstein, G. (1999). Hedonic adaptation. In D. Kahneman, E. Diener, and N. Schwarz (Eds.) *Well-being: The Foundations of Hedonic Psychology* (pp. 302–329). New York: Russell Sage Foundation.

Frederickson, J.R. and Waller, W. (2005). Carrot or stick? Contract frame and use of decision-influencing information in a principal-agent setting. *Journal of Accounting Research, 43*, 709–733.

Glassman, M. and McAfee, R.B. (2005). Pay inversion at universities: Is it ethical? *Journal of Business Ethics, 56*, 325–333.

Gneezy, U. and List, J.A. (2006). Putting behavioral economics to work: Testing for gift exchange in labor markets using field experiments. *Econometrica, 74*, 1365–1384.

Gneezy, U. and Rustichini, A. (2000). Pay enough or don't pay at all. *Quarterly Journal of Economics, 115*, 791–810.

Goldfarb, J. and Holding, R. (2011). Incentives play role in success of Netflix. *New York Times*, May 9, B2.

Gomez-Mejia, L.R., Berrone, P., and Franco-Santos, M. (2010). Risk and executive pay. In *Compensation and Organizational Performance: Theory, Research, and Practice* (Chapter 7). New York: M.E. Sharpe.

Greenberg, J. (1990). Employee theft as a reaction to underpayment inequity: The hidden cost of a pay cut. *Journal of Applied Psychology, 75*, 561–568.

Greenhouse, S. (2010a). More workers face pay cuts, not furloughs. *New York Times*, August 4, A1.

Greenhouse, S. (2010b). In Mott's strike, more than pay at stake. *New York Times*, August 18, B1.

Hannan, R., Hoffman, V., and Moser, D. (2005). Bonus versus penalty: Does contract frame affect employee effort. In R. Zwick and A. Rappoport (Eds.) *Experimental Business Research* (vol. II, pp. 151–169). Dordrecht: Springer Verlag.

Hansen, F. (2006). Companies pull back from performance-based pay. *Workforce Management*, October 23, p. 26.

Hansen, F. (2008). Where's the merit-pay payoff? *Workforce Management*, November 5, pp. 33–39.

Heath, C. (1999). On the social psychology of agency relationships: Lay theories of motivation overemphasize extrinsic incentives. *Organizational Behavior and Human Decision Processes, 78*, 25–62.

Heath, C., Knez, M., and Camerer, C. (1993). The strategic management of the entitlement process in the employment relationship. *Strategic Management Journal, 14*, 75–93.

Hewitt Associates (2010). Companies around the world focus on rewarding high performance through variable pay programs. Retrieved July 20, 2011 from http://aon.mediaroom.com/index.php?s=114&item=32.

Heyman, J. and Ariely, D. (2004). Effort for payment: A tale of two markets. *Psychological Science, 15*, 787–793.

Highhouse, S., Brooks-Laber, M.E., Lin, L., and Spitzmeuller, C. (2003). What makes a salary seem reasonable? Frequency context effects on starting salary expectations. *Journal of Occupational and Organizational Psychology, 76*, 69–81.

Highhouse, S., Luong, A., and Sarkar-Barney, S. (1999). Research design, measurement, and effects of attribute range on job choice: More than meets the eye. *Organizational Research Methods, 2*, 37–48.

Hossain, T. and List, J.A. (2009). The behavioralist visits the factory: Increasing productivity using simple framing manipulations. Working Paper 15623. Cambridge, MA: National Bureau of Economic Research.

Jenkins, G.D., Mitra, A., Gupta, N., and Shaw, J.D. (1998). Are financial incentives related to performance? A meta-analytic review of empirical research. *Journal of Applied Psychology, 83*, 777–787.

Judge, T.A., Piccolo, R.F., Podsakoff, N.P., Shaw, J.C., and Rich, B.L. (2010). The relationship between pay and job satisfaction: A meta-analysis of the literature. *Journal of Vocational Behavior, 77*, 157–167.

June, A.W. (2011). Faculty experience doesn't always pay. *Chronicle of Higher Education*, April 11.

Kahneman, D., Knetsch, J., and Thaler, R. (1986). Fairness as a constraint on profit-seeking: Entitlements in the market. *American Economic Review, 76*, 728–741.

Kahneman, D., Krueger, A.B., Schkade, D., Schwarz, N., and Stone, A.A. (2006). Would you be happier if you were richer? A focusing illusion. *Science, 312*, 1908–1910.

Kahneman, D. and Thaler, R. (1991). Economic analysis and the psychology of utility: Applications to compensation policy. *American Economic Review, 81,* 341–346.

Kahneman, D. and Tversky, A. (1979). Prospect theory: An analysis of decisions under risk. *Econometrica, 47,* 263–291.

Kepes, S., Delery, J., and Gupta, N. (2009). Contingencies in the effects of pay range on organizational effectiveness. *Personnel Psychology, 62,* 497–531.

Klaas, B. (1999). Containing compensation costs: Why firms differ in their willingness to reduce pay. *Journal of Management, 25,* 829–850.

Kube, S., Maréchal, M.A., and Puppe, C. (2008). The currency of reciprocity—Gift-exchange in the workplace. Working Paper 377, Institute for Empirical Research in Economics, University of Zurich.

Kube, S., Maréchal, M.A., and Puppe, C. (2010). Do wage cuts damage work morale? Evidence from a natural field experiment. Working Paper 471, Institute for Empirical Research in Economics, University of Zurich.

Kuhn, K.M. (2009). Compensation as a signal of organizational culture: The effects of advertising individual or collective incentives. *International Journal of Human Resource Management, 20,* 1630–1644.

Kuhn, K.M. and Yockey, M.D. (2003). Variable pay as a risky choice: Determinants of the relative attractiveness of incentive plans. *Organizational Behavior and Human Decision Processes, 90,* 323–341.

Larkin, I. and Leider, S. (2011). Incentive schemes, sorting, and behavioral biases of employees: Experimental evidence. *American Economic Journal: Microeconomics,* forthcoming.

Lee, C., Law, K.S., and Bobko, P. (1999). The importance of justice perceptions on skill-based pay effectiveness: A two-year study. *Journal of Management, 25,* 851–873.

Loewenstein, G. and Sicherman, N. (1991). Do workers prefer increasing wage profiles? *Journal of Labor Economics, 9,* 67–84.

Luft, J. (1994). Bonus and penalty incentive contract choice by employees. *Journal of Accounting and Economics, 18,* 181–206.

Merriman, K.K. and Deckop, J.R. (2007). Loss aversion and variable pay: A motivational perspective. *International Journal of Human Resource Management, 18,* 1026–1041.

Miller, S. (2011). Largest merit increases since start of financial crisis on tap. *Society for Human Resource Management Online,* February 25.

Mitra, A., Gupta, N., and Jenkins, G.D. (1997) A drop in the bucket: When is a pay raise a pay raise? *Journal of Organizational Behavior, 18,* 117–137.

Ordóñez, L.D., Connolly, T., and Coughlan, R. (2000). Multiple reference points in satisfaction and fairness assessment. *Journal of Behavioral Decision Making, 13,* 329–344.

Paolacci, G., Chandler, J., and Ipeirotis, P.G. (2010). Running experiments on Amazon Mechanical Turk. *Judgment and Decision Making, 5,* 411–419.

Parducci, A. (1965). Category-judgment: A range-frequency theory. *Psychological Review, 72,* 407–418.

Parducci, A. (1995). *Happiness, Pleasure, and Judgment: The Contextual Theory and its Applications.* Mahwah, NJ: Erlbaum.

Pazy, A. and Ganzach, Y. (2009). Pay contingency and the effects of perceived organizational and supervisor support on performance and commitment. *Journal of Management, 35,* 1007–1025.

Pfeffer, J. and Langton, N. (1993). The effect of wage dispersion on satisfaction, productivity, and working collaboratively: Evidence from college and university faculty. *Administrative Science Quarterly, 38,* 382–407.

Prendergast, C. (1999). The provision of incentives in firms. *Journal of Economic Literature, 37,* 7–63.

Rynes, S.L., Gerhart, B., and Minette, K.A. (2004). The importance of pay in employee motivation: Differences between what people say and what they do. *Human Resource Management, 43,* 381–394.

Schaubroeck, J., Shaw, J.D., Duffy, M.K., and Mitra, A. (2008). An under-met and over-met expectations model of employee reactions to merit raises. *Journal of Applied Psychology, 93,* 424–434.

Scott, K.L., Shaw, J.D., and Duffy, M.K. (2008). Merit pay raises and organization-based self-esteem. *Journal of Organizational Behavior, 29,* 967–980.

Shaffer, V.A. and Arkes, H.R. (2009). Preference reversals in evaluations of cash versus non-cash incentives. *Journal of Economic Psychology, 30,* 859–872.

Shafir, E., Diamond, P., and Tversky, A. (1997). Money illusion. *The Quarterly Journal of Economics, 112,* 341–374.

Shaw, J.D., Duffy, M.K., Mitra, A., Lockhart, D.E., and Bowler, M. (2003). Reactions to merit pay increases: A longitudinal test of a signal sensitivity perspective. *Journal of Applied Psychology, 88,* 538–544.

Shaw, J.D. and Gupta, N. (2007). Pay system characteristics and quit patterns of good, average, and poor performers. *Personnel Psychology, 60,* 903–928.

Smith, R.H., Diener, E., and Wedell, D.H. (1989). Intrapersonal and social comparison determinants of happiness: A range-frequency analysis. *Journal of Personality and Social Psychology, 56,* 317–325.

Spolsky, J. (2009). Why I never let employees negotiate a raise. *Inc. Magazine,* April 19.

Tenbrunsel, A.E. and Diekmann, K.A. (2002). Job-decision inconsistencies involving social comparison information: The role of dominating alternatives. *Journal of Applied Psychology, 87,* 1149–1158.

Thaler, R.H. (1990). Saving, fungibility, and mental accounts. *The Journal of Economic Perspectives, 4,* 193–192.

Tversky, A. and Kahneman, D. (1991). Loss aversion and riskless choice: A reference dependent model. *Quarterly Journal of Economics, 106,* 1039–1061.

Williams, M.L. and Dreher, G.F. (1992). Compensation system attributes and applicant pool characteristics. *Academy of Management Journal, 35,* 571–595.

Williams, M.L., Malos, S.B., and Palmer, D.K. (2002). Benefit system and benefit level satisfaction: An expanded model of antecedents and consequences. *Journal of Management, 28,* 195–215.

Wilson, M.G., Northcraft, G.B., and Neale, M.A. (1985). The perceived value of fringe benefits. *Personnel Psychology, 38,* 309–320.

Wiseman, R.M., Gomez-Mejia, L.R., and Fugate, M. (2000). Rethinking compensation risk. In S. Rynes and B. Gerhart (Eds.) *Compensation in Organizations* (pp. 311–347). San Francisco, CA: Jossey-Bass.

10

Combining Information and Judgments

Silvia Bonaccio and Lyn Van Swol

Whether the decision is how much to pay a new executive, or which of several job candidates to hire, it is unlikely to be made by one organizational member alone. In other words, important organizational decisions are typically a collective effort, with different organizational members contributing to varying degrees to the final decision. Hence, organizational decisions rarely occur in a "social vacuum" (Bonaccio & Dalal, 2006). In these cases, it is expected that diverse viewpoints, different information, and even unsolicited advice will be exchanged among organizational members. Combining information to arrive at a final decision is no easy task, and it is not uncommon for decision makers to struggle with this process. This chapter reviews four different research streams speaking to the process of combining information, and bringing together diverse viewpoints into a collective product.

We begin the chapter with a review of the literature on advice giving and taking, and discuss research aimed at reducing decisions makers' tendency to discount advice in favor of their own (pre-advice) opinions. We then turn to research on the common knowledge effect, which is the tendency for information known to all group members to influence the group decision to a greater extent than information known only by individual group members. We review research explaining this pervasive tendency and present ways to mitigate it. In the third section, we focus on social decision schemes, which are rules delineating a group's aggregation strategy to arrive at a group decision. Finally, we discuss research on the Delphi technique, a procedure developed to help organize group discussions to maximize the accuracy of the final decision. The four streams of research reviewed in this chapter all focus on the necessity and difficulty of combining information during the decision-making process.

The research reviewed in this chapter is relevant to two broad types of decisions: choices and judgments (see Billings & Scherer, 1988). Choices take place when decision makers need to select one among several qualitatively different options. For example, a team of selection specialists may debate which of several personality inventories to use in a new staffing cycle, and a manager may have to decide which of his or her direct reports to send to a special training course. On the other hand, judgments occur when decision makers are required to make numerical forecasts or estimates. In this case, the decision is expressed in quantitative rather than qualitative terms. For example, a team of consultants must decide at which price point to sell a new employee engagement survey, and store managers need to forecast the seasonal trends in employee turnover rates so that they can forecast how many new employees to hire.

We note that understanding how decision makers combine information is important inasmuch as it relates to several chapters in this book (for example, the chapters on making performance judgments, employee selection decision making, judgments about goals, judgments about pay), given that these organizational processes often require the combination of various pieces of information to arrive at a final choice or judgment. Consequently, we augment the review of the four above-mentioned research streams with several examples drawn from these and other organizational processes. In doing so, our goal is to encourage readers who are well versed in the organizational literature to see how traditional decision-making concepts can add to our understanding of organizational life.

ADVICE GIVING AND ADVICE TAKING

The research on advice giving and taking has grown out of a realization that both the traditional decision making and small group research areas had failed to capture some important facets of decision making. While the former had omitted the social context of decisions, the latter had not taken into account that groups are often composed of members with different roles and responsibilities vis-à-vis the decision. The research on advice giving and taking, therefore, focuses on decision making at the juncture of these two paradigms, and looks at what happens to the decision-making process and outcomes when individuals responsible for the final decision receive advice along the way.

Since the publication of Brehmer and Hagafors' (1986) article on staff decision making, a number of complementary streams of research on advice giving and taking have emerged: the judge–advisor system (e.g., Dalal & Bonaccio, 2010; Sniezek & Buckley, 1995; Van Swol & Sniezek, 2005), hierarchical team decision making (e.g., Hollenbeck et al., 1998; Humphrey et al., 2002), as well as several other foci (e.g., Budescu & Rantilla, 2000; Gino, 2008; Harvey, Harries, & Fischer, 2000; Kray, 2000; Yaniv, 2004). Given the variety of approaches, it is not surprising that different terminology has emerged. In this chapter we use the term "advisor" to denote the person giving the advice, and "decision maker" for the person receiving it. The research on advice giving and taking applies to both qualitative choices and quantitative judgments made by organizational members. The main findings of the advice giving and taking research are reviewed below. Interested readers are also referred to reviews by Bonaccio and Dalal (2006) and Humphrey et al. (2002).

Effects of Advice

Advice serves several roles in decision making. Typically, it improves decision-making accuracy (e.g., Schrah, Dalal & Sniezek, 2006). Advice also allows the decision maker to share the responsibility of the decision, reinforce or confirm his or her initial opinion, think of the decision in new ways, minimize effort, and perhaps even cope better with the decision by fulfilling the need for emotional or social support (Harvey & Fischer, 1997; Heath & Gonzalez, 1995; Horowitz et al., 2001; MacGeorge, Feng & Thompson, 2008; Schrah, Dalal, & Sniezek, 2006; Yaniv, 2004).

Given the above-mentioned functions of advice, it is surprising that decision makers typically do not follow their "advisors' recommendations nearly as much as they should have (to truly have benefited from them)" (Bonaccio & Dalal, 2006, p. 129)—an effect commonly referred to as egocentric advice discounting (Yaniv & Kleinberger, 2000). Consequently, the dependent variable having attracted most attention has been advice utilization/taking (or conversely, advice discounting). However, a number of advisor and decision-maker characteristics have been found to mitigate advice discounting. We review those below.

Advisor and Decision-maker Characteristics Influencing Advice Taking

Advisors who possess greater expert power (French & Raven, 1959) relative to the decision makers or other advisors are more influential. Indeed, advisor expertise is consistently related to advice utilization, regardless of whether expertise is operationalized in terms of greater decision-making knowledge (Van Swol & Sniezek, 2005), experience (Harvey & Fischer, 1997), training (Hollenbeck et al., 1995), or demonstrated accuracy and reputation (Bonaccio & Dalal, 2010; see also Yaniv & Milyavsky, 2007), or whether advisors are simply older or have greater life experience (Feng & MacGeorge, 2006). Similarly, novice decision makers tend to follow advice to a greater extent than their more knowledgeable counterparts do (Yaniv, 2004).

Advisors' intentions have also been shown to influence decision makers. Indeed, decision makers discount advice to a greater extent when they are suspicious of their advisors' motives or perceive the advisor to have self-interested intentions (Bonaccio & Dalal, 2010; Jodlbauer & Jonas, 2011; Van Swol, 2009a). Hence, when agency problems exist (Eisenhardt, 1989), advisors are less influential than when the decision makers' and advisors' goals are perceived to be aligned. Taken together, the ascription of good intentions to advisors and the perceived expertise (or ability) of advisors form the basis of trust (see Cook & Wall, 1980), which has been shown to be an important determinant of advice taking (Bonaccio & Dalal, 2010; Sniezek & Van Swol, 2001; Van Swol, 2011). Finally, confidence has also been linked to advice taking: confident decision makers seek out advice less frequently than less confident ones do (Cooper, 1991), and more confident advisors are more influential than less confident ones are (Phillips, 1999; Sniezek & Van Swol, 2001; Van Swol, 2009a).

Situational and Task Characteristics Influencing Advice Taking

In addition to the characteristics of the advisor and decision maker reviewed above, several additional characteristics influence decision makers' reactions to, and use of, advice. First, the advice itself matters. Dalal and Bonaccio (2010) found that advice formulated as information about decision alternatives was often better received than other forms of advice, such as an explicit recommendation to follow a particular course of action (the typical operationalization of advice), a recommendation about which alternative *not* to choose, or a recommendation about *how* to make the decision, as well as another form of interpersonal assistance, namely social support. However, when advice was explicitly solicited, or when it came from a subject matter expert, decision makers preferred an explicit recommendation *as well as* information.

Decision makers' reactions to advice also depend on the type of task at hand (see Bonaccio & Dalal, 2006 for a review of the types of tasks used in advice research). Advice utilization is greatest for difficult (versus simpler) tasks (Gino & Moore, 2007; Schrah, Dalal, & Sniezek, 2006). Moreover, Gino, Shang, and Croson (2009) found that, when a task required decision makers to judge others' behavior, decision makers used advice more heavily if it came from advisors who differed from the decision makers on key demographic variables than if it came from advisors who were similar to the decision makers, likely because demographically different advisors are perceived to provide more informative advice for this type of task (the opposite results were found for tasks requiring participants to judge their own behavior). Similarly, Van Swol (2011) found that, for judgmental tasks but not for intellective tasks (i.e., decisions for which there is not and there is a demonstrably correct answer, respectively), decision makers preferred advice from advisors whom they perceived to share their values, which in turn influenced the level of trust in the advisor. Hence, the degree to which the decision maker perceives the advisor to be (dis)similar from him or her will influence advice taking and associated outcomes, but whether dissimilarity leads to less or more advice taking depends on the type of decision being made. Finally, it is unsurprising that advice taking is improved when decision makers have purchased the advice (Gino, 2008; see also Sniezek, Schrah, & Dalal, 2004).

Implications of Advice Research for Organizations

There are many organizational domains in which advice is offered; yet, the findings reviewed above show how easy it is for advice to be discounted. Arguably, giving advice, especially when unsolicited, can be a threat to the decision maker. Indeed, decision makers often seek to balance the desire to be more accurate in their decisions with the desire to be autonomous (Dalal & Bonaccio, 2010). From a communication perspective:

> advice may threaten the recipient's positive face (the desire to be liked and included) if the message is given in a condescending or blaming manner and threaten the recipient's negative face (the desire for autonomy) if it is viewed as bossy.
>
> (Feng & MacGeorge, 2010, p. 554)

Similarly, Deelstra et al. (2003) found that unsolicited help in work contexts can be seen as inappropriate, especially when the employee considers that he or she does not require help. In addition, the colleague providing the imposed help risks being perceived unsympathetically: impatient, unpleasant to work with, and so on. Giving advice is therefore a complex and risky endeavor.

However, the research reviewed above gives some insights into when and why organizational advisors may be influential. For example, mentors might be more influential in coaching a protégé on a project that would help him or her develop new skills when the mentors emphasize both their expertise in the project domain and their good intentions vis-à-vis the protégé, thereby highlighting their trustworthiness. They may also be more influential if they appear confident to the protégé. Moreover, employees might be more likely to incorporate their supervisors' goal-setting suggestions on challenging or complex tasks. Hence, employees might be irritated by help received on routine and simple tasks (see Deelstra et al., 2003) but might appreciate input on riskier and high-profile assignments. Furthermore, employee voice may be construed as a form of advice, and whether voice has or has not been solicited, and how it is formulated (e.g., as information or as a recommendation) may influence how much weight it is given by supervisors. Advice giving and taking research might also be of interest to team/group researchers, such as those studying team mental models. Indeed, the research on advisor (dis)similarity may give insights into how team members select which colleague to consult and whether a colleague's expertise is judged to be relevant for a particular task. Finally, supervisors and leaders may also be the ones soliciting advice from their direct reports. As specified in Vroom and Yetton's (1973) normative leadership model, leaders may often fare better if they seek their subordinates' advice and input prior to making a final decision.

Whereas the advice literature has examined how decision makers incorporate others' opinions in their individual decisions, the research on the common knowledge effect, reviewed below, examines how groups discuss and incorporate information held by their members in group-level decisions.

COMMON KNOWLEDGE EFFECT

Research on the common knowledge effect has examined how group members' discussion of information impacts the group decision. The implications of the common knowledge effect have predominantly been studied with qualitative choice, but are important for both qualitative choices and quantitative judgments made by organizational members. This stream of research has found that group discussions tend to focus on shared information rather than unshared information (for reviews, see Brodbeck et al., 2007; Stasser & Titus, 2003; Wittenbaum, Hollingshead, & Botero, 2004). Shared information is information that group members know and share in common before the group discussion, and unshared information is information that is known only to one group member and only becomes known to others when mentioned during group discussion. For example, if a manager and his or her two assistant managers are discussing job applicants, some of the information (e.g., from applicants' résumés) may be shared among them, whereas other information (e.g., a lunch interview the manager had with a candidate) is unshared and only known to one group member.

Why Shared Information is More Influential

Shared information is more influential in the group for several reasons. First, by definition more members have access to shared information, so it gets mentioned more in discussion (Stasser & Titus, 1985). Second, shared information influences all group members' pre-discussion opinions, so it gets mentioned more as members provide justifications for their individual judgments. So, if all group members reviewed a job candidate's résumé, but only some of them examined the references or had an interview, then the résumé will have influenced everyone's preferences and is likely to become the focus of attention. Further, when unshared information is mentioned, group members discount it because they did not take it into account when forming their own initial opinion (Greitemeyer & Schulz-Hardt, 2003). Thus, even when both unshared and shared information are mentioned, shared information is generally more likely to be repeated and more likely to influence the group decision.

The increased focus on shared information is due to biased processing of unshared information that may be inconsistent with initial preferences. It may also be due to what Wittenbaum, Hubbell, and Zuckerman (1999) term mutual enhancement. When a group member mentions a piece of shared information, other members recognize that information and can validate it against their own knowledge, and other members often feel validated that someone mentions information that they know. Therefore, members often respond positively to shared information being mentioned and may nod or affirm the information. In this way, shared information is mutually enhancing. This brings attention to shared information and often leads to members repeating it.

Mutual enhancement highlights some benefits of shared information that professionals using groups for decision making should be aware of, and it helps explain why people gravitate towards shared information. By discovering their shared information, group members are able to develop a common ground. Due to mutual enhancement, focusing on shared information may increase group members' perception of each other's knowledge and competence. Further, the common ground and mutual enhancement established through exchanging shared information may contribute to stronger group cohesion (Wittenbaum, Hubbell, & Zuckerman, 1999). However, the focus on shared information during group discussion also reduces the group's ability to make a fully informed decision and take advantage of member diversity—the group may miss a key piece of information held uniquely by one member. Discussing predominantly shared information reduces the impact of information on the group decision because shared information has already influenced members' pre-discussion opinion, and members are not learning anything new during the discussion.

Thus, information that an individual knows and mentions during the group discussion often has much less weight in the group decision than an individual's opinion due to these biases in the discussion of information. In fact, Gigone and Hastie (1997) found that "information pooled during discussion had almost no effect on the group judgments. It was as if the group members exchanged and combined their opinions, but paid little attention to anything else" (p. 132). According to the common knowledge effect, the more shared a piece of information is before discussion, the greater impact this information will have on the group decision. However, this impact is mediated by members' pre-discussion opinions (Gigone & Hastie, 1993, 1997). Accordingly, there are two reasons that group members' discussion of information is often not influential. One is the group's focus on shared information, and the second is that groups may focus on initial opinions at the expense of information when there is a strong majority at the outset of discussion (Aramovich & Larson, 2010; Gigone & Hastie, 1993, 1997; Nijstad, 2008).

Implications of Common Knowledge Effect Research for Organizations

Discussion of unshared information can improve the quality of a group decision (Winquist & Larson, 1998), and researchers have explored ways to increase its discussion. We discuss this research and applications for professionals using groups in the workplace for decision making. First, the extent to which unshared information is pooled and affects the group decision is influenced by the uniformity of pre-group preferences. When more dissent exists and members do not have a strong majority favoring one option, there is more discussion of information and importance placed on information, rather than opinions (Parks & Nelson, 1999; Winquist & Larson, 1998). This highlights the need for professionals to compose groups with moderate to high levels of informational and opinion diversity. Informational diversity will help reduce opinions formed on the basis of the same information, and opinion diversity will increase the focus on information during discussion, as members offer facts and reasons behind their differences of opinion. In general, diversity increases information exchange. As with social decision schemes (discussed in the next section), knowing the pre-discussion composition of group opinions is extremely useful toward understanding how the group is likely to come to consensus and rely on information.

Further, researchers have emphasized how the roles that group members take on can help increase the focus on unshared information. First, research by Larson and colleagues (Larson et al., 1998; Larson, Foster-Fishman, & Franz, 1998) has found that leaders can help recognize unique information and increase the group's focus on unique information, especially when more directive leaders take an active role in managing information for the group. Other research has found that, if unique information comes from an advisor, the group may focus on it more. People expect new information and unique viewpoints from advisors, and this may make group members put in the role of advisor more comfortable discussing their unique information (Savadori, Van Swol, & Sniezek, 2001; Van Swol, 2009b). Similarly, if unshared information is introduced by an acknowledged expert in the subject area, then the group is more accepting of the unshared information (Stasser, Stewart, & Wittenbaum, 1995). Therefore, during a group discussion, members' expertise and advisor status should be made salient to other group members to increase acceptance of their unique information.

In conclusion, the role of group discussion of information in group consensus can be negligible, especially when there is a high proportion of shared information influencing pre-discussion opinions and a lack of dissent in pre-discussion opinions. Practitioners using groups should strive to use members who have both diverse information and diverse opinions. Further, leaders need to actively pool unique information in order to help overcome shared information biases. This strategy could be especially useful in contexts such as assessment centers, where the raters do not always have the possibility to observe and evaluate all candidates throughout all assessment activities. Hence, the raters might have the tendency to discuss information drawn from activities that they have all observed to the detriment of unshared information.

We now turn to research focusing on social decision schemes, which examines how individuals' diverse opinions are pooled into a collective, group-level decision.

SOCIAL DECISION SCHEMES

When trying to understand how diverse individual judgments are combined into a collective group product, social decision schemes offer a mathematical model that quantifies the relationship between individual group members' pre-discussion opinions about a discrete number of qualitative choice alternatives (i.e., yes/no; guilty/not guilty; correct/incorrect) and the decision adopted by the group (Davis, 1973, 1982). A social decision scheme (SDS) is a rule that corresponds to the process by which the group aggregates individual inputs into the group product. For example, a *majority wins* SDS states that the group will adopt the pre-discussion alternative chosen by the majority of individual group members. By knowing the initial distribution of individual judgments before the discussion and the decision reached by the group, one can determine the best-fitting SDS, and this SDS then helps understand the process used by the group to reach consensus. Although SDSs do not provide the same information as directly observing the group discussion, with an SDS one can study some group processes indirectly without the labor-intensive costs of recording, transcribing, and coding group discussion.

Types of SDS

Research has identified many different types of SDS (Davis, 1982). Table 10.1 illustrates four SDSs for a decision with a correct answer and provides the proportion of groups that will have the correct decision given that the group followed the SDSs provided as examples. In an *equiprobability* SDS, each alternative advocated by group members is equally probable to be adopted as the group choice. With *truth-wins*, the group will adopt the

TABLE 10.1

Examples of Social Decision Schemes (SDSs)

Group Distribution		Proportion of Correct Groups Predicted by SDS			
Correct	Incorrect	Truth-wins	Truth-supported Wins	Equiprobability	Majority
5	0	1.00	1.00	1.00	1.00
4	1	1.00	1.00	0.50	1.00
3	2	1.00	1.00	0.50	1.00
2	3	1.00	1.00	0.50	0.00
1	4	1.00	0.00	0.50	0.00
0	5	0.00	0.00	0.00	0.00

correct answer if it is advocated by at least one group member, and with *truth-supported wins* the group adopts the correct answer if it is advocated by at least two members. Each SDS has underlying process assumptions. For example, with *truth-wins*, it is assumed that the correct member was able to demonstrate the correct answer to the other members (Laughlin & Ellis, 1986).

Research on SDSs has helped understand the role of task type in group decision making. Specifically, the number of members who must support an alternative before it is adopted by the group differs by task type (Laughlin & Ellis, 1986). Some tasks, called intellective tasks, have a correct answer that one member may be able to demonstrate to other group members within a verbal or mathematical conceptual system, such as a math problem or engineers resolving a computer-coding problem. On intellective tasks, often one or two correct group members, even if in the minority opinion, can convince the group to adopt their choice by demonstrating its correctness. With a demonstrably correct answer, the group is predicted to use a *truth-wins* or *truth-supported wins* SDS. Other tasks, judgmental tasks, do not have a demonstrably correct answer and are based on preferences and values, such as deciding on an office dress code or deciding whether to institute more flexible scheduling for employees. On these types of tasks, the group usually picks the decision supported by the majority of group members. Other tasks fall between intellective and judgmental tasks in demonstrability. For example, memory recognition tasks and general knowledge questions are less demonstrable than math tasks but are not a matter of opinion and have a correct answer. Groups tend to follow a *truth-supported wins* SDS for these tasks (Laughlin &

Adamopoulos, 1980; Van Swol, 2008). Even when groups are assigned an explicit decision rule (e.g., unanimity for juries), the group's decision can be predicted by an implicit SDS. For example, studies with mock juries have found that juries typically follow a *two-thirds majority* (although sometimes *simple majority*) SDS for reaching conviction or acquittal (Davis, 1980).

Implications of SDS Research for Organizations

Research on SDSs has important implications for professionals using groups to make decisions. First, the research highlights the importance of knowing the pre-discussion preferences of group members and paying attention to group composition, especially in conjunction with the type of task and demonstrability of the decision. By knowing the two elements of task and group composition, one has an idea of what type of decision the group is likely to reach. Further, if consensus or voting rules are assigned by a chair leading a meeting, the rules should match the type of task. For decisions involving values and tastes, asking the group to vote by majority is a good match for the task (Laughlin & Ellis, 1986). However, for tasks that involve facts, proof, and evidence, a majority vote is a poor match because it may prevent a correct minority from influencing the group. For tasks involving facts, proof, and evidence, one would want to ensure that each group member can present their individual opinion, so that a correct minority could demonstrate the correctness of their opinion.

Thus far, this chapter has reviewed research focusing on how individuals and group members integrate various pieces of advice, information, and group members' opinions into individual-level and group-level choices and judgments. A common thread through the preceding sections is that decision accuracy can often be influenced by dyadic and group-level decision processes. Therefore, the next section focuses on a specific decision-making technique that was developed with an eye toward improving decision-making accuracy.

THE DELPHI TECHNIQUE

The Delphi technique was developed at the RAND Corporation in the 1950s to improve forecasting accuracy (Rowe & Wright, 1999). Since its first use by the U.S. Air Force, it has been applied to a variety of subjects, such as managerial decisions, healthcare, counseling, real estate, and education to name only a few (Gupta & Clarke, 1996). Delphi "involves anonymous forecasts made on two or more rounds by a group of independent hetero-geneous experts who receive feedback between rounds" (Armstrong, 1999, p. 351). Delphi groups differ from other group-based decision models, such as the nominal group technique (given Delphi's lack of face-to-face interaction) or statisticized groups (given the presence of multiple iterations in Delphi).

Goals of the Delphi Technique and Operationalizations

The driving force for the development of Delphi was to optimize human forecasting by building on the strengths of group-based interactions and minimizing its weaknesses (Rowe & Wright, 1999, 2001; see also Keeney, Hasson & McKenna, 2001; Parenté & Anderson-Parenté, 1987 for reviews). Delphi strives to (a) structure and organize group discussion and forecasts, (b) increase the accuracy of forecasts and decision making, and (c) reduce social and political pressures typically found in traditional groups.

In a classic Delphi, panel members are asked to respond to a series of questionnaires presented across several iterations. The use of questionnaires allows panel members to remain anonymous, which in turn allows freedom from the typical social pressures and process-loss found in group discussions (groupthink, social loafing, domination, and so on). After each iteration, participants receive feedback, in the form of the statistical average of group members' responses and some accompanying explanations from panel members (usually from the outliers; Martino, 1983). After several iterations during which participants revise their forecasts (typically three iterations are sufficient; Rowe & Wright, 2001), participants' estimates on the final iteration of the questionnaire are statistically aggregated. The conditions of anonymity, questionnaire iteration, controlled feedback, and statistical aggregation of responses are four necessary features of Delphi (Keeney, Hasson & McKenna, 2001; Rowe & Wright, 1999, 2001).

Traditionally, a Delphi study begins with an unstructured first iteration to generate discussion topics for the subsequent questionnaires (Martino, 1983). However, many Delphis (especially in laboratory settings; Rowe & Wright, 1999), begin with a structured first round to simplify the procedure and make it less time-consuming (Keeney, Hasson & McKenna, 2001). A second variation concerns the number of participants; although the number of participants involved can theoretically be infinite, practically speaking Rowe and Wright (2001) recommend using from five to twenty experts with a different knowledge base. In addition, the classic Delphi method suggests that qualitative feedback should only be solicited from outliers; however, soliciting it from all participants is beneficial (Rowe & Wright, 1996). Finally, whereas the Delphi method has traditionally been used to generate quantitative judgments or forecasts, one can use Delphi to generate qualitative information, such as identifying the most critical issues an industry is likely to face in the future (see, e.g., Brancheau & Wetherbe, 1987).

The operationalization of Delphi has often been criticized, most notably when laboratory settings are employed. First, much research has been conducted with non-expert (naive) panel members—often students—working on trivial tasks. Given that Delphi was designed for experts working on real forecasts, generalizability concerns have been noted (Rowe & Wright, 1999). Even when expert panel members are used, the sampling process (Keeney, Hasson & McKenna, 2001) and how expertise is defined are important considerations (Rowe & Wright, 2001). Indeed, given the time-consuming nature of a typical Delphi study, it may be that individuals who agree to participate—and remain—in the study are those who give more importance to the topic at hand, or who are more confident in their opinions (Franklin & Hart, 2007). Delphi presents a number of additional potential issues such as the possibilities of low response rates and attrition, false consensus, and unreliable/invalid findings due to poorly developed questionnaires (Keeney, Hasson & McKenna, 2001; Rowe & Wright, 2001).

Outcomes of Delphi

An impetus for using a Delphi model is decision accuracy. Although the evidence is mixed, Delphi groups tend to produce more accurate estimates than statisticized groups and traditional (interacting) groups do (the results are even more equivocal for nominal groups; Rowe & Wright, 1999). The gains in accuracy, it seems, are due to the tendency of less expert panel members to adjust their responses to converge, over the rounds, toward those of more expert (and more accurate) members (Rowe & Wright, 1996). Expecting additional rounds of questionnaires may also entice Delphi participants to "consider the problem more deeply" (Rowe & Wright, 2001, p. 136). However, these conclusions have been tempered by the fact that many so-called "technique comparison studies" have been poorly designed and executed, at best resulting in a lack of understanding of the process driving the differences between the techniques, and at worst lacking internal validity (Rowe & Wright, 1999).

Delphi also helps achieve consensus among panel members; indeed, the final round often shows convergence of opinions. However, some have questioned whether pressures for conformity were driving consensus (rather than true agreement), whether consensus is "forced" via the multiple iterations, or whether it is due to greater attrition from panel members who do not agree with the group's average (Keeney, Hasson, & McKenna, 2001; Rowe & Wright, 1999). Importantly, the goal of the technique itself need not be consensus—Delphi may be used simply for eliciting alternative positions on a topic and evaluating the merits and demerits of these alternatives (Franklin & Hart, 2007).

Implications of Delphi for Organizational Decisions

The application of Delphi could be of interest to organizational scholars and practitioners (see Rowe & Wright, 2001 for implementation guidance). Indeed, this approach to group discussion could benefit areas as diverse as salary determination, forecasting staffing needs, or product and service pricing. As another example, one could use a Delphi technique in the context of job analysis. Here, several subject matter experts would be required to provide estimates of the frequency and the importance of tasks in the job being analyzed and Delphi rounds would continue until a consensus was reached. However, industrial and organizational psychology can also contribute substantially to the study of Delphi. In particular, process-oriented research, which is much needed in this area, will necessitate an understanding of individual-level as well as group-level changes across questionnaire iterations (Rowe & Wright, 1996), and our fields' theoretical and statistical understanding of cross-level issues could be of assistance.

CONCLUSION

This chapter reviewed four research streams focusing on social aspects of decision making: the giving and taking of advice, the common knowledge effect, social decision schemes, and the Delphi technique. Although each stream makes unique contributions to decision-making research and practice, there are several common themes or findings worth highlighting. First, it is clear that initial opinions or information are often dispropor- tionally weighed in final decisions. The tendencies for decision makers to dismiss unshared information or to egocentrically discount advice are but two examples of this decision-making bias. Researchers interested in studying final (post-group discussion) decisions might therefore want to incorporate a measure of pre-discussion opinions in their research. Likewise, managers and other organizational decision makers should be aware of the general decision-making bias that anchors individuals to their initial opinions.

Second, these four research streams highlight the importance of information diversity in increasing decision accuracy. For example, the Delphi technique is particularly useful when panel members possess a different knowledge base. Similarly, it is by overcoming the tendency to discuss shared information that groups will be enabled to make more accurate and better informed decisions. That the common knowledge effect is weakened under conditions of discrepancy of information and diverse opinions between group members speaks to the importance of deep-level diversity in organizational groups. Organizational decision makers will be judicious to encourage group members to share different or additional information, and to establish an organizational culture that supports voicing concerns or disagreements. The appointment of a devil's advocate as a palliative to groupthink (Janis, 1982) is one such approach.

Third, the research streams reviewed in this chapter converge on the importance of expertise in influencing decision makers' final decisions. Hence, organizations making use of differentiated groups (e.g., cross-functional work teams, group members with varying responsibilities vis-à-vis the final decision, groups where members have access to different information) would do well to attend to the influence of expertise on decisions. For example, groups can structure their discussions such that the expert in the decision domain shares his or her opinion last so as not to unduly sway the groups' decision toward his or her own opinion.

Fourth, these streams of research emphasize, explicitly or implicitly, the importance of attending to decision makers' individual differences (e.g., their confidence, expertise, preferred decision-making strategies) as well as to the type of task at hand (e.g., intellective, judgmental). Hence, both the task and the participants are important considerations—as noted in the context of Delphi, "forecasts are the joint product of the task and the forecaster" (Ayton, Ferrell & Stewart, 1999, p. 381). At the same time, this common thread between the areas reminds us of the importance of conducting process-oriented research. It must not be forgotten that decision making is both a process that unfolds over time and an outcome. Hence, we call for future research to continue the exploration of mediating variables.

In reviewing the research on advice giving, the common knowledge effect, social decision schemes and the Delphi technique, we have tried to pay close attention to how these topics are relevant to common organizational processes. We have enumerated several areas of cross-fertilization in the preceding sections which will hopefully generate additional industrial and organizational psychology research strongly rooted in a decision-making framework.

REFERENCES

Aramovich, N.P. and Larson, J.R. Jr. (2010). Truth can win in many ways: A critique of "truth wins" and other social combination models as a basis for drawing inferences about group process. Paper presented at the 5th annual conference of the *Interdisciplinary Network for Group Research (INGroup)*, Washington, DC.

Armstrong, J.S. (1999). Introduction to paper and commentaries on the Delphi technique. *International Journal of Forecasting, 15*, 351–352.

Ayton, P., Ferrell, W.R., and Stewart, T.R. (1999) Commentaries on "The Delphi technique as a forecasting tool: Issues and analysis" by Rowe and Wright. *International Journal of Forecasting, 15*, 377–381.

Billings, R.S. and Scherer, L.L. (1988). The effects of response mode and importance on decision-making strategies: Judgment versus choice. *Organizational Behavior and Human Decision Processes, 41*, 1–19.

Bonaccio, S. and Dalal, R.S. (2006). Advice taking and decision-making: An integrative literature review, and implications for the organizational sciences. *Organizational Behavior and Human Decision Processes, 101*, 127–151.

Bonaccio, S. and Dalal, R.S. (2010). Evaluating advisors: A policy-capturing study under conditions of complete and missing information. *Journal of Behavioral Decision Making, 23*, 227–249.

Brancheau, J.C. and Wetherbe, J.C. (1987). Key issues in information systems management. *MIS Quarterly, 11*, 23–45.

Brehmer, B. and Hagafors, R. (1986). The use of experts in complex decision-making: A paradigm for the study of staff work. *Organizational Behavior and Human Decision Processes, 38*, 181–195.

Brodbeck, F.C., Kerschreiter, R., Mojzisch, A., and Schulz-Hardt, S. (2007). Group decision-making under conditions of distributed knowledge: The information asymmetries model. *Academy of Management Review, 32*, 459–479.

Budescu, D.V. and Rantilla, A.K. (2000). Confidence in aggregation of expert opinions. *Acta Psychologica, 104*, 371–398.

Cook, J. and Wall, T. (1980). New work attitude measures of trust, organizational commitment and personal need non-fulfillment. *Journal of Occupational Psychology, 53*, 39–52.

Cooper, R.S. (1991). Information processing in the judge–adviser system of group decision-making. Unpublished master's thesis, University of Illinois, Urbana-Champaign.

Dalal, R.S. and Bonaccio, S. (2010). What types of advice do decision-makers prefer? *Organizational Behavior and Human Decision Processes, 112*, 11–23.

Davis, J.H. (1973). Group decision and social interaction: A theory of social decision schemes. *Psychological Review, 80*, 97–125.

Davis, J.H. (1980). Group decision and procedural justice. In M. Fishbein (Ed.) *Progress in Social Psychology* (vol. 1, pp. 157–229). Hillsdale, NJ: Erlbaum.

Davis, J.H. (1982). Social interaction as a combinatorial process in group decision. In H. Brandstatter, J. Davis, and G. Stocker-Kreichgauer (Eds.) *Group Decision Making* (pp. 27–58). London: Academic Press.

Deelstra, J.T., Peeters, M.C.W., Schaufeli, W.B., Stroebe, W., Zijlstra, F.R.H., and van Doornen, L.P. (2003). Receiving instrumental support at work: When help is not welcome. *Journal of Applied Psychology, 88*, 324–331.

Eisenhardt, K.M. (1989). Agency theory: An assessment and review. *Academy of Management Review, 14*, 54–74.

Feng, B. and MacGeorge, E.L. (2006). Predicting receptiveness to advice: Characteristics of the problem, the advice-giver, and the recipient. *Southern Journal of Communication, 71*, 67–85.

Feng, B. and MacGeorge, E.L. (2010). The influences of message and source factors on advice outcomes. *Communication Research, 37*, 553–575.

Franklin, K.K. and Hart, J.K. (2007). Idea generation and exploration: Benefits and limitations of the policy Delphi research method. *Innovation in Higher Education, 31*, 237–246.

French, J.R. and Raven, B.H. (1959). The bases of social power. In D. Cartwright (Ed.) *Studies of Social Power* (pp. 150–167). Ann Arbor, MI: Institute for Social Research, University of Michigan.

Gigone, D. and Hastie, R. (1993). The common knowledge effect: Information sharing and group judgment. *Journal of Personality and Social Psychology, 65*, 959–974.

Gigone, D. and Hastie, R. (1997). The impact of information on small group choice. *Journal of Personality and Social Psychology, 72*, 132–140.

Gino, F. (2008). Do we listen to advice just because we paid for it? The impact of advice cost on its use. *Organizational Behavior and Human Decision Processes, 107*, 234–245.

Gino, F. and Moore, D.A. (2007). Effects of task difficulty on use of advice. *Journal of Behavioral Decision Making, 20*, 21–35.

Gino, F., Shang, J., and Croson, R.C. (2009). The impact of information from similar or different advisors on judgment. *Organizational Behavior and Human Decision Processes, 108*, 287–302.

Greitemeyer, T. and Schulz-Hardt, S. (2003). Preference-consistent evaluation of information in the hidden profile paradigm: Beyond group-level explanations for the dominance of shared information in group decisions. *Journal of Personality and Social Psychology, 84*, 322–339.

Gupta, U.G. and Clarke, R.E. (1996). Theory and applications of the Delphi technique: A bibliography (1975–1994). *Technological Forecasting and Social Change, 53*, 185–211.

Harvey, N. and Fischer, I. (1997). Taking advice: Accepting help, improving judgment, and sharing responsibility. *Organizational Behavior and Human Decision Processes, 70*, 117–133.

Harvey, N., Harries, C., and Fischer, I. (2000). Using advice and assessing its quality. *Organizational Behavior and Human Decision Processes, 81*, 252–273.

Heath, C. and Gonzalez, R. (1995). Interaction with others increases decision confidence but not decision quality: Evidence against information collection views of interactive decision-making. *Organizational Behavior and Human Decision Processes, 61*, 305–326.

Hollenbeck, J.R., Ilgen, D.R., LePine, J.A., Colquitt, J.A., and Hedlund, J. (1998). Extending the multilevel theory of team decision making: Effects of feedback and experience in hierarchical teams. *Academy of Management Journal, 41,* 269–282.

Hollenbeck, J.R., Ilgen, D.R., Sego, D.J., Hedlund, J., Major, D.A., and Phillips, J. (1995). Multilevel theory of team decision making: Decision performance in teams incorporating distributed expertise. *Journal of Applied Psychology, 80,* 292–316.

Horowitz, L.M., Krasnoperova, E.N., Tatar, D.G., Hansen, M.B., Person, E.A., Galvin, K.L., and Nelson, K.L. (2001). The way to console may depend on the goal: Experimental studies of social support. *Journal of Experimental Social Psychology, 37,* 49–61.

Humphrey, S.E., Hollenbeck, J.R., Meyer, C.J., and Ilgen, D.R. (2002). Hierarchical team decision making. In G.R. Ferris and J.J. Martocchio (Eds.) *Research in Personnel and Human Resources Management* (vol. 21, pp. 175–213). Stamford, CT: JAI Press.

Janis, I.L. (1982). *Groupthink: A Psychological Study of Policy Decisions and Fiascoes.* Boston, MA: Houghton Mifflin.

Jodlbauer, B. and Jonas, E. (2011). Forecasting clients' reactions: How does the perception of strategic behavior influence the acceptance of advice? *International Journal of Forecasting, 27,* 121–133.

Keeney, S., Hasson, F., and McKenna, H.P. (2001). A critical review of the Delphi technique as a research methodology for nursing. *International Journal of Nursing Studies, 38,* 195–200.

Kray, L.J. (2000). Contingent weighting in self-other decision making. *Organizational Behavior and Human Decision Processes, 83,* 82–106.

Larson, J.R. Jr., Christensen, C., Abbott, A.S., and Franz, T.M. (1998). Diagnosing groups: The pooling, management, and impact of shared and unshared case information in team-based medical decision-making. *Journal of Personality and Social Psychology, 75,* 93–108.

Larson, J.R., Foster-Fishman, P.G, and Franz, T.M. (1998). Leadership style and the discussion of shared and unshared information in decision-making groups. *Personality & Social Psychology Bulletin, 24,* 482–495.

Laughlin, P.R. and Adamopoulos, J. (1980). Social combination processes and individual learning for six-person cooperative groups on an intellective task. *Journal of Personality and Social Psychology, 38,* 941–947.

Laughlin, P.R. and Ellis, A.L. (1986). Demonstrability and social combination processes on mathematical intellective tasks. *Journal of Experimental Social Psychology, 22,* 177–189.

MacGeorge, E.L., Feng, B., and Thompson, E.R. (2008). "Good" and "bad" advice: How to advise more effectively. In M. Motley (Ed.) *Applied Interpersonal Communication: Behaviors that Affect Outcomes* (pp. 145–164). Thousand Oaks, CA: Sage.

Martino, J.P. (1983). *Technological Forecasting for Decision Making* (2nd ed.). New York: Elsevier.

Nijstad, B.A. (2008). Choosing none of the above: Persistence of negativity after group discussion and group decision refusal. *Group Processes and Intergroup Relations, 11,* 525–538.

Parenté, F.J. and Anderson-Parenté, J.K. (1987). Delphi inquiry systems. In G. Wright and P. Ayton (Eds.) *Judgmental Forecasting.* Chichester: Wiley.

Parks, C.D. and Nelson, N.L. (1999). Discussion and decision: The interrelationship between initial preference distribution and group discussion content. *Organizational Behavior and Human Decision Processes, 80,* 87–101.

Phillips, J.M. (1999). Antecedents of leader utilization of staff input in decision-making teams. *Organizational Behavior and Human Decision Processes, 77*, 215–242.

Rowe, G. and Wright, G. (1996). The impact of task characteristics on the performance of structured group forecasting techniques. *International Journal of Forecasting, 12*, 73–89.

Rowe, G. and Wright, G. (1999). The Delphi technique as a forecasting tool: Issues and analysis. *International Journal of Forecasting, 15*, 353–375.

Rowe, G. and Wright, G. (2001). Expert opinions in forecasting: The role of the Delphi technique. In J. Armstrong (Ed.) *Principles of Forecasting* (pp. 125–144). Boston: Kluwer Academic.

Savadori, L., Van Swol, L.M., and Sniezek, J.A. (2001). Information sampling and confidence within groups and judge advisor systems. *Communication Research, 28*(6), 737–771.

Schrah, G.E., Dalal, R.S., and Sniezek, J.A. (2006). No decision-maker is an island: Integrating expert advice with information search. *Journal of Behavioral Decision-Making, 19*, 43–60.

Sniezek, J.A. and Buckley, T. (1995). Cueing and cognitive conflict in judge–advisor decision making. *Organizational Behavior and Human Decision Processes, 62*, 159–174.

Sniezek, J.A., Schrah, G.E., and Dalal, R.S. (2004). Improving judgment with prepaid expert advice. *Journal of Behavioral Decision Making, 17*, 173–190.

Sniezek, J.A. and Van Swol, L.M. (2001). Trust, confidence, and expertise in a judge–advisor system. *Organizational Behavior and Human Decision Processes, 84*, 288–307.

Stasser, G., Stewart, D.D., and Wittenbaum, G.M. (1995) Expert roles and information exchange during discussion: The importance of knowing who knows what. *Journal of Experimental Social Psychology, 31*, 244–265.

Stasser, G. and Titus, W. (1985). Pooling of unshared information in group decision making: Biased information sampling during discussion. *Journal of Personality and Social Psychology, 48*, 1467–1478.

Stasser, G. and Titus, W. (2003). Hidden profiles: A brief history. *Psychological Inquiry, 14*, 304–313.

Van Swol, L.M. (2008). Performance and process in collective and individual memory: The role of social decision schemes and memory bias in collective memory. *Memory, 16*, 274–287.

Van Swol, L.M. (2009a) The effects of advisor motives on confidence and advice utilization. *Communication Research, 36*, 857–873.

Van Swol, L.M. (2009b). Discussion and perception of information in groups and judge advisor systems. *Communication Monographs, 76*, 99–120.

Van Swol, L.M. (2011). Forecasting another's enjoyment versus giving the right answer: Trust, shared values, task effects, and confidence in improving the acceptance of advice. *International Journal of Forecasting, 27*, 103–120.

Van Swol, L.M. and Sniezek, J.A. (2005). Factors affecting the acceptance of expert advice. *British Journal of Social Psychology, 44*, 443–461.

Vroom, V.H. and Yetton, P.W. (1973). *Leadership and Decision Making*. Pittsburgh, PA: University of Pittsburgh Press.

Winquist, J.R. and Larson, J.R. Jr. (1998). Information pooling: When it impacts group decision making. *Journal of Personality and Social Psychology, 74*, 371–377.

Wittenbaum, G.M., Hollingshead, A.B., and Botero, I.C. (2004). From cooperative to motivated information sharing in groups: Moving beyond the hidden profile paradigm. *Communication Monographs, 71*, 286–310.

Wittenbaum, G.M., Hubbell, A.P., and Zuckerman, C. (1999). Mutual enhancement: Toward an understanding of the collective preference for shared information. *Journal of Personality and Social Psychology, 77*, 967–978.

Yaniv, I. (2004). Receiving other people's advice: Influence and benefit. *Organizational Behavior and Human Decision Processes, 93*, 1–13.

Yaniv, I. and Kleinberger, E. (2000). Advice taking in decision making: Egocentric discounting and reputation formation. *Organizational Behavior and Human Decision Processes, 83*, 260–281.

Yaniv, I. and Milyavsky, M. (2007). Using advice from multiple sources to revise and improve judgment. *Organizational Behavior and Human Decision Processes, 103*, 104–120.

11

Team Decision Making in Naturalistic Environments: A Framework for and Introduction to Illusory Shared Cognition

Shirley Sonesh, Ramón Rico, and Eduardo Salas

In many professional settings, decisions are carried out by expert teams rather than individuals. Teams must often accomplish difficult, complex, and even dangerous tasks where to succeed they must engage in thorough yet rapid decision making processes. That is the case in the medical arena, where decisions for patient diagnosis or care often require the input of different specialists and the collaboration of nurse and physician teams. In the same way, decisions during military or firefighting operations that are riddled with risk, time pressure, and changing environments are the product of a team effort.

Although teamwork is essential for highly complex tasks, teams are not infallible or immune to error. In fact, Foushee and Helmreich (1988) reported that over 60 percent of airline accidents have been attributed to poor crew coordination and decision making. Moreover, the conditions in which such team decisions are made sometimes yield disastrous outcomes. In 1988, the USS Vincennes, a battleship equipped with the most sophisticated radar and battle gear of the time, mistakenly shot down a civilian jetliner in the Persian Gulf, killing 289 civilians. Despite the crew's shared intentions and goals, and even a belief that they had a shared representation of what was going on, the high stress conditions and the environmental urgency that day contributed to a lack of shared situation awareness, coordination, and a subsequent poor decision with fatal consequences. In this chapter we review several team decision making models and introduce the concept of "illusory shared cognition" (ISC) to explain situations where assumed or perceived team agreement can contribute to poor decision making.

The ways in which teams make decisions has been widely addressed in the literature since the early 1950s (Edwards, 1954; March & Simon, 1958; Klein et al., 1993; Orasanu & Salas, 1993). Thus, the literature on individual decision making is abundant with various decision models that address the many forms in which individuals make sense of data and information. In this chapter we will distinguish between classical and naturalistic decision making, review several pertinent decision models and summarize the state of the literature on team shared cognition, which includes shared mental models, shared situation assessment, and transactive memory systems that have attempted to explain how teams coordinate to reach decisions. Finally, we introduce a framework that builds on the variables of interest in the naturalistic team decision making literature and introduce the aforementioned new concept of "illusory shared cognition" to help explain poor decision outcomes despite effective teamwork and shared goals.

WHAT CONSTITUTES TEAM DECISION MAKING?

In this chapter we will refer to teams as an entity comprised of at least two individuals with individual competencies who work together toward a common goal or task. Compared to groups, team members have clearly defined roles and responsibilities and are reliant on each other with respect to task performance (Dyer, 1984; Kozlowski & Ilgen, 2006; Salas et al., 1992). Moreover, when we refer to team decision making we mean "the process of reaching a decision undertaken by interdependent individuals to achieve a common goal" (Orasanu & Salas, 1993). To be successful, team members must gather, interpret, communicate, and integrate information in support of a mutually accepted decision. Different agendas, points of view, perceptions, and preferences must be unified to reach a consensus whereby several mechanisms for achieving a shared way of thinking are utilized.

CLASSICAL DECISION MODEL VS. NATURALISTIC DECISION MODEL

The traditional approach to understanding decision making is based upon classical decision making theory or the rational economic model

(Huczynski & Buchanan, 2001). The classical view of decision making assumes that the decision maker seeks to optimize the outcome of one's choice and operates under the assumption that the options, criteria, and values are all known (Edwards, 1954; Lee, Newman, & Price, 1999). It has been argued that this theory of decision making has weaknesses when applied to real-life decision making (Beach & Lipshitz, 1997). In particular, classical decision theory fails to account for several characteristics of real-world decision settings (Orasanu & Connolly, 1993). It fails to account for ill-structured problems in dynamic environments characterized by high time pressure, conflicting goals, and incomplete information, and requires an understanding of the situation before a choice among alternatives is made (Klein, 1989).

In response to the weaknesses of classical decision models, naturalistic decision making (NDM) models were introduced (Klein, 1989). These models propose that, in environments that have limited resources or data, decision makers must maintain large amounts of information in memory under conditions of high workload and stress, and their decisions may be skewed by the lack of complete, error-free, unambiguous data. Because the situation itself either determines or constrains the response options, decision makers in these environments typically make up to 95 percent of all decisions without considering alternatives (Kaempf & Militello, 1991; Klein, 1989). In other words, NDM models investigate how people use experience to make decisions in naturalistic environments (e.g., under time pressure, shifting conditions, unclear goals, and incomplete information). We will address the prototypical NDM model as well as discuss several additional relevant team decision making models in this chapter, before introducing a new team decision framework. It should be noted that the models discussed do not represent an exhaustive set. Due to the different nature of individual and team decision making processes we excluded models that we believe do not have the potential to be elevated to the team level.

RECOGNITION-PRIMED DECISION MODEL

Although a number of models fall within the NDM framework (Lipshitz, 1993), it is fair to say that the recognition-primed decision (RPD) model can serve as the prototypical NDM model. Klein's RPD model acknowledges that decision makers rarely compare among alternatives, as classical decision theory would suggest, but rather select an appropriate action based upon the nature of the situation. The underlying assumption is that decision makers use their experiences to assess the situation, classifying it as an instance of a familiar type. Then they retrieve the most plausible response to the interpreted situation and evaluate its adequacy by using a mental simulation of the outcome. Specifically, the decision maker's process consists of three phases: situation recognition/assessment, serial option evaluation, and a mental simulation of the potential outcome of a chosen response option.

In the *situation recognition* phase, the decision maker recognizes and classifies the situation as novel or typical. Typical situations should elicit well-rehearsed actions/decisions, while novel situations may be more challenging since they require greater effort than employing old routines. The decision maker must select proper action by identifying critical cues that mark the type of situation as well as identify causal factors that explain what is happening and potentially predict what will happen. Plausible goals can then be set before proceeding to select the most appropriate decision given those goals and expectations.

The second phase consists of *serial option evaluation*, where the decision maker evaluates action alternatives until a satisfactory one is identified. These action alternatives are selected according to how typical that response is to a particular situation. These actions are then evaluated through *mental simulation*. Mental simulation is a process by which a decision maker evaluates each of the actions sorted by typicality. The decision maker must mentally simulate/imagine the steps to be taken, the potential outcomes and challenges of each of those steps, and how problems can be overcome. This simulation process helps the decision maker assess each action and informs the choice of implementing the action, modifying, or rejecting it before turning to the next most "typical" action in queue.

Applying the RPD model to teams assumes that expert teams have a shared understanding of the situation and can each subsequently mentally simulate that situation in a similar way. Team-wide collaboration opportunities can be naturally embedded into the RPD process. Evidence of teams' accounts of their decision processes were not identified as "making choices" or "considering alternatives," but rather they saw themselves acting and reacting on the basis of prior experiences (Klein & Crandall, 1990). In addition, they were generating, monitoring, and modifying plans to meet the needs of the situation. In fact, Thordsen et al. (1987) found that twenty-six of twenty-seven decisions identified in a five-hour army battalion-level planning exercise followed the RPD model, rather than any concurrent option analysis model. Nonetheless, there are some team functions that will be hindered by the added burden of communication of intent and situation assessment and, although team members may help with workload issues, there is a cost of coordination.

Although there has been evidence that real tactical decision teams use the RPD style of decision making over other models (Pascual & Henderson, 1997; Serfaty, Entin, & Johnston, 1998), Klein and Thordsen (1990) have identified eight potential barriers to team decisions within the team RPD model. These include:

- *Distorted perception*: The perceptual cues available to an individual may be lost at the team level. Since events are often communicated from outside observers, rarely will all team members, if any, experience first-hand the external event or situation that they must make decisions about. In addition to the credibility of those observers being questioned, the way the team perceives the information communicated to them may be very different from the way the actual observers perceived the situation.

- *Handoff of situation assessment*: The observer passing on critical information regarding the situation may have difficulties communicating and articulating their situation assessment (SA), especially when cues are subtle and difficult to transmit verbally.

- *Intent*: If communication of team goals is poor then teams may misunderstand the goals of a situation and the activity of a team can become confused.

- *Attention*: Teams have different individuals gathering different data depending on their role that may be irrelevant to the specific goals of the team. It is difficult then to avoid information overload, which then distracts attention from what is important.

- *Anticipation/expectancy*: Experienced individual decision makers can use expectancies to check their SA and prepare for smooth reactions. In teams, expectancies are hard to communicate and may be missed or misinterpreted so that teams operate on wrong or inadequate expectancies (e.g., not understanding how long actions take to be implemented). In addition, different teams vary on their level of anticipation of events and therefore struggle even more with correctly utilizing mental simulations to make decisions.

- *Improvisation*: Individuals are better able to understand when plans need to be abandoned or modified than teams. Teams have difficulty improvising and are much less likely to understand when plans no longer make sense and there is a need to change direction. In this case it is important to have a clear team leader who can provide sufficient overview of intent so that team members can initiate appropriate actions.

- *Synchronization*: Skilled decision makers can simulate planned actions in their minds to see if they will work. Teams on the other hand have difficulty representing all the different dimensions in a synchronized way where multiple elements and players must be sequenced in a timely fashion for all to proceed properly. Often each element is a different team member's responsibility and therefore communication is critical for proper synchronization.
- *Meta-cognition*: Individual decision makers must properly allocate resources to a task and so do teams. For a team to do this as well as individuals it must have clear communication about workload from a leader and its members to ensure assigning functions appropriately. This represents the management of decision processes rather than a stage of decision making.

SITUATION ASSESSMENT MODEL

The way decisions should be made according to the SA model is by "sizing up" a situation by combining concrete information with background "context" information. With the addition of general knowledge retrieved from the decision maker's memory an interpretation or "representation" of the situation emerges (Noble, 1989). The representation entails certain expectations concerning characteristics of a decision and outcome of that decision. These expectations are tested using additional resources and, to the extent that the expectations match the information extracted, the representation is refined or rejected in favor of a new representation. Based on this form of decision making, people can decide what to do in a current situation by comparing it to a similar situation where the decision/action worked successfully.

Applying the SA model to teams requires the consideration of an additional construct: the *team situation model* (TSM) defined as the mental representation associated with the dynamic understanding of a situation in which a team is embedded. Such representation is developed by its team members in real time (Rico et al., 2008). When a team's members highly share a TSM they can make more informed and anchored decisions since they share a common perspective regarding current environmental events, their meaning, and projected future (Wellens, 1993). TSMs' sharedness depends heavily on SA, accordingly. Salas et al. (1995), Artman (2000), and Cooke et al. (2007) further defined team SA as the collection of the perceptions (shared or not) of the elements in a particular environment and timeframe and the understanding of their meaning, in a way that the team can anticipate important future states. Thus, team members must accurately interpret task environment cues so that changes can be made when information is inconsistent with an original assumption. This ability to adapt is crucial for effective team decision making.

INFORMATION PROCESSING PERSPECTIVE

The information processing perspective of team decision making acknowledges the goals that define the context of the decision making process, the attentional resources required to process information, the acquisition of information, encoding of information, its storage, and its subsequent retrieval before a decision is made.

Thus, the first step indicated highlights how the end goal dictates what information should be processed and attended to. The next step is attention; information perceived by the team depends on its members' attentional resources and previous schemas. Although individuals have limited attentional capacity (Posner, 1982), teams may have a greater capacity for attention due to the additive effect of many individuals attending to a body of information (Duffy, 1993). That is, if teams have common schemas or shared team mental models, there should be less process loss as a result of enhanced attentional capacity. Shared task and team mental models may also increase team members' sensitivity to the information needs of others, resulting in implicit coordination allowing team members to anticipate and dynamically adapt to the actions of other team members to manage their multiple interdependencies (Rico et al., 2008).

The acquisition of information, once it has been attended to, involves at least two members of a team to have acquired the information, which is then encoded. This is the process by which information is translated into internal symbolic code, which may result in a shared mental model or shared representation and understanding of the decision problem and its context (Orasanu & Salas, 1993). Once information is encoded it is stored, which means that it is captured in a team memory system defined as a transactive memory system (TMS) (Austin, 2003; Lewis, 2003) in which the personal memory of each member is expanded to the other members of the team. Next, the team must retrieve the necessary information before making a judgment/decision. Team retrieval is thought to be superior to individual retrieval because team members can correct faulty retrievals that are susceptible to point of view errors. Moreover, when one team member may forget a crucial piece of information, there are several other team members to "back up" that information and bring it to attention.

Although the steps taken in each of the team decision models outlined are predicated on the idea that team members can clearly and explicitly share information, it is becoming increasingly apparent that there are situations in which teams must quickly come to decisions without the opportunity for much deliberation. In the next section, we review how teams achieve shared cognition, or the perception of shared cognition, in order to achieve team initiatives without explicit communication or deliberation, by means of implicit coordination mechanisms, such as shared cognition.

SHARED COGNITION IN TEAMS

Team Mental Model

Shared mental models/team mental models (TMMs) (Cannon-Bowers, Salas, & Converse, 1993; Orasanu, 1990) and team mind (Thordsen & Klein, 1989) are theoretical frameworks that have emerged from investigations of team decision making in natural environments. Teams must have a common knowledge base (Orasanu, 1994; Rouse, Cannon-Bowers, & Salas, 1992; Salas, Cooke, & Rosen, 2008) and common mission (Cannon-Bowers & Salas, 2001) to support joint decision making.

TMMs are stable organized mental representations of the key elements within a team's relevant environment that are shared across team members (Klimoski & Mohammed, 1994). A meta-analysis of over twenty empirical studies has found that teams with shared mental models consistently perform better than other teams (DeChurch & Mesmer-Magnus, 2010). There are several reasons for this. In particular, Walsh, Henderson, and Deighton (1988) suggest that TMMs play an important role in aspects of a team's shared information processes. To achieve TMMs, communication is crucial, especially in novel situations (Orasanu, 1990). When teams have highly shared TMMs it further facilitates communication about systems, standard operating procedures, and specific policies. By using a common language, communication and coordination are more efficient (Langan-Fox, 2001; Langan-Fox, Code, & Langfield-Smith, 2000), which translates into a more efficient use of information and planning for action by making it possible for team members to predict what will be required and how they should interact with the team (Klimoski & Mohammed, 1994). Moreover, shared TMMs allow for more rapid acquisition of knowledge between team members, and since the strengths and weaknesses of each team member are known it can improve the process of allocating tasks to each member. Thus, shared TMMs elucidate the process necessary to make effective team decisions (Rouse, Cannon-Bowers, & Salas, 1992).

Transactive Memory Systems

The notion of shared TMMs is related to Wegner's (1987) concept of TMSs. Transactive memory is the notion that teams can remember more information than the best individual in the team (Clark & Stephenson, 1989). The team's information processing capabilities are rooted in a shared system for encoding knowledge, where each individual is only responsible for part of what the team collectively needs to know (Wegner, Erber, & Raymond, 1991). This means that for storage and retrieval of information team members must have very well-defined roles and responsibilities. In this way, to access specific knowledge it does not have to be shared by each team member, but rather by knowing who has the idiosyncratic knowledge in the team and who is responsible for each memory domain. TMSs result in an expansion of personal memory through interdependence on other members of the group.

Although TMMs and TMSs have been shown to facilitate team decision making and enhance team performance (Cannon-Bowers, Salas, & Converse, 1993; Mathieu et al., 2000), they do not address *how* team decisions are made. In doing so, we propose a framework for team decision making drawing from the information processing, RPD, and SA models to outline the process by which teams make decisions in naturalistic environments. Moreover, the concept of ISC is introduced as a potential alternative team state contributing to erroneous or biased decision making.

FRAMEWORK OF TEAM DECISION MAKING IN A NATURALISTIC SETTING

We propose a new framework (Figure 11.1) that synthesizes the literature on team shared cognition and decision making models to elucidate the process by which teams engage in decision making. In the framework presented, a shared situation model is highlighted (Orasanu, 1990), along with shared cognition, which refers to the common modes of interpretation and shared understanding of experience that have been referred to as "shared mutual models" (Cannon-Bowers, Salas, & Converse, 1993), "team mental models" (Orasanu & Salas, 1993) "social cognition" (Larson & Christensen, 1993), "collective mind" (Weick & Roberts, 1993), and "core teamwork schemas" (Rentsch, Heffner, & Duffy, 1994). Essentially, all of

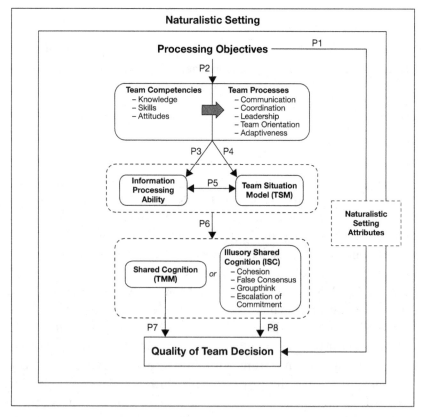

FIGURE 11.1
A framework of team decision making in a naturalistic setting.

these concepts capture one construct that we will refer to as "shared cognition," or TMM. It represents the ability for a team to have an organized knowledge structure that enables the formation of accurate expectations of the task and team, and to have a shared understanding of the problem definition, plans, strategies, information, cues, and team member roles for the purpose of creating a team-level decision.

Our framework goes on to elucidate how shared cognition and a shared assessment of the situation (TSM) contribute to selecting the decision that best matches the criteria or desired team outcome, through teamwork. This selection process is informed by synthesizing the models outlined throughout this chapter, under the assumption that, in order to make an effective team decision, the various and distinct perspectives of each team member must be integrated into a coherent representation of the situation, followed by choosing the option that best fits the situation and goals of the team.

Team Processing Objectives and Dynamic Environments

We described individual decision making theories in dynamic and changing environments and our proposed framework continues in the direction of exploring how teams make decisions in dynamic and potentially stressful situations. We highlight the importance of team goals, termed "processing objectives," as the overarching motivator behind team decisions. That is, the end goal of the team is the predominant driver of behaviors and decisions, but to reach those goals the team has to work within the constraints of the dynamic changing environment. The situation may provide an ambiguous problem with very little information that must be resolved swiftly. The team must manage stress, complexity, and high-stakes conditions. Because the situation may change quickly, bringing new values to the forefront, other than the original goals of the team, the broader goals or "processing objectives" will provide direction to the team since the decisions are typically embedded in broader tasks. Much like the information processing perspective of team decision making, teams will attend to, acquire, and encode the most relevant information as it pertains to the processing objective within the constraints of the environment. In a naturalistic setting the processing objective of a team will direct the attention of a team to focus on the attributes of a situation that are most crucial to achieving team goals, which will ultimately contribute to the quality of their decision.

Proposition 1: The processing objective of a team will be indirectly related to the quality of a team decision through attending to the attributes of a naturalistic setting that are most pertinent to the team's goal.

Processing Objective and Teamwork

In addition, shared goals are essential to teamwork because they are what tie the team together and prompt them to take an interest in each other's success. Members of a team do not act to achieve their own goals at the expense of their teammates, but rather look for synergistic opportunities to achieve overall goals as efficiently as possible. Thus, not only do team goals and objectives encourage an alignment of individual objectives, but they also encourage cooperation, team orientation, coordination, adaptation, and back up behaviors among team members (O'Leary-Kelly, Martocchio, & Frink, 1994). Generalizing the argument above, in order to achieve team processing objectives, having effective team competencies and team processes is crucial.

Team competencies are defined as the knowledge, skills, and attitudes of team members in a team (Cannon-Bowers et al., 1995). "Knowledge" refers to the factual information about the domain mission and team structure that team members must know in order to interact effectively. "Skills" are teamwork processes such as information exchange, load balancing, and conflict resolution. Finally, "attitudes" are the motivational determinants of team member's choices, such as their orientation toward teamwork, leadership, and willingness to accept advice or help. The decomposition of teamwork requirements into these three specific competencies provides a foundation on which to bridge cognition at the individual level to that at the team level. When teams have a common goal, they will collectively use their team competencies to work together, and to share information and knowledge to effectively achieve those goals.

In the same way, *team processes* are the activities explicitly oriented toward interactions among team members that are required to achieve collective success (Ioerger & He, 2003). Some examples of teamwork processes include team orientation, communication, coordination, adaptiveness, and leadership. When individuals' team competencies are high they are more suited to work well in a team setting and therefore contribute to more effective team processes. The specific competencies and processes referred to here will be discussed in greater depth in the following section. Moreover, when team members all have a vested interest in achieving a collective goal, they will have a motivation to exercise their team competencies and team processes to facilitate achieving those goals. That is, they will work harder to communicate plans, coordinate roles, anticipate team member problems, etc. to achieve collective initiatives.

Proposition 2: Processing objectives contribute to a team's engagement of team competencies and team processes.

Teamwork, Information Processing, and Shared Situation Models

Effective teamwork processes and competencies facilitate information processing, which contributes to more accurate team situation assessments, situation awareness (SA), and subsequent shared team situation models. SA describes "the human processes of gathering information (e.g., attention, pattern recognition, communication)" (Gutwin & Greenberg, 2004, p. 181). Team SA, or the collective interpretations of information gathering, is influenced by team processes such as clarity of team communications, team collaboration, and other team processes (Stout, Cannon-Bowers, & Salas, 1996). In fact, communication is contended to enhance the ability to achieve shared situation models among teams (Orasanu & Salas, 1993). Although there are myriad teamwork competencies and processes that affect decision processes, we will only highlight some salient exemplars for the purposes of the framework.

Team Orientation

Team orientation is described as the preference for working with others and the tendency to enhance individual performance, through the coordination, evaluation, and utilization of task inputs from other group members while performing group tasks (Salas et al., 2005, p. 200). Teams that are high in team collective orientation are accepting of input from their teammates, have a high level of task involvement, information sharing, and participatory goal setting and strategizing, and value team goals over individual goals (Alavi & McCormick, 2004; Driskell & Salas, 1992; Jackson et al., 2006). Thus, teams with a high level of team orientation will share more information, which will facilitate collective situation assessments.

Communication and Coordination

Teams must gather and share information to reach an effective decision, and in order to do so must use various teamwork processes, such as communication, to achieve the illusion of a streamlined information gathering process (Cannon-Bowers & Salas, 1997). In fact, evidence suggests that teams who perform effectively demonstrate consistency over time in the content of what they communicate, who they communicate with, and when they communicate (Kiekel et al., 2001). Although communication has been hypothesized as a mediator of a TMM–team performance relationship (Mathieu et al., 2000), we argue that it is also important in achieving TMM by contributing to more effective information processing abilities. Team members must communicate to build a picture of the dynamic situation, synchronize actions, assign tasks, and share information (Orasanu, 1990).

Team coordination is the process of orchestrating the sequence of timing of interdependent actions (Marks, Mathieu, & Zaccaro, 2001) and it could take place either explicitly or implicitly (Rico et al., 2008). Teams that are explicitly coordinated will communicate information about their status, needs, and objectives as often as necessary to achieve a shared TSM (Brannick et al., 1995; Malone & Crowston, 1994; Smith-Jentsch, Johnston, & Payne, 1998). In fact, Liebhaber and Smith (2000) analyzed communications among crews on battle cruisers during simulated missions and found that many messages among teammates involved information processing characteristics of recognizing, conveying, and confirming qualitative features associated with specific situations to achieve a shared situation assessment.

Adaptiveness

Adaptiveness is another important competency for effective teamwork (Klein & Pierce, 2001; Kozlowski, 1998). Team adaptation, or the ability to adjust strategies based on information gathered from the environment (Salas, Sims, & Burke, 2005), is important in naturalistic decision making contexts because team members must modify or replace routine performance strategies when they detect that the characteristics of the environment and task change (Burke et al., 2006). In addition they must make accurate assessments about underlying causes of environmental changes (Salas, Sims, & Burke, 2005). Thus, teams high in adaptiveness will be able to turn their attention to collecting and processing relevant information to more accurately understand the situation and achieve a shared team situation model.

Leadership

In addition to the aforementioned team competencies and processes, leadership may also facilitate team-level information processing to achieve a shared situation model. Team leadership refers to the "ability to direct and coordinate the activities of other team members, assess team performance, assign tasks, develop team knowledge, skills, and abilities, motivate team members, plan and organize, and establish a positive atmosphere" (Salas, Sims, & Burke, 2005, p. 560). Performing an appropriate leadership role within a team will provide frequent status updates, maintain goal orientation, or simply provide situation assessment feedback by which it strengthens the shared situation assessment. Further, Orasanu (1990) revealed that leader behavior during task performance has an impact on the extent and quality of shared problem models developed by the team.

Only through these team processes and competencies can the information gathering process be integrated to the collective level and achieve the equivalence of behavior known as "team mind" (Klein, 1999). The state of collective knowledge of the situation (shared TSM) is a reflection of the combination of knowledge collected from all team members and is facilitated by the team processes and competencies outlined above.

Proposition 3: Team processes and team competencies are directly related to a team's information processing abilities.

Proposition 4: Team processes and team competencies are directly related to the sharedness of a TSM.

Information Processing and Team Situation Models

The next part of the framework illustrates that a team's shared assessment of a situation shapes the way the team gathers and processes information and vice versa. During team tasks, teams must interpret cues and patterns in a situation (Stout, Cannon-Bowers, & Salas, 1996). Thus SA is a precursor to decision making and has three levels (Endsley, 1995). The lowest level is *perception*, in which team members making a decision become aware of basic factual information. This is followed by the *interpretation* stage, where the decision makers must fill in gaps or make inferences about what is not seen. And, finally, *comprehension* is the stage where projections of the consequences of a situation are made into the future, much like the mental simulation component of the RPD model (Klein, 1993). Developing and maintaining SA is an ongoing process, where in order to fully "comprehend" team members must continually collect more information to reduce uncertainty. Shared TSMs help to guide the team in what cues and patterns to attend to, strategies for collecting and encoding information, and developing effective ways to cope with newly acquired information (Cannon-Bowers, Salas, & Blickensderfer, 1999).

As the individual situation model suggests, individual team members acquire a specific understanding of the current situation at any one point in time and this understanding changes as the situation changes. Cannon-Bowers, Salas, and Blickensderfer (1999) refer to this as "dynamic understanding" and thus a team's collective understanding of a specific situation also changes with the changing situation.

The combination of all the team information processing steps results in a shared analysis of the naturalistic context in which the team task is embedded. Not only does the acquisition of task and contextual information help form a shared assessment of the situation and subsequent "shared cognition," shared situation models may also help teams to determine what other information is missing and thus what additional information needs to be acquired (Salas, Rosen, & DiazGranados, 2010). The team must monitor for certain threatening or dangerous situations that could develop and thus information collected must be up to date and incorporated into an evolving assessment of what the situation is most likely to be. This suggests a cyclical quality between a team's information gathering processes and the development of their shared situation model.

Proposition 5: The relationship between team information processing and TSM is cyclical, such that the more information a team gathers and processes collectively the greater the shared TSM will be, and the more accurate its shared TSM is, the greater the understanding of which additional information must be gathered and attended to.

Shared Cognition

It has been argued that the major factor that distinguishes experienced from less experienced decision makers is their situation assessment ability and shared cognition, not their reasoning processes (Chi, Glaser, & Farr, 1988; Klein, 1989; Orasanu, 1990). In fact, team situation awareness is a consistently good predictor of team performance (Cooke, Kiekel, & Helm, 2001). When information gathered and processed by a team results in an accurate collective assessment of a dynamic situation, a shared mental model or "team mind" can be achieved. Cannon-Bowers, Salas, and

Converse (1993) have noted that teams must adapt quickly to changing demands of a task and that, to do so effectively, a common or shared mental model is necessary. It is evident that some level of shared SA is necessary for achieving team shared cognition. Klimoski and Mohammed (1994) suggest that antecedents of TMMs are communication, cohesion, information sharing, participation, and negotiation. Moreover, the proximal outputs of the SA process serve as cognitive frameworks that allow team members to predict future system states (Burke et al., 2006). Thus, without shared cognition, a shared TSM is not sufficient for quality decision making, and without TSM shared cognition would not be feasible. Team members must not only share a schema of the dynamic situation, and of their overarching goals, but also each other's roles, skills, and abilities so they can extract the necessary information from the situation to make an appropriate strategic decision.

When shared cognition is achieved each team member can carry out their role in a timely and coordinated way, so to help the team function as a single unit with little need for negotiation or deliberation with the rest of the team. Shared cognition allows for the exploitation of the cognitive resources of the entire group since it provides a common platform for interpreting commands or information requests as well as a basis for predicting behavior or being sensitive to the needs of other team members (Artman & Wærn, 1998). In fact, Rouse and Morris (1986) state that the role of mental models is to provide a conceptual framework for describing, explaining, and predicting future system states without any explicit cues.

In addition, TMSs are included in the concept of "shared cognition" and are a determinant of how team decisions are made. In particular, the implicit part of TMSs refers to information that one team member may have but does not share with others. Smoothly functioning teams can address most tasks by means of implicit coordination (Rico et al., 2008) since each team member has a different role and responsibility and this facilitates the ease of making team-level decisions since teams can then collectively anticipate or "mentally simulate" the way their team members will enact potential decisions.

Even when teams have a shared situation model it is difficult for each team member to synchronize the temporal sequencing of events in their mental simulations. Nonetheless, when team members have a shared cognition with a strong TSM there is less of a need to rehash shared information and pooled yet unshared information can be accessed to develop collective mental simulations, much like the RPD model suggests (Mohammed & Dumville, 2001). Klein (1989) suggests that situation assessment sets the stage for serial selection and mental simulation of option choices. In fact, shared cognition based on accurate SA allows for decision teams to project an environment's status into the future (Artman, 1998; Brehmer, 1990).

If teams determine that their collective mental simulations match their goals within the constraints of the naturalistic setting they will implement that decision or action. If shared cognition is poor, the individual simulations will be disjointed and have a negative effect on the matching process, which may potentially end in poor team decisions. On the other hand, when teams have effective team processes and competencies that contribute to a shared assessment of the situation, a similar understanding of their ultimate goal, and high shared cognition, team members will be more successful in their initiatives and therefore the quality of their decisions.

Proposition 6: Shared TSMs and team information processing contribute to team shared cognition.

Proposition 7: Shared cognition will be directly related to the quality of team decisions.

Illusory Shared Cognition and Decision Quality

Although it has been found that shared cognition allows team members to interpret cues similarly, make compatible decisions, and take appropriate actions (Cooke et al., 2000; Klimoski & Mohammed, 1994; Mohammed & Dumville, 2001), and is therefore a strong predictor of team outcomes, the question of what is shared and what is meant by the term "shared" has been raised by team scholars (Cannon-Bowers & Salas, 2001). We propagate these questions by introducing the notion that shared cognition may be an illusion, and thus its explanatory power should be reassessed. Thus, understanding the underpinnings of shared cognition and how reliable it is in predicting quality decisions is crucial. In the same way that shared cognition among teams predicts quality decision outcomes, a *perceived* shared cognition may occur where highly cohesive teams that do not engage in sufficient information sharing fail to accurately form a shared vision of future system states. Thus a distinction between perceived and objective shared cognition is necessary. While "shared cognition" is defined as the process and outcome related to team knowledge and includes TMMs, TSMs, shared frames of reference, and schema similarity, ISC will be defined here as the false perception of shared team-level knowledge, TMMs, TSMs, shared frame of reference, and schema similarity. While managing conflict is one of the greatest challenges faced by teams, the problem of perceived rather than objective shared cognition introduces the concept that often a major source of dysfunction is the inability to accurately perceive agreement. Stated differently, ISC captures the fact that, although team members think they agree on a plan of action, an objective, or even on team members' roles and responsibilities, they may actually have inconsistent views and perspectives.

No research thus far has examined the potential ISC effect on team decision making. There are several reasons why perceived rather than objective "shared cognition" may occur, contributing to an ISC and subsequent reduced-quality decisions. We argue that ISC occurs if each team member differentially conceptualizes how "similar" their own cognition is to that of every other team member, and extrapolate those perceived "shared" cognitions to make erroneous strategic decisions without fully realizing that they diverge from the collective team's cognitive representation. In this section we discuss the potential root causes for a false illusion that teams have shared cognition, and argue that they emanate from more basic sources of team biases present in team decision making (Jones & Roelofsma, 2000).

Three sources of team biases have been introduced by Duffy (1993): cognitive, organizational, and social. First, cognitive biases are rooted in individuals' limited information processing capabilities and the consequent reliance on mental simplifying strategies known as *cognitive heuristics*. For a more comprehensive discussion of cognitive heuristics see Baron (1994) or Hogarth (1987). Second, errors emanating from the broader organization are another source of bias and subsequent decision error in teams. Many team accidents have been attributed to management-level errors. In fact, Bruggink (1985) found that 65 percent of fatal aircraft accidents were influenced by policy factors. A third source, and the one we will place the greatest emphasis on in explaining ISC, is the team biases and errors attributed to social interaction and social contextual factors within a team. Social influence and social projection comprise the two broad categories within this social source of error. Specifically, *social influence* refers to the process by which individual judgments, behaviors, and attitudes change as a result of the real or implied presence of people (Jones and Roelofsma, 2000). *Social projection* refers to the tendency for team members to make assumptions, estimates or predictions about other team members and to anchor their estimates of others on their own position. Others assert that social dysfunctions are caused by limitations inherent in the structure and form of meetings (Postmes & Lea, 2000). Examples of these processes are the false consensus effect, groupthink, and group escalation of commitment (Jones & Roelofsma, 2000), each of which will be elaborated on below.

As a consequence of having insufficient information about aspects of a group or situations, team members are forced to make assumptions, predictions, and estimates about team members, and clearly their TMMs help them to do so. These judgments help to understand how others will interpret certain pieces of information or assess situations, and what future actions of team members will be in a given situation. These judgments, though, lend themselves to potential errors in understanding one another and achieving shared cognition. Moreover, much like the concept of groupthink (Janis, 1972), which explains how team members take actions that contradict the very purpose they are trying to achieve, the illusion that a team has achieved shared cognition is just as disruptive to team objectives as *lacking* shared cognition.

First, the *false consensus effect* (Ross, 1977) refers to the tendency to overestimate the degree of similarity between self and others and may result in biased judgments or decisions. Simply put, the false consensus effect is the tendency to perceive one's own behavior as typical. A meta-analysis has shown this to be a reliable effect (Mullen et al., 1985). Team members may assume that the entire team agrees on a course of action since they themselves believe it to be a superior decision. In fact, it has been shown that the conditions in which the false consensus effect is most prevalent are when one is selectively exposed to similar others, when decisions are attributed to situational rather than dispositional attributes, and when one's focus is directed to a single position rather than alternatives (Marks & Miller, 1985). These conditions mirror those of teams in naturalistic contexts that must make immediate swift decisions and this therefore implies that these settings are most likely to contribute to "illusory shared cognition" through the false consensus effect.

Second, *cohesion* in teams may be another contributor to "illusory shared cognition." Team members take actions that contradict their ultimate purpose when they are deeply involved in a cohesive group (Janis, 1972). Groupthink is one of the most well-known biases occurring in cohesive groups (Janis, 1972). It is a mode of thinking that people engage in when they are deeply involved in a cohesive group, and when the members' striving for unanimity overrides their motivation to realistically appraise alternative courses of action. This is of particular interest in tactical decision making and planning since these activities occur in a collaborative group environment where there is mutual attraction of members. Cohesive tactical decision teams may falsely assume that cohesion indicates agreement and that their own mental simulation of potential outcomes is aligned with that of the rest of the team and therefore assume that they have achieved a shared awareness of a situation and how to proceed. Ultimately, groupthink results in defective decision making as a result of the symptom of the "illusion of unanimity," which is closely related to our conceptualization of ISC. In fact, Fischhoff, Lanir, and Johnson (1997) suggested that, where groupthink occurs, there is only the perception of completely shared TMMs, in that they don't completely overlap with other members' perceived meaning or understanding of a given situation. It is asserted that these discrepancies in understanding may appear subtle but that they may be significant enough to induce unrecognized drift in shared cognition, which ultimately results in unpredictable group decisions (Jones & Roelofsma, 2000). Moreover, it is suggested that group biases such as groupthink may be more prevalent in autonomous groups and high-ranking teams that make decisions with little external aid (Sundstrom, DeMeuse, & Futrell, 1990).

Third, *group escalation of commitment* refers to the tendency for individuals or groups to continue to support a course of action despite evidence that it is failing. Because escalating commitment can also be perceived as demonstrating consistency, and is a quality associated with good leadership (Staw & Ross, 1987), tactical decision teams are likely to commit this bias. Moreover, in a combat context, teams may escalate their decisions due to a desire to "win" or beat an opponent, without regard for the potential for heavy losses. While research has shown that this occurs at the group level (Whyte, 1993), the fact that the ultimate goal for effective decision making is muddled by the escalation of a failing decision illustrates that teams have ISC in that, although teams continue to share the notion that "winning" and being consistent is the goal, the ultimate goal of achieving task initiatives is lost.

Finally, the environments in which tactical decision teams operate contribute to the potential for the illusion of shared cognition. Much like the antecedents that predict groupthink and false consensus tendencies, tactical decision making is nested in high-stress environments with external threats, and insulated teams. Due to the high-stakes nature of the environment, cues for action may be rare and the few implicit cues that are provided are likely to be differentially interpreted by each team member. Second, because the environmental constraints preclude the opportunity for explicit and deliberate communication, the likelihood of misinterpreting hand-offs of other members' situation assessments is high. Due to insufficient time for explicit communication, team members are forced to make inferences on what each team member is thinking and what their own role in a decision should be. These may mislead team members to believe that they have a common vision, when in fact their SAs and schemas may greatly deviate from one another. Further, in a dynamic environment the iterative process between information processing and achieving a shared situation model, which we delineated earlier, may make achieving "objective" shared cognition a more time-consuming, complex, and difficult process. Moreover, obtaining more information may present a higher risk to the achievement of the team's goals than would estimating the information, thereby exacerbating the likelihood for ISC.

When ISC exists it reduces the likelihood that team members will question each other, confirm decisions, or communicate concerns, and therefore key decisions may be carried through unsuccessfully. When teams have shared cognition they "mentally simulate" the way their team members will enact potential decisions, but without adequate *objective* shared cognition, team members will erroneously anticipate each other's behaviors. They will not have compatible views of equipment, tasks, or member roles and responsibilities that allow teams accurately to mentally simulate which decisions will work and which will not (Burke et al., 2006). Thus, sharedness indicators of team cognition should be complemented with accuracy indexes. Some potential outcomes of ISC include each team member carrying out a role in what they misjudged to be part of a collective strategic decision when in fact other team members are pursuing other plans of action.

When teams carry out decisions, multiple elements and players must be sequenced in a timely fashion for the decision process to be implemented properly. In such situations communication is crucial but unlikely when there is an illusion of agreement. While individuals are better able to understand when plans need to be abandoned or modified, teams that believe they have a shared schema but don't are much less likely to understand and be wary when plans no longer make sense and require a change in direction, ultimately resulting in poor decision outcomes.

Proposition 8: Illusory shared cognition will negatively affect the quality of team decisions.

FUTURE DIRECTIONS

First, some potential applications of the proposed framework lie in training for each level in the team decision process. Although decision making in naturalistic contexts is situational and context dependent, there are some components of the decision making process that can be directly trained. Thus, future research should attempt to empirically test the propositions outlined in this chapter to better understand the links within the framework. This will greatly benefit the development of applications for several important naturalistic domains such as medical rapid response teams, military teams, and STATs (swift starting action teams) (Wildman et al., 2012), which include disaster response teams, firefighting teams, law enforcement special weapons and tactics (SWAT) teams, and many others.

Second, while literature on different forms of "shared cognition" has been fruitful, there are several future avenues for research in team decision making. Specifically, forthcoming research should pay special attention to empirically identifying the antecedents of *objective* versus *illusory* shared cognition. In addition, current approaches used to assess the sharedness of mental models may require refinement to take into account the illusion of sharedness and its correlates. It is our hope that the introduction of the ISC construct will encourage both researchers and practitioners to make a distinction between perceived and objective team agreement, further clarify and define shared cognition at a higher level of granularity, and highlight the sources and potential outcomes of ISC for both training and research initiatives.

Finally, although there have been some good initial attempts to understand how TMMs and TSMs relate to team performance outcomes (Mathieu et al., 2000; Smith-Jentsch et al., 2008), the specific process through which teams utilize and combine both cognitive structures is still nascent and just recently hypothesized (Rico et al., 2009). Future research should conduct both qualitative and quantitative research to identify when and how individual simulations of potential choices are grouped to reach one decision within a team. It would be fruitful to gather interview data, as well as non-obtrusive performance data, to assess the manner in which individual ideas influence group-level decisions and the quality of those decisions. The next steps for team researchers are to develop team assessment tools to capture cognitive phenomena during real rapid team decision contexts. Scholars focus on assessing the quality of decisions without paying heed to the process that influenced the quality, and thus more efforts should be devoted to understanding how teams aggregate their decision methods to achieve consensus for the implementation of the "winning" decision.

ACKNOWLEDGMENT

This research was supported by the United States Army Research Laboratory and the United States Army Research Office under Grant W911NF-08-1-0144. The views expressed in this work are those of the authors and do not necessarily reflect those of the organizations with which they are affiliated or their sponsoring institutions or agencies.

REFERENCES

Alavi, S.B. and McCormick, J. (2004). A cross-cultural analysis of the effectiveness of the learning organizational model in school contexts. *The International Journal of Educational Management, 18*(7), 408–416.

Artman, H. (1998). Cooperation and situation awareness within and between time scales in dynamic decision-making. In Y. Wærn (Ed.) *Cooperative Process Management: Cognition and Information Technology* (pp. 117–130). London: Taylor & Francis.

Artman, H. (2000). Team situation assessment and information distribution. *Ergonomics, 43*(8), 1111–1128.

Artman, H. and Wærn,Y. (1998). Creation and loss of cognitive empathy at an emergency control centre. In Y. Wærn (Ed.) *Cooperative Process Management: Cognition and Information Technology* (pp. 69–76). London: Taylor & Francis.

Austin, J.R. (2003). Transactive memory in organizational groups: The effects of content, consensus, specialization, and accuracy on group performance. *Journal of Applied Psychology, 88*(5), 866–878.

Baron, J. (1994). *Thinking and Deciding* (2nd ed.). Cambridge: Cambridge University Press.

Beach, L.R. and Lipshitz, R.L. (1997). Why classical theory is an inappropriate standard for evaluating and aiding most human decision-making. In G.A. Klein, J. Orasanu, R. Calderwood, and C.E. Zsambok (Eds.) *Decision Making in Action: Models and Methods* (pp. 21–35). Norwood, NJ: Ablex.

Brannick, M.T., Prince, A., Prince, C., and Salas, E. (1995). The measurement of team process. *Human Factors, 37*(3), 641–651.

Brehmer, B. (1990). Strategies in real time dynamic decision-making. In R. Hogarth (Ed.) *Insights in Decision Making* (pp. 262–279). Chicago, IL: University of Chicago Press.

Bruggink, G.M. (1985). Uncovering the policy factor in accidents. *Air Line Pilot* (May), 22–25.

Burke, C.S., Stagl, K.C., Salas, E., Pierce, L., and Kendall, D.L. (2006). Understanding team adaptation: A conceptual analysis and model. *Journal of Applied Psychology, 91*(6), 1189–1207.

Cannon-Bowers, J.A. and Salas, E. (1997). Teamwork competencies: The interaction of team member knowledge, skills, and attitudes. In H.F. O'Niel (Ed.) *Workforce Readiness: Competencies and Assessment* (pp. 151–174). Mahwah, NJ: Lawrence Erlbaum.

Cannon-Bowers J.A. and Salas, E. (2001). Reflections on shared cognition. *Journal of Organizational Behavior, 22*, 195–202.

Cannon-Bowers, J.A., Salas, E., and Blickensderfer, E. (1999). Toward an understanding of shared cognition. Unpublished manuscript, Naval Air Warfare Center Training Systems Division.

Cannon-Bowers, J.A., Salas, E., and Converse, S. (1993). Shared mental models in expert team decision making. In N.J. Castellan Jr. (Ed.) *Individual and Group Decision Making: Current Issues* (pp. 221–245). Hillsdale, NJ: LEA.

Cannon-Bowers, J.A., Tannenbaum, S.I., Salas, E., and Volpe, C.E. (1995). Defining competencies and establishing team training requirements. In R.A. Guzzo, E. Salas, and Associates (Eds.) *Team Effectiveness and Decision Making in Organizations* (pp. 333–380). San Francisco, CA: Jossey-Bass.

Chi, M.T.H., Glaser, R., and Farr, M.J. (1988). *The Nature of Expertise*. Hillsdale, NJ: Lawrence Erlbaum.

Clark, N.K. and Stephenson, G.M. (1989). Group remembering. In P.B. Paulus (Ed.) *Psychology of Group Influence* (2nd ed., pp. 357–391). Hillsdale, NJ: Lawrence Erlbaum.

Cooke, N.J., Gorman, J.C., Duran, J.L., and Taylor, A.R. (2007). Team cognition in experienced command-and-control teams. *Journal of Experimental Psychology: Applied, 13,* 146–157.

Cooke, N.J., Kiekel, P.A., and Helm, E. (2001). Measuring team knowledge during skill acquisition of a complex task. *International Journal of Cognitive Ergonomics: Special Section on Knowledge Acquisition, 5,* 297–315.

Cooke, N.J., Salas, E., Cannon-Bowers, J.A., and Stout, R. (2000). Measuring team knowledge. *Human Factors, 42,* 151–173.

DeChurch, L.A. and Mesmer-Magnus, J.R. (2010). Measuring shared team mental models: A meta- analysis. *Group Dynamics, 14,* 1–14.

Driskell, J.E. and Salas, E. (1992). Collective behavior and team performance. *Human Factors, 34,* 277–288.

Duffy, L. (1993). Team decision-making biases: An information processing perspective. In G. Klein, J. Orasanu, R. Calderwood, and C.E. Zsambok (Eds.) *Decision Making in Action: Models and Methods* (pp. 246–361). Norwood, NJ: Ablex.

Dyer, J.L. (1984). Team research and team training: A state-of-the-art review. In F.A. Muckler (Ed.) *Human Factors Review: 1984* (pp. 285–323). Santa Monica, CA: Human Factors Society.

Edwards, W. (1954). The theory of decision making. *Psychological Bulletin, 51,* 380–417.

Endsley, M.R. (1995). Toward a theory of situation awareness in dynamic systems. *Human Factors, 37,* 32–65.

Fischhoff, B., Lanir, Z., and Johnson, S. (1997). Risky lessons: Conditions for organizational learning. In Z. Shapira, R. Garud, and P. Nayyar (Eds.) *Technological Learning, Oversights and Foresights* (pp. 306–324). New York: Cambridge University Press.

Foushee, H.C. and Helmreich, R.L. (1988). Group interaction and flight crew performance. In E.L. Wiener and D.C. Nagel (Eds.) *Human Factors in Aviation* (pp. 189–227). San Diego, CA: Academic Press.

Gutwin, C. and Greenberg, S. (2004). The importance of awareness for team cognition in distributed collaboration. In E. Salas and S.M. Fiore (Eds.) *Team Cognition: Understanding the Factors that Drive Process and Performance* (pp. 177–201). Washington, DC:APA Press.

Hogarth, R.M. (1987). *Judgment and Choice* (2nd ed.). New York: Wiley.

Huczynski, A.A. and Buchanan, D.A. (2001). *Organizational Behaviour: An Introductory Text.* Harlow, UK: Pearson Education.

Ioerger, T.R. and He, L. (2003). *Modeling Command and Control in Multi-agent Systems.* 8th International Command and Control Research and Technology Symposium (ICCRTS), Washington, DC, June 17–19.

Jackson, C.L., Colquitt, J.A., Wesson, M.J., and Zapata-Phelan, C.P. (2006). Psychological collectivism: A measurement validation and linkage to group member performance. *Journal of Applied Psychology, 91,* 884–899.

Janis, I.L. (1972). *Victims of Groupthink.* Boston, MA: Houghton Mifflin.

Jones, P.E. and Roelofsma, P. (2000). The potential for social contextual and group biases in team decision-making: Biases, conditions, and psychological mechanisms. *Ergonomics, 43,* 1129–1152.

Kaempf, G.L. and Militello, L. (1991). Expert decision-making under stress. *Proceedings from the Eighth Users' Stress Workshop,* September.

Kiekel, P.A., Cooke, N.J., Foltz, P.W., and Shope, S.M. (2001). Automating measurement of team cognition through analysis of communication data. In M.J. Smith, G. Salvendy, D. Harris, and R.J. Koubek (Eds.) *Usability Evaluation and Interface Design* (pp. 1382–1386). Mahwah, NJ: Lawrence Erlbaum.

Klein, G.A. (1989). Recognition-primed decisions. In W.B. Rouse (Ed.) *Advances in Man–Machine System Research* (vol. 5, pp. 47–92). Greenwich, CT: JAI Press.

Klein, G.A. (1993). A recognition-primed decision (RPD) model of rapid decision making. In G.A. Klein, J. Orasanu, R. Calderwood, and C.E. Zsambok (Eds.) *Decision Making in Action: Models and Methods* (pp. 138–147). Norwood, NJ: Ablex.

Klein, G.A. (1999). *Sources of Power: How People Make Decisions.* Cambridge, MA: MIT Press.

Klein, G.A. and Crandall, B. (1990). *Recognition-primed Decision Strategies: First-Year Interim Report.* ARI research note 90-91, U.S. Army Research Institute for the Behavioral and Social Sciences, Alexandria, VA. Fairborn, OH: Klein Associates.

Klein, G.A., Orasanu, J., Calderwood, R., and Zsambok, C.E. (Eds.) (1993). *Decision Making in Action: Models and Methods.* Norwood, CT: Ablex.

Klein, G.A. and Pierce, L. (2001). Adaptive teams. In *Proceedings of the 6th International Command and Control Research and Technology Symposium,* Annapolis, MD, June 19–21.

Klein, G.A. and Thordsen, M.L. (1990). *A Cognitive Model of Team Decision-making.* Yellow Springs, OH: Klein Associates.

Klimoski, R. and Mohammed, S. (1994). Team mental model: Construct or metaphor? *Journal of Management, 20*(2), 403–437.

Kozlowski, S.W. (1998). Training and developing adaptive teams: theory, principles, and research. In J.A. Cannon-Bowers and E. Salas (Eds.) *Decision Making Under Stress: Implications for Training and Simulation* (pp. 115–153). Washington, DC: APA Books.

Kozlowski, S.W. and Ilgen, D.R. (2006). Enhancing the effectiveness of work groups and teams. *Psychological Science in the Public Interest, 7,* 77–124.

Langan-Fox, J. (2001). Communication in organizations: Speed, diversity, networks and influence on organizational effectiveness, human health and relationships. In N. Anderson, D.S. Ones, H.K. Sinangil, and C. Viswesvaren (Eds.) *International Handbook of Work and Organizational Psychology* (vol. 2, pp. 188–205). London: Sage.

Langan-Fox, J., Code, S., and Langfield-Smith, K. (2000). Team mental models: Methods, techniques and applications. *Human Factors, 42*(2), 1–30.

Larson, J.R. Jr. and Christensen, C. (1993). Groups as problem solving units: Toward a new meaning of social cognition. *British Journal of Social Psychology, 32,* 5–30.

Lee, D., Newman, P., and Price, R. (1999). *Decision Making in Organizations*. Glasgow, UK: Prentice Hall.

Lewis, K. (2003). Measuring transactive memory systems in the field: Scale development and validation. *Journal of Applied Psychology*, 88(4), 587–604.

Liebhaber, M.J. and Smith, C.A.P. (2000). *Naval Air Threat Assessment* (CD-ROM). In *Proceedings of Command and Control Research and Technology Symposium*, Naval Postgraduate School, Monterey, CA.

Lipshitz, R. (1993). Converging themes in the study of decision making in realistic settings. In G.A. Klein, J. Orasanu, R. Calderwood, and C.E. Zsambok (Eds.) *Decision Making in Action: Models and Methods*. Norwood, NJ: Ablex.

Malone, T.W. and Crowston, K. (1994). The interdisciplinary study of coordination. *ACM Computing Surveys*, 26(1), 87–119.

March, J.G. and Simon, H.A. (1958). *Organizations*. New York: Wiley.

Marks, G. and Miller, N. (1985). The effect of certainty on consensus judgements. *Personality and Social Psychology Bulletin*, 11, 165–177.

Marks, M.A., Mathieu, J.E., and Zaccaro, S.J. (2001). A temporally based framework and taxonomy of team processes. *Academy of Management Review*, 26, 355–376.

Mathieu, J.E., Heffner, T.S., Goodwin, G.F., Salas, E., and Cannon-Bowers, J.A. (2000). The influence of shared mental models on team process and performance. *Journal of Applied Psychology*, 85(2), 273–283.

Mohammed, S. and Dumville, B.C. (2001). Team mental models in a team knowledge framework: Expanding theory and measurement across disciplinary boundaries. *Journal of Organizational Behavior*, 22, 89–106.

Mullen, B., Atkins, J.L., Champion, D.S., Edwards, C., Hardy, D., Story, J.E., and Vanderklok, M. (1985). The false consensus effect: A meta-analysis of 155 hypothesis tests. *Journal of Experimental Social Psychology*, 21, 262–283.

Noble, D. (1989). *Application of a Theory of Cognition to Situation Assessment*. Vienna, VA: Engineering Research Associates.

O'Leary-Kelly, A.M., Martocchio, J.J., and Frink, D.D. (1994). A review of the influence of group goals on group performance. *Academy of Management Journal*, 73, 1285–1301.

Orasanu, J. (1990). *Shared Mental Models and Crew Decision Making* (Tech. Rep. 46). Princeton, NJ: Princeton University, Cognitive Science Laboratory.

Orasanu, J. (1994). Shared problem models and flight crew performance. In N. Johnston, N. McDonald, and R. Fuller (Eds.) *Aviation Psychology in Practice* (pp. 255–285). Aldershot, UK: Ashgate.

Orasanu, J. and Connolly, T. (1993). The reinvention of decision making. In G.A. Klein, J. Orasanu, R. Calderwood, and C.E. Zsambok (Eds.) *Decision Making in Action: Models and Methods* (pp. 3–20). Norwood, NJ: Ablex.

Orasanu, J. and Salas, E. (1993). Team decision making in complex environments. In G.A. Klein, J. Orasanu, R. Calderwood, and C.E. Zsambok (Eds.) *Decision Making in Action: Models and Methods* (pp. 327–345). Norwood, NJ: Ablex.

Pascual, R. and Henderson, S. (1997). Evidence of naturalistic decision making in military command and control. In C.E. Zsambok and G. Klein (Eds.) *Naturalistic Decision Making* (pp. 217–226). Mahwah, NJ: Lawrence Erlbaum.

Posner, M.I. (1982). Cumulative development of attentional theory. *American Psychologist*, 37, 53–64.

Postmes, T. and Lea, M. (2000). Social processes and group decision making: Anonymity in group decision support systems. *Ergonomics*, 43, 1152–1274.

Rentsch, J.R., Heffner, T.S., and Duffy, L.T. (1994). What you know is what you get from experience. *Group and Organization Management*, 19, 450–474.

Rico, R., Gibson, C., Sánchez-Manzanares, M., and Clark, M. (2009). On the interplay between team explicit and implicit coordination processes. Paper presented to the 4th INGRoup conference, Colorado Springs, CO.

Rico, R., Sánchez-Manzanares, M., Gil, F., and Gibson, C. (2008). Team implicit coordination processes: A team knowledge based approach. *Academy of Management Review, 33,* 163–184.

Ross, L. (1977). The intuitive psychologist and his shortcomings: Distortions in the attribution process. In L. Berkowitz (Ed.) *Advances in Experimental Social Psychology* (vol. 10, pp. 173–220). New York: Academic Press.

Rouse, W.B., Cannon-Bowers, J.A., and Salas, E. (1992). The role of mental models in team performance in complex systems. *IEEE Transactions on Systems, Man, & Cybernetics, 22,* 1296–1308.

Rouse, W.B. and Morris, N.M. (1986). On looking into the black box: Prospects and limits in the search for mental models. *Psychological Bulletin, 100,* 349–363.

Salas, E., Cooke, N.J., and Rosen, M.A. (2008). On teams, teamwork, and team performance: Discoveries and developments. *Human Factors, 50,* 540–547.

Salas, E., Dickinson, T.L., Converse, S.A., and Tannenbaum, S.I. (1992). Toward an understanding of team performance and training. In R.W. Swezey and E. Salas (Eds.) *Teams: Their Training and Performance* (pp. 3–29). Norwood, NJ: Ablex.

Salas, E., Guthrie, J.W. Jr., Wilson-Donnelly, K.A., Priest, H.A., and Burke, C.S. (2005). Modeling team performance: The basic ingredients and research needs. In W.B. Rouse and K.R. Boff (Eds.) *Organizational Simulation* (pp. 185–228). Chichester, UK: Wiley.

Salas, E., Prince, C., Baker, D.P., and Shrestha, L. (1995). Situation awareness in team performance: Implications for measurement and training. *Human Factors, 37,* 123–136.

Salas, E., Rosen, M.A., and DiazGranados, D. (2010). Expertise-based intuition and decision making in organizations. *Journal of Management, 36*(4), 941–973.

Salas, E., Sims, D.E., and Burke, C.S. (2005). Is there a "big five" in teamwork? *Small Group Research, 36*(5), 555–599.

Serfaty, D., Entin, E.E., and Johnston, J.H. (1998). Team coordination training. In J.A. Cannon-Bowers and E. Salas (Eds.) *Making Decisions Under Stress* (pp. 221–245). Washington, DC: American Psychological Association.

Smith-Jentsch, K.A., Cannon-Bowers, J.A., Tannenbaum, S.I., and Salas, E. (2008). Guided team self-correction: Impacts on team mental models, behavior, and effectiveness. *Small Group Research, 39*(3), 303–327.

Smith-Jentsch, K.A., Johnston, J.H., and Payne, S.C. (1998). Measuring team-related expertise in complex environments. In J. Cannon-Bowers and E. Salas (Eds.) *Making Decisions Under Stress: Implications for Individual and Team Training* (pp. 61–87). Washington, DC: APA Press.

Staw, B.M. and Ross, J. (1987). Knowing when to pull the plug. *Harvard Business Review, 65*(2), 68–74.

Stout, R.J., Cannon-Bowers, J.A., and Salas, E. (1996). The role of shared mental models in developing team situational awareness: Implications for training. *Training Research Journal, 2,* 85–116.

Sundstrom, E., DeMeuse, K.P., and Futrell, D. (1990). Work teams: Applications and effectiveness. *American Psychologist, 45,* 120–133.

Thordsen, M., Galushka, J., Young, S., and Klein, G.A. (1987). *Distributed Decision-making in a Command and Control-planning Environment.* (Contract MDA 903-86-C-0170 for the U.S. Army Research Institute, Alexandria, VA). Fairborn, OH: Klein Associates.

Thordsen, M. and Klein, G.A. (1989). Cognitive processes of the team mind. Paper presented at the Proceedings of the IEEE International Conference on Systems, Man, and Cybernetics, Cambridge, MA.

Walsh, J.P., Henderson, C.M., and Deighton, J. (1988). Negotiated belief structures and decision performance: An empirical investigation. *Organizational Behavior and Human Decision Processes, 42,* 194–216.

Wegner, D.M. (1987). Transactive memory: A contemporary analysis of the group mind. In B. Mullen and G.R. Goethals (Eds.) *Theories of Group Behavior* (pp. 185–208). New York: Springer-Verlag.

Wegner, D.M., Erber, R., and Raymond, P. (1991). Transactive memory in close relationships. *Journal of Personality and Social Psychology, 61,* 923–929.

Weick, K.E. and Roberts, K.H. (1993). Collective mind in organizations: Heedful interrelating on flight decks. *Administrative Science Quarterly, 38,* 357–381.

Wellens, A.R. (1993). Group situation awareness and distributed decision making: From military to civilian applications. In N.J. Castellan Jr. (Ed.) *Individual and Group Decision Making: Current Issues* (pp. 267–291). Hillsdale, NJ: Lawrence Erlbaum.

Whyte, G. (1993). Escalating commitment in individual and group decision making: A prospect theory approach. *Organizational Behavior and Human Decision Processes, 54,* 430–455.

Wildman, J., Shuffler, M., Lazarra, L., Fiore, S., and Burke, S.C. (2012). Trust development in swift starting action teams: A multilevel framework. U.S. Army Research, Paper 162. *Group & Organization Management, 37*(2), 137–170. Retrieved January 9, 2012 from http://digitalcommons.unl.edu/usarmyresearch/162.

12

Decision Making in Distributed Multiteam Systems

Stephanie Zajac, Marissa L. Shuffler,
Budd Darling, and Eduardo Salas

In August of 2005, Hurricane Katrina struck the Gulf Coast, leaving in her path a swath of destruction and devastation not previously seen by the United States (United States Congress, 2006). After the hurricane passed, additional catastrophic damage was caused to New Orleans, in particular due to flooding in much of the city and surrounding parishes. In the wake of this national emergency, cries for assistance from the stricken communities were heard by the entire country. Even prior to the hurricane making landfall, organizations such as the National Weather Service and National Hurricane Service were providing recommendations regarding evacuation needs for the region. However, in both cases, slow and uncoordinated responses from local, state, and national government leadership resulted in the most expensive natural disaster to ever hit the United States. Indeed, the Congressional Report resulting from an investigation into the aftermath of Hurricane Katrina illustrated the disorganization and disarray in the disaster's management, calling it ultimately a massive system failure (United States Congress, 2006). The total cost of damage from Hurricane Katrina was estimated to be $81 billion, with over 1,800 lives lost (Knabb, Rhome, & Brown, 2005).

So what caused this massive failure, given the vast amount of resources and leadership available to manage this event? Why would this occur when organizations such as the Federal Emergency Management Agency and others at the state and local levels have teams that prepare regularly to handle such emergencies? Most importantly, what can we learn from Hurricane Katrina in order to ensure that such a situation does not occur again?

Perhaps the most valuable lesson from Katrina is the realization of the detrimental effects that can occur to processes and performance when systems suffer from ineffective decision-making practices. Multiple teams of individuals were involved at the local, state, and national levels, yet these teams struggled to coordinate efforts in order to ensure that the overall system goals of rescue and recovery were being met. Indeed, the Congressional Report summarizing the events of Hurricane Katrina noted that "there were lapses in command and control within each level of government, and between the three levels of government" (United States Congress, 2006, p. 183).

Hurricane Katrina represents an extreme example of what can happen when there is a failure in decision making across a multiteam system (MTS). MTSs are a relatively new area of study for organizational psychology, emerging rapidly as work problems become increasingly complex (DeChurch & Marks, 2006). Several examples of MTSs can be seen in both the public and private sectors. In 2002, the U.S. government established Provincial Reconstruction Teams, which work to aid in international security and reconstruction of war-torn areas. These MTSs consist of functionally diverse component teams, including soldiers, diplomatic advisors, and civilian agencies (McNerney, 2006). In the private sector, MTSs can be found in strategic alliances, product development, and major engineering projects, with different partner organizations providing resources, distribution channels, manufacturing facilities, funding, and expert knowledge (Healey, Hodgkinson, & Teo, 2009). While the dynamic tasks performed by organizations today may necessitate the use of MTSs, decision making can become very challenging.

Certainly, decision making in distributed MTSs is an avenue ripe for theory and research, especially given its criticality in real-world situations. Thus, the purpose of this chapter is to draw upon current decision making, teams, and MTS theory in order to extrapolate key factors that may influence decision making in distributed MTSs, as well as to highlight potential antecedents that may help to improve decision-making processes and outcomes in such systems. In order to do so, we first clearly define distributed MTSs. We then introduce the antecedents that impact decision-making processes in distributed MTSs, and follow this with a discussion of key points in decision-making theories as they apply to distributed MTS decision making. Finally, we conclude with a look toward future research needs that should be investigated in relation to critical variables of MTS decision making.

DEFINING DISTRIBUTED MULTITEAM SYSTEMS

In order to understand MTSs, it is important to first define them. The most widely accepted definition of MTSs is that of Mathieu, Marks, and Zaccaro (2001): "two or more teams that interface directly and interdependently in response to environmental contingencies toward the accomplishment of collective goals." MTSs are comprised of multiple teams that maintain their own team-level goals while at the same time belonging to a network of teams who work toward at least one shared goal (DeChurch et al., 2011). In order for an MTS to be effective, team members must learn to shift their attention from within-team activities to cross-team activities (Marks et al., 2005), allowing them to transfer from their team goals to previously mentioned shared goals.

MTSs are generally tightly coupled networks of teams with specialized abilities or skills used to complete goals that would previously be considered too big for a single team to perform (DeChurch & Marks, 2006; Marks et al., 2005). As can be seen from the aforementioned examples, MTSs are not limited to working within a single organization; rather, they may include teams from other organizations so long as they are combining their efforts to accomplish a mutual goal (DeChurch et al., 2011; Mathieu, Marks, & Zaccaro, 2001). MTSs are larger than individual teams yet smaller than organizations as a whole (Mathieu, Marks, & Zaccaro, 2001). MTSs often target challenges that require multiple teams with little to no previous interaction with one another to combine their individual team expertise to help solve the issue or issues at hand (DeChurch et al., 2011).

Geographical dispersion of team and MTS members has become an increasingly prominent issue in organizational research due to numerous advances in technology (Connaughton & Shuffler, 2007). Distributed teams and MTSs are those in which members are geographically dispersed but working together interdependently to achieve a common goal (Townsend, DeMarie, & Hendrickson, 1998). Current research has focused on both the positive and negative aspects of distributed teams. Indeed, there is extensive debate as to whether distribution is a challenge or a distinct advantage (Connaughton & Shuffler, 2007). Zaccaro, Ardison, and Orvis (2004) highlight several advantages of distribution, including a greater participation of skilled participants, increased speed of response time to incidents, and increased exposure for team members to new ideas, perspectives, and experiences, which can broaden their knowledge to apply to future goals. However, there is evidence that distribution can lead to many problems in team processes, including lower levels of trust (Jarvenpaa & Leidner, 1999), increased affective conflict (Hinds & Bailey, 2003), impaired transactive memory systems (O'Leary & Mortensen, 2005), and reduced team performance (Connaughton & Daly, 2004).

Certainly, distribution can be viewed as either a challenge or an opportunity for Mtss. Systems that are able to leverage distribution in order to bring together component teams and individual members who are functionally diverse may be better able to achieve system-level and team goals, especially for complex or demanding tasks. Furthermore, distribution can enable membership fluidity where component teams and individual members can come and go as needed based on their expertise (Martins, Gilson, & Maynard, 2004). However, MTS distribution has its downfall in that it can negate these advantages if members and component teams cannot effectively coordinate, communicate, and cooperate due to decreased social presence and perceived differences caused by member geographic configuration. This can become especially problematic depending upon the richness of the media used in MTSs to facilitate the flow of information, as richer forms of media such as videoconferencing may be able to convey more information and social presence than less rich forms (Kirkman & Mathieu, 2005).

A MULTI-LEVEL FRAMEWORK OF DECISION MAKING IN MULTITEAM SYSTEMS

Given the above definition of distributed MTSs, we next move to identifying key factors involved in the decision making of such systems. While integrating the literature on individual and team decision making, we aim to move beyond current research to propose a framework of decision making in MTSs. Figure 12.1 illustrates this overarching framework, and highlights five particular components: situational context, antecedents, decision-making processes, outcomes, and task interdependency. The situational context of distributed MTSs in terms of distribution, social presence, and information flow was introduced in the previous section, thus we next explore four antecedents that ultimately lead to MTS-level outcomes, then examine critical team and MTS-level decision-making processes, and finally consider the moderating effect of task interdependence. All of these factors lead to the success of MTS outcomes, which can range from overall performance to viability and learning, and are

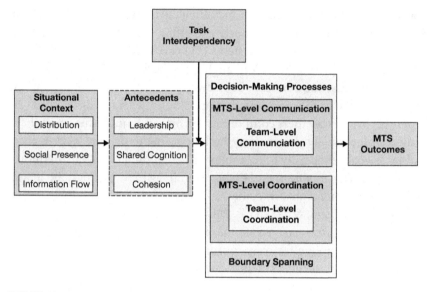

FIGURE 12.1
A multi-level framework of decision making in distributed multiteam systems.

defined by the specific outcomes of interest in a given decision-making situation. In the following sections, we provide further clarification regarding the role of antecedents, decision-making processes, and task interdependency as critical components of this framework.

ANTECEDENTS OF DISTRIBUTED MTS DECISION MAKING

Our first area of discussion is that of antecedents that may help to facilitate effective decision making. Drawing upon the teams and organization literatures, we propose that there are three such antecedents that may specifically operate in MTS environments to influence the development of effective decision-making processes. These antecedents each belong to a higher-order category of affective (i.e., cohesion), behavioral (i.e., leadership), and cognitive (i.e., transactive memory and shared mental model (SMM)) emergent states and processes, all noted in the team literature as playing critical roles in team decision making and performance.

These emergent states have become an increasing focus of team research, and are beginning to be examined in the MTS literature as well (e.g.,

DeChurch et al., 2011; DeChurch & Marks, 2006). The antecedents selected here represent specific antecedents that have previously been linked to effective distributed team and MTS processes and outcomes, and specifically have been shown to impact processes critical to decision making, such as information sharing, coordination, and communication. Of course, it is important to note that these three antecedents are not exclusive in terms of being the only antecedents to impact decision making in distributed MTSs. Instead, these antecedents are meant to provide a starting point for future researchers to begin exploring potential avenues for facilitating and improving decision making in distributed MTSs. For each of these antecedents, we provide a definition and discussion of its role in the decision-making process in distributed MTSs.

Leadership

Leadership is viewed as the enactment of necessary behaviors to establish goals and set direction that leads to the successful accomplishment of these goals (Fleishman et al., 1991). Leadership can come from one or several leaders internal or external to the team, as well as those formally acknowledged as serving in leadership positions, or informally stepping up when a need for leadership is recognized (Morgeson, DeRue, & Karam, 2010). Within MTSs, there may be multiple leaders within component teams, one MTS-level leader, or a combination of both. While leadership can be viewed from multiple perspectives, we advance this functional perspective as a critical consideration, in that it promotes an understanding of the specific behaviors that must be enacted from a leadership perspective for decision making.

From a leadership perspective, leaders of distributed MTSs can provide a critical role in ensuring effective decision-making processes, as leaders are positioned to respond to both the team-level needs and the system-level needs (Mathieu, Marks, & Zaccaro, 2001). Furthermore, leaders may also serve to coordinate across the multiple echelons, ensuring that individuals within teams are both cooperating and coordinating effectively, as well as aiding in boundary spanning to ensure that teams are also coordinating across the system (Zaccaro, Marks, & DeChurch, 2012). Thus, leaders of MTSs require skill in focusing not only at the team level of interaction to ensure effective processes and positive outcomes, but also at the larger systems level. Accordingly, it may be necessary for MTSs to invoke different forms of leadership to facilitate effective leadership functions at both levels (Zaccaro & DeChurch, 2012). Zaccaro and

DeChurch (2012) proposed that different forms of both shared and vertical leadership can occur in MTSs, and that attributes such as MTS size, composition, maturity, power distribution, and interdependence of component teams can influence which of these leadership forms are most effective.

In terms of decision making, leadership can play an especially pivotal role in distributed MTSs, as part of leadership responsibility involves motivating team members and setting the tone for how the system will interact (Zaccaro & Banks, 2001). From a decision-making perspective, this means that the role of leadership is to establish norms that will support an environment of coordination and communication that will facilitate effective decision making. This is especially critical when system members are separated by distance, as the leader can help to serve as a boundary spanner in order to promote the creation of system-level identities. Furthermore, leadership can continue to remind team members of their commitment to the goal and motivate them throughout performance periods to further ensure that coordination and communication are maintained both within and across the MTS as needed. Thus, leadership should be viewed as a key antecedent to distributed MTS decision making.

Shared Cognition

The next proposed antecedent of effective distributed MTS decision making concerns cognitive emergent states: shared mental models and transactive memory systems. Communication and coordination both contribute to a shared cognition, which enables team members to hold a common understanding of the environment and the actions required for successful execution of the task (Cannon-Bowers & Salas, 2001). In team decision-making literature this is often referred to as a *shared mental model* (SMM). An accurate SMM is depicted by individual team members possessing overlapping representations of their tasks, roles, and situational environment. SMMs provide a rich source of collective information, organized for faster processing and retrieval. Information is categorized into patterns, and is attached to salient cues in the environment (Cannon-Bowers, Salas, & Converse, 1993).

Further delineating the concept of SMMs, an effective decision-making unit must maintain a shared task representation and a shared assessment of the situation. In distributed MTSs, this may prove to be particularly challenging. As members are not always physically co-located, they may attend to different environmental cues or have disparate views of the task situation. Taking into account naturalistic decision making (NDM) models, this would cause decision makers to apply different and possibly conflicting schema.

The term *transactive memory system* (TMS) aims to describe how the "encoding, storage, retrieval, and communication of information" takes place between people (Brandon & Hollingshead, 2004, p. 633). At the team level, members serve as experts in separate domains and are often responsible for any new information that falls within their specialty (Wegner, 1986). In a well-developed TMS, team members have access to others' information through effective communication and a shared understanding or consensus of who is the expert in each field (Smith-Jentsch, Kraiger, & Salas, 2009).

Extant literature establishes the importance of efficient TMSs within decision-making teams. Although a team may be composed of individuals who collectively hold the expertise necessary to make optimal decisions, this does not guarantee they will seek and share the necessary information (Brodbeck et al., 2007). One plausible explanation may be found in the type and amount of information shared when there is a high level of expertise recognition. Often decision-making teams suffer from incomplete information because collective information (that held by all members of the team) is more likely to be shared and discussed than unique information. However, when expertise is assigned and acknowledged by team members, individuals are more likely to share critical, individually held knowledge when engaging in the decision-making process (Stewart & Stasser, 1995). In addition, the division of cognitive labor required for the encoding and storage of knowledge enables team members to gain access to a larger pool of information than they are capable of holding individually.

Extrapolating these findings to distributed MTSs, the development of highly functioning TMSs among system members should aid in facilitating a highly coordinated system, even when such systems are distributed. However, unique to MTSs is the fact that TMSs may need to be developed at both the component team and system levels. In order to accomplish both team- and system-level goals, MTSs whose members hold an understanding of expertise in regard to both their component team task and the overall goals of the MTS should be better able to coordinate appropriately and ensure that all members have the proper information required for effective decision making. These two types of TMS within distributed MTSs may be particularly necessary for facilitating information sharing across time and space, as distribution can impede such sharing of necessary information

(DeChurch et al., 2011). Thus, interventions aimed at developing such dual TMSs within distributed MTSs may be pivotal to effective decision making in these environments.

Cohesion

Cohesion is often regarded as one of the most important variables contributing to team effectiveness (Carless & DePaola, 2000; Carron & Brawley, 2000; Dion, 2001). It has been studied extensively—researchers have examined it in multiple contexts, assigning it various definitions. Indeed, there is much debate about how cohesion should be defined. At the team level, cohesion has been found to influence a range of team processes and outcomes. Of particular relevance to distributed MTS decision making, cohesion has been found to influence communication, workload sharing, and team effectiveness (Beal et al., 2003; Carless & DePaola, 2000; Evans & Dion, 1991; Mullen & Copper, 1994). However, it is important to note that, in decision making, certain aspects of cohesion are more influential in improving team decision making than others. In their meta-analysis of group cohesiveness and team performance, Mullen and Copper (1994) found that task cohesion was related to improved group decision making, while social cohesion actually impaired group decision making. This may be due to the fact that interpersonal attraction can contribute to groupthink, whereas cohesion regarding the task reflects a commitment to team goals, an important factor to consider in relation to MTSs.

Moving from the team level up to the MTS level, cohesion may influence decision making in different ways depending on the structure of the MTS. Specifically, instead of simply being concerned about the overall level of cohesion in the team, there is now an added level that may interact with the team cohesion. For example, if members of a component team identify strongly with one another and are very cohesive, this would typically be viewed as a positive factor in terms of teamwork and team performance. However, in an MTS, a team that is only cohesive within itself and not across the system may lead to the development of faultlines, bringing out differences and creating conflict within the larger system (Connaughton, Williams, & Shuffler, 2012; Lau & Murnighan, 2005). Furthermore, in large MTSs, it may be reasonable to believe that high cohesion across the entire system is not always necessary, but instead it may be more critical that there is cohesion among key players, such as those in boundary-spanning roles such as team leaders or individuals who pass information across teams. As previously discussed, these boundary spanners can be vital to the success of accomplishing large, higher-order goals (Marrone, 2010), and therefore understanding how cohesion may differ in form within MTSs is critical.

DECISION-MAKING PROCESSES IN DISTRIBUTED MULTITEAM SYSTEMS

The antecedents discussed above in turn affect particular aspects of the processes that underlie decision making in such contexts. As distributed MTSs are a new area of research, the following sections draw from current decision-making theory in order to extrapolate relevant theory and research that may be applicable to such areas. While a complete review of decision-making theory is beyond the scope of this chapter, we will use key elements of the extant literature to inform the discussion of MTS-level decision making. First, we discuss the importance of communication and coordination as critical aspects of the distributed MTS decision-making process. Next, we address issues of boundary spanning as an additional component of significance in distributed MTS decision making. Finally, we look at task interdependence as a possible moderator of the relationship between decision-making antecedents and both team- and MTS-level decision-making processes.

Communication and Coordination in Distributed MTS Decision-making Processes

As occupational requirements change with the advent of new technology and increasingly demanding tasks, work environments at times necessitate the use of teams to perform critical roles (Salas, Cooke, & Rosen, 2008). Difficult and complex tasks can be beyond the scope of any one individual's ability. They may also require expertise in more than one domain, and teams allow for a larger pool of resources and division of labor (Cooper et al., 1984; van Ginkel, Tindale, & Knippenberg 2009). According to Cannon-Bowers, Salas, and Converse (1993), the individual contributions from team members create a foundation for efficient decision making. However, engaging in effective team processes is also a critical element of performance that creates new challenges to be considered. Teams must effectively integrate their individual knowledge and expertise to make well-informed and accurate decisions (Cannon-Bowers, Salas, & Converse, 1993).

Characteristics that promote effective team processes, particularly communication and coordination, are the cornerstone of high perform- ance, and are ubiquitous in the team decision-making literature (Cannon- Bowers, Salas, & Converse, 1993; Marks, Mathieu, & Zaccaro, 2001). Information exchange could include knowledge about environmental characteristics, team resources and constraints, and mission objectives (Cooper et al., 1984). The efficacy of communication is influenced by several features, such as the communication structure, the medium used, and the nature of the messages. Technological advances have changed the face of team interaction across all domains, and have necessitated the understanding of virtual communication. Research shows that teams that do not have prior experience of working together are more likely to engage in unique knowledge sharing when they are face-to-face rather than in a technology-mediated environment (Alge, Wiethoff, & Klein, 2003). In a study conducted by Hollenbeck et al. (1995), high-performing teams were more likely to convey information while low-performing teams spent the majority of the allotted time asking questions of their team members. High-performing teams were also more likely to evaluate and process information before passing it on to a team member. This resulted in more qualitative information about the meaning of raw data, which can be more easily interpreted by non-experts.

According to van Ginkel, Tindale, and van Knippenberg (2009), failure to utilize informational resources effectively can have a detrimental effect on decision quality. Specifically, poor communication can result in incomplete knowledge when interpreting the best course of action. For example, high levels of cohesion are largely viewed as having a positive effect, but can cause problems when they lead to groupthink. This occurs when team members prefer unanimity over a thorough review of all possible options (Cannon-Bowers, Salas, & Converse, 1993). Another possible source of incomplete information is the tendency for team members to avoid discussing their individual task representations. This leads to an inability to correct misrepresentations among members and results in a lack of shared understanding (van Ginkel, Tindale, & van Knippenberg, 2009).

In addition, coordination is also considered a hallmark of effective decision making when interdependent individuals have to work together toward a common goal. High performance is indicated by synchronization in planning, action implementation, and resource management (Zaccaro, Gualtieri, & Minionis, 1995). As indicated by Fiore et al. (2003), there is an inherent difficulty in effective coordination when several members of a team work together toward a common task. This issue is even more salient when you add in the potentially limiting effects of distribution. Therefore, reducing coordination decrement in teams and team decision making continues to be a fruitful area of research.

Given these individual- and team-level decision-making approaches, we next move to the MTS level. MTSs share several key features with individual teams, and much of the empirical and theoretical literature concerning teams can be considered relevant in this emerging research domain. Moving from the team level up to the MTS level, the antecedents of effective decision making may operate in different ways, and may be more or less important based on the MTS structure. Multiteam systems are characterized in part by a goal hierarchy. Each individual team must work toward accomplishment of their distinct goals, which in turn coalesce to achieve the overarching goal of the entire system (Marks et al., 2005). This suggests that there are likely to be several independent decision makers, each having to determine where to allocate their resources in order to realize both proximal and distal goals (Baker, Day, & Salas, 2006).

Another challenge inherent to MTSs pertains to the diversity of professions and educational backgrounds represented in units that must interact cooperatively. These individuals are likely to be trained disparately, leading to differences in communication styles and possible difficulties in conveying information (Baker, Day, & Salas, 2006). Thus, these individual variations may lead to differences in how decisions are made. Indeed, Caldwell (2005) calls attention to the fact that multiple forms of expertise are present in MTSs, which from the NDM perspective may mean that decision makers may utilize their expertise differently to draw unique conclusions and decisions. Therefore, special consideration needs to be given to the way information is shared, processed, and interpreted by different individuals and units in MTSs.

In consideration of the increased importance of coordination necessary in MTSs, a "new paradigm of distributed supervisory coordination" is likely to develop (Caldwell, 2005, p. 145). Inter-team coordination is a critical component of MTS success, as teams must coordinate between one another in order to determine tasking and make decisions that will impact MTS-level goals (DeChurch & Marks, 2006). Healey, Hodgkinson, and Teo (2009) suggest that coordination may in fact be the most important element in MTS functioning, and that communication is central in facilitating coordination.

Finally, incorporating the distribution aspect of distributed MTSs, decision making may be further affected by the variance in social presence and synchronicity of communication (Kirkman & Mathieu, 2005; Zaccaro,

Marks, & DeChurch, 2012). Indeed, when members and/or component teams are distributed from one another, decision making may be conducted primarily by those who are collocated with one another, as there is a heightened level of social presence and information can be quickly relayed within and between collocated teams in the system. In their theoretical review of distributed team decision making, Stagl and colleagues (2007) proposed that distribution of team members may create feedback delays and asymmetries in the flow of information, which can negatively impact the ability of team members to interpret courses of action and decisions. This may be problematic in that critical information from distributed team members and their expertise may not be factored into important decisions. It is expected that the same may hold true for MTSs, especially when entire component teams have a delay in receiving or processing information from other component teams. As will be further discussed in the following section, decision making in MTSs may also be impeded by distribution by isolating individual members and component teams, which may make it difficult for members to identify as part of the system overall. This lack of identification can subsequently reduce the flow of information among system members, degrading the quality of shared knowledge structures and thus decisions based upon such structures (Connaughton, Williams, & Shuffler, 2012).

Boundary Spanning as a Distributed MTS Decision-making Process

A critical issue to consider when exploring distributed MTS decision making is that of boundary spanning, or the role of working across team- and system-level boundaries in order to achieve common goals and make MTS-level decisions (Marks, Mathieu, & Zaccaro, 2001). As described by Marks, Mathieu, and Zaccaro (2001), boundary spanning is referred to as an external team process that involves the interactions of a team with others who are external to the team. This differs from intra-team processes, which are the processes by which team members interact internally to distribute workloads and develop strategies. From an MTS perspective, boundary spanners may be individuals who belong to one component team but reach out to other component teams in order to share information, coordinate, or accomplish other processes (Davison et al., 2011). Boundary spanners may also be individuals external to component teams, such as the leader of an MTS, who must serve to coordinate information flow across the system in order to facilitate effective decision making at the team and MTS levels (Ancona & Caldwell, 1992).

A recent review of prior research by Marrone (2010) attempted to provide insight into the state of team boundary spanning by highlighting key factors across various studies, which included perspectives into relationships among external team activity, internal team activity, and overall team effectiveness. Marrone (2010) also makes it clear that boundary spanning is important for understanding how teams can effectively meet external demands and also maintain a productive internal climate in order to maximize both organization and team effectiveness. Extrapolating these findings to decision making in distributed MTSs, boundary spanning becomes a critical issue in MTSs as there is a need for both intra-team and inter-team horizontal coordination (Davison et al., 2012). System members, particularly leaders, must therefore be able and willing to work across boundaries in order for decision making to be based upon accurate information and input from all necessary areas of expertise within the MTS. According to JDM models, decision makers will choose an option that satisfies the current needs of the situation. If MTS-level needs are not made clear to all boundary-spanning members, then component teams may make decisions without taking into account the full range of current requirements necessary to meet the system's goals.

However, while boundary spanning is critical to distributed MTS decision making, it can also be very difficult to do effectively. Boundary spanning may be highly challenging and taxing for individuals who are participating in such activities (Marrone, 2010), as these individuals continually need to maintain their attention between internal and external demands (Choi, 2002). These same individuals may also be caught between internal and external expectations, which may be conflicting (Katz & Kahn, 1978). Ancona and Caldwell (1992) found that internal group processes predicted only team member satisfaction and performance, while external interactions were only predictive of sales revenue. Furthermore, when accounting for distribution, boundary spanners may also face a lack of social presence due to isolation from others or a lack of richness in the media being used to communicate. For example, drawing upon the original Hurricane Katrina example, it may be the case that, while leaders at the different government levels attempted to span boundaries and share information, the breakdown in landline and cellular telephone systems reduced the ability of these leaders to communicate and coordinate across distances. Thus, while boundary spanning plays a critical role in facilitating the processes necessary for effective decision making in MTSs, it can be challenging for such boundary spanning to be performed successfully.

Task Interdependence and Decision Making in Distributed Multiteam Systems

Finally, the interdependence of component teams and members within an MTS moderates the antecedents' relationship with decision-making processes, as differences in interdependency may impact how much the system is affected by emergent states such as cohesion. Interdependence is one of the key features within many definitions of teams (e.g., Kozlowski & Bell, 2003; Salas et al., 1992). It refers to the dependency among members, or the structure and degree to which members are interconnected and rely upon each other to complete the task. Task interdependence has been shown to have implications for team performance and recent work has argued that task interdependence is a useful way to classify teams in terms of their holistic team-level attributes (Wildman et al., in press). For instance, interdependence has been found to moderate the relationship between team cognition and team performance such that team cognition better predicted performance in highly interdependent teams (DeChurch & Mesmer-Magnus, 2010). Further, research has found that the collective efficacy–team performance relationship is stronger in highly interdependent teams than in those with low interdependence (Stajkovic, Lee, & Nyberg, 2009). It is thus important to evaluate the level of interdependence within and across teams within an MTS in order to gain a better understanding of decision making and how MTS task structure impacts subsequent decision-making processes.

Indeed, a key feature of MTSs involves how component teams are linked to one another and how they operate within a broader goal structure. As a defining feature, the component teams within an MTS exhibit input, process, and output interdependence with at least one other team in the MTS (Mathieu, Marks, & Zaccaro, 2001). However, this does not mean that all component teams have or need the same degree of interdependency. Further, Mathieu, Marks and Zaccaro (2001) defined three kinds of functional interdependence that can exist within MTSs. *Input interdependence* denotes the degree to which component teams in the MTS need to share task-related resources (e.g., people, facilities, information). *Process interdependence* refers to interactions that must occur between teams within the MTS in order to actually perform MTS tasks for the sake of accomplishing MTS goals. Finally, *outcome interdependence* is the extent to which the consequences of a component team performance depend upon the successful goal attainment of other component teams. According to NDM models, decision makers evaluate situational cues in the environment when responding to task demands, and apply the appropriate schema. Therefore, in interdependent teams, it is vital that all decision makers have an understanding of the task, as it will ultimately affect both team- and system-level inputs, processes, and outcomes.

Reflecting on MTS interdependencies in this sense, distributed MTSs may vary in regard to who must be connected in order to make decisions, and how coordinated component teams must be in order to make effective decisions. When considering the MTS level, it may be the case that not every member needs to be coordinated or to communicate with one another in order to obtain successful outcomes. For example, it may be the case that only component team leaders are involved in the decision-making process, as each component team is performing its own tasks that are additive in nature. Understanding how task interdependence may impact decision making in this way is critical, as it has implications for what antecedents (e.g., leadership in the aforementioned example) may influence decision-making outcomes, and how these systems should be trained and developed.

Of all the critical issues that MTSs may face in relation to decision making, perhaps these two may be in demand the most when also considering the context of physical distribution. As identity formation and boundary spanning can be challenging in face-to-face environments, the physical distribution of team members only serves further to complicate their enactment by reducing social presence. Furthermore, task interdependence may moderate the impact that distribution has on MTS decision making, as MTSs with highly interdependent and complex tasks may be much more likely to suffer communication breakdowns and coordination challenges when distributed than MTSs with less interdependency within and across component teams. Certainly, these three areas are in critical need of research, and particularly would benefit from an investigation of antecedents that may influence their impact on distributed MTS decision making.

FUTURE RESEARCH DIRECTIONS

Indeed, as has been illustrated throughout this chapter, there is much left to be learned regarding decision making in distributed MTSs. The purpose of the research framework introduced herein is to provide some organization regarding where such research may need to go in the future.

While several potential research avenues have been mentioned thus far, it is important to conclude with some overarching directions for future research that may be most critical. These include basic research necessary for understanding the functioning of decision making in distributed MTSs as well as the need for training and development interventions to enhance and improve decision making in these environments.

First, it is crucial that more basic research is conducted in order to understand these issues within distributed MTS environments. As mentioned throughout the chapter, there is very little existing empirical research regarding MTSs in general, with no real understanding of how decision making functions in these environments. Additionally, while MTSs in the real world are more often distributed in some way than not, the majority of research conducted thus far has only involved face-to-face environments.

Furthermore, much of the existing literature regarding MTSs is primarily an application of team theory and research to the system level; research is needed to investigate the qualities of decision making in distributed MTSs that may be unique to this level. In order to do this successfully, it may be necessary to conduct this research using real-world MTSs as opposed to laboratory experiments. Although it can be challenging to obtain such real-world data given the scale and complex nature of real-world distributed MTSs, there are options. For example, Dechurch and colleagues (2011) conducted a historiometric analysis of critical incidents in order to understand leadership functions within MTSs. This approach drew from historical records of real-world incidents from MTSs involved in Hurricanes Katrina and Andrew, as well as provincial reconstruction teams operating in Iraq and Afghanistan. While not a traditional field study, this analysis resulted in a unique perspective of leadership in MTSs, allowing for novel system-level issues to emerge that may not have been recognized or identified in traditional laboratory studies.

In addition to further research, it is also imperative that we begin to address the training and development needs of distributed MTSs in order to enhance decision making. It may be worthwhile to begin drawing upon what research is in existence at the team level and the current available research at the MTS level to begin identifying potential interventions that may aid in improving such decision-making processes. As discussed earlier, the historiometric approach may be necessary for improving distributed MTS decision making, particularly by drawing upon the antecedents of trust, cohesion, leadership, and transactive memory systems discussed herein. While this may not be an optimal solution given the current lack of research, it does provide a means by which to begin exploring the unique training and development needs of such systems, and to potentially improve upon and reduce the likelihood of drastic errors in decision making such as those made during Hurricane Katrina.

CONCLUSION

Certainly, there is much left to explore in the area of distributed MTS decision making. We hope that this chapter and resulting framework provide an introduction that will spark further thought and debate in this area, enriching the theory and providing empirical research in order to better understand how to prevent situations such as that experienced during Hurricane Katrina. Given the prevalence of MTSs in real-world environments and the impact that their decisions may have on others, it is imperative that we continue to expand our knowledge and theory to improve and enhance current decision-making practices in these systems.

REFERENCES

Alge, B.J., Wiethoff, C., and Klein, H.J. (2003). When does the medium matter? Knowledge-building experiences and opportunities in decision-making teams. *Organizational Behavior & Human Decision Processes, 91*, 26–37.

Ancona, D.G. and Caldwell, D.F. (1992). Bridging the boundary: External activities and performance in organizational teams. *Administrative Science Quarterly, 37*, 634–665.

Baker, D., Day, R., and Salas, E. (2006). Teamwork as an essential component of high-reliability organizations. *Health Research and Educational Trust, 4*(41), 1576–1598.

Beal, D.J., Cohen, R.R., Burke, M.J., and McLendon, C.L. (2003). Cohesion and performance in groups: A meta-analytic clarification of construct relations. *Journal of Applied Psychology, 88*, 989–1004.

Brandon, D.P. and Hollingshead, A.B. (2004). Transactive memory systems in organizations: Matching tasks, expertise, and people. *Organization Science, 15*(6), 633–644.

Brodbeck, F.C., Kerschreiter, R., Mojzisch, A., and Shulz-Hardt, S. (2007). Group decision making under conditions of distributed knowledge: The information asymmetries model. *Academy of Management Review, 32*, 459–479.

Caldwell, B. (2005). Multi-team dynamics and distributed expertise in mission operations. *Aviation, Space, and Environmental Medicine, 76*(6), 145–153.

Cannon-Bowers, J.A. and Salas, E. (2001). Reflections on shared cognition. *Journal of Organizational Behavior, 22*(2), 195–202.

Cannon-Bowers, J.A., Salas, E., and Converse, S.A. (1993). Shared mental models in expert team decision making. In N.J. Castellan Jr. (Ed.) *Current Issues in Individual and Group Decision Making* (pp. 221–246). Hillsdale, NJ: Lawrence Erlbaum.

Carless, S.A. and DePaola, C. (2000). The measurement of cohesion in work teams. *Small Group Research, 31,* 71–88.

Carron, A.V. and Brawley, L.R. (2000). Cohesion: Conceptual and measurement issues. *Small Group Research, 31,* 89–106.

Choi, J.N. (2002). External activities and team effectiveness: Review and theoretical development. *Small Group Research, 33*(2), 181–202.

Connaughton, S.L. and Daly, J.A. (2004). Leading from afar: Strategies for effectively leading virtual teams. In S.H. Godar and S.P. Ferris (Eds.) *Virtual and Collaborative Teams: Process, Technologies and Practice* (pp. 49–75). Hershey, PA: Idea Group.

Connaughton, S.L. and Shuffler, M. (2007). Multinational and multicultural distributed teams. *Small Group Research, 38,* 387–412.

Connaughton, S.L., Williams, E., and Shuffler, M. (2012). Social identity issues in multiteam systems: Considerations for future research. In S.J. Zaccaro, M.A. Marks, and L.A. DeChurch (Eds.) *Multiteam Systems: An Organizational Form for Dynamic and Complex Environments.* New York: Routledge.

Cooper, M., Shiflett, S., Korotkin, A.L., and Fleishman, E.A. (1984). *Command and Control Teams: Techniques for Assessing Team Performance* (ARRO Final Report). Washington, DC: ARRO.

Davison, R.B., Hollenbeck, J.R., Barnes, C.M., Sleesman, D.J., and Ilgen, D.R. (2012). Coordinated action in multiteam systems. *Journal of Applied Psychology, 97*(4), 808–824.

Davison, R.B., Hollenbeck, J.R., Ilgen, D.R., Barnes, C.M., and Sleesman, D.J. (2011). Role of action and transition processes in large multiteam systems. Paper presented at the annual meeting of the Society of Industrial and Organizational Psychology, Atlanta, GA.

DeChurch, L.A., Burke, C.S., Shuffler, M.L., Lyons, R., Doty, D., and Salas, E. (2011). A historiometric analysis of leadership in mission critical multiteam environments. *Leadership Quarterly, 22*(1), 152–169.

DeChurch, L.A. and Marks, M.A. (2006). Leadership in multiteam systems. *Journal of Applied Psychology, 91,* 311–329.

DeChurch, L.A. and Mesmer-Magnus, J. (2010). The cognitive underpinnings of effective teamwork: A meta-analysis. *Journal of Applied Psychology, 95,* 32–53.

Dion, K.L. (2001). Group cohesion: From "field of forces" to multidimensional construct: Erratum. *Group Dynamics: Theory, Research, and Practice, 5,* 7–26.

Evans, C.R. and Dion, K.L. (1991). Group cohesion and performance: A meta-analysis. *Small Group Research, 22*(2), 175–186.

Fiore, S.M., Salas, E., Cuevas, H.M., and Bowers, C.A. (2003). Distributed coordination space: Towards a theory of distributed team process and performance. *Theoretical Issues in Ergonomic Science, 4,* 340–363.

Fleishman, E.A., Mumford, M.D., Zaccaro, S.J., Levin, K.Y., Korotkin, A.L., and Hein, M.B. (1991). Taxonomic efforts in the description of leader behavior: A synthesis and functional interpretation. *Leadership Quarterly, 2*(4), 245–287.

Healey, M.P., Hodgkinson, G.P., and Teo, S. (2009). Responding effectively to civil emergencies: The role of transactive memory in the performance of multiteam systems. Paper presented at the 9th International Conference on Naturalistic Decision Making, London, UK.

Hinds, P.J. and Bailey, D.E. (2003). Out of sight, out of sync: Understanding conflict in distributed teams. *Organization Science, 14*(6), 615–632.

Hollenbeck, J.R., Ilgen, D.R., Sego, D.J., Hedlund, J., Major, D.A., and Phillips, J. (1995). Multilevel theory of team decision making: Decision performance in teams incorporating distributed expertise. *Journal of Applied Psychology, 80*(2), 292–316.

Jarvenpaa, S.L. and Leidner, D.E. (1999). *The Development and Maintenance of Trust in Global Virtual Teams*. Fontainebleau, France: INSEAD.

Katz, D. and Kahn, R.L. (1978). *The Social Psychology of Organizations*. New York: Wiley.

Kirkman, B.L. and Mathieu, J.E. (2005). The dimensions and antecedents of team virtuality. *Journal of Management, 31*(5), 700–718.

Knabb, R.D., Rhome, J.R., and Brown, D.P. (2005). *Tropical Cyclone Report: Hurricane Katrina, 23–30 August 2005*. Miama, FL: National Hurricane Center.

Kozlowski, S.W.J. and Bell, B.S. (2003). Work groups and teams in organizations. In W. Borman, D. Ilgen, and R. Klimiski (Eds.) *Comprehensive Handbook of Psychology* (vol. 12, pp. 333–375). New York: Wiley.

Lau, D.C. and Murnighan, J.K. (2005). Interactions within groups and subgroups: The effects of demographic faultlines. *The Academy of Management Journal, 48*(4), 645–659.

Marks, M.A., DeChurch, L.A., Mathieu, J.E., Panzer, F.J., and Alonso, A. (2005). Teamwork in multiteam systems. *Journal of Applied Psychology, 90*, 964–971.

Marks, M.A., Mathieu, J.E., and Zaccaro, S.J. (2001). A temporally based framework and taxonomy of team processes. *Academy of Management Review, 26*(3), 356–376.

Marrone, J.A. (2010). Team boundary spanning: A multilevel review of past research and proposals for the future. *Journal of Management, 36*(4), 911–940.

Martins, L.L., Gilson, L.L., and Maynard, M.T. (2004). Virtual teams: What do we know and where do we go from here? *Journal of Management, 30*(6), 805–835.

Mathieu, J.E., Marks, M.A., and Zaccaro, S.J. (2001). Multiteam systems. In N. Anderson, D.S. Ones, H.K. Sinangil, and C. Viswesvarin (Eds.) *Handbook of Industrial, Work and Organizational Psychology* (pp. 289–313). Thousand Oaks, CA: Sage.

McNerney, M.J. (2006). Reconstruction in Afghanistan: Are PRTs a model or a muddle? *Parameters, 4*(Winter), 44.

Morgeson, F.P., DeRue, D.S., and Karam, E.P. (2010). Leadership in teams: A functional approach to understanding leadership structures and processes. *Journal of Management, 36*, 5–39.

Mullen, B. and Copper, C. (1994). The relation between group cohesiveness and quality of decision making: An integration. *Psychological Bulletin, 115*, 210–227.

O'Leary, M. and Mortensen, M. (2005). *Subgroups with Attitude: Imbalance and Isolation in Geographically Dispersed Teams*. Honolulu, HI: Academy of Management.

Salas, E., Cooke, N.J., and Rosen, M.A. (2008). On teams, teamwork, and team performance: Discoveries and developments. *Human Factors: The Journal of the Human Factors and Ergonomics Society, 50*(3), 540–547.

Salas, E., Dickinson, T.L., Converse, S.A., and Tannenbaum, S.I. (1992). Toward an understanding of team performance and training. In R.W. Swezey and E. Salas (Eds.) *Teams: Their Training and Performance* (pp. 3–29). Norwood, NJ: Ablex.

Smith-Jentsch, K., Kraiger, K., and Salas, E. (2009). Do familiar teammates request and accept more backup? Transactive memory in air traffic control. *Human Factors, 51*(2), 181–192.

Stagl, K.C., Salas, E., Rosen, M.A., Priest, H.A., Burke, C.S., Goodwin, G.F., and Johnston, J.H. (2007). Distributed team performance: A multi-level review of distribution, diversity, and decision-making. In F. Dansereau and F.J. Yammarino (Eds.) *Multi-level Issues in Organizations and Time* (vol. 6, pp. 11–58). Amsterdam: Elsevier/JAI.

Stajkovic, A., Lee, D., and Nyberg, A. (2009). Collective efficacy, group potency, and group performance: Meta-analyses of their relationships, and test of a mediation model. *Journal of Applied Psychology, 94*, 814–828.

Stewart, D. and Stasser, G. (1995). Expert role assignment and information sampling during collective recall and decision making. *Journal of Personality and Social Psychology, 4*, 619–628.

Townsend, A., DeMarie, S., and Hendrickson, A. (1998). Virtual teams: Technology and the workplace of the future. *Academy of Management Executive, 2*(3), 17–29.

United States Congress (Select Bipartisan Committee to Investigate the Preparation for and Response to Hurricane Katrina; Chairman: T. Davis) (2006) *A Failure of Initiative: Final Report.* Washington, DC: U.S. Government Printing Office.

van Ginkel, W., Tindale, R.S., and van Knippenberg, D. (2009). Team reflexivity, development of shared task representations, and the use of distributed information in group decision making. *Group Dynamics: Theory, Research, and Practice, 13*, 265–280.

Wegner, D.M. (1986). Transactive memory: A contemporary analysis of the group mind. In G. Mullen and G. Goethals (Eds.) *Theory of Group Behavior* (pp. 185–208). New York: Springer-Verlag.

Wildman, J.L., Thayer, A.L., Rosen, M., Salas, E., Mathieu, J.E., and Rayne, S. (in press). Task types and team-level attributes: Synthesis of team classification literature. *Human Resource Development Review.*

Zaccaro, S.J., Ardison, S.D., and Orvis, K.L. (2004). Leadership in virtual teams. In D. Day, S. Zaccaro, and S. Halpin (Eds.) *Leader Development for Transforming Organizations: Growing Leaders for Tomorrow* (pp. 267–292). Mahwah, NJ: Lawrence Erlbaum.

Zaccaro, S.J. and Banks, D.J. (2001). Leadership, vision and organizational effectiveness. In S.J. Zaccaro and R.J. Klimoski (Eds.) *The Nature of Organizational Leadership: Understanding the Imperatives Confronting Today's Leaders* (pp. 181–218). San Francisco, CA: Jossey-Bass.

Zaccaro, S.J. and DeChurch, L.A. (2012). Leadership forms and functions in multiteam systems. In S.J. Zaccaro, M.A. Marks, and L.A. DeChurch (Eds.) *Multiteam Systems: An Organizational Form for Dynamic and Complex Environments* (pp. 253–288). New York: Routledge.

Zaccaro, S.J., Gualtieri, J., and Minionis, D. (1995). Task cohesion as a facilitator of group decision-making under temporal urgency. *Journal of Military Psychology, 7*, 77–93.

Zaccaro, S.J., Marks, M.A., and DeChurch, L.A. (2012). Multiteam systems: An introduction. In S.J. Zaccaro, M.A. Marks, and L.A. DeChurch (Eds.) *Multiteam Systems: An Organizational Form for Dynamic and Complex Environments.* New York: Routledge.

Part III

Decision Making in Action

13

Stress, Performance, and Decision Making in Organizations

Tripp Driskell, James E. Driskell, and Eduardo Salas

> *Flying is hours and hours of boredom sprinkled with a few seconds of sheer terror.*
>
> (Gregory "Pappy" Boyington, WWII Fighter Ace and Medal of Honor recipient)

Stress can impact organizations large and small. From the space program to Joe's diner, it is important that personnel respond effectively to the demands imposed by the work that they do. Sometimes the failure to meet task demands in aviation, combat, and other high-stress environments can result in loss of life, and in other cases, Joe's diner included, the failure to meet task demands can result in loss of business or revenue. Moreover, as Colonel "Pappy" Boyington described, the work environment can result in task overload or moments of "sheer terror," but can also impose conditions of task underload and boredom. We believe that both types of demands are relevant to performance in organizations.

This chapter will present an overview of the effects of stress on performance and decision making at work. We will first attempt to define the stress construct and describe its relevance to organizational performance and decision making. Second, we examine interventions to overcome stress effects, including selection, training, and job design approaches. Finally, in addition to examining overload or high demand, we address one overlooked aspect of stress in organizations—the topic of boredom.

STRESS AND PERFORMANCE

One problem in examining stress in organizations is that stress means many different things to many different people. In fact, a quick search of the PsycINFO database using the search term "stress" and "organizations" reveals over 12,091 articles related to these terms. Rest assured that we will not review them all. However, it is important to define, at least in a broad sense, what we mean when we use the term "stress." According to Driskell, Salas, and Johnston (2006), stress is defined as a high-demand, high-threat situation that disrupts performance. It is time-limited, events occur suddenly and often unexpectedly, quick and effective task performance is critical, and consequences of poor performance are immediate and often catastrophic. Note that these researchers were primarily concerned with tasks involving high demands and high arousal. Stress can also involve low demands and low arousal, leading to boredom. A transactional definition of stress incorporates both high demand and low demand: Stress is a process by which certain environmental demands evoke an appraisal process in which perceived demand is incompatible with resources, and that results in undesirable physiological, psychological, behavioral, or social outcomes. Thus, conditions in which task demands greatly exceed resources can lead to overload and high arousal, and conditions in which task demands are far below individual capabilities can lead to underload and boredom.

There is a significant difference between assessing task requirements per se, and assessing performance requirements *in context*. In other words, there is a significant difference in what it takes to perform a task in a benign task environment such as a classroom or training setting and what it takes to perform that task in a real-world setting. That difference is the *contextual environment*—the organizational, environmental, and task demands that are imposed upon the individual. Stress is a multi-dimensional construct, and this general term may be used to refer to any number of specific stressors or demands that may be present in a given task setting. These may include:

- *Time pressure*: a restriction in time required to perform a task.
- *Task load*: performing two or more tasks concurrently.
- *Role conflict*: conflicting task demands stemming from the nature of the task or from conflicting supervisor or subordinate demands.
- *Role ambiguity*: lack of clarity in job demands or procedures.

- *Threat:* the anticipation or fear of physical or psychological harm.
- *Coordination requirements:* the increased demands of coordinating task performance with multiple others.
- *Uncertainty:* unclear, shifting, or ill-defined goals.
- *Complexity/difficulty:* complexity or difficulty of the task.
- *Ambiguity:* missing, unreliable, or inaccurate information or task data.
- *Novelty:* events occur that are unique or unanticipated.
- *Fatigue:* fatigue resulting from sleep deprivation or sustained performance.
- *Environmental stressors:* noise, temperature, vibration, motion, etc.
- *Under-stimulation, repetitiveness,* and *monotony.*

Hogan and Lesser (1996) concluded, "Current job analysis methods are not very helpful for studying hazardous performance" (p. 218), yet failure to account for the role that these demands play in decision making in organizations can be costly. Accordingly, Driskell, Wadsworth, and Krokos (2009) have developed a Work Hazard Analysis Scale to assess the contextual demands that are present in various task environments. Thus, a basic step in understanding stress in organizations is to identify the types of stressors that are present in the operational environment.

Although it is useful to speak of "stress" in general terms in referring to demanding task environments, it is less useful to try to understand stress effects at this broad or unidimensional level. However, although many discrete stressors as noted above may impact performance in any given task environment, it is difficult to predict behavior on the basis of each concrete stressor. We propose that there is a limited number of cognitive, emotional, and social mechanisms through which stress impacts performance. These stress mechanisms include the following:

- *Stress may increase distraction and decrease attentional focus.* One of the more well-established findings in the stress literature is that, as stress or arousal increases, the individual's breadth of attention narrows (Combs & Taylor, 1952; Easterbrook, 1959). Perhaps the earliest statement of this phenomenon was William James's (1890) belief that the individual's field of view varied, from a broader perspective under normal conditions to a more narrow, restricted focus under stress. For complex tasks, in which the individual must attend to a relatively larger number of salient task cues, this narrowing of attention may result in the elimination of relevant task information and task performance will suffer.

- *Stress may increase cognitive load and demand on capacity.* The term "workload" refers to the individual's perception of the work demands imposed by a task environment, although the term has also been used to describe the demands of the task environment itself in terms of the volume and pace of the work to be performed (see Spector & Jex, 1998). Time-sharing, or multi-tasking, can be defined as the capacity to perform concurrent tasks or to interleave multiple tasks (Fischer & Mautone, 2005). High-stress environments often involve an increase in task load stemming from the imposition of multiple tasks that must be performed, the requirement to shift from one task to another, and having to attend to novel or unfamiliar stimuli. In brief, research suggests that concurrent tasks interfere with one another because of the increased demands on limited attentional and processing capacity.
- *Stress may increase negative emotions and frustration.* Emotional reactions to stress may include subjective feelings of anger, annoyance, tension, frustration, and increased concern for the well-being of self and others. Effective performance under stress requires the capacity to maintain one's composure and emotional control while remaining task-focused under demanding and threatening conditions (Driskell, Hogan, & Salas, 1987; Mount, Barrack, & Stewart, 1998).
- *Stress may increase fear and anxiety.* Evidence from a broad range of studies indicates that the threat of dangerous or novel environments may result in an increase in subjective stress and anxiety, increased physiological reactivity, and impaired performance (Saunders et al., 1996).
- *Stress may increase social impairment.* Social effects of stress may include a reduction in the tendency to assist others, increased interpersonal aggression, neglect of social or interpersonal cues, and less cooperative behavior among team members (Driskell, Salas, & Johnston, 1999).
- *Stress may depress performance.* Repetitive, monotonous, or understimulating task environments can lead to boredom and depressed arousal and performance (Davies, Shackleton, & Parasuraman, 1983).

Stress and Decision Making

There are two primary ways in which stress impacts decision making. First, stress can impact or disrupt normal or deliberate decision making processes. Second, extreme levels of stress can alter decision making behavior to what has been termed ballistic or hypervigilant decision making. We will consider each of these processes in turn.

Janis and Mann (1977) presented a model of decision making in which they distinguished between vigilant and hypervigilant decision making patterns. The vigilant decision making process is characterized by (a) a systematic, organized information search, (b) thorough consideration of all available alternatives, (c) devotion of sufficient time to evaluate each alternative, and (d) the re-examination and review of data before making a decision. There are many real-world settings for which such analytic strategies are applicable. For example, analytic strategies are more likely to be effective when tasks are less complex and ill-structured, data are unambiguous, and time constraints do not preclude carrying out a deliberate, analytic decision making procedure.

There are many models of stages of analytic decision making, and Janis and Mann's (1977) model is representative. According to Wheeler and Janis (1980), five broad stages of analytic decision making include: (1) identifying the problem, (2) searching for alternatives, (3) evaluating alternatives, (4) committing to a course of action, and (5) implementing and evaluating the decision. The stress mechanisms identified previously may impact decision making at each of these stages.

For example, the initial problem identification stage is a stage in which decision makers are confronted with a challenge and determine the initial procedures to follow. The effect of stress on increasing cognitive load may result in decision makers becoming overwhelmed and they may simply withdraw or reduce problem-focused efforts (Sweeny, 2008). In this case, the decision process is truncated at this point.

Stress effects may also impact the process by which initial information and alternatives are gathered. We noted that stress may increase distraction and narrow attentional focus. Under time pressure or other demand, individuals and teams may be restricted in the amount of information that can be gleaned from a situation, thus potentially relying on less information than is required to make a good decision. Cohen (1980) concluded that the narrowing of attention that occurs under stress may lead to a neglect of social or interpersonal cues required for effective team interaction, and Driskell, Salas, and Johnston (1999) found that stress led to a shift in team members' perspectives from a broad team perspective to a more narrow or individualistic self-focus. They further suggested that a tendency to neglect relevant task and social cues under stress can lead to a loss of information required for effective decision making.

Other research has suggested that the negative emotional response and frustration incurred by high demands can impact decision making. During Skylab-4's space mission in 1973/1974, astronauts Gerald Carr, William

Pogue, and Edward Gibson staged a minor mutiny against Mission Control. After their complaints about workload demands were all but ignored, the crew's frustration led to a decision to take an unscheduled day off and cut off communication for a twenty-four-hour rest period. This work stoppage was a highly questionable choice of action, and none of the crew flew a space mission again (see Connors, Harrison, & Akins, 1984).

A second primary way in which stress may impact decision making is by altering decision strategies. Janis and Mann (1977) argued that extreme stress demands can lead to adoption of a hypervigilant pattern of decision making, characterized by (a) a nonsystematic or selective information search, (b) consideration of limited alternatives, (c) rapid evaluation of data, and (d) selection of a solution without extensive review or reappraisal. Klein (1996), Payne, Bettman, and Johnson (1992), and others have argued that, under certain conditions, decision makers can make effective decisions without carrying out an elaborate and exhaustive analytic procedure. Moreover, a hypervigilant type of decision strategy may be adaptive in more realistic or naturalistic decision environments in which decisions are made under high time pressure, data are ambiguous or conflicting, and decision makers have some familiarity with the task.

In fact, in a study of hypervigilant decision making, Johnston, Driskell, and Salas (1997) argued that the shift to a hypervigilant decision strategy was an adaptive response to high-stress demands, and results of this research indicated that those who adopted a hypervigilant strategy under high demands were more effective than those who employed a more comprehensive analytic strategy. Johnston, Driskell, and Salas (1997) concluded that a hypervigilant decision strategy may in fact be an effective course of action in a high-demand task setting.

In brief, stress may degrade normal, deliberate, or analytic decision making processes by impacting performance at various stages of the decision making process. Further, high levels of stress may result in a shift to a hypervigilant pattern of decision making that is less comprehensive and time-intensive, but which may be adaptive under the pressure of high task demands.

Interventions to Reduce Stress Effects

Selection

Hogan and Lesser (1996) draw a useful distinction between a *hazardous* environment and a *stressful* environment. A hazardous environment is defined as one in which there are significant task demands and potential for injury or harm. Thus, the extent to which a task is hazardous is defined by the nature of the task environment. In contrast, the stressfulness of a situation is defined by the perceptions of the individual job incumbents, and Hogan and Lesser note that many people in hazardous jobs may or may not be stressed by their work. In fact, the objective of an effective stress selection procedure is to select personnel who perform most effectively under stress, who are less vulnerable to stress effects, and who are most resilient under high-stress conditions.

Hogan and Lesser (1996) proposed that selecting personnel for hazardous duty requires attention to four factors. The first is *job suitability*. They argue that those who perform most effectively under stress conditions are those who are most well suited for the job or task that they are engaged in. A second factor is *technical competence*. Because many high-stress environments are technically demanding, those who are technically competent are most likely to excel under high-demand conditions. A third factor is *physical capability*. Because stress can be physically demanding, those who are physically fit are more likely to excel under stress conditions. A final factor is *psychological suitability*. In a review of psychological traits that may predict effective performance under stress, Driskell, Wadsworth, and Krokos (2009) identified the following constructs as potentially useful predictors of performance under stress:

- *Stress tolerance*: The capacity to maintain one's composure and emotional control while remaining task-focused under demanding and threatening conditions. The construct of stress tolerance reflects the broader traits often termed adjustment, emotional stability, or lack of neuroticism/anxiety.
- *Hardiness/self-efficacy*: The capacity for self-sufficiency, self-confidence, and resilience in enduring hardships in demanding situations. Related traits include resilience, self-reliance, and self-esteem.
- *Sociability*: Interpersonal skill and adeptness in working or interacting with others. The trait of sociability reflects affiliation, social interest, and interpersonal skill.
- *Adaptability/flexibility*: Adaptability or flexibility in adapting one's behavior to meet changing or uncertain tasks demands. Adaptability/ flexibility is viewed as a sub-facet of the broader Big Five trait of Openness, and the negative pole is related to rigidity in behavior and unwillingness to accept change.

- *Dependability*: Tendency to be reliable, well-organized, and conscientious in carrying out tasks. Dependability reflects the responsibility/dependability component of the Big Five trait Conscientiousness.
- *Dutifulness*: Tendency to value obligations and commitments to others. Dutifulness refers to the tendency to value and adhere to obligations and duties that are held with others.
- *Achievement orientation*: Willingness to work hard to achieve goals and to persist in the face of obstacles. Achievement orientation reflects the achievement component of the Big Five trait of Conscientiousness (i.e., conscientious persons persevere and are motivated to achieve).
- *Vigilance*: Capacity to maintain alertness and awareness of actions and events over time.

Recent research to identify those who are most resilient under stress is promising, yet no clear profile has emerged of the characteristics of stress-resistant individuals. In fact, Marshall (1947) noted the difficulty of identifying those who would excel under duress on the combat battlefield: "There were men who had been consistently bad actors . . . who just as consistently become lions on the battlefield" (p. 60). Moreover, in many organizations, selection is an important tool, but attention must also be addressed to the workforce that is in place. In this case, stress training and task design become paramount.

Stress Training

The value of stress training parallels the distinction noted previously between performance in a benign or optimal environment and performance in a real-world environment. The primary goal of training is skill acquisition and retention. Therefore, most training takes place under conditions designed to maximize learning: a quiet classroom, the practice of task procedures under predictable conditions, and so on. In this manner, training typically does a good job of promoting initial skill acquisition. However, in the real world, tasks must be performed in contextual conditions quite unlike those encountered in the training classroom. For example, high-stress environments may include specific task conditions (such as time pressure or role conflict) and require specific responses (such as the flexibility to adapt to novel or changing task contingencies) that differ from those found under "normal" conditions. In brief, the primary purpose of *training* is to ensure skills acquisition. The primary purpose of *stress training* is to prepare the individual to maintain effective performance in the stress environment.

One primary objective of stress training is to provide pre-exposure to the high-demand conditions that may be encountered in the operational environment and provide the specialized skills training required to maintain effective performance under stress conditions. Kavanagh (2005) has noted that stress training can moderate the effects of stress on performance and that attention should focus on "developing training that realistically represents the environment that the individual will be expected to perform in, is targeted on particular skills, (and) builds the ability to adapt" (p. xiv).

Stress exposure training (SET) is a comprehensive approach to enhancing performance in high-demand settings that has been developed for military training applications (see Driskell, Salas, & Johnston, 2006; Driskell et al., 2008). Extensive laboratory research has documented the effectiveness of the SET approach in reducing stress effects and enhancing performance (Driskell, Johnston, & Salas, 2001; Inzana et al., 1996; Johnston, Driskell, & Salas, 1997; Saunders et al., 1996).

The SET approach incorporates three stages or phases of training:

- *Information provision*, in which information is provided to the trainee regarding stress, stress symptoms, and likely stress effects in the performance setting.
- *Skills acquisition*, in which specific cognitive and behavioral skills are taught and practiced. These are called *high performance* skills, representing those skills required to maintain effective performance in the stress environment.
- *Application and practice*, the application and practice of these skills in a graduated manner under conditions that increasingly approximate the criterion environment.

Table 13.1 provides an outline of the stress exposure training model.

There are several characteristics of the SET approach that may be particularly useful for enhancing decision making under stress in an organizational setting. First, SET is a model for stress training rather than a specific training technique. The SET model describes three stages of training, each with a specific overall objective. However, the specific content of training will vary according to the specific task and contextual requirements. Accordingly, researchers have noted the importance of designing stress training based on a comprehensive analysis of the task and contextual environment (see Johnston & Cannon-Bowers, 1996).

TABLE 13.1

Stress Exposure Training (SET)

	Objectives	Activities	Outcomes
Phase I: Information Provision	Trainee indoctrination Familiarity with stress environment Knowledge of stress effects	Provide information on value of stress training Provide preparatory information on: • Stress effects • Stress reactions • Performance effects	Increased knowledge of stress effects Less reactivity to stressors Increased confidence in ability to perform under stress
Phase II: Skills Acquisition	Develop high performance stress skills	Provide behavioral and cognitive skills training including: • Adaptability/flexibility • Overlearning • Attentional training • Mental practice • Decision skills training • Physiological control	Skills development
Phase III: Application and Practice	Graduated exposure to realistic stressors	Practice of skills under conditions that increasingly approximate the real-world environment	Successful application of skills in high-stress environment Improved cognitive and psychomotor performance under stress Reduced anxiety Increased confidence

Second, one goal of stress training is to build high-performance skills that are required to maintain effective performance under stress. A number of stress training strategies or techniques may be incorporated in this phase of training. These may include the training of time-sharing skills (Heggestad et al., 2002), attentional-focus training (Singer et al., 1991), decision making training (Johnston, Driskell, & Salas, 1997), and guided error training (Lorenzet, Salas, & Tannenbaum, 2005).

Finally, for demanding tasks, training that incorporates no stress and training that incorporates high-intensity stress are both likely to be counterproductive. Training that incorporates no stress or that does not involve the contextual factors that characterize the criterion setting does not provide the trainee the opportunity to practice skills in this environment. Training that incorporates stressors of very high intensity is likely to overload all but the most experienced trainees and may interfere with skill development and lead to loss of confidence. The SET approach provides skills practice in a graduated manner from moderate-stress low-fidelity exercises to practice that incorporates greater degrees of complexity or realism. This phased approach enhances perceived control, increases confidence, and allows the trainee to practice skills under conditions that approximate the real-world environment.

Job Design

Wickens (1996) has noted that job design solutions should be developed in the context of what we know regarding stress effects. For example, to the extent that stress may decrease attentional focus, reducing the amount of unnecessary information presented to the individual and increasing its organization should help buffer stress effects. In the following, we focus on one specific type of task design to buffer stress effects: the use of teams. As Driskell, Salas, and Hughes (2010) have noted, modern organizations have embraced an increasingly team-oriented work environment. Teams offer a number of advantages in accomplishing large, complex tasks. However, teams offer specific advantages in buffering stress effects. It has long been held that other people might provide resources necessary for coping with a stressful situation, and the very presence of others may be arousal-reducing (Mullen, Bryant, & Driskell, 1997). We examine the potential stress-reducing effects of teams in terms of three specific functions: duplication, overlap, and support. Team tasks allow for duplication of individual efforts. To the extent that individual performance is likely to falter under high-demand conditions, other team members can provide back-up, or technical redundancy, of individual performance. Such duplication of effort supports overall performance even if individual performance is degraded. Related to this function is the capacity of team members to provide overlap in task performance. Overlap occurs when two team members have overlapping responsibility, allowing each to monitor the other. As in the aviation cockpit, overlap allows errors to be discovered before they lead to negative outcomes. Finally, team members can provide valuable support resources under high-stress conditions. Research has found that affiliation with others can provide a reduction of arousal in the face of stressful environments. Team members provide useful information about what to expect and how to behave, and they may provide social support or a sense of "safety in numbers" (Mullen, Bryant, & Driskell, 1997). Teams can also be very effective at motivating their members under demanding conditions. In World War II, Stouffer et al. (1949) found that what kept soldiers going in extremely hostile conditions was not political ideals or hatred of the enemy, but primary group obligations.

BATTLING BOREDOM

Let's face it—life in the typical organization is not all excitement and over-stimulation. As our opening quote suggests, performance in even a single task setting can range from extreme task overload to extreme boredom. When we think of stress, we typically think of high-demand environments. It is safe to say that most stress researchers study the prototypical "emergency" or acute stress task conditions in aviation, combat or other high-demand task environments. Considering these extreme environments, the study of boredom can be somewhat, well, boring. However, performance in organizations can suffer as much from distraction because of overload as from distraction because of underload.

The expansive range of research conducted on stress and decision making (e.g., experimental data, Driskell & Salas, 1991; archival analysis of international politics, Holsti, 1971; real-world observations, Sperandio, 1971) suggests that stress exceeding a certain intensity adversely affects the quality of decision making. However, the same can be said for situations in which the complete absence of stimulation leads to boredom. This harkens back to the all too ubiquitous "inverted U" proposed by Yerkes and Dodson (1908), positing that human performance degrades in conditions of extreme overload or underload (albeit their research was done on mice). The following sections will briefly describe the main causes of boredom at work, its consequences, and potential interventions to mitigate its adverse effects. First, however, we will attempt to define boredom, which has been plagued by the absence of a clear definition (Loukidou, Loan-Clarke, & Daniels, 2009). Fisher (1993) has defined boredom as an "unpleasant, transient affective state in which the individual feels a pervasive lack of interest in and difficulty concentrating on the current activity" (p. 396). Davies, Shackleton, and Parasuraman (1983) defined boredom as an individual's emotional response to an environment that is monotonous, repetitive, or under-stimulating. Moreover, they noted that the association of boredom with underload distinguishes boredom from fatigue, which results from sustained overload.

Why Are We Bored?

The extant research on boredom has delineated several main categories explaining why we become bored at work. We will discuss these in sequential order, beginning with the individual and then progressing to the effects of others in the workplace, then to the task characteristics, and ending with the overall work environment.

It's Because of You

To begin, gender seems to play a role in dictating who is most susceptible to becoming bored. Specifically, research has shown that men tend to be more likely to fall victim to boredom than women (Watt & Vodanovich, 1999). This gender difference was shown to be intensified when men perceive a task to be externally under-stimulating. Additionally, an individual's predisposition to being an extravert or an introvert has been examined as a potential moderator of boredom. The basic assumption is that extraverts need more stimulation than introverts. Gardner and Cummings (1988) argue that this is the case because extraverts are conceivably more likely to be bored by monotonous and easy tasks, whereas introverts may prefer these types of tasks. This assumption has been supported by previous research investigating the effects of accompanying stimuli on extraverted or introverted performance on boring tasks. Belojevic, Jakovljevic, and Slepcevic (2003), for example, found in a twelve-year review of the literature that extraverts tend to be better adapted than introverts on mental performance tasks when those tasks are accompanied by noise. Hence, in order to combat the onslaught of boredom at work, extraverted individuals may require added stimulation to keep them adequately engaged. Intelligence has also been identified as a potential individual difference that may affect perceived boredom. Specifically, it has been suggested that intelligent individuals may be greater affected by tasks that underutilize their abilities, and thus may become more bored than less intelligent people. This suggestion has found partial support (e.g., Drory, 1982; London, Schubert, & Washburn, 1972). Similarly, an individual's level of expertise may impact their perceived boredom. Akin to how increased intelligence may impact boredom, if an individual becomes overly skilled with a task, they may feel that their abilities are being underutilized. Moreover, this may also lead to task automaticity (i.e., negligible effort being required to perform a task), which has also been suggested to lead to states of boredom (Fisher, 1993). Although tenure may be thought of as less an individual characteristic and more as a function of the work environment, it has also been identified as a potential moderator of boredom (Kass, Vodanovich, & Callender, 2001). The argument can be made that the longer one spends at a particular job, the more expertise they will develop at the tasks related to that job. In the cases where individuals may be too intelligent for a task, too expert at a task, or have been engaged in a task for too long a time, they may become subject to what Baker (1992) described as a trance-type experience. In trance-type experiences individuals perform their tasks in a robotic manner that is marked by a different level of consciousness. This may resonate with many of us during our commutes to and from work, which have likely become so routine that we sometimes forget the entire event.

We briefly note that various other individual characteristics have been linked to boredom, as shown in Table 13.2. It is also important to note that the characteristics mentioned throughout this section are not mutually exclusive and thus may combine in ways that may enhance or reduce boredom.

It's Because of Them

The social relationships we develop, or fail to develop, also affect our perceptions of boredom in the workplace. A considerable amount of research has been conducted investigating the impacts others have on one's perceived boredom. The original notion was that the presence of others would help to reduce boredom (Fisher, 1993). However, the research in this field is conflicting. For instance, Isaac, Sansone, and Smith (1999) found

TABLE 13.2
Additional Characteristics Associated with Increased Boredom

Characteristic	Reference
High Dogmatism	Leong and Schneller, 1993
Low Motivation	Pekrun, Elliot, and Maier, 2006
Low Desire to Achieve	Wendt, 1955
Younger Age	Birdi, Warr, and Oswald, 1995
Low Conscientiousness	Sansone, Wiebe, and Morgan, 1999
Low Sociability	Leong and Schneller, 1993

Note: See Loukidou et al. (2009) for a review.

that individuals find a task to be more interesting in the presence of another person, while Lee (1986) found that the presence of co-workers can have the opposite effect by potentially making a task more boring. This discrepancy can be in part explained by the types of social relationships and the types of people in the workplace. Conceivably, if we are surrounded by positive relationships and individuals whom we relate to and view positively, boredom would be less of a pressing issue. In fact, it has been shown, for example, that workers may perceive co-workers who are absent, uninteresting, unfriendly, or uncommunicative as a source of boredom (Fisher, 1987). Similarly, one's relationship with "the boss" may also be an important factor related to boredom. As noted by Loukidou, Loan-Clarke, and Daniels (2009), the employee–leadership relationship should affect feelings of self-efficacy and control, as well as a sense of belonging and sense of working toward a meaningful goal. In brief, who we are surrounded by, how many people we are surrounded by, the quality of our relationships with our co-workers and leaders, and their personalities can all affect our individual perceptions of boredom at work.

It's the Task

Although we have shown that individual differences and interpersonal relationships can affect perceptions of boredom, the conventional view that the task itself can lead to boredom still holds true. It doesn't matter if you are a highly motivated individual and find trivial, repetitive tasks to be exhilarating, the task can still lead to boredom. In her work on boredom at work, Fisher (1993) developed a theoretical framework of potential causes and consequences of boredom. Within this framework, Fisher

(1993) delineates five potential task-based causes of boredom. These include tasks that involve repetitive work, vigilance work, quantitative underload and workload variability (i.e., "having nothing to do" or "a lot to do followed by nothing to do"), qualitative underload (simple, monotonous, unchallenging jobs, and/or jobs that underutilize a worker's skills), and qualitative overload (jobs that are overly complex for the employee).

It's the Work Environment

The work environment likely becomes an important determinant in how the work experience is viewed when the task being performed provides minimal stimulation (Fisher, 1993). Thus, organizational policies and practices may either positively or negatively impact an individual's perception of boredom at work. For example, the work atmosphere can play an important role. An atmosphere that prohibits, either implicitly or explicitly, talking and social interactions may intensify feelings of burden by constraining the employee's sense of control and social influences. Moreover, limiting work breaks and employee flexibility may induce boredom. The reason these factors increase boredom is because they all serve to reduce stimulation in the workplace.

Consequences of Boredom

Grose (1988) described the boredom that can be experienced in the aviation cockpit on extended flights:

> Try to imagine being cooped up for 10 hours in a small closet with nothing to look at farther away from your nose than 18 inches, especially after you have gone through the same experience hundreds of times.
>
> (p. 35)

It is no surprise that the National Transportation Safety Board has identified boredom and monotony as a critical factor in aviation, railroad, highway, and marine accidents (NTSB, 1989). They note that the clearest instances are often seen in major highway accidents, in which fatigue is compounded by monotony and vulnerability to lapses in attention.

The consequences of boredom are numerous and have been shown to negatively impact employees and their organizations. The consequences for employees include a lower subjective rating of quality of life (Watten, Syversen, & Myhrer, 1995), more depressive symptoms (Wiesner, Windle,

& Freeman, 2005), and a greater diffusion of boredom to other areas of an individual's life (Bargdill, 2000). These adverse outcomes not only affect the individuals themselves, but unquestionably affect many of their social relationships, and thus may impact the well-being of others (e.g., family members, friends, etc.). In addition to consequences chiefly impacting employees, there are numerous outcomes that affect both employees and organizations. For example, research demonstrates that boredom can lead to a reduction in work effectiveness (e.g., Drory, 1982), job performance (e.g., O'Hanlon, 1981), and job satisfaction, as well as increases in absenteeism (e.g., Kass, Vodanovich, & Callender, 2001), work strain (Matthews et al., 2000), alcohol and drug misuse (e.g., Wiesner, Windle, & Freeman, 2005), counterproductive work behaviors (Bruursema, Kessler, & Spector, 2011), withdrawal (Spector et al., 2006), staff turnover (Mann, 2007), and accidents and subsequent injuries (Drory, 1982). Clearly, these outcomes are undesirable for both employees or organizations. In respect to individuals, each of the consequences mentioned above represents a type of stressor and without doubt adversely affects their ability to make adequate decisions. For example, Baradell and Klein (1993) showed that increasing life stress resulted in greater performance decrements and the use of hypervigilant strategies. Recall, hypervigilant strategies represent an impulsive, disorganized pattern of decision making (Janis & Mann, 1977). In regard to organizations, these outcomes may lead to higher employment costs, performance and/or production problems, and reduced organization effectiveness, all which may affect an organization's bottom line (i.e., net earnings, net income, or earnings per share).

How to Combat Boredom

We have described some of the numerous consequences associated with boredom. A wide variety of interventions have been suggested to aid in mitigating these negative consequences. Baldamus (1961) used the term *traction* to refer to the opposite of distraction, which occurs in high-demand situations. That is, in low-demand situations, traction involves connecting to the task or being pulled into the task to combat boredom. In the following, we will note some of the primary attempts to gain traction in under-stimulating environments, and emphasize the role that teams may play in overcoming boredom.

As with high-demand environments, we can apply job design, selection, and training approaches to combat the effects of boredom. In terms of job design, we may address both the task and the occupational environment.

We can begin by (re)designing the very nature of the task to be completed. Balzer, Smith, and Burnfield (2004) note, for example, that designing interesting and rewarding tasks may help in reducing boredom. If the task is repetitive in nature, steps can be taken to try to reduce the repetitiveness of the task by eliminating needless actions, ergonomic interventions, or the introduction of new technologies. If this is unachievable, a greater variety of tasks can be included in the job to make it less repetitious. Drawing from the literature on social loafing, organizations can provide a system for tracking output, thus making individual contribution more identifiable in order to increase worker motivation (Williams, Harkins, & Latané, 1982). Another intervention that can be applied, if possible, is providing opportunities to rotate, or train in how to execute, other jobs or tasks (e.g., cross-training). Cross-training occurs when co-workers rotate positions during training to develop an understanding of the knowledge and skills needed to perform the tasks of other co-workers (Cannon-Bowers et al., 1998). This can give employees the chance to gain different experiences and may prevent the monotony associated with repeatedly doing a single job or task. Having employees and the organization set goals, in addition to providing feedback regarding those goals, can be an instrumental intervention that can increase task interest and reduce boredom (Latham & Kinne, 1974). In this regard organizations can provide employees with performance goals and feedback, performance/commission-based reward systems, motivation through job enrichment (e.g., by increasing the variety of tasks to be performed), and/or job enlargement (e.g., by offering tasks previously performed by other workers), and can emphasize the importance of employee contribution for organizational success (Balzer, Smith, & Burnfield, 2004).

Research has also indicated that there are interventions that the individual can engage in to reduce boredom. For example, it has been shown that brief interruptions, either internal (e.g., daydreaming) or external (e.g., office chat), can reduce boredom. Additionally, engaging in mental games or assisting co-workers may also be useful.

As Balzer, Smith, and Burnfield (2004) note, employee selection and job placement systems have been typically underused methods to reduce boredom. Given the variance in individual differences, using selection methods may be effective interventions. However, caution should be taken in determining what variables are used for job selection. For example, by inferring from previous research that females are less susceptible to boredom and hiring personnel based on this inference, you may be engaging in gender discrimination. Moreover, it is interesting to note that the psychological traits described by Driskell, Wadsworth, and Krokos (2009) to predict effective performance under stress may be well suited to explain both overload and underload settings. For instance, individuals high in sociability may be less impacted by the effects of boredom and high stress.

As previously mentioned, boredom can be caused by work environments that frustrate social interactions. Therefore, creating an organizational climate that fosters social interactions can help reduce boredom. This can be accomplished through enacting appropriate organizational policies and practices and by physically designing the workplace to promote social interactions. The company headquarters at Google, for an extreme yet effective example, provides employees with game rooms, professional massages, and even an in-house slide.

More specifically, an intervention that we believe is of particular value in combating boredom is the use and development of teams. Organizations rely heavily on teams to perform many tasks, including complex, demanding, and coordinated efforts (Driskell, Salas, & Hughes, 2010), and can benefit from teams in combating boredom as they can provide employees with direct feedback, goal monitoring, task interdependency, and opportunities to frequently engage in coordinated social encounters. By obtaining direct feedback, team members can immediately receive information from other members of the team regarding their actions. This can allow them to gain invaluable information about their actions and how, if necessary, to modify them in order to meet task and team demands. Goal monitoring reflects the ability of team members to provide both individual team members and the team as a whole with feedback on their status of achieving a desired outcome. According to Marks, Mathieu, and Zaccaro (2001), this includes "tracking task and progress toward mission accomplishment, interpreting system information in terms of what needs to be accomplished for goal attainment, and transmitting progress to team members" (p. 366). A task is said to be interdependent if the task cannot be completed without the efforts of other team members. A high degree of task interdependency should increase team members' positive affect and motivation by making them more aware of their individual contributions to both the team and the organization (Morris & Steers, 1980). Implicit within the definition of a team—two or more individuals working together toward a shared outcome—teams afford individuals the opportunity to consistently engage in social encounters. As previously mentioned, a lack of social interaction has been identified as a boredom inducer, and thus may be mitigated through the development and use of teams. In addition to traditional advantages of teams–for example, the ability to pool resources, exchange information, coordinate actions, share responsibility for team decisions, and improve overall performance—the advantages outlined above all function to increase the stimulation, motivation, and task awareness of each team member.

RECOMMENDATIONS FOR FUTURE RESEARCH

We have been compelled in this short chapter to examine the effects of stress on decision making at a relatively high level of abstraction. We have attempted to define the stress construct, elaborate how stress may impact decision making, and examine intervention strategies to reduce negative stress effects. However, there are many more areas of research within the domain of stress and decision making that represent future opportunities that deserve at least a brief mention.

Further research is needed to examine different units of analysis, including the effects of stress on individual, team, and organizational decision making. We have implicitly adopted an individual-level approach in this chapter, primarily examining the effects of stress on individual performance in teams and in organizations. Further research is needed at the team and organizational level of analysis. For example, Driskell and Salas (1991) found that stress impacted structural aspects of decision making in teams. Sigelman and McNeil (1980) have examined how stress impacts decision making practices in organizations in government or public policy settings.

Other research has examined the effects of stress on decision making in diverse populations and applications. For example, Ganster (2005) has examined stress and executive decision making in organizations, emphasizing the impact of high job demands on leadership behavior. Moschis (2007) has examined stress and consumer decision making, adopting a model that incorporates stages of need recognition, information seeking, evaluation, purchase, and post-purchase behaviors. Similar to the approach presented in this chapter, Moschis (2007) notes that stress can impact each stage of the consumer decision making process. Porcelli and Delgado (2009) have examined the effects of stress on risk taking in financial decision making, and Preston et al. (2007) have examined stress and decision making in a gambling task. These studies provide robust tests of the effects of stress on decision making in a wide variety of domains and from various theoretical perspectives.

Stress may be viewed as existing along a continuum, from conditions in which demands are higher than normal to conditions in which demands are extreme. Extreme demands pose a special challenge for training and intervention efforts. For example, Driskell et al. (2008) described training for high-risk law enforcement encounters. In these settings, events may transition from routine to critical in an instant and require decisions on immediate actions and shoot/no-shoot judgments within seconds. Further research is needed to examine stress "at the extremes."

One area of research on stress and decision making that has been largely ignored, despite Ganster's (2005) admonitions to the contrary, is the role of stress and affect in decision making. We have noted that one effect of stress is to increase negative affect. Ganster notes that research has shown positive affect to have a beneficial effect on a number of aspects of the decision making process, and suggests that research should further examine the role of positive affect in improving decision making under stress.

There are a number of practical issues that merit further investigation. For example, understanding the effects of stress in a given work environment requires that we develop a tool to measure the demands that are relevant to a particular task. Driskell, Wadsworth, and Krokos (2009) have conducted initial analyses of the *Work Hazard Analysis Scale*, which can be administered to job incumbents or to external raters to identify contextual variables or stressors in the work environment that can impose demands on the operator. Another significant problem is how to faithfully represent realistic stressors in training scenarios. Recent research in event-based training (Fowlkes & Burke, 2005; Salas & Cannon-Bowers, 2001) provides a useful approach to representing critical decision making events and contextual demands in training simulations.

As previously mentioned, boredom is an often overlooked area of stress research. Consequently, further work should be focused on examining the effects of boredom in different work domains. One topic that has been particularly neglected and deserves just consideration is the impact of boredom on decision making in extreme environments (e.g., military, space, etc.). The lion's share of this research has been aimed at understanding how decisions are made during moments of "sheer terror." Considering that extreme environments are often akin to how "Pappy" Boyington described them—hours of boredom with a few seconds of sheer terror—research is also needed that examines the interplay between these two extremes. For example, there may be a substantial difference between shifting from a state of equilibrium to a state of high demand and transitioning from a state of boredom to a state of high stress. Furthermore, research is needed on the effects of boredom on decision making in modern organizational structures such as virtual groups or distributed organizations. With organizations shifting toward a fluid or mobile work environment (Rosen et al., 2010), it becomes evident that the nature of decision making in organizations is changing and research is needed to address these changes.

FINAL THOUGHTS

The aim of this chapter was to present an overview of the effects of stress on performance and decision making at work. In doing so, we sought to present a transactional representation of stress by examining the effects of both overload and underload as it is relevant to organizational performance and decision making. We noted at the beginning of this chapter that a search of the PsycINFO database yields over 12,000 articles related to stress and organizations. If we broaden our search outside of the scientific literature, we find that a Google search of the term "stress management" yields over 33 *million* hits. A brief review of these results tells us (a) that almost anything passes for stress management in the popular literature, but more importantly, (b) that there is clearly a huge requirement and interest in understanding and managing stress.

It is important that organizations understand how stress may impact their business and employees. Moreover, we believe that a simple understanding that the problem exists is insufficient, as organizations must be able to implement interventions to mitigate the ensuing consequences. In this chapter, we examined the effects of high-demand settings and boredom on performance and decision making in organizations. Moreover, we outlined steps that can be taken by organizations, including selection, stress training, and job design, to combat stress.

The actual costs that the demands of stress impose on organizations are difficult to determine, as many estimates include costs related to absenteeism, turnover, accidents, lost productivity, health costs, workers' compensation claims, and litigation expenses. Sometimes the costs are clearer—a railroad accident described in the previously cited National Transportation Safety Board report (NTSB, 1989) resulted in two deaths and six million dollars-worth of damage. Clearly, the personal and organizational costs of stress can be dear. Understanding the effects of stress on performance and adopting interventions to overcome these effects can lessen this impact.

ACKNOWLEDGMENT

The writing of this chapter was supported by the NASA grant (NNX09AK48G) to Dr. Eduardo Salas, Principal Investigator, Dr. Kimberly Smith-Jentsch, and Dr. Stephen M. Fiore, Co-Principal Investigators, of the University of Central Florida. The views expressed in this work are those of the authors and do not necessarily reflect the organizations with which they are affiliated or their sponsoring institutions or agencies.

REFERENCES

Baker, P.L. (1992). Bored and busy: Sociology of knowledge of clerical workers. *Sociological Perspectives, 35,* 489–503.

Baldamus, W. (1961). *Efficiency and Effort.* London: Tavistock.

Balzer, W.K., Smith, P.C., and Burnfield, J.L. (2004). Boredom. In C. Spielberger (Ed.) *Encyclopedia of Applied Psychology* (pp. 289–294). Amsterdam: Academic Press.

Baradell, J.G. and Klein, K. (1993). Relationship of life stress and body consciousness to hypervigilant decision making. *Journal of Personality and Social Psychology, 64*(2), 267–273.

Bargdill, R.W. (2000). The study of life boredom. *Journal of Phenomenological Psychology, 31,* 188–219.

Belojevic, G., Jakovljevic, B., and Slepcevic, V. (2003). Noise and mental performance: Personality attributes and noise sensitivity. *Noise Health, 6,* 77–89.

Birdi, K., Warr, P., and Oswald, A. (1995). Age differences in three components of employee well-being. *Applied Psychology: An International Review, 44,* 245–373.

Bruursema, K., Kessler, S.R., and Spector, P.E. (2011). Bored employees misbehaving: The relationship between boredom and counterproductive work behavior. *Work and Stress, 25*(2), 93–107.

Cannon-Bowers, J.A., Salas, E., Blickensderfer, E., and Bowers, C.A. (1998). The impact of cross training and workload on team functioning: A replication and extension of initial findings. *Human Factors, 40,* 92–101.

Cohen, S. (1980). After effects of stress on human performance and social behavior: A review of research and theory. *Psychological Bulletin, 88,* 82–108.

Combs, A.W. and Taylor, C. (1952). The effect of perception of mild degrees of threat on performance. *Journal of Abnormal and Social Psychology, 47,* 420–424.

Connors, M.M., Harrison, A.A., and Akins, F.R. (1984). *Living Aloft: Human Requirements for Extended Spaceflight.* Washington, DC: NASA.

Davies, D.R., Shackleton, V.J., and Parasuraman, R. (1983). Monotony and boredom. In R. Hockey (Ed.) *Stress and Fatigue in Human Performance* (pp. 1–32). Chichester, UK: Wiley.

Driskell, J.E., Hogan, R., and Salas, E. (1987). Personality and group performance. In C. Hendrick (Ed.) *Review of Personality and Social Psychology* (vol. 9, pp. 91–112). Newbury Park, CA: Sage.

Driskell, J.E., Johnston, J.H., and Salas, E. (2001). Does stress training generalize to novel settings? *Human Factors, 43,* 99–110.

Driskell, J.E. and Salas, E. (1991). Group decision making under stress. *Journal of Applied Psychology, 76,* 473–478.

Driskell, J.E., Salas, E., and Hughes, S. (2010). Collective orientation and team performance: Development of an individual differences measure. *Human Factors, 52*(2), 316–328.

Driskell, J.E., Salas, E., and Johnston, J.H. (1999). Does stress lead to a loss of team perspective? *Group Dynamics, 3,* 1–12.

Driskell, J.E., Salas, E., and Johnston, J.H. (2006). Decision-making and performance under stress. In T.W. Britt, C.A. Castro, and A.B. Adler (Eds.) *Military Life: The Psychology of Serving in Peace and Combat* (vol. 1, pp. 128–154). Westport, CT: Praeger.

Driskell, J.E., Salas, E., Johnston, J.H., and Wollert, T.N. (2008). Stress exposure training: An event-based approach. In P.A. Hancock and J.L. Szalma (Eds.) *Performance Under Stress* (pp. 271–286). London: Ashgate.

Driskell, J.E., Wadsworth, L.A., and Krokos, K. (2009). Stress assessment in hazardous environments. Unpublished report.

Drory, A. (1982). Individual differences in boredom proneness and task effectiveness at work. *Personnel Psychology, 35,* 141–151.

Easterbrook, J.A. (1959). The effect of emotion on cue utilization and the organization of behavior. *Psychological Review, 66,* 183–201.

Fischer, S.C. and Mautone, P.D. (2005). *Multi-tasking Assessment for Personnel Selection and Development* (ARI Contractor Report 2005–07). Arlington, VA: United States Army Research Institute for the Behavioral and Social Sciences.

Fisher, C.D. (1987). *Boredom: Construct, Causes, and Consequences.* Technical report ONR-9. College Station, TX: Texas A&M University.

Fisher, C.D. (1993). Boredom at work: A neglected concept. *Human Relations, 46,* 395–417.

Fowlkes, J.E. and Burke, C.S. (2005). Event-based approach to training (EBAT). In N. Stanton, A. Hedge, K. Brookhuis, E. Salas, and H. Hendrick (Eds.) *Handbook of Human Factors and Ergonomics Methods* (pp. 47.1–47.5). Boca Raton, FL: CRC Press.

Ganster, D.C. (2005). Executive job demands: Suggestions from a stress and decision-making perspective. *Academy of Management Review, 30,* 492–502.

Gardner, D.G. and Cummings, L.L. (1988). Activation theory and job design: Review and reconceptualization. *Research in Organizational Behaviour, 10,* 81–122.

Grose, V.L. (1988). Coping with boredom in the cockpit before it is too late. *Risk Management, 35,* 30–35.

Heggestad, E.D., Carpenter, S., O'Shea, W.G., DeLosh, D.L., and Clegg, B.A. (2002). *Timesharing: Its Future Implications for the Navy.* Millington, TN: Navy Personnel Research, Studies, and Technology.

Hogan, J. and Lesser, M. (1996). Selection of personnel for hazardous performance. In J.E. Driskell and E. Salas (Eds.) *Stress and Human Performance* (pp. 195–222). Mahwah, NJ: Erlbaum.

Holsti, O.R. (1971). Crisis, stress, and decision-making. *International Social Science Journal, 23,* 53–67.

Inzana, C.M., Driskell, J.E., Salas, E., and Johnston, J. (1996). Effects of preparatory information on enhancing performance under stress. *Journal of Applied Psychology, 81,* 429–435.

Isaac, J.D., Sansone, C., and Smith, J. (1999). Other people as a source of interest in an activity. *Journal of Experimental Social Psychology, 35,* 239–265.

James, W. (1890). *The Principles of Psychology* (vol. 1). New York: Holt.

Janis, I.L. and Mann, L. (1977). *Decision Making: A Psychological Analysis of Conflict, Choice, and Commitment.* New York: Free Press.

Johnston, J.H. and Cannon-Bowers, J.A. (1996). Training for stress exposure. In J.E. Driskell and E. Salas (Eds.) *Stress and Human Performance* (pp. 223–256). Mahwah, NJ: Erlbaum.

Johnston, J.H., Driskell, J.E., and Salas, E. (1997). Vigilant and hypervigilant decision making. *Journal of Applied Psychology, 82,* 614–622.

Kass, S.J., Vodanovich, S.J., and Callender, A. (2001). State-trait boredom: Relationship to absenteeism, tenure and job satisfaction. *Journal of Business and Psychology, 16,* 317–327.

Kavanagh, J. (2005). *Stress and Performance: A Review of the Literature and its Applicability to the Military.* Santa Monica, CA: RAND Corporation.

Klein, G. (1996). The effect of acute stressors on decision making. In J.E. Driskell and E. Salas (Eds.) *Stress and Human Performance* (pp. 49–88). Mahwah, NJ: Erlbaum.

Latham, G.P. and Kinne, S.B. (1974). Improving job performance through training in goal setting. *Journal of Applied Psychology, 59*(2), 187–191.

Lee, T.W. (1986). Toward the development and validation of a measure of job boredom. *Manhattan College Journal of Business, 15,* 22–28.

Leong, F.T. and Schneller, G.R. (1993). Boredom proneness: Temperamental and cognitive components. *Personality and Individual Differences, 14,* 233–239.

London, H., Schubert, D.S., and Washburn, D. (1972). Increase of autonomic arousal by boredom. *Journal of Abnormal Psychology, 80*(1), 29–36.

Lorenzet, S.J., Salas, E., and Tannenbaum, S.I. (2005). Benefiting from mistakes: The impact of guided errors on learning performance, and self-efficacy. *Human Resource Development Quarterly, 16*(3), 301–322.

Loukidou, L., Loan-Clarke, J., and Daniels, K. (2009). Boredom in the workplace: More than monotonous tasks. *International Journal of Management Reviews, 11*(4), 381–405.

Mann, S. (2007). The boredom boom. *The Psychologist, 20*(2), 90–93.

Marks, M.A., Mathieu, J.E., and Zaccaro, S.J. (2001). A temporally based framework and taxonomy of team processes. *The Academy of Management Review, 26*(3), 356–376.

Marshall, S.L.A. (1947). *Men Against Fire: The Problem of Battle Command in Future War.* Gloucester, MA: Peter Smith.

Matthews, K.A., Räikkönen, K., Everson, S.A., Flory, J.D., Marco, C.A., Ownes, J.F., and Lloyd, C.E. (2000). Do the daily experiences of healthy men and women vary according to occupational prestige and work strain? *Psychosomatic Medicine, 62,* 346–353.

Morris, J.H. and Steers, R.M. (1980). Structural influences on organizational commitment. *Journal of Vocational Behavior, 17,* 50–57.

Moschis, G.P. (2007). Stress and consumer behavior. *Journal of the Academy of Marketing Science, 35,* 430–444.

Mount, M.K., Barrick, M.R., and Stewart, G.L. (1998). Five-factor model of personality and performance in jobs involving interpersonal interactions. *Human Performance, 11,* 145–165.

Mullen, B., Bryant, B., and Driskell, J.E. (1997). The presence of others and arousal: An integration. *Group Dynamics, 1,* 52–64.

National Transportation Safety Board (NTSB) (1989). *Safety Recommendation I-81-1.* Washington, DC: Department of Transportation, National Safety Transportation Board.

O'Hanlon, J.F. (1981). Boredom: Practical consequences and a theory. *Acta Psychologica, 49,* 53–82.

Payne, J.W., Bettman, J.R., and Johnson, E.J. (1992). Behavioral decision research: A constructive processing perspective. *Annual Review of Psychology, 43,* 87–131.

Pekrun, R., Elliot, A.J., and Maier, M.A. (2006). Achievement goals and discrete achievement emotions: A theoretical model and prospective test more options. *Journal of Educational Psychology, 98,* 583–597.

Porcelli, A.J. and Delgado, M.R. (2009). Acute stress modulates risk taking in financial decision making. *Psychological Science, 20*, 278–283.

Preston, S.D., Buchanan, T.W., Stansfield, R.B., and Bechara, A. (2007). Effects of anticipatory stress on decision making in a gambling task. *Behavioral Neuroscience, 121*, 257–263.

Rosen, M.A., Salas, E., Pavlas, D., Jensen, R., Fu, D., and Lampton, D. (2010). Demonstration-based training: A review of instructional features. *Human Factors, 52*(5), 596–609.

Salas, E. and Cannon-Bowers, J.A. (2001). The science of training: A decade of progress. *Annual Review of Psychology, 52*, 471–499.

Sansone, C., Wiebe, D.J., and Morgan, C. (1999). Self-regulating interest: The moderating role of hardiness and conscientiousness. *Journal of Personality, 67*, 701–733.

Saunders, T., Driskell, J.E., Johnston, J., and Salas, E. (1996). The effect of stress inoculation training on anxiety and performance. *Journal of Occupational Health Psychology, 1*, 170–186.

Sigelman, L. and McNeil, D.M. (1980). White House decision making under stress: A case analysis. *American Journal of Political Science, 24*, 652–673.

Singer, R.N., Cauraugh, J.H., Murphey, M., Chen, D., and Lidor, R. (1991). Attentional control, distractors, and motor performance. *Human Performance, 4*, 55–69.

Spector, P.E., Fox, S., Penney, L.M., Bruursema, K., Goh, A., and Kessler, S. (2006). The dimensionality of counterproductivity: Are all counterproductive behaviors created equal? *Journal of Vocational Behavior, 68*, 446–460.

Spector, P.E. and Jex, S.M. (1998). Development of four self-report measures of job stressors and strain: Interpersonal conflict at work scale, organizational constraints scale, quantitative workload inventory, and physical symptoms inventory. *Journal of Occupational Health Psychology, 3*, 356–367.

Sperandio, J.C. (1971). Variations of operators' strategies and regulating effects on workload. *Ergonomics, 14*, 571–577.

Stouffer, S.A., Lumsdaine, A.A., Lumsdaine, M.H., Williams, R.M., Smith, M.B., Janis, I.L., Star, S.A., and Cottrell, L.S. (1949). *The American Soldier: Combat and its Aftermath.* Princeton, NJ: Princeton University Press.

Sweeny, K. (2008). Crisis decision theory: Decisions in the face of negative events. *Psychological Bulletin, 134*, 61–76.

Watt, J.D. and Vodanovich, S.J. (1999). Boredom proneness and psychosocial development. *Journal of Psychology, 133*(3), 303–314.

Watten, R.G., Syversen, J.L., and Myhrer, T. (1995). Quality of life, intelligence and mood. *Social Indicators Research, 36*, 287–299.

Wendt, H.W. (1955). Motivation effort and performance. In D.C. McClelland (Ed.) *Studies in Motivation* (pp. 448–459). New York: Appleton-Century.

Wheeler, D.D. and Janis, I.L. (1980). *A Practical Guide for Making Decisions.* New York: Free Press.

Wickens, C.D. (1996). Designing for stress. In J.E. Driskell and E. Salas (Eds.) *Stress and Human Performance* (pp. 279–295). Mahwah, NJ: Erlbaum.

Wiesner, M., Windle, M., and Freeman, A. (2005). Work stress, substance use, and depression among young adult workers: An examination of main and moderator effect models. *Journal of Occupational Health Psychology, 10*, 83–96.

Williams, K., Harkins, S., and Latané, B. (1981). Identifiability as a deterrent to social loafing: Two cheering experiments. *Journal of Personality and Social Psychology, 40*, 310–311.

Yerkes, R.M. and Dodson, J.D. (1908). The relation of strength of stimulus to rapidity of habit-formation. *Journal of Comparative Neurology, 18*, 459–482.

14

Enhancing Naturalistic Decision Making and Accelerating Expertise in the Workplace: Training Strategies that Work

Rebecca Grossman, Jacqueline M. Spencer, and Eduardo Salas[1]

In the modern work environment, performance is rarely a product of standardized actions, but instead is contingent on a series of judgments and decisions. Decision making underlies the bulk of everyday work behaviors, ranging from simple (e.g., deciding which tasks to prioritize) to complex (e.g., deciding which actions to take following an emergency). It is therefore critical to understand how decision-making processes operate and how such processes can be improved through training and development interventions. Indeed, there are multiple long-standing streams of research seeking to do just that, most falling under the formal-empiricist or rationalist paradigms (Cohen, 1993). Both approaches suggest that decision makers build and test models when selecting between concurrently available options (Cohen, 1993), with the rationalist approach emphasizing the role of human error in the construction and use of such models (Ross, Shafer, & Klein, 2006). More recently, however, the naturalistic decision making (NDM) framework has been put forward as a means of explaining how decisions are made in real-world, complex environments (Klein et al., 1993). Specifically, while other decision-making paradigms are based on controlled lab experiments, proponents of the NDM approach argue that the inherent complexity and constraints of most real-world contexts do not allow for the careful construction and con-sideration of models of choice. Instead, decision makers rely on previous experience to interpret the situation at hand and select an appropriate course of action (Klein et al., 1993).

Considering the increasing complexity of the modern work environment (Goodwin et al., 2009), the NDM paradigm appears to be the optimal lens through which decision making in work contexts should be examined. Interestingly, however, most work on NDM has been conducted outside of the industrial-organizational (I-O) and organizational behavior (OB) fields, and has remained largely absent from the corresponding literatures. Accordingly, research concerned with modeling and training decision making in these domains is generally more consistent with the formal-empiricist and rationalist paradigms as opposed to a more naturalistic framework. Specifically, much of the work in this area focuses on such things as strategic management (e.g., Escribá-Esteve, Sánchez-Peinado, & Sánchez-Peinado, 2009), ethical decision-making (e.g., Flannery & May, 2000), and personnel selection (e.g., Ployhart & Holtz, 2008), to name a few, each of which typically involves some form of cost-benefit analysis and selection among concurrently available options as the base of the decision-making process. Further, interventions designed to improve decision making in this realm tend to focus on how to effectively conduct such cost-benefit analyses, and how to reduce biases and errors while doing so. While these approaches certainly have their place, they do not seem to fit with what we know about real people who make decisions in real-world contexts. In real, complex environments, people often do not have the time or resources to engage in formal, thought-out choice procedures, but instead must rely on knowledge from previous experience to determine an appropriate course of action. The purpose of this chapter is thus to leverage findings from the NDM literature to explore how NDM can be facilitated in the modern workplace. Specifically, the goal is to draw from various NDM sources to provide a compiled, succinct collection of training and development interventions that can be effective for enhancing expert decision making at both the individual and the team level.

NDM: A BRIEF REVIEW

The NDM approach was born from a growing need to understand how people make decisions in real-world, uncontrolled settings (Lipshitz et al., 2001). Its roots can be traced to the Vincennes incident in 1988, when a U.S. Navy missile cruiser mistakenly attacked a commercial Iranian flight, ultimately killing 290 innocent passengers (Salas & Rosen, 2008). The incident, and others like it, could not be understood through traditional models of the decision-making process (i.e., formalist-empiricist paradigm, rationalist paradigm). While such models were certainly valuable, they were not compatible with the dynamic, stressful, and uncertain nature of most real-world environments. Decision making was seen as the process of evaluating and selecting an alternative from a set of concurrently available options (Salas & Rosen, 2008). In reality, however, time pressure and other constraints do not allow for the careful consideration of all possible courses of action. Additionally, traditional decision-making models did not consider the expertise of the decision maker, viewing previous experience and other decision points as unrelated (Salas & Rosen, 2008). The NDM approach was thus initiated to move beyond what was known about controlled, laboratory contexts, and to begin explaining how "people use their experience to make decisions in field settings" (Zsambok, 1997, p. 4).

As alluded to above, the NDM approach is defined by two primary factors that characterize the settings in which naturalistic decisions are made (Lipshitz et al., 2001). First, the expertise of the decision maker is central to the decision-making process (Salas & Rosen, 2008). In the recognition-primed decision (RPD) model, for example, a prominent NDM approach, expert decision makers are thought to rely on previous experience to carry out two overarching processes: pattern recognition and mental simulation (Klein, Calderwood, & Clinton-Cirocco, 1986). Specifically, the decision maker matches cues in the current environment to those from a past experience to identify previous courses of action that might apply to the present domain. The decision maker then evaluates the effectiveness of the chosen action given the unique aspects of the present situation by engaging in a mental simulation, or a "cognitive walkthrough" of what might result if such an action were implemented (Salas & Rosen, 2008). This process results in either the implementation of the chosen course of action, or the rejection of it, in which case the decision maker returns to the pattern recognition phase.

The second distinguishing feature of the NDM paradigm is the emphasis on the real-world context in which decision making takes place. Specifically, such real-world settings can be characterized by the presence of eight features put forth by Orasanu and Connolly (1993): ill-structured problems, uncertain and dynamic environments, shifting and ill-defined or competing goals, action/feedback loops, time constraints, high stakes, multiple players, and organizational goals and norms. While each of these features has been deemed central to naturalistic contexts, all of them do not need to be present or at their extreme in any one situation in order for that situation to be classified as an NDM setting (Fritzsche, Wicks, & Salas, in press; Orasanu & Connolly, 1993). Rather, for a decision to be considered naturalistic, some or all of these features may be present at differing extremes. NDM is thus relevant to a range of contexts characterized by varying degrees of complexity.

WHY IS NDM RELEVANT TO THE WORKPLACE?

Although the NDM approach has primarily been applied to research on fireground, military, aviation, and medical decision making (Carvalho, dos Santos, & Vidal, 2005), it also has important implications for more traditional organizational contexts. Technological advances, increasing globalization, shifting work demands, and the increasingly distributed nature of work (Goodwin et al., 2009) have rendered organizational environments highly dynamic and complex. Such environments are thus becoming less and less conducive to more traditional models of decision making, and increasingly in need of an NDM framework through which decision making should be examined. Relevant to this discussion, one of the early NDM models, cognitive continuum theory (Hammond et al., 1987), asserts that whether decision making requires the use of intuitive (i.e., NDM) or analytical (i.e., formal-empiricist, rationalist paradigms) processes depends on where they fall on a complexity continuum. Specifically, conditions such as the amount of information available and the degree of time pressure determine where decisions fall on this continuum, and ultimately which type of decision-making process is utilized (Klein, 2008). Further, as described above, Orasanu and Connolly's (1993) description of features that define complex environments specifically notes that all eight features need not be present or extreme for a situation to require the use of NDM. These propositions point to the relevance of NDM in organizational settings, given the increasing complexity of such contexts in the modern day. Indeed, various authors have argued for the application of NDM research to organizational contexts through both empirical and theoretical insights (e.g., Carvalho, dos Santos, & Vidal, 2005; DiBello, Missildine, & Struttman, 2009; Lipshitz, Klein, & Carroll, 2006; Phillips, Klein, & Sieck, 2004; Rosen, Shuffler, & Salas, 2010), suggesting that NDM not only has a place in work settings, but also that it is greatly needed if we hope to thoroughly understand decision making in the modern workplace.

ENHANCING EXPERT DECISION MAKING

The NDM approach suggests that extensive experience, or expertise, is required to make effective decisions in naturalistic environments. However, such expertise can take years to develop, posing an issue for organizations seeking to maintain relevance and competitive advantage. Researchers have thus begun to explore mechanisms through which the development of expertise can be accelerated in organizational settings (Salas & Rosen, 2010). Building on this work, we describe a variety of interventions that can be used to train or develop the expertise needed to make naturalistic decisions. Specifically, we refer to decision making in naturalistic settings as *expert decision making*, and delineate strategies that can be used to enhance such expert decision making at both the individual and the team level. As depicted in Figure 14.1, we begin by describing what it means to be an expert as well as what it means to be an expert team. Leveraging theoretical and empirical insights from the NDM literature, we then present an integrated collection of training and development interventions that can be used to enhance expert decision making at each level (i.e., individual and team). In doing so, we also draw from literature on situation awareness, pattern recognition, metacognition, intuition, and, most importantly,

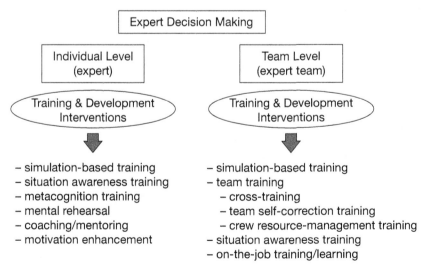

FIGURE 14.1
Organizing framework for expert decision making.

expertise—factors that are fundamental to the expert decision-making process. More broadly, we utilize the literature on training and other developmental strategies (e.g., coaching) to provide specific information about how each intervention can be optimally executed. Specifically, for each developmental intervention, we describe what it is, why it is effective for enhancing expert decision making, and how it can best be implemented. First, however, we briefly discuss our theoretical reasoning for identifying these specific interventions, among the many, as effective mechanisms for enhancing expert decision making in individuals and teams.

SELECTION OF TRAINING AND DEVELOPMENT INTERVENTIONS

There are a variety of training and development techniques that can be used to enhance trainees' knowledge, skills, and abilities of interest; those included in this chapter were selected because they facilitate some contextual feature or underlying process that is fundamental to NDM theory. As described above, the NDM approach is distinguished by its emphasis on the expertise of the decision maker and the complexity of the naturalistic setting in which decision making takes place. Given these characteristics, the NDM process primarily involves pattern recognition and mental simulation, not more structured processes (e.g., building and testing mathematical models) that characterize other decision-making theories. Thus, we selected training and development interventions that are compatible with the basic tenets of NDM theory—they provide experience in naturalistic settings, they help develop expertise, and they facilitate the pattern recognition and mental simulation processes that are required to make decisions in the real world.

More specifically, we include situation awareness (SA) training because it teaches individuals to identify the presence of cues and ongoing changes in those cues in a given environment, facilitating pattern recognition, and subsequent mental simulation. This technique is included as both an individual- and a team-level intervention, as it is important for decision makers to be aware not only of the situation itself, but also of their team members. SA training also helps team members attain shared cognition, enabling them to interpret the situation and act in ways that are compatible with one another. Further facilitating these processes, metacognition training is included because it enables individuals to recognize short-comings in their thinking, prompting them to collect additional information before making a decision, when necessary. Within this, mental rehearsal is discussed as a means of providing additional experiences and increasing motivation to engage in continuous learning. We include simulation-based training, perhaps the most powerful of the techniques, because it provides trainees with relevant experience, helping to build the level of expertise that is necessary for making decisions in naturalistic settings. Such experience can consist of exposure to the environment itself, practice engaging in pattern recognition and mental simulation, and practice coordinating with team members in team settings, facilitating all aspects of the expert decision-making process. Simulation-based training is thus included as both an individual- and a team-level intervention—it can provide experience in the processes required for expert decision making in both individuals and teams.

Particularly important for expert teams is team training, included because it develops the teamwork processes and emergent states that are required for teams to make decisions in complex, dynamic situations using minimal time and overt communication. Cross-training, team self-correction training, and crew resource management training, all types of team training, are thus included in our discussion. Each of these techniques provides team members with some type of knowledge, skill, and/or ability that enables individuals to quickly interpret the situation, coordinate with each other, recognize and correct shortcomings, and, ultimately, make effective decisions within naturalistic settings. Finally, we include coaching and mentoring, motivation enhancement techniques, and on-the-job training and learning because they facilitate the continued development of expertise, central to the ability to make decisions in naturalistic settings. While coaching/mentoring and motivation enhancement techniques can encourage the behaviors that promote expertise (e.g., feedback seeking), on-the-job training/learning, and, to some extent, coaching/mentoring can provide additional experiences that can ultimately feed into the decision-making process. Thus, each training and development intervention that we include ties into the foundational elements of NDM theory, making them ideal techniques for enhancing expert decision making in both individuals and teams.

INDIVIDUAL-LEVEL EXPERT DECISION MAKING

What is an Expert?

Experts are individuals who have the ability to "perform repeatedly and reliably at high levels on a specific set of tasks within the boundaries of a domain" (Salas & Rosen, 2010, p. 105). A variety of characteristics enable experts to reach this level of performance. Specialized analytical reasoning skills, for example, are one of many dimensions thought to contribute to expertise. Rosen and colleagues (2008) identify nine key characteristics that experts possess that contribute to effective decision making, suggesting that developing and maintaining expertise is far from simple:

- Ability to connect cues and contextual features of the environment more effectively to decision making than novices.
- A more robust knowledge base as compared to novices, allowing experts not only to pull the information that is needed, but also to organize the information conceptually for more proficient use.
- Ability to recognize patterns in order to make decisions based on similar, previously encountered situations.
- Engaging in dedicated practice aimed at improving knowledge and skills.
- Striving for opportunities to receive feedback.
- Greater ability to identify and define the situation and issue as compared to novices.
- A larger memory capacity compared to novices.
- Possessing previously thought-out steps for how to handle minor issues that will be encountered.
- Desire to self-evaluate continuously.

In addition to these, Cannon-Bowers and Bell (1997) propose that situation awareness, organized knowledge structures, mental simulation, strategy selection/modulation, and reasoning skills can all be considered mechanisms of expert decision making. Interventions designed to enhance expert decision making can thus focus on a variety of knowledge, skills, and abilities (KSAs) and behaviors, all of which contribute to the development and maintenance of expertise. In the following sections, we delineate training and development interventions that can be used to enhance expert decision making at the individual level, describing their relevance to expert decision making, and explaining how they can best be implemented. Mirroring this information, in Table 14.1, we provide a summary of the interventions, guidelines for how they should be implemented, and information about why they are useful for training expert decision making.

Interventions for Enhancing Individual-level Expert Decision Making

Simulation-based Training

At the broadest level, a highly effective approach to training expert decision making is simulation-based training (SBT), as it emphasizes extended opportunities for practice and feedback (Salas et al., 2008a). Specifically, trainees develop target competencies by practicing in a simulated environment that is representative of the actual work setting in which such skills will ultimately be applied (Salas et al., 2006b). In the past, the ability to make expert decisions was accomplished by gaining extensive real-world experience in complex situations. SBT enables the individual to practice specified tasks or competencies that will be encountered in real work settings. Through SBT, individuals are able to acquire skills necessary for success at a much quicker rate than would normally be possible by relying on regular work activities (Salas, Wildman, & Piccolo, 2009). Simulations can vary in the degree of fidelity they possess and can be classified into three categories—role-playing simulations, physically based simulations, and computer-based simulations (Summers, 2004). Sometimes referred to as scenario-based or event-based training, the defining feature of SBT is that the simulations, or scenarios, themselves essentially comprise the training curriculum rather than some form of reading or lecture (Salas et al., 2006c). SBT can also be distinguished by its reliance on practice and feedback to elicit target competencies in lieu of more traditional methods (e.g., lectures). The benefits of using simulations in training are abundant, including such things as the safety of the simulated environment, the ability to practice relevant tasks, and the inclusion of feedback opportunities that can lead to the discovery of strengths and weaknesses (DiBello, Missildine, & Struttman, 2009).

Simulation-based training has been used in a variety of settings such as aviation (Salas et al., 1999), management education (Salas, Wildman, & Piccolo, 2009), healthcare (Rosen et al., 2010), and military training (Salas, Cannon-Bowers, & Smith-Jentsch, 2006), to name a few. Particularly

TABLE 14.1

Interventions for Enhancing Individual-level Expert Decision Making

Training Strategy	Guidelines	How Does It Enhance Individual-level Expert Decision Making?
Simulation-based training	• Design training to target adaptability, intuitive expertise, and cognitive agility • Cater practice scenarios, feedback, and the degree of fidelity to the specific job of interest • Develop scenarios with training objectives in mind • Allow for the measurement of training process and outcomes • Provide feedback • Incorporate role-play and behavioral modeling; incorporate both positive and negative examples of behavior	• Provides experience relevant to decision making in the operating environment • Accelerates the development of expertise • Provides opportunities to engage in deliberate and guided practice, self-regulation, feedback-seeking behaviors, motivation, and goal setting
Situation awareness training	• Training should involve attention sharing, task management, contingency planning, information seeking/filtering, self-checking, and other meta-skills • Focus on developing mental models of the importance, consequences, timing, risk levels, and capabilities associated with potential events and options that will be encountered in the naturalistic environment • Provide practice opportunities and feedback	• Facilitates cue recognition and pattern recognition • Promotes the ability to project what will occur next in a situation

Metacognition training	• Deliver training in the form of guidelines indicating how trainees can increase their metacognitive ability during problem-solving • Guidelines should involve steps trainees can take such as monitoring the reading and understanding of the question or problem, assessing what information is necessary to reach a conclusion, using a strategy or plan to organize the information gathered, monitoring the use of this strategy, and calculating a solution, followed by rechecking each step to ensure that an appropriate decision has been made • Provide a decision-making task that enables trainees to practice following the guidelines	• Promotes self-awareness and self-regulation • Develops the ability to identify one's own strengths, weaknesses, and gaps in understanding, indicating when more information is needed to make a decision
Mental rehearsal	• Prompt trainees to mentally rehearse both positive and negative decision situations and outcomes during and after training	• Provides experience that serves as a foundation for pattern recognition and mental simulation during expert decision making • Motivates trainees to engage in continuous learning and practice
Coaching and mentoring	• Provide ample opportunities for supervised practice • Provide extensive, diagnostic feedback • Prompt trainees to engage in behaviors that contribute to the development of expertise • Coaches and mentors should share information from their own experiences with trainees	• Supplements trainees' own repertoire of experiences with those shared by their coach/mentor • Prompts trainees to engage in behaviors that facilitate the development of expertise
Motivation enhancement	• Implement goal-setting activities prior to, and following, NDM training	• Motivates trainees to engage in behaviors that help develop and maintain expertise over time

relevant to expert decision making, DiBello, Missildine, and Struttman (2009) discuss the use of an accelerated learning Operational Simulation (OpSim) as a method for training individuals to make effective decisions in the workplace. The authors argue that "experts rel[y] on a more intuitive, adaptive decision-making process as opposed to the analytic deductive approach" (p. 15). Consistent with the broader NDM literature, this suggests that experts use their experience and previously learned knowledge to make decisions in naturalistic environments. SBT is thus an ideal approach for training expert decision making, as it places individuals in an environment that allows them to practice actual events that will be encountered on the job, thereby allowing them to gain relevant task-related expertise without having to accumulate years of experience to make a comparable decision. As an empirical example of its effectiveness, other researchers have shown that SBT is more effective than more guided role-playing training, arguably because it is more realistic, provides automatic feedback, and allows for paced learning (Murthy et al., 2008). Specifically, in two call centers at *Fortune 50* firms, training type impacted trainees' speed ($F = 4.47$, $p < .05$) and accuracy ($F = 5.56$, $p < .05$) during customer service calls, with those who underwent SBT performing better than those who didn't in both domains.

Various researchers have provided guidance indicating how SBT can best be used to train expert decision making at the individual level. DiBello, Missildine, and Struttman (2009), for example, list the mechanisms they feel are needed to develop expertise-based intuition. Such mechanisms include deliberate and guided practice, self-regulation, feedback-seeking behaviors, motivation, and goal setting. Training designed to target these characteristics can thus serve to enhance the development of expertise and, in turn, expert decision making. Further, they note that, in order for training to be effective, it must address adaptability, intuitive expertise, and cognitive agility (i.e., "the ability to rapidly revise one's mental model in the face of changing feedback," p. 16). Another important approach to training expert decision making through SBT is to cater the practice scenarios, feedback, and degree of fidelity to the specific job of interest. These features should thus be representative of the specific job, not generic naturalistic settings. Similarly, Salas and Cannon-Bowers (2001) note that SBT should be developed with training objectives in mind, should allow for the measurement of both processes and outcomes, and should provide diagnostic feedback. An instructional feature also identified by these authors is behavior role-play in which "role-playing and other elements of behavior modeling" are implemented and characterized through the emphasis on practice and performance feedback (p. 485). Additionally, demonstrating and practicing both positive and negative examples of behavior that trainees might encounter on the job can lead to greater behavioral generalization and transfer (Salas & Cannon-Bowers, 2001).

Situation Awareness Training

Another, more specific, approach that can be used to train individuals to engage in expert decision making is situation awareness training. Research on expert decision makers has revealed that experts tend to have a greater understanding of the situations in which they operate. Referred to as situation awareness (SA), this understanding is defined as "the perception of the elements in the environment within a volume of time and space, the comprehension of their meaning, and the projection of their status in the near future" (Endsley, 1995, p. 31). SA is regarded as a critical driver of performance in complex environments, thus has been the focus of various studies examining how it can best be trained. Relevant to its training are insights put forth by Salas et al. (1995) regarding their model of SA's developmental process. Specifically, the authors state that:

> SA occurs as a consequence of an interaction of an individual's preexisting, relevant knowledge and expectations; the information available from the environment; and cognitive processing skills that include attention allocation, perception data extraction, comprehension, and projection. This results in an increase in the individual's knowledge, a change in expectations, and another cycle of information extraction.
>
> (1995, p. 125)

This implies that, among other things, SA training should teach individuals how to recognize cues in the current environment, relate them to previous experiences, project potential outcomes, and respond to the demands of a dynamic environment.

Consistent with this model, two aspects of SA have been highlighted in the literature—cue recognition and pattern recognition. These processes are foundational elements of expert decision making, as they drive the first phase of the process, feeding into subsequent mental simulations, and ultimately decisions. Indeed, the ability of decision makers to recognize cues quickly and holistically has been identified as a critical component of the NDM approach (Meso, Troutt, & Rudnicka, 2002). Once such cues are perceived, pattern recognition enables decision makers to compare the components of the current situation to those that they experienced in another domain. These skills are developed through experience and training—experts are better able to identify patterns when making decisions in naturalistic environments than are novices (Meso, Troutt, & Rudnicka, 2002). Ultimately, the recognition of events, cues, and patterns that results from SA allows individuals to pull from experiences and anticipate what might occur next in order to make a more informed decision (Salas et al., 1995). Supporting these ideas, SA training has shown success in improving elements of SA that relate to decision making in naturalistic environments. Through a series of training modules for aviation pilots, for example, Bolstad et al. (2010), showed that SA training improved such things as knowledge of current aircraft altitude ($t = 1.86$, $p < .05$), knowledge of current winds ($t = 1.72$, $p < .05$), and time to react while monitoring ($t = -2.578$, $p < .01$), among other variables indicative of situation awareness.

SA training tends to focus on developing the component skills that enable individuals to achieve and maintain SA in the operating environment. For example, enhancing the cognitive skills that drive SA involves teaching attention sharing, task management, contingency planning, information seeking/filtering, self-checking, and other meta-skills deemed important for SA (Endsley & Robertson, 2000). Similarly, Endsley and Robertson (2000) argue that training should be devoted to developing mental models of the importance, consequences, timing, risks levels, and capabilities associated with potential events and options that will be encountered in the naturalistic environment. While there are many insights about which KSAs should be trained to facilitate SA, much less is known about the methods by which the desirable KSAs may be cultivated (Bolstad et al., 2010). Unfortunately, research in this area is sparse compared to other training techniques, making practical guidance and best practices for SA training more difficult to come by.

Nonetheless, there are some insights that can inform the development of SA training. Intensive pre-briefings and structured feedback, for example, have been identified as valuable features that should be included in SA training interventions (Endsley et al., 1998). Providing feedback about trainees' SA levels is a critical strategy for increasing SA due to the unrealistic perceptions that individuals often have of their own SA levels (Endsley & Robertson, 2000). Additionally, practice is critical to the development of SA, particularly for the abilities to identify relevant cues and recognize patterns. Practice-based instructional features, such as scenarios and simulations, should therefore be incorporated into SA training programs. Practice does not necessarily need to be high fidelity, but should psychologically represent the task and transfer environment. Additionally, they should be embedded with instructional features (e.g., performance measurement) to ensure their value as a training tool (Salas & Burke, 2002).

Metacognition Training

Another technique that targets expert decision making is metacognition training. Salas, Rhodenizer, and Bowers (2000, p. 496) define metacognition as "having knowledge about one's own cognitive processes or thinking." Adding to this definition, Alessi (2000, p. 202) defines metacognition as "self-awareness about one's cognitive activities and *ability to modify them consciously*. This includes reflection, self-assessment, planning, and selecting fix-up strategies to correct problems." Metacognition has also been described as a type of self-awareness in which individuals possess knowledge of their own knowledge, cognitive processes, and performance (Salas & Rosen, 2010). While there are slight variations in how metacognition is defined, metacognition training generally focuses on calling attention to cognitive processes and training individuals to consider them, and potentially alter them in real-life situations.

In a discussion of experts in the workplace, Salas and Rosen (2010) argue that self-monitoring and metacognitive skills are essential components of expertise. Further, they describe metacognition as "essential to expert performance as well as to the development of expertise" (pp. 111–112). Metacognition training is thus critical for developing not only the expertise, but also the self-awareness and self-regulation skills that are needed for carrying out the decision-making process. In the decision-making context, metacognition enables individuals to identify their own strengths, weaknesses, and gaps in understanding, facilitating their ability to self-correct in situ, without assistance from other actors. Further, metacognition assists individuals in determining whether or not they have obtained sufficient information to make a decision, or whether it is necessary to collect additional data and restart the mental simulation component of the expert decision-making process before proceeding. Evidence of the usefulness of metacognition training has been seen within the aviation industry (Salas et al., 1999; Salas, Rhodenizer & Bowers, 2000), as well as in mathematical problem solving (Pennequin et al., 2010), computer-based problem solving (Veenman, Elshout, & Busato, 1994), and error management (Keith & Frese, 2005). There is also evidence for a link between metacognition training and enhanced decision making—metacognitive strategy instructions have been reported to increase individuals' meta-cognition levels and, in turn, to improve decision-making performances (r = 0.389; Batha & Carroll, 2007). Further, through metacognitive training, improvements have been reported in backup behaviors and the problem-solving skills of airline crews (Salas et al., 1999; Salas, Rhodenizer, & Bowers, 2000), both of which indicate that individuals are more prepared to handle complex situations when they occur in their natural work settings, after receiving training.

While we could not locate specific guidelines or best practices for implementing metacognition training, information about previous training programs in the literature can serve to guide the design and delivery of future interventions targeting expert decision-making. Batha and Carroll (2007), for example, describe their strategy for training metacognition as guidelines that are given to trainees, teaching them how to increase their metacognitive ability during problem solving. The authors recommend that trainees be given these instructions prior to engaging in a decision-making task. The steps included in the training guidelines involve:

> monitoring the reading and understanding of the question or problem, assessing what information is necessary to reach a conclusion, using a strategy or plan to organize the information so gathered, monitoring the use of this strategy, and calculating a solution, followed by re-checking every step of the strategy used to ensure the right decision has been made.
> (Batha & Carroll, 2007, p. 65)

While each of these steps cannot be taken in the real decision-making environment, practicing them through training can provide the experience needed for them to be more fluid and automatic upon returning to the naturalistic setting. Interestingly, Batha and Carroll (2007) found that trainees' regulation of cognition was more conducive to decision making than was mere knowledge of cognition, suggesting that particular emphasis should be placed on the regulation component during metacognition training.

Mental Rehearsal

Related to metacognition training is mental rehearsal, the process of using mental imagery to practice, or imagine one's self performing a particular task or behavior without actually engaging in overt actions (Cohn, 1990). Mental rehearsal has been used extensively in the realm of sports, exhibiting the ability to improve performance when used either independently, or in combination with other training and practice techniques (Jones & Stuth, 1997). It has also demonstrated effectiveness in more traditional training settings, used alongside behavioral modeling techniques, for example. Davis and Yi (2004) showed that adding a mental rehearsal component to computer skills training led to significant improvements in both declarative knowledge and task performance. Support has also been found in meta-analyses; Driskell, Copper, and Moran (1994) reported a positive, significant relationship between mental practice and task performance ($d = .527, p < .001$).

Though mental rehearsal has not been used to train expert decision making specifically, its ability to provide additional practice likely makes it a valuable technique for doing so. Because mental rehearsal essentially affords a limitless number and range of "experiences," it can help build the level of expertise that is needed to make effective decisions in naturalistic contexts. This is because the neural representations the brain builds when imagining a task and actually executing a task are thought to be functionally equivalent (Jeannerod, 1994). Thus, mentally rehearsing different decision scenarios can help build a foundation for pattern recognition and mental simulation in real-world situations. Interestingly, athletes have reported engaging in negative imagery as a way of helping them cope with possible negative events in the future (MacIntyre & Moran, 2007). Consistent with error management training (Keith & Frese, 2008) then, mentally rehearsing both positive and negative decision situations and outcomes may be an ideal approach for developing expertise. Also relevant is research showing that mentally envisioning successful task performance can increase trainees' motivation and learning (e.g., Cumming et al., 2005). Because expertise development requires extensive effort, such imagery may serve to motivate trainees to engage in continuous learning and practice efforts once the formal training period is over. Overall then, prompting trainees to engage in mental rehearsal both within the training context and on their own can help build experience banks and can increase motivation, both of which contribute to the ability to engage in expert decision making in the real world.

Coaching and Mentoring

Expert decision making can also be developed through the use of coaching and mentoring. Coaching involves a one-on-one relationship where the coach guides the trainee toward behaviors that are necessary for effective performance. In the past, coaching was used primarily with individuals who were seen as troublesome or deficient in some way. Today, however, coaching is used for "developing the capabilities of high-potential performers" (Coutu & Kauffman, 2009, p. 1), suggesting that it can be particularly effective in complex environments. Indeed, coaching is becoming a valuable resource for organizations seeking to enhance the skills and capabilities of their workforces. Coaching utilizes aspects of consulting and therapy to provide individuals with the tools necessary for success. Similar to consulting, the coach advises the individual on business matters, involves the individual in goal setting, and frames learning material around the ethics and goals of the organization. Similar to therapy, the coach prompts target behaviors by asking the "right question[s]" (p. 3), addresses the individual's behavioral changes, and explores the individual's subjective experiences to help him or her learn from them (Coutu & Kauffman, 2009).

Similar to coaching, expert decision making can also be enhanced through a mentoring relationship. A mentor is a senior individual who guides the development and learning of a protégé. He or she is often an influential person, either within the organization, or outside of the organization but within the field, has extensive experience and knowledge, and has a vested interest in the career of the protégé (Ragins & Cotton, 1999). Mentoring relationships can be formal (i.e., appointed by an organization) or informal (i.e., the relationship forms naturally) (Ragins & Cotton, 1999). Traditional mentoring was based on a one-on-one relationship between mentor and protégé, but new thinking is that having multiple mentors may be of benefit because the protégé is able to have access to a few individuals who possess expert knowledge in different areas, thereby enabling the protégé to gain a larger perspective on topics. This might be the optimal approach for facilitating expert decision making, as trainees need to gain a range of knowledge and experience that can feed into decision making in the future.

Coaching and mentoring can be effective strategies for enhancing expert decision making because they facilitate experiences and behaviors that drive the components of the decision-making process. Specifically, because NDM operates on the basis of one's previous experience, it is important that individuals acquire a repertoire of experiences that they can draw from in the naturalistic environment. In addition to their own experiences, coaching and mentoring can expose trainees to a whole new set of experiences—those encountered by their coach or mentor. Coaches/mentors can share their experiences with trainees, providing examples of positive and negative critical incidents, and ultimately expanding trainees' knowledge bases pertaining to their domains of interest. Coaching and mentoring can also enhance expert decision making by prompting trainees to engage in behaviors that contribute to the development of expertise. Specifically, because deliberate and continuous effort is required to become an expert (e.g., deliberate practice, feedback-seeking behaviors), whether or not an individual develops expertise is often largely contingent on their motivation to do so. Guidance from a coach or mentor, however, can prompt trainees to engage in the necessary behaviors, allowing them to depend less on their own motivation, and more on external reinforcement. Sport is one area that comes to mind when thinking of the effects of coaching. In an attempt to understand what practice activities make an expert decision maker in sports, Baker, Côté, and Abernethy (2003) found that those participants considered experts had significantly more individual instruction with a coach than those considered non-experts ($d = .99, p < .005$).

Research on how best to implement coaching and mentoring tends to be very broad, and has not focused specifically on the development of expertise. However, based on knowledge of expert decision making and the science of training, such techniques are likely most effective for developing expertise when they provide ample opportunities for practice and feedback. Trainees should acquire a range of experiences through the coaching/mentoring relationship, and should receive diagnostic feedback in relation to established performance criteria. Coaching/mentoring are unique mediums, as they allow for extensive supervision and feedback that are not always easy to come by in the hustle and bustle of modern work settings. Further, as described above, coaches/mentors should not only focus on the performance of the trainee, but should also describe their own performance by sharing information about their own experiences that are relevant to the current context.

Motivation Enhancement

Though not necessarily a form of training, it is possible that interventions designed to increase motivation can also serve to enhance the development of expertise. As alluded to above, a common theme in the expertise literature is the critical role of individuals' motivation for carrying out the components of the developmental process. In their chapter on the development of expertise, for example, Salas and Rosen (2010) discuss four different types of motivation that are important for becoming an expert. Specifically, these include the learners' self-efficacy beliefs, the learner's goal orientation, the degree to which the learner values the ultimate outcomes of the developmental process, and the degree to which the learner values the task in and of itself (p. 115). In other words, in order for individuals to effectively become experts, they must believe in their ability to do so and must develop and focus on learning goals rather than on outcome or performance goals. Further, they should be interested in positive outcomes rather than avoiding negative outcomes, and should possess an intrinsic interest in the task that is not contingent on external praise or rewards. Each of these forms of motivation is important for becoming an expert because the development of expertise is largely dependent on sustained, self-directed behaviors, such as engaging in continuous, effortful practice. It thus stands to reason that enhancing one's level of motivation can also serve to enhance the development of expertise and, in turn, the ability to engage in expert decision making.

The primary means through which motivation can be enhanced is the implementation of goal-setting activities. Goal setting provides opportunities for trainees to formally describe what they will derive from the training, or how they will apply what they learn to the real world (Wexley & Latham, 2002). For example, trainees might be prompted to set proximal and distal goals regarding the application of newly acquired behaviors and skills. Goals that are difficult and specific, when paired with diagnostic feedback, are considered to be a primary source of motivation (Robbins & Judge, 2009). Moreover, goal setting increases the probability that trained KSAs are transferred, as they help direct attention, stimulate action, increase persistence, and ultimately prompt trainees to utilize such KSAs when they return to the work environment. Hence, goal-setting activities can motivate trainees to engage in behaviors that facilitate the development of expertise, and thus might be beneficial to include as a component of expert decision making training.

TEAM-LEVEL EXPERT DECISION MAKING

What is an Expert Team?

To manage the growing complexity of the modern work environment, organizations are increasingly relying on teams (Weaver, Wildman, & Salas, 2009). Expert decision making is therefore important not only at the individual level, but also at the team level. Like individual experts, expert teams are defined by a variety of characteristics and abilities that facilitate the decision-making process. For example, members of expert teams are able to be adaptable when applying existing knowledge to novel situations such that they can make predictions about system functioning and can generate new procedures on the basis of these predictions (Salas et al., 2006a). Expert teams are also able to coordinate implicitly, as they possess shared cognitions regarding their task, the situation, their teammates, and their equipment. Salas et al. (2006b) list the characteristics of expert teams as:

- Team members' ability to combine their individual expertise and coordinate their actions to fluidly achieve a common goal.
- Ability to solve problems quickly and accurately.
- Ability to be flexible when applying existing knowledge to novel situations.
- Possessing shared mental models (SMMs) that facilitate implicit coordination.
- Adaptability; possessing deep conceptual understanding of the target domain that promotes the ability to make predictions about system functioning and develop new solutions based on predictions.

Below, we describe various mechanisms for developing these characteristics, and ultimately enhancing team-level expert decision making. A summary of the interventions, guidelines for how they should be implemented, and information about why they are useful for training team-level expert decision making can be found in Table 14.2. While each of the individual-level interventions described in the first half of this chapter should be provided to the individuals comprising the team, simply ensuring that each team member has received such training is not sufficient. Working and making decisions in team contexts requires a unique set of skills, thus unique approaches to enhancing them.

Interventions for Enhancing Team-level Expert Decision Making

Simulation-based Training

Like individual-level expertise, a highly effective approach to training expert decision making in teams is simulation-based training (Salas et al., 2008a). SBT at the team level differs from that at the individual level in that it focuses on developing teamwork competencies, in addition to

TABLE 14.2

Interventions for Enhancing Team-level Expert Decision Making

Training Strategy	Guidelines	How Does It Enhance Team-level Expert Decision Making?
Simulation-based training	• Target specific competencies • Incorporate performance measurement tools • Generate opportunities for practice and feedback • Adopt a systems approach by considering the surrounding context before, during, and after the training takes place • Carefully craft scenarios to be representative of the transfer environment • Embed practice scenarios with multiple scenario cues, measurement opportunities, and timely feedback • Provide opportunities for teams to practice engaging in decision making as a team • Encourage team members to implement feedback and self-correction strategies	• Provides team experience relevant to decision making in the operating environment • Accelerates the development of team expertise • Facilitates the development of SMMs
Team training	• Design training on the basis of a team task analysis • Incorporate performance measurement tools • Utilize pre-practice tools • Align organizational messages with training goals • Promotes clear, valued, and shared visions • Create systematic opportunities for practice • Emphasize key teamwork competencies	• Facilitates the development of SMMs • Promotes the ability to learn and adapt as a team • Promotes the establishment and maintenance of clear roles and responsibilities • Trains teams to engage in a cycle of pre-brief, performance, debrief • Promotes a sense of collective trust, teamness, and confidence

Training type	Guidelines	Outcomes
	• Facilitate a shared understanding among team members • Encourage the use of closed-loop communication • Evaluate the training's effectiveness	• Develops the ability to cooperate and coordinate • Develops teamwork behaviors such as information exchange, communication, and supporting behavior • Promote attitudes and behaviors that characterize a learning climate
Cross-training	• Base training choices on a team task analysis in order to identify team interdependencies and the level of interpositional knowledge required for effective team performance • The higher the interdependence and complexity of the task, the more immersive the training should be • Provide information not only about *what* roles and responsibilities are assigned to other team members, but also *how* those members operate in order to achieve them • Provide information explaining why team members must operate the way they do, and identifying which team member should be depended on for different types of knowledge and skills • Provide opportunities for trainees to engage in cycles of practice and feedback in order to develop informed expectations of their fellow teammates	• Promotes teams' ability to engage in implicit coordination • Helps team members anticipate the needs of other teammates • Promotes teams' ability to communicate and maintain shared awareness
Team self-correction training	• Identify and define target team self-correction skills prior to designing and delivering the training • Provide both positive and negative examples of teamwork dimensions during team performance episodes	• Develops teams' ability to generate continuous, diagnostic feedback with self-correction • Facilitates the development of accurate SMMs

TABLE 14.2 continued

Interventions for Enhancing Team-level Expert Decision Making

Training Strategy	Guidelines	How Does It Enhance Team-level Expert Decision Making?
	• Training facilitators should classify and prioritize observations, diagnose strengths and weaknesses, and identify goals for improvement before beginning the formal debriefing period • Design the debrief to encourage team participation and to solicit examples of teamwork behaviors • Utilize lecture, demonstration, practice, and feedback	• Promotes a shared understanding of what constitutes an error and what actions can be taken to correct an error • Facilitates implicit coordination
Crew resource management training	• Conduct a training needs analysis in order to accurately identify teamwork competencies that should be targeted in training • Focus on KSAs pertaining to teamwork, not taskwork • Utilize presentation, demonstration, practice, and feedback • Incorporate simulation-based practice, when possible • Design practice opportunities to be both guided and unguided and to incorporate both positive and negative examples of relevant behavior • After practice, provide and elicit debriefs and constructive feedback in a team setting, highlighting both successes and failures • Evaluate training at multiple levels • Repeat training—it should be ongoing	• Develops team adaptability • Facilitates shared situational awareness • Develops SMMs • Promotes teams' ability to fully utilize available resources, minimizing reliance on outside members • Promotes implicit coordination

	• Incorporate training into the performance appraisal process by building teamwork competencies into evaluation criteria	
Team situation awareness training	• Focus on developing SMM's team coordination processes • Incorporate cue-recognition training techniques • Utilize both informational and experiential learning techniques • Include demonstration, guided-practice, and feedback opportunities	• Helps team members develop a shared understanding of the operating environment • Helps team members attend to the same cues, recognize similar patterns, and select courses of action that are compatible with one another
On-the-job training and learning	• OJT/L should be rooted in the science of training such that it targets specific KSAs derived from a needs analysis, incorporates performance measurement tools, and provides opportunities for practice and feedback • Performance criteria and feedback pertaining to the team should be embedded in the work environment • For informal OJL, organizational support and performance feedback should be provided	• Provides shared team experiences with engaging in expert decision making • Facilitates SMMs and coordination processes

taskwork competencies. As discussed, SBT is particularly effective for training expert decision making because it affords opportunities for trainees to obtain experience, the primary mechanism through which such decision making operates (Salas & Rosen, 2008). Experiences gained during the training period can later form the basis of pattern recognition and mental simulation in the actual work environment. The feedback component of SBT is also central to the development of expert decision-making competencies. Indeed, Klein (1998) proposed that expertise is learned by engaging in deliberate practice, compiling extensive experience banks, obtaining accurate, diagnostic, and timely feedback, and reviewing experiences (Phillips, Klein, & Sieck, 2004), all of which are facilitated through SBT. In terms of team training, it is crucial for trainees to obtain experience engaging in decision making alongside the actual teammates with whom they will be working in the real world. Not only does this help ensure that each teammate obtains the requisite experience, but it also contributes to the development of shared mental models (SMMs), a construct that has been shown to enhance decision-making performance in teams (Stout, Cannon-Bowers, & Salas, 1994; Volpe et al., 1996). Specifically, SMMs help teammates develop a shared understanding of what their task is, who is responsible for what, and which resources are required (Lipshitz et al., 2001). Once this shared understanding is formed, team members are able to anticipate each other's needs without engaging in overt strategizing, a skill that is critical for making decisions in fast-paced, complex environments. SBT thus facilitates the development of expert decision-making competencies in teams by providing trainees with experience with both taskwork and teamwork.

Various theoretical and empirical insights point to the value of using SBT to train expert decision making in team settings. Freeman and Cohen (1996), for example, improved the decision-making processes of Navy teams through training that incorporated highly realistic, computer-based simulations. Specifically, the authors assessed a variety of decision-making processes (i.e., identification of conflicting evidence, explanation of conflicting evidence, generating arguments, and generating alternative assessments), finding that trainees performed significantly better in each of these domains after completing the training (i.e., t = 5.48, 4.92, 3.81, and 4.18, respectively; $p \leq .001$). Additionally, consistent with subject matter experts (SMEs), trained participants chose to engage in actions that were more accurate, or appropriate, than did those in the control condition (i.e., $F = 2.64, p = .08$). Training therefore enabled team members to better assess, thus better act in situations characterized by high complexity and intense time pressure. In another setting, DiBello, Missildine, and Struttman (2009) used SBT to develop expertise and enhance decision making in teams of low-level workers in a biotech company. Interestingly, the experience gained through simulation served to generate a foundation for expert decision making in workers who otherwise lacked the requisite expertise. Other authors have made theoretical arguments for the use of SBT to improve naturalistic decision processes in teams. Oser et al. (1999), for instance, offer an event-based approach to training teams to problem solve in naturalistic environments. Similarly, Schaafstal, Johnston, and Oser (2001) also suggest SBT for training teams to make decisions in emergency management contexts.

While the simulation itself is the driving force behind SBT, simply introducing simulation alone does not guarantee that training will be effective (Oser et al., 1999). Various authors have thus offered strategies and guidelines for designing and implementing SBT to ensure that it is in fact effective (e.g., Salas & Burke, 2002; Salas, Guthrie, & Burke, 2007; Salas, et al., 2006c; Salas, Wildman, & Piccolo, 2009). The general theme of this work is that SBT should be grounded in the science of training such that it targets specific competencies, incorporates performance measurement tools, generates opportunities for practice and feedback, and adopts a systems approach by considering the surrounding context before, during, and after the training takes place. Further, scenarios should be carefully crafted to be representative of the transfer environment and should be embedded with various instructional features (e.g., multiple scenario cues, measurement opportunities, timely feedback; Salas & Burke, 2002). Critical to the enhancement of team expertise, scenarios should provide opportunities for trainees to practice engaging in decision making as a team, and should encourage team members to implement feedback and self-correction strategies (Salas, Guthrie, & Burke, 2007). Overall, the literature suggests that properly executed SBT is an optimal strategy for developing expert decision-making competencies at the team level. Simulations provide a shared environment where team members are able to develop SMMs and to accumulate similar experiences that later feed into the decision-making process in the real work environment. Another prime advantage of this approach is that teams are able to generate such expertise in the safety of the simulation environment, without incurring the potential consequences inherent in the real world.

Team Training

A primary difference between training expert decision making at the team, versus the individual level is the need to target teamwork competencies in addition to taskwork competencies. Even if each team member is highly skilled at decision making, this does not guarantee that the team as a whole will be successful—a team of experts does not necessarily constitute an expert team (Salas, Cannon-Bowers, & Johnston, 1997). To be effective, expert teams must possess a high degree of shared cognition regarding what's expected of them and which strategies and processes should be implemented (Cannon-Bowers & Salas, 2001; Weaver, Wildman, & Salas, 2009). One of the most widely used strategies for developing such expertise is the implementation of team training (Weaver, Wildman, & Salas, 2009). Team training is a "set of tools, methods, and content that together create an instructional strategy for enhancing teamwork" (Salas, Cannon-Bowers, & Smith-Jentsch, 2006, p. 2245). Specifically, it is a systematic intervention designed to develop both latent teamwork KSAs, and manifest team processes that have been deemed critical to team performance (Goldstein & Ford, 2002; Weaver, Wildman, & Salas, 2009). This approach is generally regarded as a necessary component of any training intervention designed to enhance performance at the team level and is supported by a variety of empirical findings. A recent meta-analysis, for example, showed that team training was generally effective, exhibiting positive relationships with team cognitive, affective, process, and performance outcomes ($r = .38$ across all outcomes; Salas et al., 2008b).

Team training is especially critical for interventions targeting expert decision making because the demands of naturalistic environments often require team members to make decisions without directly communicating or strategizing with one another. Team members therefore must be highly skilled at maintaining a shared awareness of the operating environment and coordinating their actions under various constraints. Indeed, researchers have identified a set of primary mechanisms through which expert team performance and decision making operates (Rosen et al., 2008; Salas, Rosen, & DiazGranados, 2010). Specifically, members of expert teams (1) develop shared mental models, (2) learn and adapt, (3) maintain clear roles and responsibilities, (4) possess clear, valued, and shared visions, (5) develop a cycle of pre-brief, performance, debrief, (6) are led by strong team leaders, (7) have a strong sense of collective trust, teamness, and confidence, and (8) cooperate and coordinate (Rosen et al., 2008). Each of these competencies can be greatly enhanced through the use of team training strategies. Similarly, Schaafstal, Johnston, and Oser

(2001) describe four teamwork dimensions, originally put forth by Cannon-Bowers and Salas (1998), that distinguish expert teams from novice teams. These include information exchange, communication, supporting behavior, and team initiative/leadership. Among other techniques, the authors suggest the use of team training to develop such competencies and, in turn, to enhance team decision-making performance. Essentially, team training enhances teamwork cognitions, attitudes, and behaviors that enable team members to draw similar conclusions and anticipate each other's actions following the pattern recognition and mental simulation stages of the expert decision-making process without directing communicating in great length. This level of implicit coordination is critical for teams operating in complex, dynamic environments.

There are various steps that can be taken to ensure that team training effectively develops target KSAs. Like other training techniques, team training should be rooted in the science of training such that it is designed on the basis of a team task analysis, it incorporates performance measurement tools, and it is evaluated following the training period (Burke et al., 2004), among other procedures. Further, Burke and colleagues (2004) present a series of guidelines for facilitating team training that include recommendations to utilize pre-practice tools, to align organizational messages with training goals, and to create systematic opportunities for practice throughout the training. Additionally, team training should emphasize key teamwork competencies, facilitate a shared understanding among team members, encourage the use of closed-loop communication, and promote attitudes and behaviors that characterize a learning climate (Burke et al., 2004). There are also several different types of team training that can be utilized (Salas, Cannon-Bowers, & Smith-Jentsch, 2006). Most relevant to expert decision making are cross-training, team self-correction training, and crew resource management training. Each of these methods will be discussed below.

Cross-training

Cross-training is a strategy in which team members are exposed to the basic tasks, duties, and responsibilities of their fellow teammates (Salas, Cannon-Bowers, & Smith-Jentsch, 2006). Especially critical for teams operating in complex environments, cross-training seeks to develop functional knowledge of the tasks, roles, and communication patterns performed by other team members in order to facilitate a shared understanding of the team's overall process and structure (Weaver, Wildman, & Salas,

2009). There are three different approaches through which cross-training can be implemented, each varying in the degree to which trainees are exposed to the roles of their team members (Weaver, Bedwell, & Salas, 2010). Specifically, *positional clarification* involves learning about the roles of teammates through simple information exchange, while *positional modeling* incorporates actual models of members' tasks and duties. The most involved approach, *positional rotation*, allows trainees to "walk in each other's shoes" by actively engaging in the tasks and duties assigned to other teammates. The type of cross-training that is most appropriate will depend on the level of interdependency present in the team, and the setting in which the team will be operating.

When incorporated into a larger program of instruction, cross-training is an effective strategy for training expert decision making because it facilitates the implicit coordination processes that are so critical for team decision making in naturalistic environments. Indeed, research suggests that full cross-training (i.e., including positional rotation) is especially effective when team tasks are highly interdependent and complex (Cooke et al., 2000), rendering it particularly valuable for developing team-level expertise. Specifically, when team members are required to perform complex tasks within dynamic environments, they must be able to anticipate the needs of other teammates, provide necessary support, and clearly communicate in order to maintain a shared awareness and, in turn, to operate effectively (Weaver, Bedwell, & Salas, 2010). For this to be possible, team members must possess a clear understanding of the various roles and responsibilities that are ascribed to each of their teammates. Cross-training meets this need by helping team members develop a shared awareness of each other's role requirements and necessary degrees of task interdependence. The effectiveness of cross-training has been empirically demonstrated in a variety of studies. Volpe and colleagues (1996), for instance, found that teams who underwent cross-training received better teamwork process ratings ($F = 4.40$, $p < .05$) and performed better ($F = 6.98$, $p < .05$) than teams who did not. Additionally, the average correlation between cross-training and training outcomes in a meta-analysis on team training strategies was .43 (Salas et al., 2008b).

Various best practices have been presented in the literature that can be used to guide the design and delivery of cross-training strategies (e.g., Stagl, Salas, & Fiore, 2007; Weaver, Wildman, & Salas, 2009). A common theme is the need to base training choices on a team task analysis in order to identify team interdependencies and the level of interpositional knowledge required for effective team performance. Information derived from this process should drive the type of cross-training that is selected—the higher the interdependence and complexity of the task, the more immersive the training should be (Weaver, Wildman, & Salas, 2009). It is also recommended that information provided during cross-training should not only include *what* roles and responsibilities are assigned to other team members, but also *how* those members operate in order to achieve them. Information should also be provided explaining why team members must operate the way they do, and identifying which team members should be depended on for different types of knowledge and skills. Finally, trainees should have opportunities to engage in cycles of practice and feedback in order to develop informed expectations of their fellow teammates.

Team Self-correction Training

Another prominent approach to team training is teaching teams how to correct their own shortcomings and errors. Specifically, team self-correction training is an intervention in which team members learn to diagnose their team's problems and develop effective strategies for solving them (Smith-Jentsch et al., 1998; Weaver, Wildman, & Salas, 2009). Such training generally focuses on developing the skills needed to carry out the four stages of self-correction identified by Blickensderfer, Cannon-Bowers, and Salas (1997), including (1) reviewing past events to highlight what has occurred and set the tone for the following analysis, (2) identifying errors and engaging in problem solving, (3) exchanging feedback, and (4) planning for future improvement (Weaver, Wildman, & Salas, 2009). Ultimately, the goal of team self-correction training is to enable teams to generate their own feedback, and to correct their own errors without enlisting the help of an outside member.

Team self-correction training has been identified as an effective strategy for developing expert teams (e.g., Weaver, Bedwell, & Salas, 2010; Weaver, Wildman, & Salas, 2009). Although self-correction generally takes place after a performance episode is complete, doing so habitually can ultimately serve to facilitate decision-making processes in situ. Generating continuous, diagnostic feedback through self-correction plays a key role in the development of accurate shared mental models (Weaver, Wildman, & Salas, 2009), which are critical for team decision making in fast-paced, ambiguous environments. Further, through team self-correction training, team members can develop a shared understanding of what constitutes an error, and what actions can be taken to correct an error, types of SMMs that are critical for implicitly coordinating when selecting courses of action in naturalistic settings. Indeed, empirical evidence supports the positive impact of team self-correction training on key processes and outcomes. Smith-Jentsch et al. (2008), for example, showed that teams who learned how to self-correct based on an expert model of teamwork demonstrated more accurate mental models ($t = -3.37, p < .01$), better teamwork processes ($t = -1.98, p < .05$), and greater performance outcomes ($t = -6.72, p < .01$) than teams who did not.

Weaver, Wildman, and Salas (2009) present a series of best practices that can be utilized to optimize team self-correction training efforts. Specifically, to begin, target team self-correction skills should be identified and defined prior to the delivery of the training intervention. Once the training begins, both positive and negative examples of teamwork dimensions should be recorded during team performance episodes. Additionally, training facilitators should classify and prioritize observations, diagnose strengths and weaknesses, and identify goals for improvement before beginning the formal debriefing period. Finally, the debrief should be designed to encourage team participation and solicit examples of teamwork behaviors. Related to this, Salas, Cannon-Bowers, and Smith-Jentsch (2006) note that team self-correction training is typically delivered through a combination of lecture, demonstration, practice, and feedback. Through such methods, team members are taught how to observe their own performance, how to categorize their behavior as effective and ineffective in a structured manner, and how to use this information to provide each other with feedback (Cannon-Bowers & Salas, 1998).

Crew Resource Management Training

Crew resource management training, or CRM, is a strategy for training teams in complex, high-reliability organizations (Shuffler, Salas, & Xavier, 2010). Specifically, it was designed to increase team reliability and reduce errors by teaching teams to better perform teamwork behaviors and, in turn, to better utilize available resources (Weaver, Bedwell, & Salas, 2010). Through the science of training (e.g., job/task analysis), CRM is designed to improve specific teamwork competencies by utilizing a collection of instructional features (Helmreich, 1997). While CRM is particularly common in the safety, aviation, and medical communities (Weaver, Wildman, & Salas, 2009), it can be applied to any environment requiring reliable team outcomes, suggesting that it is of value to many modern organizations.

CRM training is typically used to train teamwork KSAs such as team adaptability, shared SA, and SMMs (Shuffler, Salas, & Xavier, 2010; Weaver, Wildman, & Salas, 2009), all critical for expert decision making at the team level. While CRM is, in essence, a form of team training, it is particularly relevant to expert decision making because it was designed specifically for high-stress, high-risk environments (Salas et al., 2006d). As described earlier, to make decisions in complex environments, teams must engage in key coordination processes, and develop SMMs and shared SA in situ, through minimal overt communication. CRM targets KSAs that facilitate these processes. Further, through such processes, team members are taught to fully utilize available resources, thereby minimizing their reliance on outside members, and enhancing their ability to operate as an expert team. While all organizations are not characterized by extreme danger, or risk, it seems that the growing complexity of many organizations is sufficient to warrant the use of CRM training. For example, Salas and colleagues (2006d) suggest that national culture can influence the performance of team KSAs that are typically trained using CRM approaches. As globalization is rapidly changing the workforce and work locale, culture is a key factor contributing to the complexity of the modern work environment. In this example alone then, CRM seems necessary for ensuring that team competencies are appropriately developed in culturally diverse teams. Beyond theoretical reasons for using CRM, there is a variety of empirical evidence that speaks to its effectiveness. In a set of evaluation studies, for instance, researchers showed that CRM training improved naval pilots' and aircrewmen's attitudes toward teamwork ($t = 6.93$, $p < .05$; $t = 2.13$, $p < .05$), knowledge of teamwork ($F = 26.7$, $p < .05$), and behavioral performance ($z = 2.53$, $p < .05$) (Salas et al., 1999). More recently, meta-analyses revealed an average correlation between CRM training and outcomes of .43 (Salas et al., 2008b).

Because CRM is a broad approach, guidelines for how it can best be implemented largely focus on utilizing the science of training. For example, Weaver, Wildman, and Salas (2009) present a set of best practices, the first emphasizing the need to conduct a training needs analysis in order to accurately identify teamwork competencies that should be targeted in training. Importantly, CRM should focus on developing KSAs pertaining to teamwork, not taskwork. The authors also suggest that training should include presentation, demonstration, practice, and feedback, and should incorporate simulation-based practice when possible. Moreover, practice opportunities should be both guided and unguided, and should incorporate both positive and negative examples of relevant behavior. After practice, debriefs and constructive feedback should be provided and elicited in a team setting, highlighting both successes and failures. Finally, to enhance the effectiveness of CRM, training should be evaluated at multiple levels, should be ongoing, and should be incorporated into the performance appraisal process by building teamwork competencies into evaluation criteria.

Team Situation Awareness Training

Underlying many of the training strategies outlined above is the importance of developing and maintaining shared situation awareness for team-level expert decision making. Though it can incorporate a variety of team training strategies, team situation awareness (TSA) training is an intervention designed specifically for this purpose. TSA training involves many of the same competencies as does individual SA training (e.g., cue recognition), but also incorporates coordination processes that are critical for attaining a shared awareness at the team level. Shared, or team situation awareness, essentially means that the individuals comprising a team have each attained SA, and that such perceptions are consistent with one another. Specifically, it has been defined as "the degree to which team members possess the same SA on shared SA requirements" (Endsley & Jones, 1997). TSA is considered to be critical for performance in complex settings, particularly in aviation (Endsley & Rodgers, 1994) and military contexts (Pleban et al., 2009). A number of errors and accidents in aviation have been attributed to a lack of shared SA (Endsley & Robertson, 2000; Hartel, Smith, & Prince, 1991), for example, demonstrating the importance of training teams to acquire this skill.

As described throughout this chapter, situation awareness is central to the process of expert decision making. When NDM occurs at the team level, the team's SA is equally as important. TSA training thus represents an optimal strategy for preparing teams to make naturalistic decisions in real-world settings. To draw comparisons between cues in current and past situations, as required for effective decision making, one must first attain an awareness of the cues that are present in the current situation. Further, such cues are not static—more or fewer cues might become available, and remaining cues might be altered over time. At the team level, members are required not only to attend to the same dynamic cues, but also to interpret them in the same manner, recognizing patterns, and ultimately selecting courses of action that are compatible with one another. Shared SA is essentially the mechanism through which this can occur, making TSA training a critical component to include in team expert decision making training efforts.

Though researchers generally agree that team SA is important, only a handful of studies have examined how to train it. Those that have done so, however, have used a variety of techniques, showing each to be largely effective. Endsley and Robertson (2000), for example, successfully trained team SA in aviation teams using classroom-based instruction and experiential techniques that allowed for interaction and participation among trainees. Importantly, the training was based on a detailed needs analysis that identified TSA requirements specific to the aviation context. In another example, Bolstad and colleagues (2005) used cross-training to improve shared mental models and, in turn, TSA in a military setting (i.e., trainees' SA was higher after undergoing cross-training; $F = 36.28$, $p < .01$). Still others have used games and simulators to effectively train SA at the team level (Proctor, Panko, & Donovan, 2004).

In addition to empirical findings, there are various theoretical insights that can inform the development of TSA training interventions. Stout, Cannon-Bowers, and Salas (1996), for example, present a variety of strategies that can be used to train TSA based on their ability to enhance shared knowledge bases and to foster the development of team processes that facilitate TSA. Such strategies include direct information presentation (e.g., lectures), positional knowledge training (e.g., cross-training), demonstration/modeling, task simulation, guided task practice, communication training, planning training, team leader training, and team self-correction training. Building on their work, Salas and colleagues (2001) suggest that cue-recognition training can effectively enhance TSA, as it can help link the cognitive components of individual SA with the interdependent, behavioral components of TSA. Drawing from previous findings, they argue that such training can be delivered through passive techniques, such as lectures or demonstrations, or through active techniques, such as behavioral coaching or instructor-guided practice. Overall, it is apparent that a number of techniques can be used to enhance SA at the team level. A common theme running throughout this work is that training should focus on developing SMMs among teammates in order to facilitate coordination processes.

On-the-job Training and Learning

Team training is not limited to formal training environments, but can also take place in the context of the job itself. Specifically, on-the-job training

(OJT) involves the implementation of training in the exact physical and social contexts relevant to the target job tasks (De Jong & Versloot, 1999). OJT and on-the-job learning (OJL) can occur through various mediums. Apprenticeship training, for example, is one form of OJT that involves classroom learning, such as a lecture or demonstration, followed by close supervision of job tasks (Salas et al., 2006e). While the apprenticeship model is typically applied to individual-level training, it can also be applied to teams, where members attend training sessions together, and are subsequently supervised and evaluated on team performance. Mentoring is another form of OJT, though it may not be as applicable to team settings. As described earlier, mentoring involves a working relationship between job novices and experts (Wilson & Johnson, 2001). If utilized for training teams, each team might be assigned a mentor to supervise their performance and provide feedback, thereby ensuring that they engage in appropriate behaviors. On the less formal side, OJL can occur through informal learning, the process in which employees engage in learning outside of any specific training effort (Salas et al., 2006e). Tannenbaum et al. (2010) recently presented a model of informal learning suggesting that such learning takes place through the following components: (1) the learner has intentions to learn or improve, (2) the learner engages in an action or experience relevant to what he or she intends to learn, (3) the learner receives feedback related to that action or experience, and (4) the learner reflects, or engages in thoughtful consideration to seek to understand his or her experience. Informal learning is thus largely self-directed, but also requires support and feedback from the organization. At the team level, members can engage in each component of the informal learning process as a group, facilitating team learning.

Team OJT and OJL are ideal mechanisms for enhancing expert decision making because they enable team members to gain experience in relevant environments, the driving force behind expert decisions (Salas & Rosen, 2008). The more experiences members gain as a group, the easier it will be to recognize patterns and conduct mental simulations when engaging in decision making. Additionally, these shared learning experiences facilitate SMMs and team coordination, allowing team members to quickly enact decisions that are compatible and effective while operating in naturalistic environments. Notably, the components of informal learning proposed by Tannenbaum and colleagues (2010) coincide nicely with the developmental mechanisms of expertise, suggesting that it is a highly effective approach to enhancing expert decision making (Klein, 1998; Salas & Rosen, 2010). Specifically, expertise is thought to be developed through the motivation to learn, deliberate practice, the seeking of feedback, and the review of experiences (Phillips, Klein & Sieck, 2004; Salas & Rosen, 2010), all of which are components of the informal learning process.

While there are few best practices specific to OJT and OJL, it can be expected that those pertaining to other types of training are applicable to formal OJT interventions. Specifically, OJT should be rooted in the science of training such that it targets specific KSAs derived from a needs analysis, it incorporates performance measurement tools, and it provides opportunities for practice and feedback. Rather than embedding performance criteria and feedback into practice scenarios, however, such things should be embedded in the actual job environment. Additionally, practice, performance measurement, and feedback should all be conducted as a team in order to promote shared team experiences and team learning. For informal OJL, it seems the key to facilitating training is through organizational support and performance feedback. Specifically, because informal learning is largely self-directed, characteristics of the organization can play an influential role in its effectiveness. The organizational climate, through learning opportunities, time and resources, and supervisor support, for example, can all influence whether or not learners develop the intention to learn, have opportunities to obtain experience, receive feedback, and are able to reflect on their experiences, at each phase of the informal learning process (Tannenbaum et al., 2010). As part of such organizational characteristics, it is critical that learners receive feedback in order for them to learn. If they do not receive feedback, they might miss opportunities to learn, learn incorrect or incomplete material, falsely assume their level of competence, and/or lose motivation if they do not recognize their own progress (Tannenbaum et al., 2010). Thus, to facilitate informal OJL at the team level, the organizational climate should be designed to encourage teams to engage in each component of the informal learning process, and should provide team feedback, whether through automatic means, or through supervisors directly.

A CAUTIONARY NOTE

Throughout this chapter, we have argued for the value of using the NDM approach to understand and improve decision making in the modern work environment. It is important to note, however, that NDM should *supplement*, not replace, our current understanding of workplace decision making. Specifically, there remain many organizational decision-making situations for which the NDM approach is not ideal, or even applicable. Decisions related to budgets, personnel selection, and mergers and acquisitions, for example, all require more thought-out, strategic decision making, thus are better understood through the formal-empiricist and/or the rationalist paradigms (Cohen, 1993). In these instances, decision making is based less on pattern recognition and mental simulation, and more on mathematical models and detailed cost-benefit analyses. The NDM approach is therefore not suited for all decision situations that arise in the organizational context. Rather, it is most appropriate for the day-to-day decision situations that arise within the fast-paced, complex environments to which we refer throughout this chapter (Orasanu & Connolly, 1993). Thus, while we focus on the benefits of the NDM approach for understanding decision making in such environments, the reader should note that there are also drawbacks, as it is not applicable to all aspects of decision making that can arise in the workplace.

FUTURE RESEARCH DIRECTIONS

While much is known about how expert decision making can be trained, much also remains to be further explored. Many of the training techniques described in this chapter have largely been employed in extreme environments (e.g., military) and have not yet been utilized in more traditional work settings. As the work environment becomes increasingly complex, or naturalistic, however, it is important to consider how these techniques apply to organizational contexts, and to explore how additional training techniques, not previously applied to expert decision making training, might be used to enhance it. Beyond that, many questions remain regarding the types and combinations of interventions required to develop expertise at both the individual and the team level. Thus, in the following paragraphs, we describe what we believe are key areas of research that should be examined in order to move the science and, ultimately, the practice of enhancing expert decision making forward.

First, additional training and development interventions that might be effective for enhancing expert decision making should be explored. Emotion-regulation training and other types of self-regulation training, for example, may be particularly beneficial. A common theme throughout the relevant literature is that individuals need to engage in self-regulation not only to acquire expert decision-making skills, but also to apply them when operating in complex situations. Specifically, because the development of expertise requires continuous effort (e.g., deliberate practice, seeking feedback), trainees might benefit from training that teaches them to regulate their behavior so that they can sustain these activities over long periods of time. Additionally, decision making training, particularly simulation-based training, can be stressful for trainees, as it requires them to actively participate, often under highly complex, ambiguous conditions. Such training can be difficult and anxiety provoking, making it particularly important to consider the role of emotion, which can consume cognitive resources, thereby hindering learning and performance (Kanfer & Ackerman, 1989). To fully benefit from a developmental intervention then, trainees might first need to learn how to regulate their emotions. Beyond training, emotion regulation is likely critical in the operating environment as well, where individuals face real threats and risk real consequences. Indeed, the ability to regulate one's emotions may be a key driver of one's capacity to implement, or transfer, trained skills to the real world. We thus propose that future research should explore the effectiveness of self-regulation and emotion-regulation training for developing expertise.

Beyond the formal training setting, another important area in need of future research is how training opportunities can be extended into the work environment. While we described current knowledge of this in the OJT/OJL section, we believe this is a topic that warrants additional attention, as it affords opportunities for continuous learning, which is particularly beneficial for the development of expertise. Because expert decision making is grounded in extensive experience, it is critical that individuals and teams continue to add to their repertoire of experiences once the formal training has been completed. Further, as described throughout this chapter, the value of such experiences often hinges on the availability of diagnostic feedback, to ensure that trainees acquire the appropriate KSAs and form accurate perceptions of their abilities. We thus suggest that research is needed to explore ways in which these features can be incorporated into the work environment. Utilizing synthetic learning environments and other technological advances, for instance, may be particularly effective for embedding learning opportunities into the work setting. For example, perhaps realistic practices scenarios could intermittently appear on employee's computers, prompting them to complete the exercises, and generating automated feedback that could later be supplemented with supervisor feedback. Research is needed to determine whether this type of activity could be effective, how different activities can be delivered, and how often they should be implemented, among other things. In addition to the example we provided, we suggest that research should move toward exploring new and innovative ways of enhancing expertise and, in turn, expert decision making.

Second, research is needed to determine the types, amounts, and frequencies of training and development interventions that are needed to best facilitate expert decision making. Specifically, over ten different strategies were identified in this chapter; it is currently not clear whether implementing one strategy will suffice, or whether several are needed in order to develop expertise. Further, it is possible that certain combinations of interventions may be particularly effective while others may not produce much additional value beyond that of the individual interventions. Along these lines, determining which intervention or combination of interventions to use may depend on a variety of factors. For example, the degree to which the job requires the use of expert decision making may help determine the type(s) and number of interventions that are necessary—whereas one or two sessions of simulation-based training might be sufficient for jobs that require less expertise, multiple sessions paired with ongoing coaching or mentoring might be more effective for jobs that are more complex.

Additionally, determining the appropriate intervention may also depend on trainees' existing levels of expertise, as there are various stages to the process of becoming an expert. Specifically, Dreyfus and Dreyfus (1986) propose a five-stage model of the development of expertise, with such stages describing the learner as a novice, as an advanced beginner, as competent, as proficient, and, finally, as an expert. It is possible, then, that different types of training and development interventions may be more or less effective depending on the learner's current phase in the developmental process. For example, practicing and receiving diagnostic performance feedback (i.e., simulation-based training) might be particularly important in the early stages, whereas motivation and support (i.e., motivation enhancement, mentoring) might be more important in the later stages. This would suggest that there is not a "one size fits all" solution to facilitating the development of expert decision making, but rather that interventions might need to be tailored to meet the needs of specific individuals and teams. Related to this is the question of how often refresher interventions are needed in order to maintain expertise over time. Is a few times a year sufficient? Do interventions need to be built into the job monthly, or even weekly? The answer to this will likely depend on the variety of factors described above—the type of job, the trainees' current level of expertise, and so on. With this, we also must consider the point at which training becomes exhausting, and potentially counterproductive. There are thus various questions surrounding the development of expertise that remain unanswered, and in need of future research.

In a similar vein, the balance between individual interventions and team interventions that is required to best enhance team expertise is not currently well understood. It is well documented in the literature that a team of experts does not necessarily culminate in an expert team (e.g., Salas, Cannon-Bowers, & Johnston, 1997). Thus, we know that team training is critical for developing the shared cognition and teamwork behaviors that are required for teams to coordinate and make decisions in complex environments. What is less clear, however, is how much individual training versus team training is needed to best enhance the development and maintenance of an expert team. For example, do the individuals comprising a team already need to possess a certain level of expertise in the relevant domain, and thus require a certain amount of individual training before being trained as a team? Once the team has been trained together, is it more important for future interventions to focus on maintaining teamwork skills or on individual levels of domain-specific expertise? We argue that research is needed to better understand how to determine the optimal combination of individual and team training needed to best enhance expert decision making in teams.

Third, non-traditional, innovative research methods are needed to better understand the development of expertise. Each of the research questions identified above points to the fact that we simply do not know enough about how expert decision making operates and develops. This is likely because it cannot easily be studied through the same methods that are traditionally used to understand decision making (e.g., experiments)—it does not occur in a systematic, rational manner that can readily be manipulated or measured. Rather, expert decision making is largely an intuitive process that might operate differently in one context from the next. Thus, we argue that to better understand expert decision making, researchers should utilize methods and tools that may be less often used in this field of research. Specifically, qualitative methods, such as interviews or diary tools, can be used to garner first-hand knowledge of how the expert decision-making process operates. Further, such methods can also contribute to our understanding of what constitutes effective decision making in complex environments. Because expert decision making does not involve carefully selecting the "best" decision from a range of alternatives, it is not always clear what can be considered an effective decision. Thus, because expert decision making cannot be measured objectively, we suggest that qualitative methods should be used to better understand potential variance in levels of decision-making performance. Overall then, qualitative methods can help us gain a deeper understanding of how expert decision making operates "in the wild," which can help us understand how it can be developed and measured, and ultimately can inform the design of training and development interventions.

PRACTICAL IMPLICATIONS

We have now presented a wealth of information about different training and development interventions that can be used to enhance expert decision making, and have followed with a description of questions about them that have yet to be answered. What, then, can the reader conclude about how to develop expert decision making in practice? Which of the many interventions should organizations implement in order to accelerate expertise in their workforces? While these questions have not been empirically answered, as noted above, certain techniques can be considered more important, or valuable, than others based on the knowledge and skills that they enhance. Specifically, if an organization had to choose one technique, we believe that simulation-based training holds the most promise for enhancing expert decision making in both individuals and teams. SBT is flexible—it can be used as a platform for practicing each element of the expert decision-making process (i.e., pattern recognition, mental simulation, team coordination, etc.). In this way, it provides the trainee with experience not only with engaging in these processes, but also with the naturalistic setting itself, as simulations take place within realistic environments. Each of these things helps build expertise, the foundation of decision making within the NDM framework. As a standalone intervention, SBT thus provides more experience and KSAs that contribute to expert decision making than do any of the other interventions on their own.

Of the remaining techniques, situation awareness training can also be considered particularly valuable for enhancing expert decision making in both individuals and teams. Such training helps sensitize individuals to certain cues in the environment that are important for recognizing patterns and projecting potential outcomes that can result from different courses of action. At the team level, it helps team members stay "on the same page" in decision situations, and allows them to coordinate by anticipating each other's actions and needs. These processes are critical for expert decision making, thus critical to train if one aims to enhance it. Not surprisingly, team training is also highly important for enhancing expert decision making at the team level. Teams need to possess certain attitudes, behaviors, and cognitions to effectively coordinate and make decisions within complex settings, making team training especially valuable for organizations to include in efforts to develop expert teams. Thus, while we believe that all of the training and development interventions presented in this chapter are ideal for enhancing expert decision making, from a practical standpoint, simulation-based training, situation awareness training, and team training can be considered the most important to implement, or the most likely to generate advancements in individuals' and teams' expert decision making.

CONCLUSION

As the face of the modern work environment becomes increasingly complex, traditional models of decision making are becoming less and less relevant for understanding how individuals and teams make effective decisions. Rather, the NDM paradigm, though historically applied only to extreme, high-risk environments, is fast becoming the more appropriate lens through which the decision-making process should be examined in more traditional workplaces. Adopting an NDM approach can not only enable a more accurate understanding of decision making at work, but can also inform training efforts designed to accelerate expertise and facilitate decision making in fast-paced, naturalistic environments. However, much of the research on expert decision making to date has occurred outside of the realm of I-O/OB, remaining in relatively separate fields. The purpose of this chapter was thus to summarize NDM-relevant research indicating how expert decision making operates, and how it can best be enhanced at the individual and the team levels, thereby providing an accessible resource for those less exposed to the NDM literature. Consistent with other authors (e.g., Lipshitz, Klein, & Carroll, 2006; Shuffler, Salas, & Xavier, 2010), we believe that expert decision making has an important place in the workplace and, in turn, in I-O/OB research and practice. Our hope is that this chapter will serve as a resource from which researchers and practitioners can leverage findings that originate from more traditional NDM disciplines, as well as a foundation for future research efforts.

NOTE

1. This work was supported by NASA Grant NNX09AK48G awarded to the University of Central Florida.

REFERENCES

Alessi, S. (2000). Simulation design for training and assessment. In H.F. O'Neil and D.H. Andrew (Eds.) *Aircrew Training and Assessment* (pp. 199–224). Mahwah, NJ: Lawrence Erlbaum Associates.

Baker, J., Côté, J., and Abernethy, B. (2003). Learning from the experts: Practice activities of expert decision makers in sport. *Research Quarterly for Exercise and Sport, 74,* 342–347.

Batha, K. and Carroll, M. (2007). Metacognitive training aids decision making. *Australian Journal of Psychology, 59*(2), 64–69.

Blickensderfer, E.L., Cannon-Bowers, J.A., and Salas, E. (1997). Theoretical bases for team self-correction: Fostering shared mental models. In M. Beyerlein, D. Johnson, and S. Beyerlein (Eds.) *Advances in Interdisciplinary Studies in Work Teams* (vol. 4, pp. 249–279). Greenwich, CT: JAI Press.

Bolstad, C.A., Cuevas, H.M., Costello, A.M., and Rousey, J. (2005). Improving situation awareness through cross-training. Paper presented at the Human Factors and Ergonomics Society 49th Annual Meeting, Orlando, FL.

Bolstad, C.A., Endsley, M.R., Costello, A.M., and Howell, C.D. (2010). Evaluation of computer-based situation awareness training for general aviation pilots. *International Journal of Aviation Psychology, 20*(3), 269–294.

Burke, C.S., Salas, E., Wilson-Donnelly, K.A., and Priest, H.A. (2004). How to turn a team of experts into an expert medical team: Guidance from the aviation and military communities. *Quality Safety in Healthcare, 13*(Suppl. 1), i96–i104.

Cannon-Bowers, J.A. and Bell, H.H. (1997). Training decision makers for complex environments: Implications of the naturalistic decision making perspective. In C.E. Zsambok and G.A. Klein (Eds.) *Naturalistic Decision Making* (pp. 99–110). Mahwah, NJ: Lawrence Erlbaum.

Cannon-Bowers, J.A. and Salas, E. (Eds.) (1998). *Making Decisions Under Stress: Implications for Individual and Team Training.* Washington, DC: American Psychological Association.

Cannon-Bowers, J.A. and Salas, E. (2001). Reflections on shared cognition. *Journal of Organizational Behaviour Special Issue: Shared Cognition, 22,* 195–202.

Carvalho, P.V.R., dos Santos, I.L., and Vidal, M.C.R. (2005). Nuclear power plant shift supervisor's decision making during microincidents. *International Journal of Industrial Ergonomics, 35,* 619–644.

Cohen, M.S. (1993). Three paradigms for viewing decision biases. In G. Klein, J. Orasanu, R. Calderwood, and C.E. Zsambok (Eds.) *Decision Making in Action: Models and Methods* (pp. 36–50). Norwood, NJ: Ablex.

Cohn, P.J. (1990). Preperformance routines in sport: Theoretical support and practical applications. *Sport Psychologist, 4,* 301–312.

Cooke, N.J., Salas, E., Cannon-Bowers, J.A., and Stout, R. (2000). Measuring team knowledge. *Human Factors*, 42, 151–173.

Coutu, D. and Kauffman, C. (2009). What can coaches do for you? *Harvard Business Review*, January, 1–8.

Cumming, J., Clark, S.E., Ste-Marie, D.M., McCullagh, P., and Hall, C. (2005). The functions of observational learning questionnaire (FOLQ). *Psychology of Sport and Exercise*, 6, 517–537.

Davis, F.D. and Yi, M.Y. (2004). Improving computer skill training: Behavior modeling, symbolic mental rehearsal, and the role of knowledge structures. *Journal of Applied Psychology*, 89(3), 509–523.

De Jong, J.A. and Versloot, B. (1999). Structuring on-the-job training: Report of a multiple case study. *International Journal of Training and Development*, 3(3), 186–199.

DiBello, L., Missildine, W., and Struttman, M. (2009). Intuitive expertise and empowerment: The long-term impact of simulation training on changing accountabilities in a biotech firm. *Mind, Culture, and Activity*, 16, 11–31.

Dreyfus, H.L. and Dreyfus, S.E. (1986). *Mind Over Machine: The Power of Human Intuition and Expertise in the Era of the Computer*. New York: The Free Press.

Driskell, J.E., Copper, C., and Moran, A. (1994). Does mental practice enhance performance? *Journal of Applied Psychology*, 79, 481–492.

Endsley, M.R. (1995). Situation awareness in dynamic human decision making: Theory. In J.M. Koonce (Ed.) *Proceedings of the Center for Applied Human Factors Aviation (CAHFA)* (pp. 77–58). Daytona Beach, FL: University of Central Florida.

Endsley, M.R., Farley, T.C., Jones, W.M., Midkff, A.H., and Hansman, J. (1998). *Situation Awareness Information Requirements for Commercial Airline Pilots* (ICAT-98-1). Cambridge, MA: Massachusetts Institute of Technology International Center for Air Transportation.

Endsley, M.R. and Jones, W.M. (1997). *Situation Awareness, Information Dominance, and Information Warfare* (AL/CF-TR-1997-0156). Wright-Patterson AFB, OH: United States Air Force Armstrong Laboratory.

Endsley, M.R. and Robertson, M.M. (2000). Training for situation awareness in individuals and teams. In M.R. Endsley, D.J. Garland, M.R. Endsley, and D.J. Garland (Eds.) *Situation Awareness Analysis and Measurement* (pp. 349–365). Mahwah, NJ: Lawrence Erlbaum.

Endsley, M.R. and Rodgers, M.D. (1994). *Situation Awareness Information Requirements for En Route Air Traffic Control* (DOT/FAA/AM-94/27). Washington, DC: Federal Aviation Administration, Office of Aviation Medicine.

Escribá-Esteve, A., Sánchez-Peinado, L., and Sánchez-Peinado, E. (2009). The influence of top management teams in the strategic orientation and performance of small and medium-sized enterprises. *British Journal of Management*, 20, 581–597.

Flannery, B.L. and May, D.R. (2000). Environmental ethical decision making in the U.S. metal-finishing industry. *Academy of Management Journal*, 43, 642–662.

Freeman, J.T. and Cohen, M.S. (1996). Training for complex decision-making: A test of instruction based on the recognition/metacognition model. In *Proceedings of the 1996 Command and Control Research and Technology Symposium*. Monterey, CA: Naval Postgraduate School.

Fritzsche, B.A., Wicks, K., and Salas, E. (in press). Judgment, classical and naturalistic decision making in organizations. In C.L. Cooper and J. Barling (Eds.) *Handbook of Organizational Behavior*. Thousand Oaks, CA: Sage.

Goldstein, I.L. and Ford, J.K. (2002). *Training in Organizations: Needs Assessment, Development, and Evaluation* (4th ed.). Belmont, CA: Wadsworth.

322 • *Rebecca Grossman et al.*

Goodwin, G.F., Burke, C., Wildman, J.L., and Salas, E. (2009). Team effectiveness in complex organizations: An overview. In E. Salas, G.F. Goodwin, and C. Burke (Eds.) *Team Effectiveness in Complex Organizations: Cross-disciplinary Perspectives and Approaches.* New York: Routledge.

Hammond, K.R., Hamm, R.M., Grassia, J., and Pearson, T. (1987). Direct comparison of the efficacy of intuitive and analytical cognition in expert judgment. *Proceedings of IEEE Transactions on Systems, Man, and Cybernetics, SMC-17,* 753–770.

Hartel, C.E., Smith, K., and Prince, C. (1991). Defining aircrew coordination: Searching for mishaps for means. Paper presented at the 6th International Symposium on Aviation Psychology, Columbus, OH, April.

Helmreich, R.L. (1997). Managing human errors in aviation. *Scientific American, 276,* 62–67.

Jeannerod, M. (1994). The representing brain: neural correlates of motor intention and imagery. *Behavioural and Brain Sciences, 17,* 187–245.

Jones, L. and Stuth, G. (1997). The uses of mental imagery in athletics: An overview. *Applied & Preventive Psychology, 6,* 101–115.

Kanfer, R. and Ackerman, P.L. (1989). Motivation and cognitive abilities: An integrative/ aptitude-treatment interaction approach to skill acquisition. *Journal of Applied Psychology, 74*(4), 657–690.

Keith, N. and Frese, M. (2005). Self-regulation in error management training: Emotion control and metacognition as mediators of performance effects. *Journal of Applied Psychology, 90*(4), 677–691.

Keith, N. and Frese, M. (2008). Effectiveness of error management training: A meta-analysis. *Journal of Applied Psychology, 93,* 59–69.

Klein, G.A. (1998). *Sources of Power: How People Make Decisions.* Cambridge, MA: MIT Press.

Klein, G.A. (2008). Naturalistic decision making. *Human Factors, 50,* 456–460.

Klein, G.A., Calderwood, R., and Clinton-Cirocco, A. (1986). Rapid decision making on the fireground. *Proceedings of the Human Factors and Ergonomics Society 30th Annual Meeting, 1,* 576–580.

Klein, G.A., Orasanu, J., Calderwood, R., and Zsambok, C.E. (Eds.) (1993). *Decision Making in Action: Models and Methods.* Norwood, CT: Ablex.

Lipshitz, R., Klein, G., and Carroll, J.S. (2006). Introduction to the Special Issue. Naturalistic decision making and organizational decision making: Exploring the intersections. *Organization Studies, 27,* 917–923.

Lipshitz, R., Klein, G., Orasanu, J., and Salas, E. (2001). Taking stock of naturalistic decision making. *Journal of Behavioral Decision Making, 14,* 331–352.

MacIntyre, T. and Moran, A. (2007). A qualitative investigation of meta-imagery processes and imagery direction among elite athletes. *Journal of Imagery Research in Sport and Physical Activity, 2*(1), 1–20.

Meso, P. Troutt, M.D., and Rudnicka, J. (2002). A review of naturalistic decision making research with some implications for knowledge management. *Journal of Knowledge Management, 6*(1), 63–73.

Murthy, N.N., Challagalla, G.N., Vincent, L.H., and Shervani, T.A. (2008). The impact of simulation training on call center agent performance: A field-based investigation. *Management Science, 54*(2), 384–399.

Orasanu, J. and Connolly, T. (1993). The reinvention of decision making. In G.A. Klein, J. Orasanu, R. Calderwood, and C.E. Zsambok (Eds.) *Decision Making in Action: Models and Methods* (pp. 3–20). Norwood, NJ: Ablex.

Oser, R.L., Gualtieri, J.W., Cannon-Bowers, J.A., and Salas, E. (1999). Training team problem solving skills: An event-based approach. *Computers in Human Behavior, 15,* 441–462.

Pennequin, V., Sorel, O., Nanty, I., and Fontaine, R. (2010). Metacognition and low achievement in mathematics: The effect of training in the use of metacognitive skills to solve mathematical word problems. *Thinking and Reasoning, 16*(3), 198–220.

Phillips, J.K., Klein, G., and Sieck, W.R. (2004). Expertise in judgment and decision making: A case for training intuitive decision skills. In D.J. Koehler and N. Harvey (Eds.) *Blackwell Handbook of Judgment and Decision Making* (pp. 297–315). Malden, UK: Blackwell.

Pleban, R.J., Tucker, J.S., Johnson, V., Gunther, K., and Graves, T.R. (2009). *Training Situation Awareness and Adaptive Decision-making Skills Using a Desktop Computer Simulation* (Research Report 1889). Arlington, VA: U.S. Army Research Institute for the Behavioral Social Sciences.

Ployhart, R.E. and Holtz, B.C. (2008). The diversity-validity dilemma: Strategies for reducing racioethnic and sex subgroup differences and adverse impact in selection. *Personnel Psychology, 61*, 153–172.

Proctor, M.D., Panko, M., and Donovan, S.J. (2004). Considerations for training team situation awareness and task performance through PC-gamer simulated multiship helicopter operations. *The International Journal of Aviation Psychology, 14*(2), 191–205.

Ragins, B.R. and Cotton, J.L. (1999). Mentor functions and outcomes: A comparison of men and women in formal and informal relationships. *Journal of Applied Psychology, 84*(4), 529–550.

Robbins, S.P. and Judge, T.A. (2009). *Organizational Behavior*. Upper Saddle River, NJ: Pearson Prentice Hall.

Rosen, M.A., Salas, E., Lyons, R., and Fiore, S.M. (2008). Expertise and naturalistic decision making in organizations: Mechanisms of effective decision making. In G.P. Hodgkinson and W.H. Starbuck (Eds.) *The Oxford Handbook of Organizational Decision Making: Psychological and Management Perspectives* (pp. 211–230). Oxford: Oxford University Press.

Rosen, M.A., Shuffler, M.L., and Salas, E. (2010). How experts make decisions: Beyond the JDM paradigm. *Industrial and Organizational Psychology: Perspectives on Science and Practice, 3*, 438–442.

Rosen, M.A., Weaver, S.J., Lazzara, E.H., Salas, E., Wu, T., Silvestri, S., Schiebel, N., Almeida, S., and King, H.B. (2010). Tools for evaluating team performance in simulation-based training. *Journal of Emergencies, Trauma, and Shock, 3*, 353–359.

Ross, K.G., Shafer, J.L., and Klein, G. (2006). Professional judgments and "naturalistic decision making." In K. Ericsson, N. Charness, P.J. Feltovich, R.R. Hoffman, K. Ericsson, N. Charness, and R.R. Hoffman (Eds.) *The Cambridge Handbook of Expertise and Expert Performance* (pp. 403–419). New York: Cambridge University Press.

Salas, E. and Burke, C.S. (2002). Simulation for training is effective when . . . *Quality Safety Health Care, 11*, 119–120.

Salas, E. and Cannon-Bowers, J.A. (2001). The science of training: A decade of progress. *Annual Review of Psychology, 52*, 471–499.

Salas, E., Cannon-Bowers, J.A., Fiore, S.M., and Stout, R.J. (2001). Cue-recognition training to enhance team situation awareness. In M. McNeese, E. Salas, and M. Endsley (Eds.) *New Trends in Cooperative Activities: Understanding System Dynamics in Complex Environments* (pp. 169–190). Santa Monica, CA: Human Factors and Ergonomics Society.

Salas, E., Cannon-Bowers, J.A., and Johnston, J.H. (1997). How can you turn a team of experts into an expert team? Emerging training strategies. In C.E. Zsambok and

324 • *Rebecca Grossman et al.*

G. Klein (Eds.) *Naturalistic Decision Making* (pp. 359–370). Mahwah, NJ: Lawrence Erlbaum.

Salas, E., Cannon-Bowers, J.A., and Smith-Jentsch, K.A. (2006). Principles and strategies for team training. In W. Karwowski (Ed.) *International Encyclopedia of Ergonomics and Human Factors, 2,* 2245–2248.

Salas, E., DiazGranados, D., Klein, C., Burke, C.S., Stagl, K.C., Goodwin, G.F., and Halpin, S.M. (2008b). Does team training improve team performance? *Human Factors, 50*(6), 903–933.

Salas, E., Fowlkes, J.E., Stout, R.J., Milanovich, D.M., and Prince, C. (1999). Does CRM training improve teamwork skills in the cockpit?: Two evaluation studies. *Human Factors, 41,* 326–343.

Salas, E., Guthrie, J., and Burke, S. (2007). Why training team decision making is not as easy as you think: Guiding principles and needs. In M. Cook, J. Noyes, and Y. Masakowski (Eds.) *Decision Making in Complex Environments* (pp. 225–232). Burlington, VT: Ashgate Publishing.

Salas, E., Priest, H.A., Wilson, K.A., and Burke, C.S. (2006c). Scenario-based training: Improving military mission performance and adaptability. In A.B. Adler, C.A. Castro, and T.W. Britt (Eds.) *Minds in the Military: The Psychology of Serving in Peace and Conflict* (vol. 2, pp. 32–53). Westport, CT: Praeger Security International.

Salas, E., Prince, C., Baker, D.P., and Shrestha, L. (1995). Situation awareness in team performance: Implications for measurement and training. *Human Factors, 37,* 123–136.

Salas, E., Prince, C., Bowers, C., Stout, R.J., Oser, R.L., and Cannon-Bowers, J.A. (1999). A methodology for enhancing crew resource management training. *Human Factors, 41,* 161–172.

Salas, E., Rhodenizer, L., and Bowers, C.A. (2000). The design and delivery of crew resource management training: Exploiting available resources. *Human Factors, 42,* 490–511.

Salas, E. and Rosen, M.A. (2008). Naturalistic decision making, expertise, and homeland security. In J.G. Voeller (Ed.) *Wiley Handbook of Science and Technology for Homeland Security.* Hoboken, NJ: Wiley.

Salas, E. and Rosen, M.A. (2010). Experts at work: Principles for developing expertise in organizations. In S.W.J. Kozlowski and E. Salas (Eds.) *Learning, Training, and Development in Organizations.* Mahwah, NJ: Erlbaum.

Salas, E., Rosen, M.A., Burke, C.S., Goodwin, G.F., and Fiore, S. (2006a). The making of a dream team: When expert teams do best. In K.A. Ericsson, N. Charness, R. Hoffman, and P. Fletovich (Eds.) *The Cambridge Handbook of Expertise and Expert Performance* (pp. 439–453). New York: Cambridge University Press.

Salas, E., Rosen, M.A., and DiazGranados, D. (2010). Expert-based intuition and decision making in organizations. *Journal of Management, 36,* 941–973.

Salas, E., Wildman, J.L., and Piccolo, R.F. (2009). Using simulation-based training to enhance management education. *Academy of Management Learning and Education, 8,* 559–573.

Salas, E., Wilson, K.A., Burke, C.S., and Priest, H.A. (2006b). What is simulation-based training? *Forum, 24,* 12.

Salas, E., Wilson, K.A., Burke, C.S., Wightman, D.C., and Howse, W.R. (2006d). Crew resource management training research, practice, and lessons learned. In R.C. Williges (Ed.) *Review of Human Factors and Ergonomics* (vol. 2, pp. 35–73). Santa Monica, CA: Human Factors and Ergonomics Society.

Salas, E., Wilson, K.A., Lazzara, E.H., King, H.B., Augenstein, J.S., Robinson, D.W., and Birnbach, D.J. (2008a). Simulation-based training for patient safety: 10 principles that matter. *Journal of Patient Safety, 8,* 3–8.

Salas, E., Wilson, K.A., Priest, H.A., and Guthrie, J. (2006e). Training in organizations: The design, delivery, and evaluation of training systems. In G. Salvendy (Ed.) *Handbook of Human Factors and Ergonomics* (3rd ed., pp. 472–512). Hoboken, NJ: Wiley.

Schaafstal, A.M., Johnston, J.H., and Oser, R.L. (2001). Training teams for emergency management. *Computers in Human Behavior, 17,* 615–626.

Shuffler, M.L., Salas, E., and Xavier, L. (2010). The design, delivery, and evaluation of crew resource management training. In E.Weiner, B. Kanki, and R. Helmreich (Eds.) *Crew Resource Management* (pp. 205–232). San Diego, CA: Elsevier.

Smith-Jentsch, K.A., Cannon-Bowers, J.A., Tannenbaum, S.I., and Salas, E. (2008). Guided team self-correction: Impacts on team mental models, processes, and effectiveness. *Small Group Research, 39,* 303–327.

Smith-Jentsch, K.A., Zeisig, R.L., Acton, B., and McPherson, J.A. (1998). A strategy for guided team self-correction. In J.A. Cannon-Bowers and E. Salas (Eds.) *Making Decisions Under Stress: Implications for Individual and Team Training* (pp. 271–297). Washington, DC: American Psychological Association.

Stagl, K.C., Salas, E., and Fiore, S.M. (2007). Best practices for cross-training teams. In D.A. Nembhard (Ed.) *Workforce Cross Training* (pp. 155–179). Boca Raton, FL: CRC Press.

Stout, R.J., Cannon-Bowers, J.A., and Salas, E. (1994). The role of shared mental models in developing shared situational awareness. In R.D. Gilson, D.J. Garland, and J.M. Koonce (Eds.) *Situational Awareness in Complex Systems* (pp. 297–304). Daytona Beach, FL: Embry-Riddle Aeronautical University Press.

Stout, R.J., Cannon-Bowers, J.A., and Salas, E. (1996). The role of shared mental models in developing team situational awareness: Implications for training. *Training Research Journal, 2,* 85–116.

Summers, G.J. (2004). Today's business simulation industry. *Simulation & Gaming, 35*(2), 208–241.

Tannenbaum, S.I., Beard, R.L., McNall, L.A., and Salas, E. (2010). Informal learning and development in organizations. In S.W.J. Kozlowski and E. Salas (Eds.) *Learning, Training, and Development in Organizations* (pp. 303–331). New York: Mahwah, NJ: Erlbaum.

Veenman, M.V.J., Elshout, J.J., and Busato, V.V. (1994). Metacognitive mediation in learning with simulations. *Computers in Human Behavior, 10*(1), 93–106.

Volpe, C.E., Cannon-Bowers, J.A., Salas, E., and Spector, P. (1996). The impact of cross training on team functioning: An empirical investigation. *Human Factors, 38,* 87–100.

Weaver, S.J., Bedwell, W.L., and Salas, E. (2010). Training teams to cope with errors: A framework for instructional strategies and transfer. In D. Hofmann and M. Frese (Eds.) *Errors in Organizations: SIOP Frontiers Series.* Mahwah, NJ: Lawrence Erlbaum.

Weaver, S.J., Wildman, J.L., and Salas, E. (2009). How to build expert teams: Best practices. In R.J. Burke and C.L. Cooper (Eds.) *The Peak Performing Organization* (pp. 129–156). New York: Routledge.

Wexley, K.N. and Latham, G.P. (2002). *Developing and Training Human Resources in Organizations.* Upper Saddle River, NJ: Prentice Hall.

Wilson, P.F. and Johnson, W.B. (2001). Core virtues for the practice of mentoring. *Journal of Psychology and Theology, 29*(2), 121–130.

Zsambok, C.E. (1997). Naturalistic decision making: Where are we now? In C.E. Zsambok and G. Klein (Eds.) *Naturalistic Decision Making* (pp. 3–16). Mahwah, NJ: Erlbaum.

15

Assessing Decision-making Competence in Managers

Christopher J. Lake and Scott Highhouse

Peter Drucker (1954, p. 351) notably said that "management is always a decision making process." That is, managers are charged with the important task of making the decisions that will either facilitate or inhibit effective business operations. Managerial decision making may have an impact upon a wide variety of organizational stakeholders including employees, investors, and customers. A competent decision maker, therefore, can shape a company's strategy and create a path toward greater organizational effectiveness or efficiency. In contrast, an incompetent decision maker can be disastrous for organizational profits and employee well-being.

In this chapter, we examine the history and current knowledge of tools that may be used to predict competent decision making in organizational managers. Specifically, we examine (a) various ways in which competent decision making has been defined in the organizational and psychological literature, (b) predictor constructs relevant to competent managerial decision making, and (c) three methods that have been used to assess decision-making competence in managerial applicants. We also attempt to connect the predictor constructs to on-the-job decision-making performance. Our goal is to set the direction for theory regarding the relation between applicant competence and managerial decision-making performance.

DEFINING COMPETENT DECISION MAKING IN MANAGERS

The ability to make good decisions is desirable for all employees, but there are at least two reasons why this quality is especially important for managerial employees. First, nearly every organization imposes some elements of the "classical" hierarchical structure, wherein policies, procedures, goals, and other directives flow from higher-level to lower-level employees. Thus, as an employee's hierarchical level rises, so too does his or her capacity to make influential decisions. Second, it is frequently acknowledged that managers spend considerable time planning, strategizing, and making decisions (Brown, 1966; Campbell et al., 1970; Drucker, 1954; McGregor, 1960). Rather than directly creating products or providing services, managerial jobs entail making decisions regarding others' creation of products and delivery of services. In his classic book, *The Functions of the Executive*, Chester Barnard (1938) described managerial decision making as follows:

> The fine art of executive decision consists in not deciding questions that are not now pertinent, in not deciding prematurely, in not making decisions that cannot be made effective, and in not making decisions others should make.

> (p. 194)

Barnard was clearly emphasizing the importance of timing in managerial decision making. As described below, the importance of timing in organizational decisions has long been weighed against the importance of making fully informed and thorough decisions.

Psychologists and management researchers have traditionally thought about decision making in terms of a decision maker's use of intuition or analysis. Intuition emphasizes the speed and confidence with which a decision is made (e.g., Elaydi, 2006; Ghiselli, 1971; Hammond, 1996). In contrast, analysis emphasizes the use of a systematic process by which the expected costs and benefits of possible options are compared (von Neumann & Morgenstern, 1947). Analysis involves the use of option maximization; the single decision with the lowest cost and greatest benefit is considered the best (Baird, 1989; Hastie & Dawes, 2010). It is apparent that intuition and analysis represent competing demands upon the decision maker. An analytical decision will take time as the costs and benefits of various options must be estimated and compared. Such a decision may not seem very decisive to subordinates or other managers. Conversely, by relying on gut instincts, an intuitive decision may not seem very rational. Management scholars have had different views about which approach is best.

The Decisive Manager

Intuitive decision making is often described as "decisive" in the literature (e.g., Ghiselli, 1971) and we adopt that term here to describe a management decision-making style that relies on intuition. Decisiveness is the willingness, confidence, and desire to make a quick intuitive decision (House et al., 1999). One early organizational scholar, Ordway Tead (1935, p. 121), emphasized the need for decisiveness when he commented "the studiously and 'scientifically' minded who are in posts of leadership will never stop taking evidence and accumulating and weighing facts." Tead said that it is all too often that managers are afraid to make important decisions or are perhaps stricken with a chronic indecision resulting from the (over)analysis of problems. Barnard (1938, p. 190) similarly lamented a reluctance of some managers to decide due to "a persistent disposition to avoid responsibility and their fear of criticism." Present-day scholars, too, have noted the problems associated with decision delay, indecisiveness, and outright refusal to make decisions (see Anderson, 2003; Baron, 1993; Brooks, 2011; Elaydi, 2006; Hammond, Keeney, & Raiffa, 1999).

The decisive manager, according to Ghiselli (1971), is one who stands ready to make difficult decisions and acknowledges the benefits of taking immediate action rather than attempting the arduous or blatantly impossible task of collecting enough factual data to make a purely analytical decision. Indeed, one of the key characteristics of intuitive decisions is that they are automatic; they do not require timely calculations and they therefore provide a relatively quick decision upon which one can act (Hastie & Dawes, 2010). Ghiselli (1959, 1963) found that managers scoring high on his measure of decisiveness and self-confidence were more apt to hold upper-level than lower-level managerial jobs. Robertson et al. (2000) found that self-reported decisiveness was related to managerial job performance and promotability, as rated by those managers' immediate supervisors. Considering decisive decisions at the organizational level, Bourgeois and Eisenhardt (1988) analyzed data from eight companies and found that quick decisions from powerful management teams (rather than slower decisions from democratic teams) were related to positive organizational performance in the rapidly changing technology sector.

The Analytical Manager

In contrast to the quick and intuitive processes involved with decisiveness, analytical decision making involves careful analysis and systematic consideration of possible decision options (Baird, 1989; Hastie & Dawes, 2010; Tetlock, Peterson, & Berry, 1993). Tannenbaum, Weschler, and Massarik (1961, p. 267) described the analytical decision-making process as one in which a manager "must become aware of relevant behavioral alternatives, define them, and fully evaluate them" before making a decision. Tannenbaum and his associates suggested that good managerial decision making has two defining elements: (1) the decisions themselves are rational, and (2) the decisions influence subordinate decision making toward rationality.

Because analytical decisions are intended to be objective, one particularly salient aspect of analytical decision making is freedom from sources of irrationality (e.g., emotion, stress, personal biases, and heuristics). Brown (1966) noted that "coolness and calmness are . . . companions of good judgment," while warning of the dangers of making decisions under stress or emotional duress. The key benefit of analytical decision making is that, because such decisions are systematically examined and free from bias, they have the highest probability of success. Deviations from purely analytical decisions, of course, introduce error into the decision process and can create disastrous problems (Milkman, Chugh, & Bazerman, 2009). Pacini and Epstein (1999) found that people who use a more analytical approach are more likely to engage in optimal responses to games of chance. Furthermore, Parker and Fischhoff (2005) found that decision makers who integrate information consistently and avoid impulsive responding also score high on real-world markers of good decision making.

The Adaptive Manager

A contingency view of managerial decision making is presented by Hammond (1996), who rejects the analysis–intuition dichotomy in favor of a continuum. Hammond proposed that judgment is conducted on a continuum anchored at one pole by intuition and on the other by analysis. He argued that the most common mode of judgment is *quasirationality*, which includes elements of both intuition and analysis. Kahneman (2003) similarly distinguished between System 1 (intuitive) and System 2 (analytical) processing (see Stanovich & West, 2000). According to Kahneman, System 1 is the default, operating continuously until it is interrupted. At this point System 2 is engaged. Such a perspective suggests that a manager can be both decisive and analytical. Indeed, research by Pacini and Epstein (1999) has shown that individual differences in the use of experiential (i.e., intuitive) decision making are only modestly correlated with individual differences in the use of analytical decision making—people can be high or low on both dimensions.

We suggest that an adaptive manager is one who is cognizant of the tradeoff between decisiveness and analysis, and is comfortable transitioning between both modes of processing in accordance with environmental demands (Payne, Bettman, & Johnson, 1993). Given the wide array of problems with which managers must deal, it is likely that managers will regularly encounter situations that demand a quick response or that are relatively inconsequential such that devoting time to a thorough analysis would not be worth the investment. Other problems, especially those that are broad in scope and those with important consequences for the company's finances or morale, may call for intensive consideration of all options. In short, we propose that adaptive managers are those who adjust their decision-making technique appropriately to a given situation. Theory in this area, therefore, requires a consideration of both decision style and work context (see Johns, 2006).

Summary

The preceding discussion of managerial decision making presents decisiveness, analysis, and adaptivity as three constructs relevant to performance in managerial decision making. Below we discuss the specific methods that have been used to assess decision-making competence in managerial job candidates, and research on the utility of these methods. After we present these methods, we consider how they may be used to assess the decisiveness, analysis, and adaptivity constructs.

METHODS OF ASSESSING DECISION-MAKING COMPETENCE

In this section, we review three primary methods that have been used to assess the decision-making competence of managerial applicants. We use the term *methods* here to refer to testing instruments or protocols. This is in keeping with the increased recognition of the need to make clear distinctions between the measures themselves, and the conceptual variables they were designed to assess (see Arthur & Villado, 2008, for an extended discussion). As we will discuss later, multiple methods may be used to assess the constructs of decisiveness, analysis, and adaptivity.[1]

It is important to note that the methods used in organizational research and practice are very different from measures of decision-making competence that focus on a person's resistance to common decision traps (e.g., Bruine de Bruin, Parker, & Fischhoff, 2007; Parker & Fischhoff, 2005). The methods we discuss here receive no mention in the JDM literature on how to assess decision-making competence. And, they are not used as criteria in decision-making research (see MacCrimmon & Wehrung, 1984, for an exception). One goal of this chapter, therefore, is to provide awareness of these predictors to scholars in the field of judgment and decision making.

Although the methods we discuss are generally well known to organizational researchers and practitioners, they receive less attention than commonly used assessments such as mental-ability tests and personality scales. As such, a second goal of this chapter is to review the relations between measures of decision-making competence and measures of mental ability and personality. Because much of managerial and executive assessment is practical in orientation, the various instruments and protocols used to assess decision-making competence have been designed based on either (a) analysis of the tasks managers are likely to engage in on the job, or (b) identification of the skills and abilities believed to be possessed by good decision makers. Three such tools are discussed now.

In-basket Tests

For over a half-century, industrial-organizational (I-O) psychologists have used the "in-basket" method to assess managers' decision-making competence. The in-basket presents managers with a hypothetical work situation requiring a series of decisions that must be made without consultation or delegation of such responsibility to others.

In 1952, the United States Air Force contracted the Educational Testing Service (ETS) to assess its training program at the Air Command and Staff School. Norman Frederiksen and his colleagues at ETS (Frederiksen, Saunders, & Wand, 1957) set about developing a test that could measure one's ability to organize information and balance a large number of considerations to arrive at decisions. Frederiksen, Saunders, and Wand created simulations of problems for the Air Force officers to solve based on a study of typical problems encountered by Air Force officers. These problems were translated into memos and reports that were presented in the form of a managerial in-basket.

The ETS in-basket was later adapted for use by the New York Port Authority to assess prospective police lieutenants (see Lopez, 1966). It also became part of large-scale executive assessment programs at Sears & Roebuck (Bentz, 1967) and AT&T (Bray, Campbell, & Grant, 1974). Although the format has been modernized to correspond with the electronic workspace, the in-basket remains a commonly used work sample for managerial assessment (Prien, Schippmann, & Prien, 2003), and it has become a staple of the widely used "assessment center" for identifying managerial talent (Howard, 1997; Thornton & Byham, 1982).

In the prototypical in-basket, a candidate is presented with a wide variety of documents that might appear on the desk (or in the in-box) of a manager. There are a number of sources for guidance on developing an in-basket (e.g., Moses & Byham, 1977; Thornton & Mueller-Hanson, 2004), but the typical one might include letters, reports, budgets, and memos designed to represent common issues faced by people in the targeted position. The candidate decides how to prioritize the tasks and then writes responses, schedules meetings, or assigns duties to others. Time pressure is created by giving the candidate two or three hours to complete the task. Afterward, the candidate is interviewed to learn how problems were handled, what he or she learned, and the reasoning behind actions taken or not taken. Within the assessment center, the in-basket is linked with multiple other situational assessment devices in order to derive overall trait or dimension scores. The in-basket, however, often serves as the primary indicator of a managerial candidate's decision-making competence.

Given that the in-basket is often studied as part of an assessment center program, research on the in-basket *alone* is quite scarce. In a study of fifty-one Sears & Roebuck executives, Bentz (1967) found a small non-significant correlation ($r = .25$) between in-basket performance and scores on a general mental ability test. Lopez (1966) and Crooks (1971) reported that in-basket scores were significantly related to cognitively loaded college entrance tests. Similarly, few studies have been conducted on the personality correlates of performance in an in-basket. And the research that does exist was conducted over forty years ago (Bentz, 1967; Frederiksen, 1966; Lopez, 1966). Frederiksen, for example, found significant positive correlations (rs ranging from .20–.40) with traits labeled *active, dominant,* and *calm and confident.* Lopez found a significant correlation ($r = .26$) with *aggressiveness.* Bentz's study of fifty-one executives found significant positive correlations ($r = .30$) with *seriousness* (vs. carefree) and *general activity* (vs. inactivity). He reported a similar-sized negative correlation with *creativity.* Translating these into "Big 5" traits, there appear to be consistent relations between in-basket performance and extraversion/surgency, suggesting that people who demonstrate managerial decision-making competence are more active, aggressive, and leader-like. Past findings are also suggestive of relations with emotional stability and low openness to experience.

Critical Thinking Tests

Educational scholar Robert Ennis described critical thinking as "reasonable reflective thinking focused on deciding what to believe or do" (1993, p. 180). There is a wide variety of critical thinking assessments that are specifically designed for administration to primary and secondary school students. One measure, however—the Watson-Glaser Critical Thinking Appraisal (Watson & Glaser, 2009)—has a long history of use in organizational hiring and promotions beginning from its original development in 1925. Among I-O psychologists conducting individual (managerial) assessments, the Watson-Glaser is the single most popular form of ability testing used in organizations (Ryan & Sackett, 1987). Kline (1994) speculated that the popularity of the Watson-Glaser in employment contexts is due to the test's divergence from conventional intelligence tests. Specifically, the Watson-Glaser primarily involves reading short scenarios and answering follow-up questions regarding those scenarios. This is in contrast to conventional intelligence tests, which may involve manipulating geometric shapes, solving math problems, or applying the rules of English grammar.

Scoring well on the Watson-Glaser requires careful, thorough, and reflective evaluation of arguments. In spite of its emphasis on analytical judgment, one potential criticism of the Watson-Glaser is that it measures one's ability to think critically while not measuring one's propensity to use those skills. The argument goes that critical thinking requires more mental effort than heuristic thinking and thus some people may be resistant to using it, even if they possess the ability to do so (Halpern, 1998).

In spite of differences in testing formats, the Watson-Glaser can be expected to substantially relate to measures of intelligence. For example, the Watson-Glaser relates to scores on other measures such as the Raven's Advanced Progressive Matrices ($r = .53$) and the WAIS intelligence test ($r = .52$) (Watson & Glaser, 2009). Regarding its relation with personality, at least three studies have demonstrated significant relations between Watson-Glaser scores and measures of openness to experience; r values ranged from .15 to .36 (Clifford, Boufal, & Kurtz, 2004; Moutafi, Furnham, & Crump, 2003; Spector et al., 2000). There seem to be far weaker and less consistent relations between Watson-Glaser scores and other personality traits. Furnham et al. (2007) observed no significant relations between Watson-Glaser scores and Big 5 traits in a sample of approximately 8,000 managerial and professional employees.

Situational Judgment Tests

In the typical SJT, a managerial applicant is presented with a short paragraph describing a hypothetical dilemma and a list of possible actions. The applicant's task is to evaluate the list of actions and choose the one that is most likely to result in success. Depending on the wording of a particular test, the applicant is asked to report the best and/or worst action, evaluate the quality of every individual action, or to indicate which action he or she would personally employ. SJTs have been described as a type of work simulation because they present the applicant with scenarios that are apt to be encountered in a particular job (McDaniel et al., 2001). Consider an example SJT item from McDaniel and Whetzel (2005):

> You assigned a very high profile project to one of your project managers. The project is very complex and involves the coordination of several other project managers. During each of the project update meetings, your project manager indicates that everything is going as scheduled. Now, one week before the project is due, your project manager informs you that the project is less than 50 percent complete.
>
> (p. 520)

Possible actions include: (a) firing the project manager, (b) personally taking on the project manager's work, (c) coaching the project manager, and (d) keeping the project manager from participating in future projects. Applicants earn points for correctly identifying an effective action—usually identified by a sample of experts.

The scenario-presentation format of the SJT first appeared in a social judgment test in the 1920s. A particular subscale of the George Washington Social Intelligence Test required respondents to analyze scenarios and select from a multiple-choice list the single solution that seemed most appropriate. During World War II the German and American militaries administered SJTs to soldiers to assess "effective" or "practical" intelligence (Highhouse, 2002; McDaniel et al., 2001). During this same period, SJTs were developed by the Standard Oil Company of New Jersey and the United States Office of Personnel Management to measure managerial potential. Although SJTs have been around for many decades, it is only in the past twenty years that such tests have become a relatively widespread means of assessing decision-making competency in organizations (Weekley & Ployhart, 2006).

Although some view SJTs as merely low-fidelity work samples, others have noted that SJTs provide the potential to capture a practical intelligence that is not captured by standard intelligence and personality measures (see Lievens & Chan, 2010, for a review). Brooks and Highhouse (2006, p. 40) asserted that "the use of SJTs is based on the assumption—either explicit or implicit—that judgment ability varies across candidates, and that this ability can be measured." Although SJTs differ in content from test to test, meta-analyses suggest that scores tend to relate substantially to cognitive ability, $\rho = .32$ (McDaniel et al., 2007). In terms of personality traits, it seems that SJT scores relate fairly strongly to agreeableness ($\rho = .25$), conscientiousness ($\rho = .27$), and emotional stability ($\rho = .22$), and relate less so to extraversion ($\rho = .14$) and openness ($\rho = .13$).

CONNECTING METHODS AND CONSTRUCTS

Earlier in this chapter, we discussed three constructs related to decision-making competence in managers. They are: decisiveness, analysis, and adaptivity. The left portion of Figure 15.1 proposes connections among these three constructs and the three methods of assessing managerial decision-making competence discussed here. As the figure suggests, the in-basket is tied to all three constructs. The in-basket requires a person to (a) make decisions and take action versus deferring decisions and actions, (b) produce high work output versus low work output, and (c) act independently versus seeking advice and guidance (Siegel, 1969). Thus, successful performance in the in-basket requires decisiveness, as well as the ability to analyze problems (Thornton & Byham, 1982). The flexibility in development and administration allows for one to create time pressure and vary the importance of one task relative to another (Thornton & Mueller-Hanson, 2004). As such, the in-basket is well suited to assess an applicant's adaptivity.

Next, the critical thinking test is directly tied to the analysis construct. The Watson-Glaser and other measures of critical thinking assess one's ability to recognize assumptions, evaluate arguments, and draw conclusions from evidence. When completing the Watson-Glaser, managerial

Predictor Methods	Predictor Constructs	Narrow Criterion Construct	Broad Criterion Construct

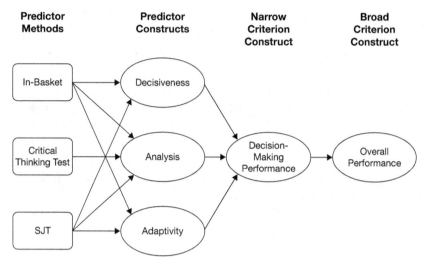

FIGURE 15.1
Connections among decision constructs and three methods of assessing managerial decision-making competence.

applicants (a) determine the level of factuality in assumptions made based on data provided, (b) identify when assumptions are being made, (c) determine whether statements logically follow from a given paragraph, and (d) evaluate the strength of arguments made about a certain topic. Thus, successful performance on the Watson-Glaser requires the ability to analyze problems and make informed choices.

Finally, Figure 15.1 shows that, like the in-basket, the SJT method is connected to all three constructs. SJTs may be used to assess one's propensity for decisiveness or analysis. Consider an SJT item from Ployhart and MacKenzie (2011) that emphasizes decisiveness:

> A customer wishes to return some expensive clothing but does not have a receipt. Store policy is to never accept returns without a receipt. You state this to the customer, who quickly becomes so irate that he or she starts to make other customers leave the store. Unfortunately, the store manager is out to lunch and you have to do something fast.
>
> (p. 241)

This scenario requires that some form of immediate action be taken. In contrast, an item used in the FBI special agent selection process reads:

- You are shopping when you notice a man robbing the store. What would you do?
  - Leave the store as quickly as possible and call the police.
  - Try to apprehend the robber yourself.
  - Follow the man and call the police as soon as he appears settled somewhere.
  - Nothing, as you do not wish to get involved in the matter.

This item expects the special agent candidate to consider the circumstances surrounding the robbery attempt, weigh the proposed alternatives, and consider possible outcomes associated with each. Such an item requires considerable analysis.

Wagner and Sternberg (1987) demonstrated that SJTs can also be used to assess one's adaptivity. Their theory of tacit knowledge emphasizes the ability to tradeoff idealism for pragmatism, as well as the ability to balance local (short-term) concerns with more global (long-term) ones. Tetlock, Peterson, and Berry (1993) similarly noted that "good judgment" requires knowing when to consider subtle tradeoffs, versus taking a decisive or principled stand. Like the in-basket, the SJT can be modified to capture one's ability to adapt decision style to situational demands.

The connections between methods and constructs described above were admittedly made *post hoc*. Unfortunately, applied psychologists have constructed and used these sorts of methods without regard to any theory of human reasoning. Industrial-organizational psychologists would do well to examine the JDM literature on axiomatically correct and incorrect decisions. They might examine whether succumbing to decision traps, for example, is related to on-the-job decision-making performance. Perhaps integrating the attention to measurement theory, characteristic of applied psychologists, with the decision-making focus on problem solving and reasoning would result in more powerful methods of assessment.

CONNECTING PREDICTOR CONSTRUCTS TO CRITERION CONSTRUCTS

A theoretical approach to personnel selection requires connecting the constructs assessed by the predictors with the performance constructs one wants to predict (Schmitt & Chan, 1998). As briefly discussed in our introduction, many organizational scholars have observed that competent decision making plays a key role in work performance (e.g., Campbell et al., 1970; Drucker, 1954; Tett et al., 2000). Dill (1964) described five different functions of management: (1) the detection and prioritization of problems requiring a solution, (2) determining how solutions to problems should be sought, (3) deciding how to best devote resources (money, employee time) to the resolution of problems, (4) deciding how to best execute the solution to the problem, and (5) examining the repercussions of the solution after some time has passed. Clearly judgment and decision making constitutes a considerable portion of these activities. Those interested in predicting managerial job performance, however, rarely consider decision making as a separate performance dimension.

Recent scholarly work has argued for taking a fine-grained approach to the measurement of work performance by specifying precisely which elements of performance a given method might assess (e.g., Bartram, 2005; Tett et al., 2000). Applying this approach, we expect that the constructs decisiveness, analysis, and adaptivity would relate to on-the-job decision-making performance—a narrow criterion construct. This relation is shown in the right-hand portion of Figure 15.1. We were only able to find two studies that used an on-the-job decision-making performance measure as the criterion for evaluating the effectiveness of the predictors we reviewed (Meyer, 1970; Watson & Glaser, 2009). Meyer's study of eighty-one General Electric plant managers showed that decision-making performance on the in-basket was correlated substantially ($r = .38$) with the planning and decision-making component of work performance. The Watson-Glaser test manual (Watson & Glaser, 2009) reports that scores on the critical thinking test were related to supervisor ratings of judgment and decision-making job performance ($r = .23$) in a sample of 142 job incumbents across multiple industries.

The far more common method of criterion validation is to relate method scores to measures of *overall* work performance—a broad criterion construct (see Figure 15.1). Regarding the ability of the in-basket to predict overall job performance, Bentz's (1967) Sears & Roebuck executive study showed a solid positive relation ($r = .34$) with management ratings of overall effectiveness. There is also evidence that SJTs predict overall work performance. McDaniel et al.'s (2007) meta-analysis shows a fairly strong relation, $\rho = .26$, between SJT scores and measures of overall work performance.

CONCLUSIONS

Given the overlap of mental ability and personality measures with the decision-making assessment methods discussed here, one may wonder why such methods are necessary. In other words, one might believe that they are indirectly assessing individual differences in decision-making competence when they assess general mental ability and personality. We believe there are both practical and theoretical reasons for going beyond typical ability and personality predictors. Although there is no research on the in-basket per se, research on the assessment center has shown that use of dimension scores based on situational exercises (which often include in-baskets) produce significant incremental validity in predicting job performance—over and above cognitive ability and personality (Dilchert & Ones, 2009). Research on the SJT has also demonstrated incremental validity, over and above cognitive ability and personality (e.g., Weekley & Ployhart, 2005).

We believe that decisiveness, analysis, and adaptivity are more *proximal* constructs than cognitive ability and personality (see Lievens & Chan, 2010). Generally speaking, broad constructs predict broad criteria and narrow constructs predict narrow criteria. More specific constructs related to decision-making competence will be more useful when trying to predict specific performance related to managerial decision making. This also fosters understanding of the underlying mechanisms, and brings us closer to a theory of managerial decision-making competence. Guion (1998) noted that it is possible to make valid decisions without understanding the constructs we are measuring, "[but] at this point in the history of employment psychology we should be getting tired of not knowing what we are doing, no matter how carefully we do it" (p. 618). We look forward to a better evidence base for making informed decisions about managerial decision making.

NOTE

1. We are using the term "constructs" to refer to these three decision-making typologies because it allows for us to make the important distinction between predictor constructs and the methods used to assess them. We use the term construct to refer to decisiveness, analysis, or adaptivity in the sense that it has been used in the past to describe broad predictor variables such as "adaptability" (Pulakos et al., 2000), or various dimensions assessed in assessment centers.

REFERENCES

Anderson, C.J. (2003). The psychology of doing nothing: Forms of decision avoidance result from reason and emotion. *Psychological Bulletin, 129*, 139–167.

Arthur, W. Jr. and Villado, A. (2008). The importance of distinguishing between constructs and methods when comparing predictors in personnel selection research and practice. *Journal of Applied Psychology, 93*, 435–442.

Baird, B.F. (1989). *Managerial Decisions Under Uncertainty: An Introduction to the Analysis of Decision Making*. New York: John Wiley.

Barnard, C.I. (1938). *The Functions of the Executive*. Cambridge, MA: Harvard University Press.

Baron, J. (1993). *Morality and Rational Choice*. Boston, MA: Kluwer Academic Publishers.

Bartram, D. (2005). The great eight competencies: A criterion-centric approach to validation. *Journal of Applied Psychology, 90*, 1185–1203.

Bentz, V.J. (1967). The Sears experience in the investigation description and prediction of executive behavior. In F.R. Wickert and D.E. McFarland (Eds.) *Measuring Executive Performance* (pp. 147–205). New York: Apppleton-Century-Crofts.

Bourgeois, L.J. III and Eisenhardt, K. (1988). Strategic decision processes in high velocity environments: Four cases in the microcomputer industry. *Management Science, 34*, 816–835.

Bray, D.W., Campbell, R.J., and Grant, D.L. (1974). *Formative Years in Business: A Long-term AT&T Study of Managerial Lives*. New York: John Wiley.

Brooks, M.E. (2011). Management indecision. *Management Decision, 49*, 683–693.

Brooks, M.E. and Highhouse, S.E. (2006). Can good judgment be measured? In J.A. Weekley and R.E. Ployhart (Eds.) *Situational Judgment Testing*. Mahwah, NJ: Lawrence Erlbaum.

Brown, R.E. (1966). *Judgment in Administration*. New York: McGraw-Hill.

Bruine de Bruin, W., Parker, A.M., and Fischhoff, B. (2007). Individual differences in adult decision-making competence. *Journal of Personality and Social Psychology, 92*, 938–956.

Campbell, J.P., Dunnette, M.D., Lawler, E.E. III, and Weick, K.E. Jr. (1970). *Managerial Behavior, Performance, and Effectiveness*. New York: McGraw-Hill.

Clifford, J.S., Boufal, M.M., and Kurtz, J.E. (2004). Personality traits and critical thinking skills in college students. *Assessment, 2*, 169–176.

Crooks, L.A. (1971). *The In-basket Study: A Pilot Study of MBA Candidate Performance on a Test of Administrative Skills as Related to Selection and Achievement in Graduate Business School*. (Brief No. 4, ATGSB Research and Development Committee). Princeton, NJ: Educational Testing Services.

Dilchert, S. and Ones, D. (2009). Assessment center dimensions: Individual difference correlates and meta-analytic incremental validity. *International Journal of Selection and Assessment, 17*, 254–270.

Dill, W.R. (1964). Decision-making. In D.E. Griffiths (Ed.) *Behavioral Science and Educational Administration* (Part II, pp. 199–222). Chicago, IL: University of Chicago Press.

Drucker, P.F. (1954). *The Practice of Management*. New York: Harper.

Elaydi, R. (2006). Construct development and measurement of indecisiveness. *Management Decision, 10*, 1363–1376.

Ennis, R.H. (1993). Critical thinking assessment. *Theory into Practice, 32*, 179–186.

Frederiksen, N. (1966). Validation of a simulation technique. *Organizational Behavior and Human Performance, 1*, 87–109.

Frederiksen, N., Saunders, D.R., and Wand, B. (1957). The in-basket test. *Psychological Monographs, 71*, 1–28.

Furnham, A., Dissou, G., Sloan, P., and Chamorro-Premuzic, T. (2007). Personality and intelligence in business people: A study of two personality and two intelligence measures. *Journal of Business Psychology, 22*, 99–109.

Ghiselli, E.E. (1959). Traits differentiating management personnel. *Personnel Psychology, 12*, 535–544.

Ghiselli, E.E. (1963). The validity of management traits in relation to occupational level. *Personnel Psychology, 16*, 109–113.

Ghiselli, E.E. (1971). *Explorations in Managerial Talent.* Pacific Palisades, CA: Goodyear.

Guion, R.M. (1998). *Assessment, Measurement, and Prediction for Personnel Decisions.* Mahwah, NJ: Lawrence Erlbaum.

Halpern, D.F. (1998). Teaching critical thinking for transfer across domains: Dispositions, skills, structure training, and metacognitive monitoring. *American Psychologist, 53*, 449–455.

Hammond, J.S., Keeney, R.L., and Raiffa, H. (1999). *Smart Choices: A Practical Guide to Making Better Decisions.* Boston, MA: Harvard Business School Press.

Hammond, K.R. (1996). *Human Judgment and Social Policy: Irreducible Uncertainty, Inevitable Error, Unavoidable Injustice.* New York: Oxford University Press.

Hastie, R. and Dawes, R.M. (2010). *Rational Choice in an Uncertain World: The Psychology of Judgment and Decision Making* (2nd ed.). Thousand Oaks, CA: Sage.

Highhouse, S. (2002). Assessing the candidate as a whole: A historical and critical analysis of individual psychological assessment for personnel decision making. *Personnel Psychology, 55*, 363–396.

House, R.J., Hanges, P.J., Ruiz-Quintanilla, S.A., Dorfman, P.W., Javidan, M., Dickson, M., Gupta, V., and GLOBE (1999). Cultural influences on leadership and organizations: Project GLOBE. In W.F. Mobley, M.J. Gessner, and V. Arnold (Eds.) *Advances in Global Leadership* (vol. 1, pp. 171–233). Stanford, CT: JAI Press.

Howard, A. (1997). A reassessment of assessment centers: Challenges for the 21st century. *Journal of Social Behavior and Personality, 12*, 13–52.

Johns, G. (2006). The essential impact of context on organizational behavior. *Academy of Management Review, 31*, 386–408.

Kahneman D. (2003). A perspective on judgement and choice. *American Psychologist, 58*, 697–720.

Kline, P. (1994). *The Handbook of Psychological Testing.* London: Routledge.

Lievens, F. and Chan, D. (2010). Practical intelligence, emotional intelligence, and social intelligence. In J.L. Farr and N.T. Tippins (Eds.) *Handbook of Employee Selection.* New York: Routledge.

Lopez, F. (1966). *Evaluating Executive Decision Making: The In-basket Technique.* New York: American Management Association.

MacCrimmon, K.R. and Wehrung, D.A. (1984). The risk in-basket. *Journal of Business, 57*, 367–387.

McDaniel, M.A., Hartman, N.S., Whetzel, D.L., and Grubb, W.L. III (2007). Situational judgment tests, response instructions, and validity: A meta-analysis. *Personnel Psychology, 60*, 63–91.

McDaniel, M.A., Morgeson, F.P., Bruhn Finnegan, E., Campion, M.A., and Braverman, E.P. (2001). Use of situational judgment tests to predict job performance: A clarification of the literature. *Journal of Applied Psychology, 86*, 730–740.

McDaniel, M.A. and Whetzel, D.L. (2005). Situational judgment test research: Informing the debate on practical intelligence theory. *Intelligence, 33,* 515–525.

McGregor, D. (1960). *The Human Side of Enterprise.* New York: McGraw-Hill.

Meyer, H.H. (1970). The validity of the in-basket test as a measure of managerial performance. *Personnel Psychology, 23,* 297–307.

Milkman, K.L., Chugh, D., and Bazerman, M. (2009). How can decision making be improved? *Perspectives on Psychological Science, 4,* 379–383.

Moses, J.L. and Byham, W.C. (1977). *Applying the Assessment Center Method.* New York: Pergamon Press.

Moutafi, J., Furnham, A., and Crump, J. (2003). Demographic and personality predictors of intelligence: A study using the NEO Personality Inventory and the Myers-Briggs Type Indicator. *European Journal of Personality, 17,* 79–94.

Pacini, R. and Epstein, S. (1999). The interaction of three facets of concrete thinking in a game of chance. *Thinking and Reasoning, 5,* 303–325.

Parker, A.M. and Fischhoff, B. (2005). Decision-making competence: External validation through an individual-differences approach. *Journal of Behavioral Decision Making, 18,* 1–27.

Payne, J.W., Bettman, J.R., and Johnson, E.J. (1993). *The Adaptive Decision Maker.* Cambridge: Cambridge University Press.

Ployhart, R.E. and MacKenzie, W.I. Jr. (2011). Situational judgment tests: A critical review and agenda for the future. In S. Zedeck (Ed.) *APA Handbook of Industrial and Organizational Psychology* (vol. 2, pp. 237–252). Washington, DC: American Psychological Association.

Prien, E.P., Schippmann, J.S., and Prien, K.O. (2003). *Individual Assessment: As Practiced in Industry and Consulting.* Mahwah, NJ: Lawrence Erlbaum.

Pulakos, E.D., Arad, S., Donovan, M.A., and Plamondon, K.E. (2000). Adaptability in the workplace: Development of a taxonomy of adaptive performance. *Journal of Applied Psychology, 85,* 612–624.

Robertson, I.T., Baron, H., Gibbons, P., MacIver, R., and Nyfield, G. (2000). Conscientiousness and managerial performance. *Journal of Occupational and Organizational Psychology, 73,* 171–180.

Ryan, A.M. and Sackett, P.R. (1987). A survey of individual assessment practices by I/O psychologists. *Personnel Psychology, 40,* 455–488.

Schmitt, N. and Chan, D. (1998). *Personnel Selection: A Theoretical Approach.* Thousand Oaks, CA: Sage.

Siegel, L. (1969). *Industrial Psychology.* Homewood, IL: Irwin.

Spector, P.E., Schneider, J.R., Vance, C.A., and Hezlett, S.A. (2000). The relation of cognitive ability and personality traits to assessment center performance. *Journal of Applied Social Psychology, 30,* 1474–1491.

Stanovich, K.E. and West, R.F. (2000). Individual differences in reasoning: Implications for the rationality debate. *Behavioral and Brain Sciences, 23,* 645–665.

Tannenbaum, R., Weschler, I.R., and Massarik, F. (1961). *Leadership in Organization.* New York: McGraw-Hill.

Tead, O. (1935). *The Art of Leadership.* New York: McGraw-Hill.

Tetlock, P.E., Peterson, R.S., and Berry, J.M. (1993). Flattering and unflattering personality portraits of integratively simple and complex managers. *Journal of Personality and Social Psychology, 64,* 500–511.

Tett, R.P., Guterman, H.A., Bleier, A., and Murphy, P.J. (2000). Development and content validation of a "hyperdimensional" taxonomy of managerial competence. *Human Performance, 13,* 205–251.

Thornton, G.C. III and Byham, W.C. (1982). *Assessment Centers and Managerial Performance*. San Diego, CA: Academic Press.

Thornton, G.C. III and Mueller-Hanson, R.A. (2004). *Developing Organizational Simulations: A Guide for Practitioners and Students*. Mahwah, NJ: Lawrence Erlbaum.

von Neumann, J. and Morgenstern, O. (1947). *Theory of Games and Economic Behavior*. Princeton, NJ: Princeton University Press.

Wagner, R.K. and Sternberg, R.J. (1987). Tacit knowledge in managerial success. *Journal of Business and Psychology, 1*, 301–312.

Watson, G. and Glaser, E.M. (2009). *Watson-Glaser II Critical Thinking Appraisal: Technical and User's Manual*. San Antonio, TX: Pearson.

Weekley, J.A. and Ployhart, R.E. (2005). Situational judgment: Antecedents and relationships with performance. *Human Performance, 18*, 81–104.

Weekley, J.A. and Ployhart, R.E. (2006). *Situational Judgment Tests: Theory, Measurement, and Application*. Mahwah, NJ: Lawrence Erlbaum.

Commentary

16

Apollo, Dionysus, or Both?: The Evolving Models and Concerns of JDM

Kevin R. Murphy

Apollo and Dionysus were sons of Zeus. Apollo was the god of the sun, or dreams, and of reason, while Dionysus was the god of wine, ecstasy, and intoxication. The great German philosophers and historians of the nineteenth century (e.g., Nietzsche, 2008; Spengler, 1991) used the terms *Apollonian* and *Dionysian* to refer to two modes of thinking, one rational and analytic, and the other intuitive, emotional, and chaotic, and they argued that entire civilizations and epochs of history could be characterized in similar terms. Nietzsche (2008) claimed that the highest forms of art (Greek tragedy, in particular) required a synthesis of both the Apollonian and Dionysian mindsets.

In this chapter, I compare the theories, models, and concepts that dominated judgment and decision making (JDM) research at the time I entered the field (the late 1970s) with those that appear to dominate the field of JDM today. My purpose is to ask the question of what JDM really represents, and whether the field is making significant and meaningful progress. Ultimately, the answer may depend on what you think of Nietzsche's (2008) conclusion that a synthesis of the rational/analytic and the intuitive/emotional produces a product that is superior to that produced by either mode of thinking alone.

In a nutshell, I will argue that JDM research and theory was for the most part concerned with rational models of JDM (i.e., Apollonian) at the time that I entered the field, and that the current field of JDM exhibits a mix of concerns for the rational and the intuitive side of how we make decisions (i.e., Apollonian at times, Dionysian at others). This can lead to a splintered and fragmented body of research, or it can provide the springboard for a synthesis of the two traditions to create something of real value. It may be too soon to tell whether we are heading for chaos or synthesis, but there are reasons for confidence in the future of JDM research and for its relevance to understanding behavior in organizations.

JDM IN THE 1970S AND 1980S

I started my career as a JDM researcher (Balzer, Rohrbaugh, & Murphy, 1983; Lane, Murphy, & Marques, 1982; Murphy, 1982; Nystedt & Murphy, 1979). At that time, the JDM fraternity was small, learned, exclusive, and, to tell the truth, nasty. After receiving some withering reviews of my early attempts to crack this fraternity, I decided that life as an untenured faculty member would be a lot easier and more rewarding if I switched fields. My brief and largely unsuccessful foray into the field of JDM left some decided impressions, both of the promise and of the limitations of this area of research.

The goal of this chapter is to lay out some of the big questions that dominated JDM research forty years ago and take stock of how things have progressed since then. Like my initial impressions, my take on the current field of JDM is that there is still a tantalizing mix of promise and limitations. Significant progress has been made on many fronts, but the field of JDM is still a decidedly mixed bag. It is not always clear what holds this field together, or how the efforts of various subdisciplines in the field are interrelated. The best and tightest theories don't seem to explain very much in terms of real-world JDM, while the most useful models and theories are collections of interesting but disparate phenomena in JDM, more like curio cabinets than theories.

THE BIG PICTURE, THEN AND NOW

In the 1970s and 1980s, the big questions in JDM often revolved around the inadequacies of human decision making, at least in comparison to formal models of judgment and decision. These formal models, mainly described under the heading of subjective expected utility (SEU) theory, had developed quickly in the years following World War II, and by the mid 1970s there were well-specified models of judgment and choice that appeared to provide insight into both how people should make decisions (normative) and how they *did* make decisions (descriptive). Keeney and Raiffa (1976) provided the definitive overview of the development and application of expected utility models as understood at that time.

Historically, the first formalization of models of decision making involved the concept of expected value, in which the expected value of an outcome was a product of the payoff associated with an outcome and the probability of that outcome occurring. As early as the eighteenth century, Bernoulli recognized that the perceived value of money or similar outcomes reflected a subjective evaluation of outcomes, and that the utility of money was not linear. That is, the difference between winning nothing and winning $5 is much bigger, subjectively, than the difference between winning $100 and winning $105 (Kahneman & Thaler, 1991). In the 1940s and 1950s, von Neumann and Morgenstern formulated a modern version of SEU theory that allowed them to derive individual utility functions from the preferences and choices of individual decision makers.

Despite the steady progress in developing rigorous and rational models of human decision making, since at least the 1950s there had been hints that, when making high-stakes decisions, human decision makers often performed poorly in comparison to even simple statistical models (Meehl, 1954). More generally, the image of humans as efficient and rational information processors was under steady assault (Newell & Simon, 1972). In particular, social judgments (i.e., judgments that involved relationships among individuals or groups) seemed to conform poorly to normative models of efficient judgment (Nisbett & Ross, 1980).

The 1970s and 1980s was the heyday of research demonstrating non-rational, non-optimal, and sometimes downright illogical patterns in the behavior of human decision makers. For example, Staw (1976) showed how decision makers tend to escalate commitment to courses of action they have chosen, even when these actions are clearly likely to fail. Arkes and Blumer (1985) explored the psychology of sunk cost, in which previous investments of time, energy, or resources to a particular goal increased the attractiveness and importance of that goal. As in the escalation literature, research on sunk cost phenomena provided many illustrations of the tendency to persist even when a particular course of action is clearly failing. Huber, Payne, and Puto (1982) studied decoy effects and showed how including irrelevant information in a decision scenario could consistently mislead decision makers. All of these phenomena violate the assumption thatdecision makers are following (albeit sometimes inefficiently) rational policies when making judgments and decisions.

The big-picture question that dominated this era was the meaning of frequently observed differences between formal and normative models of decisions and decision making and the actual behavior of decision makers. For example, throughout the 1950s and 1960s the usual interpretation of the poor performance of human judges in comparison to robust statistical models was that humans simply did not have insight into their own decision policies, and that the weight they gave to various cues in the environment was best defined in terms of statistical relationships between cues and decisions rather than in terms of judges' descriptions of the way their own policies and preferences operated (Nystedt & Murphy, 1979). Similarly, differences between formal models of optimal decision strategies and actual decisions were often interpreted as evidence that human judges were simply not very good at implementing the optimal model.

The work of Kahneman, Tversky, and their colleagues dealt a substantial blow to the argument that people functioned in a way that was similar to, but less efficient than, formal statistical models (Kahneman, Slovic & Tversky, 1982; Kahneman & Tversky, 1973). Their studies of heuristic biases in JDM led to the realization that cognitive shortcuts could often lead to judgments and decisions that looked superficially like the outcomes of inefficient application of optimal statistical models, but in fact were reflections of much simpler and less analytic processes. Heuristics such as availability (Tversky & Kahneman, 1973), anchoring (Tversky & Kahneman, 1974), and representativeness (Kahneman & Tversky, 1972) came to replace rational analytic models as depictions of what human judges and decision makers actually do. Kahneman and Tversky's (1972) conclusion that man is not an inefficient Bayesian, he is not a Bayesian at all, is emblematic of this shift from formal mathematical models to heuristic processes.

Prospect Theory (Kahneman & Tversky, 1979) illustrates both the strengths and weaknesses of JDM research at that time. Prospect Theory is a relaxation of expected utility theory that:

- emphasizes changes in the value of outcomes (e.g. gains vs. losses) rather than the absolute value of outcomes;
- replaces event probabilities (with all of their axiomatic structure) with decision weights in describing judges' integration of information about the likelihood and value of different outcomes;
- describes value functions in terms of a concave relationship between the size of a gain and the value attached to that gain and a convex

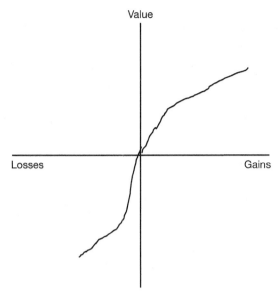

FIGURE 16.1
The Prospect Theory value function.

relationship between the size of a loss and the value attached to that loss (see Figure 16.1);

• on the basis of this value function, predicts that people are risk averse when it comes to gains and risk seeking when it comes to losses;

• includes preliminary analysis and editing of prospects to simplify their comparison (e.g., by cancelling out apparently identical elements, or by decomposing prospects into risky and riskless elements).

The obvious strength of Prospect Theory is that it accommodates many of the well-known violations of classic SEU theory. The obvious weakness of the theory is that it does so by sometimes interposing concepts and terms that have little clear justification other than a demonstration that they tend to work. That is, the theory is inductive rather than deductive. For example, decision weights are inferred from choices, and do not reflect any stated policy or preference on the part of the decision maker. The value function that is central to this theory is not a product of any specified decision process, but rather is an empirical summary of the way decision makers end up treating nominally equivalent gains vs. losses. In other words, Prospect Theory provided a masterful description of *what* people do, but a less convincing one of *why* they do it.

In contrast to their work on decision heuristics and biases, which emphasized departures from formal rationality, Prospect Theory is (warts and all) highly similar in its structure to standard SEU theories. That is, Prospect Theory assumes that, once a decision maker has formulated his or her understanding of the problem (which can involve complex processes of editing and framing), the actual choice among options unfolds in a manner von Neumann and Morgenstern would have recognized. In particular, this theory assumes that, in the final stage of decision making, the anticipated payoffs for alternative choices are compared, and the decision maker chooses the course of action with the highest anticipated payoff. From this point of view, Prospect Theory can be viewed as Apollo's Last Stand. It is a theory that is at its heart rational, tweaked to account for the many failures of human decision makers to act in what appears to be a rational fashion. Interestingly, this theory stands in sharp contrast to the Dionysian theme of Kahneman and Tversky's work on heuristics and biases in decisions, which focused on the intuitive, non-rational side of judgment and decision making.[1]

In sum, my understanding of the state of JDM in the 1970s and 1980s is that the field had to some extent come to grips with the fact that models that formalized and optimized the process of combining information to reach judgments and decisions (e.g., Bayesian models, Brunswik lens model, expected utility models) did not provide an adequate description of how people make decisions. The work of Kahneman, Tversky and their colleagues had catalogued a number of systematic violations of the rational-analytic processes assumed in the 1950s and 1960s. Important questions about how and why people made decisions still seemed to be open questions, and on the whole the 1970s and 1980s provide more convincing answers about what did not work (Bayesian models, expected utility models) than about what did. Nevertheless, if Prospect Theory is taken as a statement of JDM principles in the late 1970s and early 1980s, it is fair to say that JDM researchers were still very much attached to the idea that even actions that seemed to defy rationality could best be understood with a model that was rational in its heart.

JDM TODAY

What is the current state of JDM theory and research, and how does current JDM research help us understand behavior in organizations?

I approached this task inductively, trying to identify the JDM concepts, theories, and models that seemed to make useful contributions to the chapters in this volume. Even the most superficial examination makes it clear that different authors have a very different idea of what JDM is, what its proper concerns are, and how it contributes to our understanding of behavior in organizations. It seems harder now than it was thirty years ago to identify the big picture issues, the most important theories and models, or the core of JDM. This is not to say that there has been no progress. Rather, the field of JDM, which was starting to show some fragmentation thirty years ago, seems in some respects to have become even more fragmented in the ensuing decades, making considerable progress in addressing particular issues (e.g., the role of emotion in decision making), but without any clear progress on building the sort of grand model that could replace the expected utility models that dominated the early history of JDM.

It is clear today that any adequate model of human judgment and decision making must include both rational (Apollonian) and instinctive (Dionysian) components (Chaiken, 1980; Hammond, 1996; Kahneman, 2003). Topics such as emotion in decision making (e.g., Forgas, 1995; Forgas & George, 2001), heuristic decision making (e.g., Gigerenzer, 2008; Gigerenzer & Selten, 2002), decision making styles (e.g., Kozhevnikov, 2007; Mohammed & Schwall, 2009), and dual-systems theory (Kahneman, 2011) are firmly fixed in the mainstream of JDM research. It is no longer a question of whether or not people act rationally when making judgments and decisions. They clearly sometimes follow Apollo (rational approaches), and sometimes follow Dionysus (instinctive approaches). It seems to me that the big picture question in contemporary JDM research is not whether people are sometimes rational and sometimes not, but rather *when* or *why* they adopt Apollonian vs. Dionysian approaches to decision making.

UNDERSTANDING THE MIX OF RATIONAL AND INSTINCTIVE STYLES

The chapters in this volume suggest three broad explanations for when and why people use rational vs. instinctive strategies for making decisions. There are person-centered explanations, which suggest that it is characteristics of the decision maker that determine whether particular judgments and decisions will be attacked in a rational vs. instinctive manner.

Alternatively, there are environment-centered explanations, which suggest that it is the characteristics of the tasks and the environment in which judgment and decision tasks are performed that determine whether particular judgments and decisions will be attacked in a rational vs. instinctive manner. Finally, there are explanations that focus on the decision maker's understanding or representation of the task and the task environment. Each of these is explored below.

Person-centered Explanations

Person-centered explanations of the use of rational vs. instinctive decision making styles draw on concepts that have been explored in research on expertise (e.g., Chi, Farr, & Glaser, 1988). Experts are not necessarily smarter than non-experts, but they have acquired skills that allow them to solve problems within their domain of expertise quickly and accurately. The critical insight from this literature is that the process of practice and skill acquisition allows experts to develop complex representations of problems and methods of solving them. The classic example of this ability comes from studies of novice vs. expert chess players. Novices tend to plan and play one move at a time, each time looking for the best choice, whereas experts recognize the game in terms of complex sets of moves and strategies, and tend to play many moves at a time. They can recognize patterns in sets of moves and structure their game in terms of these patterns rather than approaching the game on a move-by-move basis.

Person-centered explanations for the use of rational vs. intuitive decision making strategies suggest that the dominant mode of decision making depends on the person's experience with the task. Tasks that are novel require a step-by-step rational approach, whereas tasks that are more familiar can be solved on the basis of applying one's experience in similar situations in the past. In other words, Apollo is for beginners and Dionysus is for experts.

Several of the chapters in this volume refer to person-centered explanations for the use of rational vs. intuitive decision strategies. For example, research shows that there are consistent individual differences in decision making strategies (Mohammed & Schwall, 2009), and that these may be related to broader differences in cognitive styles (e.g., habitual strategies for interpreting and attacking problems). This body of research suggests that some individuals prefer rational decision making across a wide variety of tasks, whereas others prefer intuitive decisions. Still others are spontaneous in their decision styles, showing no clear or discernible preference. Finally, many decision makers prefer to procrastinate and avoid decisions whenever possible.

The emerging body of research on naturalistic decision making (Klein, 2008; Klein et al., 1993) pays careful attention to the chaotic, time-pressured environment in which real-world decisions are made, but at its heart it is a person-centered model, in which the key construct is the decision maker's experience with the task. As in the broader body of literature on expert decision making, experienced decision makers tend to be intuitive in their approach, while less experienced decision makers tend to be rational.

Environment-centered Explanations

Environment-centered explanations for the use of rational vs. intuitive decision making strategies focus on the demands of the task rather than the characteristics of the individual. These explanations draw on concepts that have been articulated in two very different lines of research—i.e., in studies of dual information processing systems and in studies of the preference vs. inference.

Schneider and Shiffrin (1977) suggested that there were both controlled and automatic systems for managing the task of processing information. Automatic processing operates independently of the subject's conscious control, and it minimizes the consumption of limited cognitive resources (e.g., short-term memory). Controlled processing requires more cognitive resources, is serial in nature (i.e., one stimulus at a time is processed), and is under the control of the individual. Controlled processing is effortful, but is necessary for novel tasks, whereas automatic processing is both fast and essentially effortless.

Zajonc (1980) argued that affective reactions (e.g., the evaluation of whether something is good or bad, the attractiveness of one thing vs. another) can and do occur independently of and prior to any cognitive assessment of people, objects, or events. Simply put, the argument is that we often like or dislike things before we even know what they are. The systems we use to respond affectively to stimuli are fast, basic, and instinctive, whereas the systems we use to respond cognitively are slower and more deliberative.

Schneider and Shiffrin (1977) and Zajonc (1980) studied very different phenomena, and their theories involve quite different processes, but they agree on a central point. Some decision tasks will involve quick, basic, and instinctive processes and others will involve processes that are controlled and deliberate. Tasks that are familiar, that are done under time pressure, or that involve emotional stimuli will tend to be handled by decision making systems that are simple, fast, and intuitive, whereas tasks that are novel, abstract, and unhurried will tend to attract rational, deliberative decision strategies.

Several chapters in this volume refer to studies of heuristic vs. analytic cognitive systems (e.g., Chaiken, 1980; Kahneman, 2011), or to related concepts, such as hypervigilant decision making (Janis & Mann, 1977). Heuristic systems are fast, are low in computational power, require little concentration, and do not interfere with other ongoing cognition. Analytic systems are slow, are high in computational power, require much concentration, and interfere with other ongoing cognition. In these theories, the best predictor of the use or one system versus another tends to be the characteristics and demands of decision tasks. As noted above, decision tasks that are familiar, are poorly structured, or that involve time pressure tend to be attacked using heuristic systems, whereas decision tasks that are rich in relevant information, are novel, or that allow decision makers plenty of time tend to be attacked using analytic systems. Thus, it is the task that pushes decision makers to choose between Apollo and Dionysus.

A comparison of the person-centered and environment-centered approaches suggests that the distinction between the two may not always be simple. Tasks that are novel or unemotional for some decision makers may be familiar and emotion-laden to others. The lack of an ironclad distinction between persons and environments as explanations for the use of rational vs. intuitive decision strategies suggests the need to consider a third possibility—i.e., that it is not the environment per se that influences decision makers, but rather the decision maker's mental representation and understanding of that environment.

Environment as Understood or Represented by the Decision Maker

Brunswik's (1955) lens model is one of many approaches to understanding individual behavior (including decision making) that devotes detailed attention to the way individuals represent environments rather than to the environments themselves as causes of behavior. In particular, he directed researchers' attention to the relationships between the cues by which environments are represented and the decisions that are made, and noted that there were at least two ways in which decisions could turn out badly: (1) when the cues do not faithfully represent the environment, and (2) when decision makers use cues in ways that do not reflect the true relationship between environments and the cues that characterize them.

A number of the chapters in this volume refer to the mental representation of environments as the key to understanding the use of rational vs. intuitive decision strategies. The clearest example of this approach is in research on shared mental models in team decision making. This body of research argues that, when team members share the same basic mental representation of their task and their task environment, they are more likely to succeed than when they have divergent understandings of their tasks and the environments in which they function. It also suggests that interventions to improve decision making should include assessments of how team members perceive their tasks and training to improve the consistency of these representations across decision makers.

One of the major developments in JDM in the last forty years has been a recognition that emotions and affective states are a very important component of how decisions are made (Au et al., 2003; Forgas, 1995; Forgas & George, 2001; Seo & Barrett, 2007). The question that is not always explicitly asked in this body of research is what makes decisions affectively or emotionally charged. Both person-centered and task-centered explanations are possible (i.e., some people are more emotional than others when making decisions; some tasks elicit emotion, regardless of the characteristics of the individual decision maker), but I believe the decision maker's mental representation of the task and the task environment provides the best predictor of whether decisions will be driven by emotions. If this is true, it should follow that changing the way individual decision makers mentally represent the task and the task environment can make decisions either more emotion-based or less emotion-based. I am not aware of studies that have tested this conclusion, but it offers a tantalizing possibility for adding emotion where it is needed and tamping down emotion where it is not needed in decision making.

A final example of an "environment as mentally represented" approach to understanding the use of different decision making strategies comes from the work of Lichtenstein and Slovic (2006), which examines preferences. They argue that people seldom "have" preferences; rather, preferences are constructed in the process of making a particular choice (see also, Payne, Bettman, & Johnson, 1992). This construction of preference can lead to reversals in choice: Sometimes people prefer option A to option B; sometimes they prefer B to A. I would argue that the on-the-fly construction of preferences is likely to be a manifestation of the individual's mental representation of the task and the task environment, and that reversals of preferences would be much less likely in two decisions that are mentally represented in consistent terms than in two decisions that are mentally represented as quite different. Again, this is pure speculation; I am not aware of studies that specifically address this prediction.

FRACTURING VS. SYNTHESIS

Collectively, the chapters in this volume suggest that the field of JDM has become increasingly splintered. Reading these chapters, it is hard to complete the sentence "The main concerns of JDM research and theory are . . ." Different chapters cite and rely on quite different theories, models, and research literatures. Some chapters barely touch on JDM research at all. The question is whether this is a fair representation of the field. Do different JDM researchers and those who apply this research in organization contexts share a core set of assumptions and concerns? I think the answer depends on one's time frame. Thinking of JDM research as a snapshot, in which the key questions, assumptions, and beliefs of JDM researchers do not seem to show much communality, seems to lead to the conclusion that the field is highly fractured, and that there is no common core to JDM research. Thinking about JDM research as a process that unfolds over time leads to a somewhat more optimistic conclusion.

I believe that there are several core assumptions that are shared across virtually all of the JDM studies reviewed in this volume, and that these provide a basis for the synthesis of rational and intuitive decision making strategies. These assumptions are deeply embedded in the conduct of JDM research, and while they are rarely made explicit in any specific study, they seem apparent when programs or research are examined. First, modern JDM researchers seem to agree that both the Apollonian and Dionysian systems are at play in decision making. I do not believe that there are many (if any) serious JDM researchers who would argue that decisions are purely rational, or that decisions are purely intuitive. Second, modern JDM researchers seem to agree that not all decision tasks are created equal, and that some tasks are more likely to elicit particular decision making strategies than others. Third, modern JDM researchers seem to agree that not all decision makers are created equal, and that some decision makers are better at the task of making particular decisions than others.

If these three assumptions are shared among JDM researchers, I believe that both the big-picture questions in current JDM research and the most likely route to addressing those questions are reasonably clear. The big question is what prompts decision makers to follow Apollo or Dionysus, and I think that the most likely route to an answer will involve an interaction between people and environments, with the mental models of the task and the task environment emerging as the key driver. That is, it is not enough to look at either persons or tasks in isolations. People are not experts in general; they are experts in particular domains. Tasks are not novel or emotion-laden in general; they are novel or emotion-laden for some decision makers and not for others. I believe that studies of the mental representations of tasks and task environments (e.g., shared mental models) are by their nature interactive, and my money is on person × task interactions as the best explanation for whether and when decision makers will follow rational or intuitive strategies in making particular decisions. Time will tell whether I am right.

NOTE

1. It is notable that Prospect Theory, at least in its original formulation, says virtually nothing about the role of heuristics and biases in decision making.

REFERENCES

Arkes, H.R. and Blumer, C. (1985). The psychology of sunk cost. *Organizational Behavior and Human Decision Processes, 35,* 124–140.

Au, K., Chan, F., Wang, D., and Vertinsky, I. (2003). Mood in foreign exchange trading: Cognitive processes and performance. *Organizational Behavior and Human Decision Processes, 91,* 322–338.

Balzer, W.K., Rohrbaugh, J., and Murphy, K.R. (1983). Reliability of actual and predicted judgments over time. *Organizational Behavior and Human Performance, 32,* 109–123.

Brunswik, E. (1955). Representative design and probabilistic theory in a functional psychology. *Psychological Review, 62,* 193–217.

Chaiken, S. (1980). Heuristic versus systematic information processing and the use of source versus message cues in persuasion. *Journal of Personality and Social Psychology, 39,* 752–766.

Chi, M.T.H., Farr, M.J., and Glaser, R. (1988). *The Nature of Expertise.* Hillsdale, NJ: Lawrence Erlbaum.

Forgas, J.P. (1995). Mood and judgment: The affect infusion model (AIM). *Psychological Bulletin, 117*(1), 39–66.

Forgas, J.P. and George, J.M. (2001). Affective influences on judgments and behavior in organizations: An information processing perspective. *Organizational Behavior and Human Decision Processes, 86*(1), 3–34.

Gigerenzer, G. (2008). Why heuristics work. *Perspectives on Psychological Science, 3,* 20–29.

Gigerenzer, G. and Selten, R. (Eds.) (2002). *Bounded Rationality: The Adaptive Toolbox.* Cambridge, MA: MIT Press.

Hammond, K.R. (1996). *Human Judgment and Social Policy: Irreducible Uncertainty, Inevitable Error, Unavoidable Injustice.* New York: Oxford University Press.

Huber, J., Payne, J.W., and Puto, C. (1982). Adding asymmetrically dominated alternatives: Violations of regularity and the similarity hypothesis. *Journal of Consumer Research, 9*, 90–98.

Janis, I.L. and Mann, L. (1977). *Decision Making: A Psychological Analysis of Conflict, Choice, and Commitment.* New York: Free Press.

Kahneman, D. (2003). A perspective on judgement and choice. *American Psychologist, 58*, 697–720.

Kahneman, D. (2011). *Thinking, Fast and Slow.* New York: Farrar, Straus, and Giroux.

Kahneman, D., Slovic, P., and Tversky, A. (1982). *Judgment Under Uncertainty: Heuristics and Biases.* New York: Cambridge University Press.

Kahneman, D. and Thaler, R. (1991). Economic analysis and the psychology of utility: Applications to compensation policy. *American Economic Review, 81*, 341–346.

Kahneman, D. and Tversky, A. (1972). Subjective probability: A judgment of representativeness. *Cognitive Psychology, 3*, 430–454.

Kahneman, D. and Tversky, A. (1973). On the psychology of prediction. *Psychological Review, 80*, 237–251.

Kahneman, D. and Tversky, A. (1979). Prospect theory: An analysis of decision under risk. *Econometrica, 47*, 263–291.

Keeney, R.L. and Raiffa, H. (1976). *Decisions with Multiple Objectives: Preferences and Value Tradeoffs.* New York: Wiley.

Klein, G.A. (2008). Naturalistic decision making. *Human Factors, 50*, 456–460.

Klein, G.A., Orasanu, J., Calderwood, R., and Zsambok, C.E. (Eds.) (1993). *Decision Making in Action: Models and Methods.* Norwood, CT: Ablex.

Kozhevnikov, M. (2007). Cognitive styles in the context of modern psychology: Toward an integrated framework of cognitive style. *Psychological Bulletin, 133*, 464–481.

Lane, D., Murphy, K., and Marques, T. (1982). Measuring cue importance in policy capturing. *Organizational Behavior and Human Performance, 30*, 231–240.

Lichtenstein, S. and Slovic, P. (Eds.) (2006). *The Construction of Preference.* Cambridge, MA: Cambridge University Press.

Meehl, P.E. (1954). *Clinical Versus Statistical Prediction: A Theoretical Analysis and a Review of the Evidence.* Minneapolis, MN: University of Minnesota.

Mohammed, S. and Schwall, A. (2009). Individual differences and decision making: What we know and where we go from here. *International Review of Industrial and Organizational Psychology, 24*, 249–312.

Murphy, K. (1982). Assessing the discriminant validity of regression models and subjectively weighted models of judgments. *Multivariate Behavioral Research, 17*, 354–370.

Newell, A. and Simon, H.A. (1972). *Human Problem Solving.* Englewood Cliffs, NJ: Prentice Hall.

Nietzsche, F. (2008). *The Birth of Tragedy* (trans. Douglas Smith). New York: Oxford University Press.

Nisbett, R.E. and Ross, L.D. (1980). *Human Inference: Strategies and Shortcomings of Social Judgment.* Englewood Cliffs, NJ: Prentice Hall.

Nystedt, L. and Murphy, K. (1979). Some conditions affecting the utility of subjectively weighted models in decision making. *Perceptual and Motor Skills, 49*, 583–590.

Payne, J.W., Bettman, J.R., and Johnson, E.J. (1992). Behavioral decision research: A constructive processing perspective. *Annual Review of Psychology, 43*, 87–131.

Schneider, W.E. and Shiffrin, R.M. (1977). Controlled and automatic human information processing: 1. Detection, search, and attention. *Psychological Review, 84*, 1–66.

Seo, M.G. and Barrett, L.F. (2007). Being emotional during decision making—good or bad? An empirical investigation. *Academy of Management Journal, 50*(4), 923–940.

Spengler, O. (1991). *The Decline of the West.* New York: Oxford University Press.

Staw, B.M. (1976). Knee deep in the big muddy: A study of escalating commitment to a chosen course of action. *Organizational Behavior and Human Performance, 16*, 27–44.

Tversky, A. and Kahneman, D. (1973). Availability: A heuristic for judging frequency and probability. *Cognitive Psychology, 5*, 207–232.

Tversky, A. and Kahneman, D. (1974). Judgment under uncertainty: Heuristics and biases. *Science, 185*, 1124–1131.

Zajonc, R.B. (1980). Feeling and thinking: Preferences need no inference. *American Psychologist, 35*, 151–175.

Author Index

Subject Index

Printed in the United States
by Baker & Taylor Publisher Services